T0235841

The Rise of Politically Motivated Cyber Attacks

This book outlines the complexity in understanding different forms of cyber attacks, the actors involved, and their motivations. It explores the key challenges in investigating and prosecuting politically motivated cyber attacks, the lack of consistency within regulatory frameworks, and the grey zone that this creates, for cybercriminals to operate within.

Connecting diverse literatures on cyberwarfare, cyberterrorism, and cyber-protests, and categorising the different actors involved – state-sponsored/supported groups, hacktivists, online protestors – this book compares the means and methods used in attacks, the various attackers, and the current strategies employed by cybersecurity agencies. It examines the current legislative framework and proposes ways in which it could be reconstructed, moving beyond the traditional and fragmented definitions used to manage offline violence.

This book is an important contribution to the study of cyber attacks within the areas of criminology, criminal justice, law, and policy. It is a compelling reading for all those engaged in cybercrime, cybersecurity, and digital forensics.

Tine Munk is a senior lecturer in the Criminology and Criminal Justice Department at Nottingham Trent University, UK. Tine is predominately teaching and researching cybercrime and cybersecurity. Her overarching research interest is cybercrimes in a political context focusing on these crimes' power, responses, and impacts.

Routledge Studies in Crime and Society

For more information about this series, please visit: www.routledge.com/Routledge-Studies-in-Crime-and-Society/book-series/RSCS

The Rise of Politically Motivated Cyber Attacks

Actors, Attacks and Cybersecurity

Tine Munk

Routledge
Taylor & Francis Group

LONDON AND NEW YORK

First published 2022
by Routledge
4 Park Square, Milton Park, Abingdon, Oxon OX14 4RN

and by Routledge
605 Third Avenue, New York, NY 10158

Routledge is an imprint of the Taylor & Francis Group, an informa business

© 2022 Tine Munk

British Library Cataloguing-in-Publication Data
A catalogue record for this book is available from the British Library

Library of Congress Cataloging-in-Publication Data
Names: Munk, Tine, 1970– author.
Title: The rise of politically motivated cyber attacks :
actors, attacks and cybersecurity / Tine Munk.
Description: Milton Park, Abingdon, Oxon ; New York, NY :
Routledge, 2022. | Includes bibliographical references and index.
Identifiers: LCCN 2021046395 (print) | LCCN 2021046396 (ebook) |
ISBN 9780367648695 (hardback) | ISBN 9780367648701 (paperback) |
ISBN 9781003126676 (ebook)
Subjects: LCSH: Cyberterrorism. | Computer crimes–Political aspects. |
Political crimes and offenses. | Computer crimes–Law and legislation.
Classification: LCC HV6773.15.C97 M86 2022 (print) |
LCC HV6773.15.C97 (ebook) | DDC 363.325–dc23
LC record available at https://lccn.loc.gov/2021046395
LC ebook record available at https://lccn.loc.gov/2021046396

ISBN: 978-0-367-64869-5 (hbk)
ISBN: 978-0-367-64870-1 (pbk)
ISBN: 978-1-00-312667-6 (ebk)

DOI: 10.4324/9781003126676

Typeset in Times New Roman
by Newgen Publishing UK

Inge Højsgaard Munk
22.11.1942–06.01.2018

Contents

Tables

Acknowledgements

This book would never have been written if I did not have support and help from several people. I want to thank my family and friends for their constant support: you know who you are. A special thank goes to my Danish friends in 'Blå Gruppe' for meeting up consistently on Zoom Friday evenings during the corona virus disease 2019 (COVID-19) pandemic and afterwards. These meetings and conversations allowed me to test book ideas and get instant feedback. Thank you, Maibritt and Jan Falkesgaard, Inge and John Ankjær Bertz, and Laura and Jesper Munk, and generation 2.0: Emma, Emil, Jeppe, Marcus, and Sarah. Also thanks to Evald Munk and Ruth Rousing.

Writing this book has been an interesting journey during the COVID-19 pandemic, where new personal and professional challenges sometimes felt overwhelming. Going back to my main research interest area and exploring a developing cybercrime field kept my mind occupied. Although the proposal was written before the pandemic, it soon became apparent during that time that politically motivated cybercrimes were escalating, and I was writing while key events unfolded.

I am very grateful for the assistance and support I received from Dr Magali Peyrefitte, Dr Angus Nurse, and Professor Vincenzo Ruggiero in developing the proposal. I would also thank Dr Angus Nurse for his feedback on the chapters during the writing up period. A special thanks for the support I have received should go to the team at Routledge, Thomas Sutton, Jessica Phillips, Zoe Thomson, and the anonymous reviewers involved in the process.

During this book research and writing process, several people have supported me. This helped me through the long hours in front of the computer screen. Therefore, I would like to express my gratitude to Tine Lee Senft, Lene Dam, Bettina Jacobsen, Georgia Mouskou, Dr Magali Peyrefitte, Sara Rodriguez, Dr Naomi Graham, Professor Karen Duke, Sue Mew, and Dr Graham Smith. Thank you for the patience, enthusiasm, and interest you have offered me.

Finally, my academic network's encouragement, discussions, and ideas have been instrumental for my development as an academic. I want to express my appreciation to all the people in this network. I would also like to thank the undergraduate and postgraduate cybercrime students from Middlesex

University, the Criminology and Sociology Department. These students listened and engaged in my teaching about politically motivated cybercrime. I want to thank all the MSc Cybercrime and Digital Investigation students from 2016 to 2021. In particular, I would thank the group from 2019 to 2020 for their excitement and enthusiasm when I started the research.

Abbreviations

APTs	Advanced Persistent Threats
ARPANET	Advance Research Project Network
ASEAN	The Association of Southeast Asian Nations
AU	The Africa Union
AUCCPDP	The AU Convention on Cybersecurity and Personal Data Protection
BLM	Black Lives Matter
CaaS	Crime-as-a-Service
CAC	The Office of the Central Cyberspace Affairs Commission
China	The People's Republic of China
CI	Critical Infrastructure
CIA	US Central Intelligence Agency
CII	Critical Information Infrastructure
CIP	Critical Infrastructure Protection
CNCERT	National Computer Network Emergency Response Team
CNCI	The Comprehensive National Cybersecurity Initiative
CNI	Critical National Infrastructure
DCCC	The Democratic Congressional Campaign Committee
DDoS	Distributed-Denial-of-Service
DDoSecrets	Distributed-Denial-of-Secrets
DHS	The Department of Homeland Security
DISA	Defense Information Systems Agency
DNC	The Democratic National Committee
DoD	Department of Defence
DoJ	Department of Justice
DoS	Denial-of-Service
EC	European Comisssion
EMA	The European Medicine Agency
EU	The European Union
FBI	Federal Bureau of Investigation

FSB	Federal Security Service
GCHQ	The Government Communications Headquarters
GTsSS	The 85th Main Centre for Special Services of the Main Directorate of the General Staff of the Armed Forces of the Russian Federation
GTsST	The Main Centre for Special Technologies of the Main Directorate of the General Staff of the Armed Forces of the Russian Federation (GU/GRU)
GU/GRU	The Armed Forces of the Russian Federation
HfH	Hacking-for-Hire
HSE	The Health Service Executive
ICS	Industrial Control Systems
ICT	Information and Communication Technologies
ITU	International Telecommunication Union
MaaS	Malware-as-a-Service
MSS	The Ministry of State Security
NAO	The National Audit Office
NATO	North Atlantic Treaty Organisation
NCSC	The National Cyber Security Centre
NHS	National Healthcare Service
North Korea	Democratic People's Republic of Korea
NSA	National Security Agency
OAS	The Organisation of American States
RaaS	Ransomware-as-a-Service
RGB	The Reconnaissance General Bureau
SCADA	Supervisory Control and Data Acquisition
SVR	The Foreign Intelligence Service
TOR	The Onion Router
TTP	Tactic, Technique, and Procedures
UK	The United Kingdom
UN	United Nations
US	United States of America
USCYBERCOM	US Cyber Command
VPN	Virtual Private Network
WWW	World Wide Web

1 Introduction

Introduction

Politically motivated cyber attacks are escalating. For years there has been an assumption that these attacks were linked to geopolitics, national states, or minor conflicts with no noticeable effect on ordinary online users or populations. Therefore, not much attention has been given to these attacks compared with personal and financial types of cybercrime. Yet, the number of attacks is rising, and it is becoming apparent that the impact of these attacks spills over to the other domains. These attacks are not just another form of cybercrime to be managed using the current cybercrime legislation. The attacks are much more complicated, involving numerous different actors, targets, and attack routes. Attacks are conducted in a borderless environment where geopolitics makes it impossible to reach international agreements to limit the attacks.

Public awareness about these attacks is rising. Currently, the attacks make headlines in mass media, placing politically motivated attacks high on the agenda. Headlines dominate tech reporting in mass media, and there is not a week without doomsday headings, such as "Barely able to keep up: America's cyberwarriors are spread thin by attacks" (Collier, 2021); "New Ransomware Attack By Russian Hackers Highlights Cybersecurity Challenges" (Segal, 2021); "U.S. to Treat Cyber Attacks With Same Urgency as Terrorism" (Paytoncular, 2021).

This book aims to provide an understanding of the various actors, the targets, and the cybersecurity strategies developed to manage these complex areas. Chapter 1 introduces a complex area intending to create a general fundament by conceptualising the actors, cyberspace and attacks, targets, cyber strategies, and security. Finally, this chapter also provides an outline of the book's different chapters.

Politically Motivated Actors

Politically motivated attacks are increasing rapidly where the attacks have a substantial impact. There is a growing awareness about how dangerous they

DOI: 10.4324/9781003126676-1

can become (Kale, 2021). The different types of politically motivated actors fall under the scope of war and warfare, terrorism, or activism. However, these online actions cannot be compared with those conducted in the offline environment. Currently, there is no precise classification of these actors, and they are considered in isolation without seeing the pattern and considering the groups' means and methods. Still, there are different levels of sophistication used in the attacks. The least intrusive, low impact attacks are easier to detect and prosecute as they are likely to be conducted by non-state actors as a part of a political protest. In contrast, there is a low probability of prosecuting the national state, state-sponsored/supported actors conducting the most sophisticated and intrusive attacks.

There has been a significant setback in diplomacy and transnational collaborations between states to develop comprehensive norms and practices for managing this area. Warmongering rhetoric is being used, which sounds like a return to the Cold War, albeit online. Actors are increasing their online capabilities and capacities and showing off their powers through actions. The United States (US) President Biden has warned that significant cyber attacks would lead to a real conventional war on the ground (Tung, 2021a). This argument is supported by the North Atlantic Treaty Organization (NATO), which has stated that the series of cyber attacks directed at Western states should be considered similar to a threat of armed attacks (Tung, 2021b). The US agencies, the National Security Agency (NSA), and the Federal Bureau of Investigation (FBI) have warned about hacking campaigns tied to the Russian military. In particular, the SolarWinds attack in 2020 demonstrated the impact of supply-chain attacks. The Russian state-sponsored group, Fancy Bear, was subsequently attributed for the attacks on Western states' public and private entities. In particular, it has caused concerns that SolarWind targets included the US Justice, State, Energy, and Commerce Departments (Corera, 2021; Gagliordi, 2021; Whitaker, 2021). Some of the attributions of attacks have increased tension and harsh verbal exchanges between the different actors. The US, NATO, the European Union (EU), and the United Kingdom (UK) have accused China of being behind the Microsoft Exchange hack. In return, China accused the US of being behind several attacks against China (Janofsky, 2021; Vincent, 2021).

Ransomware groups have intensified their attacks on critical infrastructure (CI) and essential services with a frequency and severity that has surpassed other cybersecurity concerns. Of all the Western states, the US has experienced an unusually high number of ransomware attacks, directly impacting the public. The 2021 attacks on the Colonial Pipeline and the meat plant JBS prompted the US authorities to raise concerns about the attacks originating from Russia. This led to the Western security actors classifying ransomware attacks as a national security threat. The US took this one step further by directly linking ransomware attacks with terrorism (Barnes, 2021; Bing, 2021; Chapple, 2021; Palmer, 2021; Security, 2021).

Politically motivated cyber attacks are not only associated with state, state-sponsored, and state-supported actors. Non-state actors also use the online environment for political protests, affecting public and private entities, services, and infrastructures. In 2020–2021, hacktivists and other political activists conducted several legal and illegal attacks, which caught worldwide attention. Older, established hacktivist groups, like Anonymous, emerged from the shadows along with new groups showing that hacktivism still constitutes a threat online (Molloy & Tidy, 2020). However, new groups have emerged which are more engaged in collecting data troves in the public spare or accessing open-source codes online (Reuters, 2021; Stone, 2020). Contrary to the hacktivist groups, another breed of political actors launched innovative attacks that did not break the law, i.e. Gen Z and K-pop stans (Alexander, 2020; Lorenz et al., 2020).

Cyberspace and Attacks

The term 'cyberspace' was coined in 1984 by the sci-fi writer Gibson in his novel 'Neuromancer'. Gibson describes the space as a 'consensual hallucination' by referring to the ability of the online space to alter the offline reality by those engaging in virtual chat rooms or virtual environments (Cavelty, 2013, p. 107; Gibson, 1984; Puyvelde & Brantly, 2019, p. 2; Shires, 2020, p. 89). Yet, the term, cyberspace, originates from cybernetics using the Greek word kybernētēs, which means rudder, pilot, a device used to steer a boat or support human governance. For example, a self-steering mechanism is applied to techniques to keep ships on the course during the night watch (Cyber Security Intelligence, 2017; Green, 2001, p. 199; Marinescu, 2017). Plato used kybernētēs to describe the governance of people (Marinescu, 2017). In a more contemporary context, the word 'cyber' is associated with the digital environment creating an intellectual and emotional interactional space within a technological realm (Green, 2001, p. 199).

Cyberspace is now considered a global domain that creates an information environment of independent networks of systems infrastructure, interlinking Internet telecommunication networks, computer systems, and various embedded processors and controllers (Clark, 2010, p. 1; US DoD 2016; NIST, 2020). The online space comprises an ecosystem blending network technologies and online users based on organic technological evolutions. Different technologies coexist and influence each other within the ecosystem, combined with external forces fuelled by social and technological changes. Technological innovations, computer technologies, interconnectivity, and interdependency create immediate changes to the online ecosystem. These changes are based on a fusion of all communication networks, databases, and information sources in a universal context (Cavelty, 2013, p. 108; Lapointe, 2011, pp. 2–3).

The technology used is instrumental in understanding cyberspace. The material and physical aspects, the electronics used in hardware, software, and the applications linked to the actual operative technologies are defining aspects. Equally important are the language, the interpersonal interactions, the use, and the performance (Manning, 2019, p. 291). Global connectivity is linked to various communication pathways where software is used on millions of computers controlling cyberspace's storage devices and pathways. These computers continually sense the status of interlinked routers, which means that the online traffic does not follow a linear and direct route. Instead, the data are being routed through various global pathways to arriving at a destination only miles away in the shortest time possible (Inglis, 2016, p. 19).

Cyber Attacks

The distinction between illegal activities of states and organised crime groups is becoming blurred, and various groups are coving their activities behind a false front, making the attribution difficult. Many foreign state-sponsored groups are threatening other states' interests. Attempts from states, state-sponsored and state-supported attacks penetrating networks for political, diplomatic, technological, commercial, and strategic advances are also a growing concern. These groups are principally targeting governments, defence, finance, energy, and telecommunication sectors. According to the UK National Cyber Security Strategy 2016–2021, the capacity and impact of these state/state-sponsored actors vary. The most technologically advanced states continue to update their capabilities and methods using encryption and anonymised services to remain covert. Other actors do not have the same abilities. However, they can archive similar impacts using basic tools and techniques because of the low level of cybersecurity imposed by the targets (HM Government, 2016, p. 18).

The interconnectivity and interdependencies on computer technologies enables cyber attacks to be conducted on an unprecedented scale which impact states, groups, and individuals. The accessibility of computer devices, networks, and the architecture of cyberspace and the Internet means that more online users can communicate and share information globally. The online spaces provide the attackers with global resources to move data and information around and find safe havens for conducting attacks (Clough, 2015, pp. 7–9; Gillespie, 2019, p. 13; Munk, 2018).

Cyber Targets: Critical Infrastructure

Attacking infrastructures and services is becoming common, and everything linked to the online environment are at risk. For years, the attackers have targeted political and private entities, groups, and individuals. Yet, politically motivated attacks are not confined to governmental and military entities; commercial and economic interests and industries, such as finance, high-technology, biotechnology, and telecommunications, have faced a substantial amount of attacks (Anderson, 2008). Large-scale attacks such as the 2007 attack against Estonia and the 2017 WannaCry and NotPetya ransomware attacks demonstrated the vulnerabilities of interconnected systems and networks.

Defining Critical Infrastructure (CI), Critical National Infrastructure
(CNI), Critical Information Infrastructure (CII), and Information
and Communication Technologies (ICTs)

The online and interconnected environment is changing, and various CIs constitute significant risks. The frequency of politically motivated attacks proves the need for managing this area by building up resilience and preparedness to increase cybersecurity. CI systems, such as those linked to power generators, water treatments, electricity production, and other platforms, are considered vital for modern societies (Allianz, 2021). The attacks on these vital assets have a detrimental effect on society. There might be direct damages to the actual target, but the services provided are equally disrupted.

These targets become more attractive to attackers, who have various tools available to conduct attacks, such as distributed-denial-of-service (DDoS), advanced persistent threats (APTs), supply-chain attacks, etc. The variety and complexity of these attacks increase the pressure on CI providers and governments to improve security, enhance protection, and develop strategies to manage online risks. The different forms of CI are classified due to the particular providers and contexts where they are developed. CI is classified as an essential service, and states, businesses, and organisations must develop a robust framework to anticipate and mitigate disaster across the entire CI architecture (Forcepoint, 2020).

Attacks against CI systems and services have generated changes to strategies, processes, and practices. However, cyber attackers outsmart cybersecurity actors by constantly upgrading their cyber capabilities and capacities. There have been several attacks on CI and services in the past. For example, in the 2003 attack, the SQL Slammer worm infected a monitoring and control system at the Davis–Besse nuclear power plant in Ohio, US (Poulsen, 2014). The most well-known politically motivated attack was the Stuxnet worm discovered in 2010. This worm was launched against Iranian power plants to sabotage centrifuges, and the operation demonstrated the powers and impact of malware attacks (Liu et al., 2017, p. 14; Zetter, 2015). In 2013, Iranian hackers breached the Bowman Avenue Dam in New York and took over the control of the floodgates. Although the attack was not sophisticated and could not have caused significant damage, it is concerning how easily attackers can seek out vulnerabilities and exploit old CIs running of retrofitted software connected to the online environments (Prokupecz et al., 2015).

Another significant attack on CI was in 2020 launched against Israeli water stations where a few pumps malfunctioned by turning on and off without being activated. An Iranian-written code travelled through servers in the US and Europe before targeting the water pumping stations attempting to modify chlorine levels (Goud, 2020; Srivastava, 2020). If the attacks were successful, the populations could have suffered a mild poising by drinking the water (Cimpanu, 2020; Goud, 2020; Srivastava, 2020). A similar attack was prevented in Florida in 2021, where hackers briefly increased the amount of sodium hydroxide (Lye) in Oldesmar's water system. After a couple of attempts, the hacker managed to access the treatment software and changed the sodium hydroxide content from 100 to 11,100 ppm. This attack was detected by an employee who reversed the action (BBC News, 2021; Porterfield, 2021; Vallejo, 2021).

Most of the politically motivated cyber attacks are launched against CI, CNI, CII, and ICTs. These CIs and services are primarily embedded in the daily activities of the global economy and society, i.e. sharing/developing ICTs, services, networks, and infrastructures (EC, 2013, p. 1). In the offline environment, the main threat is terrorism, espionage, cyberthreats, and the proliferation of weapons of mass destruction. These concerns can be transferred to the online environment, where CIs constitute a more complex system reliant on computer technology and networks (Allianz, 2021).

The various aspects of CIs can be distinguished into the following groups. CI is an umbrella term covering several essential structures, systems, and services, such as CNI, CII, and ICTs. CI covers a wide range of material systems, such as delivering communication, energy, water, food, transport, emergency services, and healthcare provisions. All these areas create a body of systems, networks, and assets essential to the functioning of a state, its economy, public health, and service (US DHS, 2020). CIs are controlled and monitored by industrial control systems (ICSs), including supervisory control and data acquisition (SCADA) systems.

The CI systems are predominately based on standard embedded system platforms usually based on commercial off-the-shelf software. Although ICS and SCADA systems have reduced the costs and made them easier to use, the risk of exposure to cyber attacks has increased (ENISA, 2021). An example is the supply-chain attacks where the attackers seek out vulnerabilities in the weakest link of the chain, which allows the attack access to a substantial number of entities simultaneously, i.e. SolarWind supply-chain attack and Kaseya ransomware attack (2021) have both used the companies supply-chain to gain access to a more extensive network (Constantin, 2021; Paganini, 2020; Whitney, 2021).

CNIs are a part of the CI framework that covers facilities, systems, sites, information, and processes essential for the everyday running of a state (Pratt, 2019). These can be chemicals, civil nuclear communications, defence, emergency services, energy, finance, food, government, health, space, transport, water, etc. CNI covers a complicated network beyond the actual structures, systems, and services. Subunits of third parties are involved in the development of these structures and services. Contractors and third parties still need to be protected because of the potential danger to the public if they are attacked (CPNI, 2020). Ransomware attacks have reinforced the need for protecting CNIs. Attacks on these vital services can have physical consequences on society beyond the actual target. Managing and building up resilience against cyber attacks are challenging, as it is impossible to shut down these services to maintain and update the systems without cause disruptions to society.

Unfortunately, the safety of these services is often prioritised over security (Price, 2021).

Another essential part of the structure is CIIs, which provides the functions that enabled CI and CNI operations. CIIs are any form of physical or virtual information systems that control, process, transmit, receive, or store information (US DHS, 2011, p. 10). CII is linked to the information structure, such as telecommunication, computer/software, the Internet, satellites, fibre optics, which allows the CIs to communicate and function due to their dependency on technologies and networks (Yar & Steinmetz, 2019, p. 91). CIIs' physical infrastructure is entangled in a complex structure by its transnational and cross-sectoral relationships (Clemente, 2013, p. 16). Attacking CII could significantly impact citizens' health, safety, security, or economic well-being and the effective functioning of society (OECD, 2008).

Finally, ICTs are infrastructure and components facilitating computing, such as telecommunication devices and Internet-enabled and mobile devices. ICTs cover all devices, including networking components, applications, and systems that enable online users and organisations to interact in the online environment, such as the Internet, wireless networks, mobile phones, and other communication forms (TechTerms, 2020; UNESCO, 2020). The growing use and dependencies of ICT have also created problems and challenges for organisations, online users, and society as technological developments open up new attack routes.

THE RELATIONSHIP BETWEEN PUBLIC AND PRIVATE CI, CNI, CII, AND ICTS

The CI sectors depend on each other and exist in an interdependent and interconnected environment determined by their functions, products, and services. These areas are linked to specific structure parts, such as physical, geographic, cyber, and logical interdependencies. These dependent areas could generate a domino effect if one CI is disrupted, damaged, or destroyed; the consequences would impact other services (Alcaraz & Zeadally, 2015).

Societies' reliance on global networks has led to new attack levels. Attackers persistently target vulnerabilities in CI structures allowing them to change electronically enabled systems and networks – or gain unauthorised access to systems to steal money, intellectual property, information, or disrupt CI control systems (Pratt, 2019). Cyber–physical interactions within these different domains enable the possibilities for cross-domain attacks. For example, attackers can conduct an attack causing disruptions or damages to the physical domain or target the cyber domain. These two types of attacks can amplify the damage in an interlinked cyber–physical attack (Liu et al., 2017, p. 14). Vulnerabilities in the CI structures have been exposed during the COVID-19 pandemic, where several health facilities have been attacked. Of course, these attacks caused significant damage at a time, where societies relied on hospital services. Attacks had caused other facilities to close down, and they have impacted offline and online services. The ransomware attack against the American Universal Health Service facilities caused sub-stantial disruptions. Hospitals were forced to use manual backups, redirect ambulances, and cancel or reschedule surgeries (CSIS, 2020; Newman, 2020).

Critical infrastructure protection (CIP) has become an issue of strategic importance, and protection needs to be imposed on multiple levels. A high level of CIP is needed to protect CI systems and services early in the pro-cess. Every government and governmental actors and institutions worldwide are responsible for protecting those against natural disasters, terrorist activi-ties, and cyberthreats. It is not only a governmental responsibility; public and private actors are engaged to ensure processes and practices are developed to ensure the reliability, performance, continuous operation, safety, mainten-ance, and protection of CIs (Alcaraz & Zeadally, 2015; Forcepoint, 2020). The protection should be considered a cross-sectoral activity closely coordinated between multiple actors using a holistic approach. The multi-agency and cross-sectoral approach should be used rather than limit the protection to specific sectors (Alcaraz & Zeadally, 2015; EC, 2005; Munk, 2015, p. 69).

Cyber Strategies and Security

International and national governmental institutions have failed to develop a comprehensive definition of cybersecurity. According to the International Telecommunication Union (ITU), cybersecurity is

> [T]he collection of tools, policies, security concepts, security safeguards, guidelines, risk management methods, actions, training, best practices, assurance and technologies that can be used to protect the cyber environ-ment, as well as organisations' and users' assets.
>
> (ITU, 2020; Munk, 2015, p. 47)

Cybersecurity is the practice of protecting critical systems and sensitive information. Disparate technologies add to the complexity of securing vital interests, systems, and assets in a public and private context (Carr, 2016, p. 49; IBM, 2021). The core function of cybersecurity is to protect hardware, soft-ware, and data from cyberthreats, including various connected computer devices, infrastructures, applications, services, clouds, and telecommunication systems (Shea et al., 2021).

Cybersecurity has been introduced to effectively control cyberspace and provide online users with a reliable, resilient, and trustworthy digital infra-structure. However, cyberspace is not secure and resilient in its current form. Several control mechanisms are missing, creating an absent, incomplete, or poorly designed structure, and it is often compared with the wild west of the digital era. Cyber professionals are managing cyberspace in a fragmented and differentiated way linked to isolated areas. One of the core problems is the lack of an overarching system to control cyberspace, the Internet, and online platforms as a whole (Bayuk et al., 2012, p. 1). Various practices and processes are imposed to prevent the misuse of computers or data where attackers target the integrity of computers, networks, or data to violate the intended state of data or systems, such as espionage or sabotage (Puyvelde & Brantly, 2019, pp. 57–58). Most of the attacks used by politically motivated actors are based on malware designed to (Puyvelde & Brantly, 2019, p. 59).

Currently, only a limited number of states have developed highly sophisticated cyberweapons and capabilities. These states have capacities and resources available that enable them to conduct large-scale multilayered attacks over a long period (HM Government, 2016, p. 18; Park & Walstrom, 2017). Other states are in the process of recognising the powers of cyberweapons by developing low-cost and high-impact weapons using the available capacities and capabilities. However, these weapons should not be underestimated as they can cause a significant impact on the targets. Yet, these states are in the process of producing sophisticated means and methods for more damaging large-scale attacks (HM Government, 2016, p. 18). States like North Korea and Iran are important cyber powers and have been behind significant attacks on foreign entities – just as other states have also targeted them.

Risk, Nodal Governance, and Complexity

Whether a system is a physical facility or a collection of cyberspace components, the role of a security professional assigned to that system is to plan for potential attacks and prepare for its consequences (Bayuk, 2012, p. 1). Dissimilar to conventional territorial conflicts, the ability to develop and deploy various forms of malware is not limited to state actors. In online attacks, actors can range from cybercriminals, individual hackers, to terrorist organisations or online activists. All online users can create, reuse, or purchase cyber capabilities instrumental for conducting an attack (Munk, 2019; Puyvelde & Brantly, 2019, p. 60). Traditional political conflicts have primarily been linked to war and warfare or conventional terrorism. In cyber-conflicts, the groupings and the means and methods used are blurred, and there is no clear legal division between groups and actions (Guiora, 2017, p. 16)

The attack forms are hybrid, interlinked with national and geopolitics, local conflicts or dissatisfaction with how incidents and problems are managed in the offline environment, and conflicts merging offline and online activities. The attack forms and motivations change depending on the attackers underlying agenda, i.e. personal, political, and economic gain; espionage; disruption; and destruction (Munk, 2015, p. 74). Assessing risks is a critical component in cybersecurity decision-making; these include risk assessments on the strategic, operational, and information system levels. Risk management is constantly ongoing, and the risk assessments are conducted through the whole life cycle from pre-system acquisition through the system acquisition, the maintenance of the system until it is retired (NIST, 2012, p. ix).

PUBLIC–PRIVATE PARTNERSHIPS

Cybersecurity calls for a multilayered approach where actors work together to enhance cyber resilience, both with deterrence and defence. Public–private partnerships are deeply integrated into protective frameworks drawing on a joint effort by key players from various sectors and industries. Previously, cooperation between public and private actors has been problematic as the actors have been reluctant to share information and develop best practices. There are many explanations for this reluctance, fear of compromising national security or reveal corporate secrets that can jeopardise the actors' competitiveness (Carr, 2016, p. 46; EC, 2020, p. 5). Public and private actors need to interact, exchange knowledge, communicate, and pull resources to protect these vital areas. Cybersecurity requires constant collaboration and cooperation between key actors and entities to constant review and apply new security solutions and plans (Forcepoint, 2020; US DHS, 2020).

Information sharing enables the victims and security actors to create coordinated and effective countermeasures to enhance resilience and prepare for future attacks against CIs. The exploitation of known vulnerabilities in software is the most likely source of attacks. The cybersecurity actors should ensure that the security systems are up to date, and known vulnerabilities are patched as soon as they are communicated. Often actors underestimate the importance of constantly updating the security level. If this is not done, there will be free entry into the system for zero-day exploits (NCSC, 2015, 2016). Another issue is the underinvestments in hardware and software and the use of outdated police and preparedness plans. Technological development progresses rapidly, which requires constant assessment of resilience and preparedness. Investments in cybersecurity are critical for all actors to ensure the integrity, confidentiality, and availability of data assets (Fedele & Roner, 2021). Outdated software might not resist a sophisticated attack as the product would no longer receive updates or security measures are not developed (NCSC, 2021).

The success of CIP is linked to different partnerships developed between public and private actors and their abilities to manage and implement security initiatives. It is, therefore, essential to take a proactive stance and include risk assessments and risk classifications of the different procedures and practices. Often the online threats are linked to hacking, but other threats need to be considered, such as equipment failures, human errors, and natural causes.

The Structure of This Book

Part 1

This book is organised into two parts. The first part of this book covers Chapters 1–4. These chapters set out definitions and problem areas for understanding how the different politically motivated actors are organised. The focus is centred around the actors, their motivation, and the means and methods used in the attacks. These three areas are linked to the strategic position of the actors. The theoretical foundation derives from risk and anticipatory governance forms imposed to decrease the attacking actors' payoff, such as the developed deterrence and defence measures. Chapter 1 sets out the framework for understanding critical aspects in this book, covered in depth in the following chapters. Notably, this chapter defines the distinct elements in CIs essential for understanding how these structures and services underpin the online environment and societies dependency on the consistent function of these structures and services. Therefore, these entities are increasingly vulnerable to attacks, which require a high level of protection and security measures. Chapter 2 moves on to defining the actors in the online environment and applies the definitions to key online groups. The aim is to understand the complex offline groups and their foundation applicable to online groups. Likewise, this chapter also outlines how the actors are exploring the online environment. Chapter 3 follows this conceptualisation of actors by adding the different attack forms to the context. The actors are innovative and constantly exploring new ways to exploit the victims. Hence, the chapters outline a list of current means and methods. Chapter 4 is the final definitional chapter. The core elements generate an understanding of the anticipatory governance forms based on risk. This book's theoretical foundation aligns with the complexity theory and game theory introduced to the security strategies, deterrence and defence policies.

Part 2

The second part of this book covers three case studies outlined in Chapters 5–7. The three main areas included in the chapters are motivation, actors, and means and methods. Each of the three chapters includes discussions about influential attacks conducted within a short time frame, classifications of actors, key legislations, and strategic positions to decrease the risks. The three areas are distinct, and the discussion points are not directly comparable. However, key elements apply to all three areas, and there are overlaps between the areas. Chapter 5 focuses on how state-sponsored actors are used in cyberwar and warfare, where groups operate in the grey zone of international law. This exposes a significant absence of regulations, cyber norms, and practices. Chapter 6 explores a new area where ransomware attackers are considered a national security threat and can be linked to terrorism. The actors are not state-sponsored. Instead, they are state-supported, operating with more autonomy. Again, this is a borderline concept where the legislation and norms are underdeveloped. The actors are usually associated with financial cybercrime, but this has changed, and they are categorised as politically motivated actors. Chapter 7 covers non-state actors engaged in online activism of various forms. The focus is predominately on new groups conducting attacks that have a significant impact; however, this chapter converging on two directions, the legal, political activist and the hacktivist conducting illegal attacks. The legislation is developed to manage illegal intrusion/hacking. However, those who are conducting the legal action are protected by the right to protest. Chapter 8 is the final chapter, which concluded on previous discussions included in the three case studies and sets out future directions.

Limitations

This book only included a selection of states, actors, and attacks as the number of attacks launched cannot be included. It is not possible to analyse all state and non-state actors engaged in politically motivated attacks. Therefore, some need to be excluded. The selection process is based on the dominance of actors, attributions, and media coverage these attacks have received, predominately in 2020 and 2021. The selection process has been conducted objectively based on media attention, attack attribution, and targets. Therefore, the selection does not represent the author's own opinion.

Most of the events included in this book have been unfolding during the research period, making this book topical. However, this has led to a limitation in the use of academic books and journal articles. Nevertheless, updated information about legislations, policy papers, reports, and online material from key institutions are included. The cases studies are being supported by mass media reporting of significant cyber attacks. Yet, the sources are being subjected to a credibility selection process. The media websites used are well-established news outlets, computing news magazines used within the tech industry, and blogs written by experts in this field. The information from these sources have been double checked to ensure the validity of the information.

References

Alcaraz, C. & Zeadally, S., 2015. Critical infrastructure protection: Requirements and challenges for the 21st century. *International Journal of Critical Infrastructure Protection*, 1, pp. 53–66.

Alexander, J., 2020. *K-pop stans overwhelm app after Dallas police ask for videos of protesters.* [Online] Available at: www.theverge.com/2020/6/1/21277423/k-pop-dallas-pd-iwatch-app-flood-review-bomb-surveillance-protests-george-floyd [Accessed 01 04 2021].

Allianz, 2021. *Cyber attacks on critical infrastructure.* [Online] Available at: www.agcs.allianz.com/news-and-insights/expert-risk-articles/cyber-attacks-on-critical-infra-structure.html [Accessed 07 07 2021].

Anderson, K., 2008. *How do we tackle political cyber-crime?* [Online] Available at: www.computerweekly.com/opinion/How-do-we-tackle-political-cyber-crime [Accessed 09 07 2021].

Barnes, J. E., 2021. *F.B.I. director compares danger of ransomware to 9/11 terror threat.* [Online] Available at: www.nytimes.com/2021/06/04/us/politics/ransomware-cyberattacks-sept-11-fbi.html [Accessed 28 06 2021].

Bayuk, J. L. et al., 2012. *Cyber Security. Policy Guidebook.* Hoboken: John Wiley & Sons Inc.

BBC News, 2021. *Hacker tries to poison water supply of Florida city.* [Online] Available at: www.bbc.co.uk/news/world-us-canada-55989843 [Accessed 17 06 2021].

Bing, C., 2021. *Exclusive: U.S. to give ransomware hacks similar priority as terrorism.* [Online] Available at: www.reuters.com/technology/exclusive-us-give-ransomware-hacks-similar-priority-terrorism-official-says-2021-06-03/ [Accessed 04 06 2021].

Carr, M., 2016. Public–private partnerships in national cyber-security strategies. *International Affairs*, 92(1), pp. 43–62.

Cavelty, M. D., 2013. From cyber-bombs to political fallout: Threat representations with an impact in cyber-security discourse. *International Studies Review*, 15(1), pp. 105–122.

Chapple, M., 2021. *Ransomware is a national security risk. It's time to treat it like one.* [Online] Available at: https://amp-cnn-com.cdn.ampproject.org/c/s/amp.cnn.com/cnn/2021/06/10/perspectives/ransomware-attacks-national-security/index.html [Accessed 12 06 2021].

Cimpanu, C., 2020. *Two more cyber-attacks hit Israel's water system.* [Online] Available at: www.zdnet.com/article/two-more-cyber-attacks-hit-israels-water-system/ [Accessed 17 06 2021].

Clark, D., 2010. *Characterising cyberspace: Past, present and future.* [Online] Available at: https://ecir.mit.edu/sites/default/files/documents/%5BClark%5D%20Characterizing%20Cyberspace-%20Past%2C%20Present%20and%20Future.pdf [Accessed 14 06 2020].

Clemente, D., 2013. *Cyber Security and Global Interdependence: What Is Critical?* London: Chatham House.

Clough, J., 2015. *Principles of Cybercrime.* 2 ed. Cambridge: Cambridge University Press.

Collier, K., 2021. *Barely able to keep up: America's cyberwarriors are spread thin by attacks.* [Online] Available at: www.nbcnews.com/tech/security/ransomware-attacks-leave-cybersecurity-experts-barely-able-keep-rcna1337 [Accessed 06 08 2021].

Constantin, L., 2021. *SolarWinds attack explained: And why it was so hard to detect.* [Online] Available at: www.csoonline.com/article/3601508/solarwinds-supply-chain-attack-explained-why-organizations-were-not-prepared.html [Accessed 05 07 2021].

Corera, G., 2021. *The US and UK agencies accuse Russia of political cyber-campaigns.* [Online] Available at: www.bbc.co.uk/news/technology-57658656 [Accessed 06 08 2021].

CPNI, 2020. *Critical national infrastructure.* [Online] Available at: www.cpni.gov.uk/critical-national-infrastructure-0 [Accessed 21 10 2020].

CSIS, 2020. *Significant cyber incidents.* [Online] Available at: www.csis.org/programs/technology-policy-program/significant-cyber-incidents [Accessed 26 08 2020].

Cyber Security Intelligence, 2017. *The difference between cyberspace and the Internet.* [Online] Available at: www.cybersecurityintelligence.com/blog/the-difference-between-cyberspace-and-the-internet-2412.html [Accessed 13 06 2020].

Department of Defense, 2016. *Department of defense dictionary of military and associated terms.* [Online] Available at: https://fas.org/irp/doddir/dod/jp1_02.pdf [Accessed 13 07 2020].

EC, 2005. *Green paper on a European programme for critical infrastructure protection.* [Online] Available at: https://eur-lex.europa.eu/legal-content/EN/TXT/?uri=celex%3A52005DC0576 [Accessed 27 10 2020].

EC, 2013. *Directive 2013/40/EU of the European Parliament and of the Council of 12 August 2013 on attacks against information systems and replacing Council Framework Decision 2005/222/JHA.* [Online] Available at: https://eur-lex.europa.eu/legal-cont ent/EN/ALL/?uri=CELEX%3A32013L0040 [Accessed 12 08 2020].

EC, 2020. *Communication from the Commission to the European Parliament, the European Council, The Council, the European Economic and Social Committee and the Committee of the Regions on the EU Security Union Strategy.* [Online] Available at: https://eur-lex.europa.eu/legal-content/EN/TXT/PDF/?uri=CELEX:5202 0DC0605&from=EN [Accessed 02 11 2020].

ENISA, 2021. *Critical infrastructures and services.* [Online] Available at: www.enisa. europa.eu/topics/critical-information-infrastructures-and-services [Accessed 07 07 2021].

Fedele, A. & Roner, C., 2021. Dangerous games: A literature review on cybersecurity investments. *Journal of Economic Surveys*, pp. 1–31. https://doi.org/10.1111/ joes.12456

Forcepoint, 2020. *What is Critical Infrastructure Protection (CIP)?* [Online] Available at: www.forcepoint.com/cyber-edu/critical-infrastructure-protection-cip [Accessed 27 10 2020].

Gagliordi, N., 2021. *NSA, FBI warn of ongoing brute force hacking campaign tied to Russian military.* [Online] Available at: www.zdnet.com/article/nsa-fbi-warn-of-ongoing-brute-force-hacking-campaign-tied-to-russian-military/ [Accessed 06 08 2021].

Gibson, W., 1984. *Neuromancer.* New York: ACE.

Gillespie, A. A., 2019. *Cybercrime. Key Issues and Debate.* 2 ed. Abingdon: Routledge.

Goud, N., 2020. *Cyber attack on Israel water system.* [Online] Available at: www.cybersecurity-insiders.com/cyber-attack-on-israel-water-system/ [Accessed 18 06 2021].

Green, L., 2001. *Communication, Technology and Society.* London: Sage.

Guiora, A. N., 2017. *Cybersecurity. Geopolitics, Law and Policy.* Abingdon: Routledge.

HM Government, 2016. *The UK National Cyber Security Strategy 2016–2021.* London: GOV.UK.

IBM, 2021. *What is cybersecurity?* [Online] Available at: www.ibm.com/topics/ cybersecurity [Accessed 11 07 2021].

Inglis, C., 2016. Cyberspace – Making some sense of it all. *Journal of Information Warfare*, 15(2), pp. 17–26.

ITU (2020) *Definition of cybersecurity.* [Online] Available at: www.itu.int/en/ITU-T/studygroups/com17/Pages/cybersecurity.aspx#:~:text=Cybersecurity%20 is%20the%20collection%20of,and%20organization%20and%20user's%20assets [Accessed 15 11 2021]

Janofsky, A., 2021. *China accuses US of launching cyberattacks, denies Microsoft Exchange hack.* [Online] Available at: https://therecord.media/china-accuses-us-of-launching-cyberattacks-denies-microsoft-exchange-hack/ [Accessed 20 07 2021].

Kale, S., 2021. *'It's quite feasible to start a war': Just how dangerous are ransomware attacks?* [Online] Available at: www.theguardian.com/technology/2021/aug/ 01/crypto-criminals-hack-the-computer-systems-of-governments-firms-even-hospitals [Accessed 03 08 2021].

Lapointe, A., 2011. *When good metaphors go bad: The metaphoric "branding" of cyber-space.* [Online] Available at: www.csis.org/analysis/when-good-metaphors-go-bad-metaphoric-branding-cyberspace [Accessed 19 11 2021].

Liu, X., Zhang, J. & Zhu, P., 2017. Modeling cyber-physical attacks based on probabilistic colored Petri nets and mixed-strategy game theory. *International Journal of Critical Infrastructure Protection*, 16, pp. 13–25.

Lorenz, T., Browning, K. & Frenkel, S., 2020. *TikTok teens and K-pop stans say they sank trump rally*. [Online] Available at: www.nytimes.com/2020/06/21/style/tiktok-trump-rally-tulsa.html [Accessed 01 04 2021].

Manning, P. K., 2019. Technology, law and policing. In: *Comparative Policing from a Legal Perspective*. 1 ed. Cheltenham: Edward Elgar Publishing, pp. 290–305.

Marinescu, D. C., 2017. Complex systems. In: *Complex Systems and Clouds*. London: Elsevier.

Molloy, D. & Tidy, J., 2020. *George Floyd: Anonymous hackers re-emerge amid US unrest*. [Online] Available at: www.bbc.co.uk/news/technology-52879000 [Accessed 28 03 2021].

Munk, T., 2018. Policing virtual spaces: Public and private online challenges in a legal perspective. In: *Comparative Policing from a Legal Perspective*. Cheltenham: Edward Elgar, pp. 228–254.

Munk, T., 2019. *Cyber terrorism: Definitional problems*. [Online] Available at: https://counterterrorbusiness.com/features/cyber-terrorism-definitional-problems [Accessed 17 08 2020].

Munk, T. H., 2015. *Cyber-security in the European region: Anticipatory governance and practices*. [Online] Available at: www.escholar.manchester.ac.uk/api/datastream?publicationPid=uk-ac-man-scw:266937&datastreamId=FULL-TEXT.PDF [Accessed 12 08 2020].

NCSC, 2015. *Understanding vulnerabilities*. [Online] Available at: www.ncsc.gov.uk/information/understanding-vulnerabilities [Accessed 06 08 2021].

NCSC, 2016. *Vulnerability management*. [Online] Available at: www.ncsc.gov.uk/guidance/vulnerability-management [Accessed 06 08 2021].

NCSC, 2021. *Device security guidance*. [Online] Available at: www.ncsc.gov.uk/collection/device-security-guidance/managing-deployed-devices/obsolete-products [Accessed 06 08 2021].

Newman, L. H., 2020. *A ransomware attack has struck a major US hospital chain*. [Online] Available at: www.wired.com/story/universal-health-services-ransomware-attack/ [Accessed 08 07 2021].

NIST, 2012. *Information Security*. Gaithersburg: US Department of Commerce.

NIST, 2020. *Cyberspace*. [Online] Available at: https://csrc.nist.gov/glossary/term/cyberspace [Accessed 13 06 2020].

OECD, 2008. *OECD Recommendation of the Council on the Protection of Critical Information Infrastructures*. London: Organisation for Economic Co-Operation and Development.

Paganini, P., 2020. *US agencies and FireEye were hacked with a supply chain attack on SolarWinds software*. [Online] Available at: https://securityaffairs.co/wordpress/112275/apt/solarwinds-supply-chain-attack.html [Accessed 26 12 2020].

Palmer, D., 2021. *Ransomware is now a national security risk. This group thinks it knows how to defeat it*. [Online] Available at: www.zdnet.com/article/ransomware-is-now-a-national-security-risk-this-group-thinks-it-knows-how-to-defeat-it/ [Accessed 30 04 2021].

Park, D. & Walstrom, M., 2017. *Cyberattack on critical infrastructure: Russia and the Ukrainian power grid attacks*. [Online] Available at: https://jsis.washington.edu/news/cyberattack-critical-infrastructure-russia-ukrainian-power-grid-attacks/ [Accessed 08 07 2021].

Paytoncular, C. E., 2021. *U.S. to treat cyber attacks with same urgency as terrorism.* [Online] Available at: www.teiss.co.uk/u-s-to-treat-cyber-attacks-with-same-urgency-as-terrorism/ [Accessed 10 07 2021].

Porterfield, C., 2021. *Hacker tried to raise chemicals in drinking water 'to dangerous levels' at Florida treatment plant.* [Online] Available at: www.forbes.com/sites/carlieporterfield/2021/02/08/hacker-tried-to-raise-chemicals-in-drinking-water-to-dangerous-levels-at-florida-treatment-plant/?sh=350432441f21 [Accessed 18 06 2021].

Poulsen, K., 2014. *'Cyber-war' and Estonia's Panic Attack.* [Online] Available at: www.wired.com/2007/08/cyber-war-and-e/ [Accessed 15 11 2021].

Pratt, M. K., 2019. *ICT (information and communications technology, or technologies).* [Online] Available at: https://searchcio.techtarget.com/definition/ICT-information-and-communications-technology-or-technologies [Accessed 07 07 2021].

Price, C., 2021. *How to protect our critical infrastructure from attack.* [Online] Available at: www.ifsecglobal.com/borders-infrastructure/how-to-protect-our-critical-infrastructure-from-attack/ [Accessed 07 07 2021].

Prokupecz, S., Kopan, T. & Moghe, S., 2015. *Former official: Iranians hacked into New York dam.* [Online] Available at: https://edition.cnn.com/2015/12/21/politics/iranian-hackers-new-york-dam/index.html [Accessed 07 07 2021].

Puyvelde, D. V. & Brantly, A. F., 2019. *Cybersecurity. Politics, Governance and Conflicts in Cyberspace.* 1 ed. Cambridge: Polity Press.

Reuters, 2021. *New generation of angry & youthful hackers join the 'hacktivism' wave, adding to cyber-security woes.* [Online] Available at: https://economictimes.indiatimes.com/magazines/panache/new-generation-of-angry-youthful-hackers-join-the-hacktivism-wave-adding-to-cyber-security-woes/articleshow/81707844.cms?from=mdr [Accessed 31 07 2021].

Security, 2021. *US to treat ransomware like terrorism.* [Online] Available at: www.securitymagazine.com/articles/95366-us-to-treat-ransomware-like-terrorism [Accessed 12 06 2021].

Segal, E., 2021. *New ransomware attack by Russian hackers highlights cybersecurity challenges.* [Online] Available at: www.forbes.com/sites/edwardsegal/2021/07/02/new-report-the-challenges-companies-face-to-prevent-and-respond-to-cyberattacks/?sh=340a8b4473b5 [Accessed 06 08 2021].

Shea, S., Gillis, A. S. & Clark, C., 2021. *Cybersecurity.* [Online] Available at: https://searchsecurity.techtarget.com/definition/cybersecurity [Accessed 11 07 2021].

Shires, J., 2020. Cyber-noir: Cybersecurity and popular culture. *Contemporary Security Policy,* 41(1), pp. 82–107.

Srivastava, M., 2020. *Israel-Iran attacks: 'Cyber winter is coming'.* [Online] Available at: www.ft.com/content/3ea57426-40e2-42da-9e2c-97b0e39dd967 [Accessed 18 06 2021].

Stone, J., 2020. *DDoSecrets' mission is 'unchanged' in wake of 'BlueLeaks' Twitter ban.* [Online] Available at: www.cyberscoop.com/blue-leaks-ddosecrets-twitter-ban-anonymous/ [Accessed 01 08 2021].

TechTerms, 2020. *ICTs.* [Online] Available at: https://techterms.com/definition/ict [Accessed 13 08 2020].

Tung, L., 2021a. *Biden: Major cyber attack could lead to a 'real shooting war'.* [Online] Available at: www.zdnet.com/article/biden-major-cyber-attack-could-lead-to-a-real-shooting-war/ [Accessed 03 08 2021].

Tung, L., 2021b. *NATO: Series of cyberattacks could be seen as the same threat as an armed attack.* [Online] Available at: www.zdnet.com/article/nato-series-of-cyberattacks-could-be-seen-as-the-same-threat-as-an-armed-attack/ [Accessed 02 08 2021].

UNESCO, 2020. *Information and communication technologies (ICT).* [Online] Available at: http://uis.unesco.org/en/glossary-term/information-and-communication-technologies-ict [Accessed 13 08 2020].

US DHS, 2011. *Blueprint for a Secure Cyber Future: The Cybersecurity Strategy for the Homeland Security Enterprise.* Washington, DC: US Department of Homeland Security.

US DHS, 2020. *Critical infrastructure security.* [Online] Available at: www.dhs.gov/topic/critical-infrastructure-security [Accessed 27 10 2020]. Vallejo, J., 2021. Hunt for hackers who seized Florida city's water supply in online attack to poison it. [Online] Available at: www.independent.co.uk/news/world/americas/hacker-poison-florida-water-supply-b1799450.html [Accessed 18 06 2021].

Vincent, J., 2021. *US and allies accuse Chinese government of masterminding Microsoft Exchange cyberattack.* [Online] Available at: www.theverge.com/2021/7/19/22583251/us-government-blames-china-cyberattacks-microsoft-exchange-hack [Accessed 19 07 2021].

Whitaker, B., 2021. *SolarWinds: How Russian spies hacked the justice, state, treasury, energy and commerce departments.* [Online] Available at: www.cbsnews.com/news/solarwinds-hack-russia-cyberattack-60-minutes-2021-02-14/ [Accessed 03 08 2021].

Whitney, L., 2021. *Kaseya supply chain attack impacts more than 1,000 companies.* [Online] Available at: www.techrepublic.com/article/kaseya-supply-chain-attack-impacts-more-than-1000-companies/ [Accessed 07 07 2021].

Zetter, K., 2015. *A cyberattack has caused confirmed physical damage for the second time ever.* [Online] Available at: www.wired.com/2015/01/german-steel-mill-hack-destruction/ [Accessed 07 07 2021].

2 The Growing Online Threat
The Actors

Introduction

Politically motivated cyber attacks are not a new phenomenon. However, online attacks are increasing in frequency and severity where the attackers exploit the technological development, interconnectivity, and interdependencies on computer systems and services. The motivation for attacking and how the online attackers operate is essential to understand how they use the online environment, developing means and methods to access, exploit, disrupt, and destroy vital online assets and services.

This chapter sets out critical questions for understanding problems related to the current classification of the groups and the legal and strategical issues, which are focus points throughout this book. The chapter focuses on defining different groups and actors offline and online and takes it outset in the classifications of offline groups. The groups are very diverse, but they are either state or non-state actors. The critical part of the classification is whether the groups have links to state actors or act purely outside the state apparatus. This chapter also includes a brief introduction to the architecture of the Internet platforms to understand the usefulness of the virtual space to launch attacks and communicate.

Cyberspace and Politically Motivated Actors

Cyberspace is often perceived from two contrasting perspectives, increasing the complexity of defining activities and actors. Cyberspace creates opportunities for new ways of carrying out attacks. It is widely recognised as a strategic environment for future conflicts: irregular and traditional (Macdonald & Mair, 2015, p. 10). There is a diversity of actors involved in cyber attacks; some individuals or groups are engaged in the thrill, the challenge, or the money. Other actors conduct attacks to damage or destroy critical infrastructures (CIs), such as power grids, water supplies, hospitals, etc. The dangers are numerous, spanning from stealing sensitive data or holding it hostage to potentially damage nuclear power plants, which can constitute a threat to everyday life – or have the ability to kill people (Parker & Kremling, 2017, p. 89). The groups

DOI: 10.4324/9781003126676-2

Table 2.1 Actor characteristics

Groupings	Characteristics
State actors	Sophisticated attacks
	More resources are available to develop and conduct high-level attacks
	Hierarchical command lines
Non-state actors	Less sophisticated attacks
	Innovative activities, using operational capabilities to develop new methods
	No or limited hierarchical command lines

Source: Holt et al. (2018, p. 392).

are often separated due to their involvement with the state, i.e. state actors and non-state actors.

The state actors are operating within the confinement of the hierarchical structure of the state. Non-state actors come together in loosely formed networks to communicate and plan their actions using web forums, instant messaging, and social networking sites to enable new networked formations useful for the attack. This formation is beneficial to these actions as the actors can quickly join the network to complete the attack to disband the collaboration upon completion (Holt et al., 2018, p. 392). This is also a tactic that has been used by the state-supported groups who are enjoying a high level of freedom as longs as they operated within the overarching strategies of the state.

The Definitional Lacuna

The lack of clear definitions of cyber attacks has been an issue from the early days of using the Internet for politically motivated attacks. In 1999, the then US President Clinton used the term 'computer hackers' about 'cyberterrorists'. Yet, no definition was developed to distinguish hackers and terrorists. At the same time, Clarke, the US' national coordinator for counterterrorism efforts, used information warfare in relation to hackers. Clarke linked information warfare to rogue states, terrorist groups, or criminal cartels that could carry out an illegal intrusion into computer systems on the national level. The overall effect could be compared with the strategic bombing of CIs during World War II (WWII) (Bowman-Grieve, 2015, p. 93; Ranger, 2018). The number of attacks has increased significantly, and new means and methods makes it important to define groups and attack forms.

Just as several cybercrime groups and individuals expose the online environment for personal and financial gain, the political actors do the same. Politically motivated cybercrime crimes have developed since the late 1980s, but online attacks have dominated the area since the late 2010s, where reports of new attacks are constantly being broadcasted. Cyberspace, the Internet, and virtual spaces are progressively embedded in political actors' strategies within the online environment. There are significant overlaps between political groupings in the offline environment and those developing online. However, there are also distinct features. The threats come from national states, groups, and individuals following a political agenda (Anderson, 2008). The actors embrace technological developments to expose gaps in computer systems, networks, and infrastructures underpinning the online environment. New large-scale attacks have emerged based on known means and methods, whereas new types develop parallel to them, making the area difficult to define. Understanding the different online politically motivated attacks and groupings needs to be considered in light of offline political systems and offences.

Politically Motivated Actors

Politically motivated groups can be challenging to conceptualise. There are several different groupings, motivations, and activities, spanning from warfare situations to activism. This broad political spectrum includes state actors, para-militant or patriotic groups, terrorists, hacktivists, and activists groups. Regarding ordinary and political crime, the "law is formal expression

Table 2.2 Outline of war and warfare groups and tactics

Types	Characteristics	Actors
War and warfare	War is defined as large-scale violence	Organised between political units
Proxy war	The product of a relationship between a state and non-state actors external to a conflict. Providing weapons, training, and fundings to a proxy	The proxy replaces the state Avoiding being dragged into a costly and often lengthy war.
Hybrid war	Low-level conflict that includes the full spectrum of capabilities Synchronise various instruments of powers simultaneously and intentionally	Combines state and non-state actors under the state authority Merging conventional and unconventional warfare
Irregular warfare	Consisting of surprise attacks, guerrilla tactics, and terrorism to reach a political objective	Predominately used by non-state actors who do not have the monopoly of the legitimate use of force

Sources: Bull (1977); Hoffmann (2009); Kiras (2019, pp. 184–185); Mumford (2013a, p. 11, 2013b); Najžer (2020); Williams (2008, p. 157).

of the value system of the prevailing social power" (Schafer, 1969). Changes to political systems sometimes happen as a natural development. At other times, changes are fuelled by shifts in social and political opinions, morals, and systems. The rise and fall of political systems, leaders, races, classes, and social systems have predominately been the trigger for changes – and most of these changes involve political crimes (Schafer, 1971, p. 381).

Politically motivated attacks can be carried out over a short period or part of a more extended campaign for changes. Attacks can be launched against one particular target in a discriminatory operation or attacks can be carried out indiscriminately against random targets. Yet, it is essential to investigate massive scale attacks from the outset of the offline environment to understand the offline attack types. See Table 2.2.

Politically Motivated State and Non-state Actors: War and Warfare

War and Warfare

According to Von Clausewitz's definition, "[W]ar is … an act of force to compel our enemies to do our will" (Von Clausewitz, 1997, p. 5; Williams, 2008, p. 152). War is distinct from peace, as war is a legal dispute using military means. Yet, this is not the same as military engagement. The parties in a conflict can legally be in a state of war, although no violence occurs between them; for example, the relationship between South Korea and North Korea (Williams, 2008, p. 157). The motive of entering a war conflict are the standard for determining the aim for using military force and the amount of effort used (Von Clausewitz, 1997, p. 13). State-based armed conflicts are those where the recognised government is one of the warring parties. In comparison, non-state armed conflicts are based on organised, collective armed violence without the involvement of a recognised government. Still, war and warfare can be linked to other actors outside the use of military force. Grey (2006) differentiates war and warfare by arguing that "War is a relationship between belligerents, not necessarily states. Warfare is the conduct of war, primarily, though not exclusively, by military means" (Grey, 2006, p. 37; Najžer, 2020).

Regarding war or other types of armed conflicts, the legality of using force is not necessarily the predominant question that the politicians consider. It is more likely that the considerations are centred around whether the policy objectives would be archived through the use of force, and it would be done at a reasonable cost. However, this would also depend on the situation's perceived aim: use force or not use force. If the state is fighting for ultimate survival, any cost would be reasonable. If the situation is linked to political empowerment and growth or to secure the welfare of non-nationals, it would be less acceptable to consider a high level of costs. There are direct costs allocated to offline conflicts that are much higher in comparison with online conflicts. In the offline environment, for example, modern weapons' destructive powers are limitless and destructive, which can cause significant damage to lives and properties, both military and civilian. There are political costs linked to the decision of entering an armed conflict. It is essential to consider what the response would be nationally and internationally. Here the considerations might be linked to the possible outcome of the actions weighing up the payoffs' probabilities. Even a victory might come with too high a price – and therefore, there will be a negative political impact on the actions taken. If the action is perceived to violate the internationally accepted norms and laws, politically, allies might act negatively. They might even interfere or support the opponent in the conflict, and there is a risk of direct sanctions being imposed (Morris, 2019, pp. 114–115).

PROXY WARS

Proxy wars are indirect involvement in a conflict, where states are trying to further their own strategic goals by using third parties operating outside the state apparatus (Mumford, 2013a, p. 11). Proxy warfare is described by the former US President Eisenhower as being a 'cheap insurance'. He suggested that this form of warfare is cheaper than conventional wars where the whole military apparatus is invoked. Thereby, there is a distance between the state and the actual combatant (Mumford, 2013b). The actors included can be a state using another state as a surrogate or activate non-state actors, such as terrorist organisations, militia groups or private contractors, or vice versa (Mumford, 2013a, p. 45). An emerging between traditional and proxy warfare is hybrid warfare. In this form of war, the actors invoke several different weapons and tactics to exploit creativity, ambiguity, non-linearity, and cognitive elements of warfare using state and non-state actors. The activities are designed to remain below the apparent detections and response threshold (Cullen & Reichborn-Kjennerud, 2017).

HYBRID WARFARE

Hybrid warfare includes multiple attacks route using various means, methods, and actors. Notably, the activities are conducted under central authority, such as the state or state-like actors. Hybrid warfare is aiming to archive political goals that would not be archivable using conventional means and methods. Blending the different attack routes allows the actors to exploit the opponents' weaknesses (strategic and doctrinal) while upholding a level of strategic surprise and deniability of involvement (Najžer, 2020, p. 20). Hoffmann (2009) has defined two definitive and conceptually interconnected areas used to define hybrid war and threats. The first area highlights that hybrid war "Incorporates a range of different modes of warfare including conventional capabilities, irregular tactics and formations, terrorist acts including indiscriminate violence and coercion, and criminal disorder" (Friedman, 2018; Hoffmann, 2009, p. 5). The second area is linked to the hybrid threats. Hybrid threats are defined as "Any adversary that simultaneously and adaptively employs a fused mix of conventional weapons, irregular tactics, terrorism, and criminal behaviour in the battlespace to obtain its political objectives" (Friedman, 2018, p. 31; Hoffmann, 2009, p. 5; Hoffmann, 2010, p. 443).

Other groupings and activities are linked to modern warfare. Irregular warfare is distinct from warfare describes types of violence conducted by substate actors. In contrast to conventional wars, irregular wars are linked to the modus operandi employed by one or all of the combatants. The weaker part of the conflict often prefers this method. This tactic is helpful to groups that fight to change a political system or administration by organising and fighting in small units, which are more effective than their state-based opponent (Kiras, 2009, 2019, pp. 184–185).

Cyberwar and Warfare

There is a risk of politically motivated attacks becoming normalised because cyberwar is sanitised and moved outside the public sphere. Online warfare and political attacks are operational in a grey zone outside the Geneva and Hague conventions regulating war and warfare. There is no ethical accountability associated with online politically motivated attacks. The public and private victims of these attacks are not protected. Contrary to conventional warfare, no attempts are made to shield the civilian victims from the long-lasting effects of these attacks. Moreover, the nature of cyber attacks is not catching the attention of mass media in the same way as territorial disputes, just war, civil unrest, terrorism, and other attacks in the offline environment. Instead, these incidents are mostly unreported. The reporting is circulated after the incident, which predominately is linked to the after-effect of the attacks and how the political actors have yielded the attack (Merrin, 2018, pp. 40–43; Porche III, 2019).

Table 2.3 Outline of cyberwar and warfare groups and tactics

Types	Characteristics	Actors
Cyberwarfare	Linked to attackers using computer code to attack an adversary's infrastructure and to support conventional warfare on the ground	State and state actors are using cyber attacks against a nation-state
Hybrid cyberwarfare	Cyberspace and computer technologies enable states to be involved in these activities without more expensive conventional forces and weapon	States that lack conventional military can still cause damage and chaos using asymmetric cyberwarfare

Sources: Hanna et al. (2021); Manjikian (2021, p. 276); Ranger (2018).

The complexity of cyberspace and computer software to attack adds a new layer to international relations and cybersecurity. Cyberspace and various technological advances in cyberespionage and cybercrimes create a new strategic game where actors include cyberspace and online platforms to their already vast numbers of weapons. Various CI structures and services are using the online architecture beyond the nation-states. Interlinked economies play an essential role as states are working together to accomplish economic growth. This makes states more vulnerable to attacks from other states. However, there is mistrust between state actors due to geopolitics, making them potential political targets for increasing cyber attacks. Due to cyberspace's nature and different tools to cover identities, it is difficult to identify the attackers, and therefore, several attacks remain undetected. Governmental actors are aware of the benefits of cyberspace to operate in secrecy. This means that cyberspace is useful to conduct large-scale attacks and operate in secret to spy on each other. Yet, the interconnectivity and the interdependence also make the states more vulnerable to direct cyberwar and warfare. These types of wars can have significant economic and political consequences for everyone involved, where counterattacks can be equally damaging to the attackers if CIs are targeted (Parker & Kremling, 2017, p. 113).

Governments and state actors work closely together in transnational formations to share information, harmonise rules, processes, and practices to reduce the frictions associated with globalisation and borderless cyberspace. These actions of these groupings are based on mutual trust. Yet, there are also limitations to the collaborations due to the failure of developing global rules, processes, and practices to manage the growing threats deriving in and from cyberspace (Bach & Newman, 2010; Kshetri, 2014, p. 8; Munk, 2015). Therefore, this dependency can act as a deterrence mechanism that needs to be factored into the strategic planning where the payoff can quickly change if the conflict escalates (Kshetri, 2014; Parker & Kremling, 2017, p. 113). The diversity of the cyber attacks deployed is manifold, with public and private targets and many different attack groupings. Cyber attacks can be designed to damage CIs. Examples of the diversity span over hacking systems of private companies, such as the 2014 attack against Sony Entertainment's planned cinema release of 'the Interview' that made fun of the North Korean leader Kim Jong-un. The revenge from the state-sponsored hackers was a hybrid attack on multiple levels (BBC News, 2014; Hautala, 2016; Sang-Hun, 2014). So was the hacks against Ukrainian power grinds in 2015 and 2016, where there are clear links to the conflict between Ukraine and Russia (BBC News, 2017; Hautala, 2016; Zetter, 2016). This hybrid warfare included attacks launched simultaneously online and offline to meet a political end.

Politically Motivated Non-state Actors in War and Warfare

While the rules and norms about war and warfare are usually based on state actors operating within the legal framework of war and warfare. These rules regulated state actors, while several conflicts and politically motivated attacks are based on interstate conflicts conducted by rebel groups, insurgents, and violent non-state actors. These non-state actors are usually not bound by these rules. Therefore, governments cannot hold them responsible for their actions under international law. Instead, the activities might be regulated under domestic law (Jakobi, 2020, p. 137). Several groupings, such as guerrilla warfare, insurgencies, state-sponsored activities/para-military actions, share characteristics with terrorism rather than armed forces.

Although the state acts outside the context of war and warfare in internal matters, state-supported violence policies characterise these activities, repression, and importation prompted by official government actors. The violence and coercion are launched against perceived enemies that threaten the interest or security of the state. Although official state actors can be involved in these activities, the activities are often conducted by unofficial agents contracted or encouraged by the state. The role of state actors is to direct these groups or set out the goal for the activities, but leaving the actual operation to the state-sponsored groups (Martin & Prager, 2019, p. 137). Non-governmental groups, organisations, or individuals acting consistently with state actors' aims are perceived as a part of the organisation of the state. This means that there is no delegation of power between the state and the groups unless the state has granted the non-governmental organisation or actor the authority of acting on its behalf. Different actors outside the state's realm might have particular technical or political expertise that makes them more efficient to undertake the task. It might be that the state is unwilling to invest in obtaining these capabilities, they are unable to do so themselves or the state-sponsored actors have conventional solid military capabilities, and by engaging with the groups outside the established areas of the state, it is believed that the state-sponsored group would have the ability and experience to deploy unconventional tactics or additional niche skills (Byman & Kreps, 2010, p. 3).

Armed actors emerging during armed conflicts are fighting on behalf of the state or against the rebel in support of the states to shield the local population from rebel demands or depredations. There is an increase in non-state groups and individuals operating in para-military units (Martin & Prager, 2019, p. 159). The groups have different size, location of operation, levels of professionalism, tasks, and their use of weapons and violence. They also vary in their actual formation, recruitment, membership, and relationship with the state and the population (Jentzsch et al., 2015). These groups are used in various types of civil wars, including irregular civil wars where states are pursuing high-quality local information, ethic or separatist insurgencies, insurgencies or military actions against foreign occupiers, and conventional and symmetric nonconventional civil wars (Fearon & Laitin, 2003; Jentzsch et al., 2015, p. 757; Kalyvas, 2006, 2008; Kalyvas & Balcells, 2010). The distinction between state-orchestrated and community-driven militia formation and organisation is not stable over time. Just as militias formed by communities might need assistance from state agents to continue to mobilise recruitments, state agents might have supported state-orchestrated militants in the formation but later progress independently of the state (Jentzsch et al., 2015).

Although states are widely involved in cyberwar, state-sponsored actors are linked closely to the state apparatus. These groups are essential for the state to distance itself from the online attacks. However, the use of the groups cannot be underestimated as they are creating an essential buffer zone, which enables the state to act outside the constraints of international law. The groups can be enacted through military deployment, contractually hired for the job, or sponsored by the state. In all these formations, the actors might be given direct or indirect support, but they are not acting directly on behalf of the state or through delegated authority (Holt & Bossler, 2016). Groups that claim to be independent have been attributed to the actual state and particular departments. The close links to the state raise questions about whether they are included in the state apparatus pursuing its political agenda or acting independently with its blessing.

Advanced persistent threat (APT) groups have claimed to be independent hacker groups. However, closer investigations show close links to intelligence agencies, distinguish between state actors and independent groups. Groups, such as the Russian Guccifer 2.0, Fancy Bear, and Cozy Bear, were all involved in the hacks into the US Democratic National Committee's servers during the US presidential election in 2016. For example, it was believed that Guccifer 2.0 was a Romanian hacker, but investigations in 2018 traced the hacker to the Russian GRU intelligence department (Lavorgna, 2020, p. 176). Russian cyber attacks have included major components of cyberwarfare activities, including cyberespionage and influence operations. The actors involved and their motivations reveal a very complex structure, where actors are directly linked to Russia's Federal Security Service, where other groups have been

Table 2.4 Outline of terrorist and insurgency groups and tactics

Type	Characteristics	Actors
Terrorism	A violent, secretive, surprise-based tactic carried out by non-national groups or individual	Primarily but not exclusively, a tactic deployed to influence governments' political climate, system and policies, communities of particular groups in society
Insurgency	Attempts to make changes through force of arms and the adversaries are asymmetric and weaker	Organised movement to overthrow of a legitimate through use of insurrection and armed conflict

Sources: Kiras (2019, pp. 184–195); Manning (2006, pp. 61–62); US DoD (2008).

backed by GRU (Porche III, 2019). As most of the states are operating below the threshold of cyberwarfare, such a declaring war online, they engage in irregular warfare by using state-sponsored actors.

Politically Motivated Non-state Actors and Terrorism

The term 'terrorism' is contested. The word covers conflict situations where one side's actions are considered legitimate while the other is illegitimate. The problems with the classification of terrorism occur in determining which audience or population recognises this clause as legitimate. Both the demographic and the support for the case can change over time. Although terrorism often spreads fear, they also seek to get domestic and international support and empathy from the population they aim to 'free' by the actions (Kiras, 2019, pp. 184–185). The notion 'one man's terrorist, another man's freedom fighter' covers two ends of the spectrum that cannot be combined. The question is 'who is the terrorist?' and the answer would depend on which side of the conflict asked. This also illustrates the difficulties of defining terrorism (Townshend, 2002, p. 23). There are different motivations and groupings classified as terrorists. For example, vigilante terrorism is politically motivated violence conducted by non-governmental groups and individuals. In comparison, vigilante violence committed by state-sponsored groups on behalf of the regime is often linked to the defence of a demographic group or political or cultural establishment, and vigilante state terrorism is used to preserve a preferred order (Martin & Prager, 2019, p. 159).

In an objective definition of terrorism, it can be argued that terrorism can be based on the acceptance of international laws and principles related to behaviours permitted in armed conflicts between nations (wars). This position could then be extended to conflicts between non-governmental organisations and states, differentiating between guerrilla warfare and terrorism, targeting military goals. In comparison, the terrorists' primary goal is civilians (Ganor, 2010). It is clear that terrorist organisations have a political motive, regardless of their other motives. They use political means and methods to reach their political, ideological, or religious goal (payoffs). These political objectives distinguish terrorism from other criminal activities, i.e. terrorist attacks vs pointless criminal killings. Terrorism can, on the one hand, be an element of a large military or guerrilla warfare strategy, but it can also be confined to more limited goals. The political motivation goes in multiple directions, from systematic terrors to pursuit a political goal, such as changing political systems, overthrowing colonial or oppressive rulers, destroying unjust economic regimes to more limited goals, such as demand prisoners' release, revenge, publicity, political statements, ethnic autonomy, etc. (Lenard, 2020, p. 4; Townshend, 2002, p. 13). See Table 2.3.

The target can also be broader than the actual target, as the terrorist activities produce fear within a large group of people beyond the immediate victims. This tactic is widely used as terrorists believe that associated fear can erode and threaten the quality or stability of the existing societal and political order (Lenard, 2020, p. 4; Scheffler, 2006, p. 5; Wilkinson, 2011, p. 4). Finally, terrorism often aims to target and harm civilians, and they continuously threaten the population with the risk of more violence. This is an area where terrorism is clearly distinguished from warfare, where the rules of warfare are introduced to prevent combatants from targeting civilians (Lenard, 2020, p. 4).

Insurgency

Insurgency is not conventional war or terrorism. However, it shares the foundation of using force to archive a political end. Insurgencies are characterised by the support and mobilisation of a significant part of the population. However, the character of the groups and the means and methods used vary depending on the aim. The operations can be linked to social, cultural, and economic aspects by using revolutionary, partisan, guerrilla, liberation, or civil war tactics. However, these groups have the means to contest, hold, and govern the territory. In this context, political control is essential, and the external physical and moral support for the goal is the prerequisite for the groups' success (Kiras, 2019, pp. 184–185).

Cyberterrorism

Cyberterrorism can be used by actors engaging in cyberwarfare, but not all cyberwarfare types can be categorised as terrorism. The categorisation is also linked to the distinction between cybercrime and cyberterrorism based on the attacker's intentions, targets, and level of harm. It is considered that it is more likely that cyberterrorists would focus on attacking CIs using conventional war and warfare means and methods compared with the traditional cybercriminal (Parker & Kremling, 2017, p. 131). However, in 2020, the distinction has been blurred by the increase in ransomware attacks targeting CIs. Ransomware has traditionally been considered a financial cybercrime. However, due to groups constant attacks on vital services, the impact on society and the fear of the targets, the frequency, and the level of protection offered by states, they are now considered national security threats and sidelined with terrorism, and levelled with national security threats. The whole process related to the ransomware attacks is getting considerable attention, i.e. cryptocurrency exchanges, illicit online forums or marketplaces, and botnets linked to these attacks (Paytoncular, 2021).

The motivation behind cyberterrorism is similar to conventional offline terrorism. However, the means and methods differ, and the reach and scope of these activities have changed as it is possible to conduct attacks from a considerable distance. The various cyber-dependent malware and software to conduct attacks are also different from offline terrorism. Similar to traditional offline terrorism, online attacks would also include several preparatory strategies and methods to ensure that the attack can be launched. These would include target choice, reconnaissance; entrance and exit routes; and knowledge about processes and practices. The preparations constitute a high level of risk, as the attackers might be exposed to cybersecurity actors and internal alarm systems. Yet, they are still more secure than preparing for an attack on the ground (Macdonald & Mair, 2015, p. 21). Undoubtedly, the online environment and the Internet's architecture are beneficial to terrorism planning and execution of various acts, such as recruiting, circulating propaganda, communicating, and conducting cyber attacks. Modern technologies amplify the terrorist organisations to communicate effectively online, broaden their message by reaching out to a broader audience because of the different anonymising software available (Jakobi, 2020, p. 207).

Groups, such as Aum Shinrikyo (Japan), al-Qaeda, and IS (worldwide), have used technology for recruitment, propaganda dissemination, and fundraising. The online environment allows these groups and individuals to use unconventional weapons in unexpected ways through asymmetrical warfare (Hamilton, 2017; Martin & Prager, 2019). Clearly, the unlimited access to the Internet, the connectivity, and the anonymity provided by various platforms and encryption software make computer technologies attractive for terrorists, which have emerged from using basic surveillance to more damaging tools while hiding on the Dark Web to avoid detection (Parker & Kremling, 2017, p. 133). There are limited data available about the level of cyberterrorism beyond the focus on religious terrorism using the online environment. Cyber attacks are rising in new settings, such as attacks on CI structures and services. Yet, individuals and policymakers tend to pay attention to high-risk scenarios on behalf of the probability of low-risk scenarios – even though with high probability. Hence, attacks might be unnoticed or classified as cybercrime rather than cyberterrorism (Jakobi, 2020, p. 207).

Politically Motivated Non-state Actors: Political Movements and Activism

Although political and social movements are distinct from terrorism and war and warfare, this area is rising. The majority of the actors are using peaceful means and methods to engage in political debates and activism. Despite being on the other side of the spectrum, protests can include violence. However, these are criminalised in the national criminal justice system and weighed against the right to freedom of assembly, protest, and freedom of speech. Civil unrest develops when social, economic, and political stress accumulate slowly until the pressure is released spontaneously as a form of social unrest (Braha, 2012).

Social and political movements enable people to collectively voicing their grievances and concerns about rights, welfare, and well-being of themselves and others. Social and political movements create an outlet for people to engage in actions that are an essential vehicle for articulating and pressing a collective's interests and claims (Snow et al., 2004, p. 3). In the 1970s,

Table 2.5 Outline of political activist groups and tactics

Type	Characteristics	Actors
Anarchism	A process whereby authority and domination are being replaced with non-hierarchical, horizontal structures, with voluntary associations between human beings	Political anarchists view the state's centralised, monopolistic, coercive powers and illegitimate
Civil disobedience	Both a political tactic and the foundation for a movement for social change A non-violent action where an individual refuses to comply with the law for moral or philosophical reasons	A group or individual that wilfully and openly refuses to comply with the law to highlight what is considered to be unjust
Activism	Intentionally taking actions to be about social or political change	A feeling by an individual, group, or nation of a cause of injustice that must be changed

Sources: Fiala (2017); Sliwinski (2016); Tindall et al. (2008); Wittel (2015).

political action was characterised as 'protest', and actions were defined as the willingness to engage in dissent, including unofficial strikes, boycotts, petitions, the occupation of buildings, mass demonstrations, and, if needed, acts of political violence (Nolas et al., 2017, p. 3; Norris, 2009, p. 11). In the 1960s and 1970s, a number of social movements were rooted in collective action, such as feminist, environmentalist, disability, antiwar, and gay rights – and more recently, the Occupy Wall Street and Black Lives Matter (BLM) demonstrations. These social movements have deployed successful strategies and tactics developed during the civil rights movement; predominately non-violent protests, boycotts, sit-ins, freedom rides, and mass demonstrations (Clayton, 2018; Sitkoff, 2008). On the other side of the spectrum, there has been a rise in political movements linked to the 'extreme right', 'far-right', and 'populist radical right'. The common denominators for these groups are their exclusionist and ethnic-nationalist notion of citizenship. This can be seen in the notion of 'own people first' (Arzheimer, 2009; Bélanger et al., 2019, p. 910; Mudde, 2007). See Table 2.5.

Anarchism

Anarchism is a sceptical theory of political legitimation linked to the justification of authority and power – and in particular political power grounded in moral claims about the importance of individuals' liberties and the idea of human flourishing deriving from an ideal of non-coercive consensus-building (Fiala, 2017; Wittel, 2015). A surge in anarchism is promoted by different social movements linking First and Third World struggles over the last decade. These movements have resulted in the formation of several new global political alliances blending the politics of globalisation. Political anarchism has enjoyed a renaissance where activists are deeply integrated into political movements, such as Global Justice, Occupy (Bowen & Purkis, 2018, p. 3; Scheuerman, 2018, p. 81). For some anarchist movements, violence is a part of the game where violence sometimes arises as a part of the activities. This is seen as an unfortunate and, to some extent, an unavoidable fact of political life (Scheuerman, 2018, p. 88; Wittel, 2015).

Civil Disobedience

Civil disobedience and activism are different from anarchism, although there are some similarities. Civil disobedience is a public, non-violent, and conscientious breach of the law to change political systems or governmental policies. The politically motivated participants are willing to accept that their actions might have legal consequences. This notion demonstrates their fidelity to the rule of law – contrary to the anarchist who disobeys the political consensus and the legal strains on their liberties. It can be argued that civil disobedience, on the one hand, falls between legal protest (Brownlee, 2013; Delmas & Brownlee, 2021). Due to conscientious refusal of accepting the status quo, civil disobedience also includes revolutionary action, militant protest, and organised forcible resistance (Brownlee, 2013).

Activism

There is a rise in alternative forms of activism based on cause-oriented politics, which has become mainstream. Political engagement in society is predominately linked to voting rights. Activism in this context is civic engagement within representative democracy in national states, including the channels influencing elections, governments, and parties where citizens are involved in the actual voting but also in campaign work, organised events in communities, lobbying politicians, etc. (Nolas et al., 2017, p. 3; Norris, 2009, p. 10). However, value-based political activism is also increasing. Value-based activism can be understood as political activism linked to assemblages of meanings and practices people feel about the world and the areas that matter most. This is linked to the normative challenges people face every day and what is important to them, i.e. what is good and wrong, how to act, and what to do. Decisions about individual ethics play in everyday value-based activism. For example, where to live, how to live, what to eat, and environmental issues can be lived experiences and social norms linked to political statements and activism (Nolas et al., 2017, p. 4; Sayer, 2011, p. 1).

Online Activism: Politically Motivated Hackers or Hacktivist Groups

The threat to cybersecurity spills over to the more private part of the spectrum. The actors are not linked to military units or political causes where violence and harm are promoted to spear a political or ideological fear (Parker & Kremling, 2017, p. 89). The majority of online activism is not related to cyber attacks. Instead, this form of online activisms circulate information that fed into a particular narrative to enhance a specific political or sociological perspective. For example, influencing votes as part of a large-scale attempt to affect public opinion or voting plans. The Internet provides a valuable platform for information favouring a preferred political candidate playing with the voters' fear and prejudice. Some issues of this practice are state-sponsored attacks, where politically motivated campaigns can quickly reach a global audience (Lavorgna, 2020, p. 174).

HACKER/HACKTIVIST COLLECTIVES

Hacktivism can broadly be defined as a combination of offline grassroots movements merged with computer hacking (Li, 2013, p. 305). Hacktivism has been defined as hackers using legal and/or illegal digital tools to archive a political goal, free speech, and promote human rights by moving offline demonstrations, civil disobedience, and low-level information warfare into cyberspace. Therefore, the activism activities are considered a modern equivalent of political protesters using the Internet as a means of communication (Trend Micro, 2015; Yar & Steinmetz, 2019, pp. 87–88).

Hacktivism combines a hack with activism where hacktivism turns traditional forms of radical protest into cyberspace-generated non-violence actions, such as virtual sit-ins or blockades. There are two forms of activism. One is mass action hacktivism. The other is digitally correct activism. Mass action hacktivism is close to traditional mass protests where activists defy the physical barriers by using the online environment. In this context, hacktivists reinvent the traditional political protest or civil disobedience and add a new online dimension to the political and social movements, whereas digitally correct hacktivism is the political application of hacking against online infrastructures. This is predominately used to ensure that online information remains free and accessible to everyone echoing the original ethical hackers' incitement to engage in online actions (Jordan & Taylor, 2004, pp. 68–69; Lavorgna, 2020, p. 60; Yar & Steinmetz, 2019, pp. 85–86). The means used are linked to cyber-dependent methods and malware that enables the attacks. Email bombs, website defacements, viruses, worms, doxxing, and leaking information are all methods used by various hacking groups. Using these tools, hackers can circumvent traditional activism forms with innovative actions to reach their goal globally (Yar & Steinmetz, 2019, pp. 86–88).

The Internet and Internet Platforms

The development has gone fast from the early computers, which could perform limited tasks and were expensive, to the current use of computer technologies, networks, and devices. Three decades ago, most people did not own a personal mobile phone or computer as they were still costly. The people who had access to these computer devices faced limited use and functionality compared with the current use of multiple devices and Wi-Fi systems in everyday life. The impact of computer technologies, networks, and devices cannot be underestimated. One of the significant innovations is the development of the Internet. The Internet and various online forums are instrumental for politically motivated actors similar to the architecture of cyberspace that enables cyber attacks.

The Internet

The online environment is not only computer technologies such as hardware and software. Equally important is the Internet, enabling online users to communicate, exchange knowledge, and search for information. In the same way as the development of computers, the military has influenced one of the most important innovations: The Internet. The forerunner to the World Wide Web (WWW) is the Advance Research Project Network (ARPANET). The US Department of Defence (DoD) foundered in 1969 research on networking computers with new processing capabilities. However, at the time, there was little interest from businesses to use computer systems to develop their commercial potential (Norman, 2017, p. 26; Yar & Steinmetz, 2019, pp. 7–8). The breakthrough of creating a networking computer system for sharing and processing information came in 1989 when Berners-Lee started creating the World Wide Web (WWW). WWW is based on an interlinked hypertext document system that forms the Internet. This is also defined as the networks of networks for multimedia access. (Gohel, 2014, p. 23). The Internet is a computer system that can process vast amounts of data traffic across a worldwide network. The global network ensures that computers worldwide are connected despite the different devices and persons operating them (Ropolyi, 2013, p. 2).

Today, it is possible to share information commercially and privately worldwide instantaneously (Puyvelde & Brantly, 2019, p. 3). The creation, obtaining, and transferring information is critical in cyberspace and the Internet, where the information flow takes various forms. The interconnected computer devices on multiple levels created a structure of processed data. Today, data are floating around in cyberspace and are also indexed on hard drives or memory sticks and clouds – continuously transmitted between various computers and stored externally on business, governmental, or private sever spaces. Thus, data structures are more complex and dynamic, in which the physical location is less critical (Gálik & Tolnaiová, 2019). However, interconnectivity and the way the Internet is used facilitate cyber attacks.

The accessibility of computer devices, the Internet and networks, and the architecture of cyberspace and the Internet means that people worldwide can communicate and share information. At the same time, cyberspace and the Internet provide attackers with global resources for moving data and information around and finding safe havens for conducting cybercrimes and attacks. Legal obstacles and judiciary challenges set up limitations for investigating these offences. Communications are routed through multiple jurisdictions, requiring assistance from local and national law enforcement and security actors. This makes it challenging to investigate or prosecute the different illegal activities. The inconsistent criminalisation of online behaviours and disharmonised cyber laws also create obstacles for effective policing of the Internet and virtual spaces. It is increasingly easy to cover up an identity, take on a fake identity or hide behind virtual private network (VPNs) or the Dark Web. Portability and transferability of devices and data make it difficult to trace the offenders as data can be stored on various portable devices, cloud storage, and the Internet (Clough, 2015, pp. 7–9; Gillespie, 2019, p. 13; Munk, 2018).

The Internet, a Vector for Attacks

Web-based or online threats are vectors for causing undesirable actions using the Internet and virtual spaces for attacks. These attacks are possible because of the architecture of the Internet, end-user vulnerabilities, web-serviced developers/operators, or the actual web services. All these areas can cause significant damage to individuals, groups, corporations, and governments (Kaspersky, 2021).

Various cybersecurity systems are often costly and challenging to integrate and manage. The vulnerabilities in the different systems come from insuring operating systems and network architecture to flaws in servers and hosts, misconfigured wireless action points and firewalls, and insecure network protocols. Yet, hardware vulnerabilities and software and applications vulnerabilities where coding errors or the software respond to particular requests unintendedly. Zero-day vulnerabilities adds to the complexity as attackers exploit gaps in the system unknown to the software vendors. As long as these exploits are unpatched, the attackers have free access to the systems and networks (ENISA, 2020, p. 2; IT Governance, 2021). These means and methods open various parts of the Internet to cyber attackers who can continue to use the web for malicious activities (Mimecast, 2021). The attackers can quickly move parts of their infrastructure, alter aspects of the code, adapt the functionality, gather more victim data, etc. (Europol, 2020, p. 12). Normal channels for communication have also been infected with malware. Any messenger can be manipulated to send dangerous messages, attachments, and links. Online users should always be suspicious about links and attachments. WhatsApp has been used in the past, and attackers use Telegram's bot account operating by software as an attack vector. These attacks are conducted by advanced threat actors on a sophisticated attack level to control malware (Doffman, 2021; Hofman, 2021).

Politically motivated attackers do not need to have a high level of computing skills to conduct attacks. According to Europol (2020), cyberthreats range from social engineering and phishing to ransomware and other forms of malware. The different threat actors are operating online with different levels of skills, capability, and adaptability. The top-tier attackers manage their operations professionally, where the less sophisticated threat actors rely on off-the-shelf materials to conduct their criminal activities (Europol, 2020, p. 7). Various vulnerabilities are available online for both attackers and cybersecurity professionals. However, attackers can buy the different tools and vulnerabilities online, enabling them to exploit them using a malware toolkit and online tutorials; both are offered on various forums on the Dark Web. More advanced attacks require a high level of sophistication and would be more lab intensive, but many of these attacks rely on the available tools (IT Governance, 2021).

The web threats expose the interconnectivity of systems and services where the threats travel the systems to amplify the attacks. The attacks are often caused by a mixture of human manipulation and technical commands. The malicious actors usually place the threats in locations where the users will engage with them, such as public web pages, social media, web forums, and emails. Thereby, the online users play an active role in enabling the infection and spreading the web threats. Often the threats are being spread by innocent online users who unknowingly spread the threats to other users and networks (Europol, 2020, p. 15; Kaspersky, 2021). By targeting online users, social engineering and phishing have a high impact on society. Attackers are using two ways to conduct their activities online. One method is to conduct untargeted attacks, where they are indiscriminately using the online environment to attack as many devices, services, and users as possible. These techniques enable most attacks, from extortion to acquiring sensitive information, to execute more advanced malware attacks (Europol, 2020, p. 15; NCSC, 2016; Pratt, 2021). The second method uses targeted attacks, where the targets are singled out because the attacker has a particular interest in the victims. The groundwork for these attacks can take months, where the attackers seek out the best routes for infecting the systems. These attacks are more damaging than untargeted attacks, as the exploits are designed to access the target's system (NCSC, 2016; Pratt, 2021). An example of a targeted attack is the hacktivist group Anonymous that re-emerged in the aftermath of violent protests in Minneapolis after the death of George Floyd in 2020. The group threatened to expose crimes committed by the police force (Molloy & Tidy, 2020; Pratt, 2021).

Attackers are employing a holistic approach to their attacks and the initial parts of the different schemes. In terms of phishing, the attackers demonstrate a high level of competency by combining the different tools, systems, and vulnerabilities. Collaborations are also developing, and the actors are sharing tools and platforms. The groups are also conducting attacks together, which increased the challenges for blocking or tracing the groups. Moreover, skilled attackers are increasingly targeting preselected victims instead of attacking randomly to optimise their gains. Information gathering and victim profiling have become integrated into operations (Europol, 2020, p. 15).

The attackers are conducting repeated stages as a part of their operations. The attacks started on the survey stage, where the attackers are using any possible means available to find the technical, procedural, or physical vulnerabilities. Having obtained these initial types of information, the attackers move to the developer stage to identify a path for exploiting the vulnerabilities. The actual breach stage depends on the nature of the vulnerability and the explosion method. The attack can open up the affect stage allowing the attackers to explore the system further. The attacker might exit the system and remove all evidence of the intrusion or create backdoors for future exploitation by them or other attackers (NCSC, 2016). The large-scale supply-chain attack against SolarWind provides a clear example of how more than one actor can use these attack routes. In 2020, the SolarWind attack was discovered, which has been attributed to Russian threat actors. At the same time, Chinese attackers were using the zero-day vulnerability to install the SUPERNOVA web shells on the IT monitoring platforms. This attack is unrelated to the SUNBURST attack by the Russian attackers against SolarWinds Orion businesses software updates. Yet, due to the complexity of the attack, it took time to separate the two attack groups. The Chinese group, the Spiral threat group (DEV-0322), targeted software companies and entities within the base sector of US Defence (Cimpanu, 2021; Secureworks, 2021).

ONLINE PLATFORMS AND INTERACTIONS

Cyberspace and the Internet are attractive to users for several reasons. First, it has developed into an important place for communication that encompasses distinct social dynamics. Cyberspace and the Internet open for communication display a different pattern compared with traditional offline communication forms. Everyday associations are created which trigger assumptions or connotations regarding the degree or quality of interaction of online users, their social relationship, or the temporal and spatial belongings. However, these are defined in the context of the interactions and purposes of the communications (Chmiel et al., 2011). The use of computer technologies and online platforms varies. Online communities developed because online communications coexist with the physical world. Due to changes in the ecosystems and how computer technologies are embedded in everyday life, it becomes challenging to separate offline and online experiences as they are inherently blended. Online user's perceptions and experiences of computer-mediated use change depending on the different tasks they undertake and how they communicate and interact at a given time (Croon, 1999).

Political network societies are centred around digitalisation, connectivity, nodes, transfer of information, power, space, and culture. These areas create a new wealth production, enable debates, manage populations, and sharpen relations between groups and individuals. Compared with offline communities, networked societies are decentred social systems where connectivity binds people together. The existence within these online spaces requires an omnipotent ability to change. Flexibility to adjust is vital when involved with these online communities to embrace the constant flow of information, ideas, technologies, and shifting connectivity patterns (Athique, 2013, pp. 16–17). Networked societies are instrumental for politically motivated online users, who groups online with like-minded people across traditional offline boundaries. The interconnectivity and borderless societies create opportunities for political actors. Everyone with a political agenda has the potential to become a cyberwarrior. Technological evolution has unleashed repressed desires from an online user to engage in various politicised activities. Moreover, the evaluation has removed barriers to creating and participating by enabling several people to access the various platforms and the opportunity for sharing tools, knowledge, and skills (Merrin, 2018, p. 189).

Online users create virtual societies to promote political and/or social issues and mobilise like-minded citizens in the online environment. The web creates an opportunity for politically motivated online users to be involved in permanent campaigns and interactions in both a global, regional, national, or local context, depending on the area of concern. The decentralised nature of the online environment spills over this area, and these groups of people often act without clear leadership (Siapera, 2018, pp. 54–55). The online media enables the actors to be engaged with no physical barriers, and they can work beyond the different groupings, shifting in and out of the online spaces.

These movements are more based on individual experiences and narratives rather than ideological theories and goals. This change is in line with a broader historical shift where social movements are grounded in identity policies that offer flexibility to adjust, regroup, and reconfigure themselves with the case and the end goal (Siapera, 2018, p. 55). Most online political activism is non-violent civil disobedience and protects very similar to offline social movements (Yar & Steinmetz, 2019, p. 85). However, the actual means and methods are different – and so is the way they are organised. This change of social movements is reflected in hacktivism that illustrates the group's decentralised establishment and how they align with and embraces modern technologies. The information flows to reach their goals. Hacktivism projects are based on online users who support projects and particular viewpoints in line with their own identities, and they show the imagination and depth of their political interactions (Siapera, 2018, p. 56).

POLITICALLY MOTIVATED GROUP ACTIVITIES FUELLED BY ONLINE PLATFORMS

There are groups of online users conducting actions to meet a political end. These are not linked to the military or terrorist organisations – hacking or hacktivism. Instead, online users and political actors created their collective subunit to pursue an overall goal. Promoters of Western activism have welcomed the Internet and online platforms to circulate human rights, and democratic values and activities are praised. Before developing the Internet, there were several ways people could communicate their disdain with political decisions by writing letters to media outlets or their parliamentary representatives. People could also raise their opinion in public settings. The web has extended this form of protest as various online platforms, and communication boards enable online users to express their viewpoints on politics and social issues (Holt et al., 2018, p. 85).

Other groupings have also adopted the Internet to promote their political end without being classified as cyberterrorism. The radical right movements are often associated with white supremacist groups (Holt et al., 2018, p. 405). These activist groups, such as the far-right hate groups, are often based on the concept of leaderless resistance, where the individual and autonomous activity is encouraged, and all can claim involvement with the group. Therefore, they are organisationally and conceptually different from terrorist groups, which have some form of a hieratical structure. Leaderless resistance enables online users to communicate in a wider geographical sphere enabled by cyberspace and its interconnectedness (Bowman-Grieve, 2015, p. 89).

THE INTERNET: THE DARK WEB

The different layers of the Internet allow different actors to operate in open or closed encrypted societies. Both open and closed communications and interactions can provide a space for pursuing political interests. Internet users are most familiar with the Surface Web. The Surface Web is content indexed by search engines, and it is a part of the WWW, which everyone can access (Yar & Steinmetz, 2019, p. 10). Compared with the Surface Web, the Deep Web contains a more significant amount of hidden data (Chang & Cho, 2006, p. 804). The data on the Deep Web are not accessible through static URL links. Instead, data are assembled into web pages where the online users can enter by using personal log in details or other types of authorisation to access the underlying databases and the Surface Web crawlers are prohibited from accessing these databases (Bin He et al., 2007, pp. 95–96; Yar & Steinmetz, 2019, p. 10).

Despite the Deep Web providing more security for the political actors when online, the Dark Web has predominately been used for secret communications and activities due to the protection offered on these spaces. The Dark Web is placed within the Deep Web. However, the access and the actual space differ from both the surface and the Deep Web. The Dark Web consists of a large number of unindexed information that is only accessible through the Onion Router (TOR) and the Invisible Internet Project (I2P), which hides the IP addresses of the online users (Lavorgna, 2020, p. 141;

Table 2.6 The Surface, Deep, and Dark Web

Levels	Characteristics
The Surface Web	Part of the WWW that is readily available to the general public
	Searchable with standard web search engines
	Widely used in regular day-to-day activity for standard searches
	Do not require particular configurations
The Deep Web	Part of the WWW
	Contents are not indexed on search engines
	No links are visible on the Surface Web
	Includes all of the Internet pages which cannot be searched or opened by other users, i.e. webmail, online banking, and services
The Dark Web	Part of the WWW but as a restricted-access network.
	Less accessible subset of the Deep Web
	Relies on connections made between trusted peers
	Requires specialised software, tools, or equipment to access
	Only accessed through 'overlay networks'; these run on top of the regular Internet and hide access.

Sources: CIS (2021); Grustniy (2021); Varma (2018).

Yar & Steinmetz, 2019, p. 10). Multilayered encryption is enabled to ensure that all data traffic is relayed and encrypted three times through the process. The way the online traffic is routed allows the users to browse freely and accessing web pages that otherwise might be blocked on the Surface Web and the Deep Web (Andress & Winterfeld, 2014; Perera, 2015; TOR, 2020). The Dark Web offers a high level of anonymity, valid for the political actors' communication, planning, and execution of their online attacks. Accessing the Dark Web requires special encryption software and browser protocols to authorise access to space. This access is produced by the software, part of TOR's free service (Faizan & Khan, 2019; TOR, 2020; Wallance, 2016, p. 9). The dangers developing in and deriving from the Dark Web are real. Europol (2019) highlighted the problems stating that this space remains a critical online enabler for criminal products and services.

Encrypted communication applications allow the users to pursue illegitimate goals which are not possible on the Surface and Deep Web. Encrypted communication helps users access various services and create secret groups online. The anonymity and the interconnectivity are vital for politically motivated groups (Europol, 2019, p. 49, 2020, p. 43). Carding markets and forums on the Dark Web create relevant web communication platforms for these actors, i.e. terrorist organisations, politically motivated hackers, and hacktivists. The Dark Web enables these actors to manoeuvre in and out of these spaces undetected. The actors use the carding forums to enable individuals to share information regarding means and methods to engage online, carry out attacks, spread information – spy on victims and collaborate, as seen with the emerging ransomware groups. These forums and spaces enable politically motivated actors and cybercriminals to develop and share practices, buy and sell software, malware, etc. These include forums, file sharing, creative and website hosting sites, URL shortening applications and services, video and live streaming/sharing, news, and social media sites and platforms developed for legitimate purposes. Various political actors and cybercriminals have embraced these spaces for their illegal activities. The activities are also extended to the use of VPNs, anonymised cryptocurrencies, and DDoS mitigation (Europol, 2019, p. 50).

There is an increasing market on the Dark Web in the provision of digital and cybercrime elements. Personal data, access to compromised systems, attack services providing malware, ransomware, and DDoS attacks are essential elements to facilitate cyber attacks (Europol, 2020, p. 59). However, there is a shift in the use of the Dark Web by some of the groups. There are more options for using anonymous forums and market spaces not necessarily placed on the Dark Web. Organised cyber-groups have moved communications to private encrypted channels such as Telegram, Jabber, and WickR (Sharma, 2021). Some platforms exist on the surface or Deep Web interlinked with Dark Web goods and services, which offers additional benefits to the criminal enterprises and business models. Surface Web e-commerce platforms are used for increased accessibilities. These online shopping windows post links to the online digital e-commerce stores offering stolen accounts, databases, carding, crypters, malware, ransomware, and botnets (Europol, 2020, p. 59). The shift has been generated by increased Law Enforcement presence on the Dark Web, where marketplaces have been infiltrated and taken down in joint policing operations. The increased use of the Dark Web by 'wannabe' cybercriminals has also generated these changes, as the more advanced actors want to distance the newbies. Today, malware developers and political groups are relying less on the Dark Web for distributing their malware. Instead, they use black hat forums operating on the Deep Web and Dark Web to establish their brand and develop online communities. The Dark Web facilitates recruitments and acts to vet potential affiliates (Sharma, 2021).

By mid-2020, hundreds of organisations have been targeted by ransomware groups using double extortion attacks by exfiltrating the data before injecting the malware into the system. The use of Dark Web communities and services has been instrumental for these ransomware groups operating as 'ransomware-as-a-service' (RaaS), where the developers have sold and rented newly developed malware (Leddy, 2021). Various web pages have been created for leaking the data if the ransom was not paid. The ransomware groups are also developing their forums for communication on the Dark Web. For example, the REvil RaaS group communicates on its 'Happy Blog' placed on the Dark Web. The group uses its blog to increase the pressure on victims by posting information about the data extorted in the attacks (Mendrez & Kazymirskyi, 2021).

Conclusion

Different online groups emerge from the offline typologies; some are slightly different; however, the main characteristics are using the online environment to conduct the different attacks. Online warfare, terrorism, and activism are similar to offline definitions, so it is possible to transfer them to the new forms of groups that emerge. In contrast, the new inclusion of ransomware groups, hacktivism, and hackers differentiates in names but not their underlying foundation. The online environment acts as a vector for the actions, which links to the Surface, the Deep, and the Dark Web. These spaces are instrumental for facilitating actions in a borderless online environment where actors can operate anonymously and without being traced. Without cyberspace and the virtual spaces and communities, these actions would not have the impact as it has today. The ground can operate undetected to spy, disrupt, and damage their target's assets, structures, and services.

References

Anderson, K., 2008. *How do we tackle political cyber-crime?* [Online] Available at: www.computerweekly.com/opinion/How-do-we-tackle-political-cyber-crime [Accessed 09 07 2021].

Andress, J. & Winterfeld, S., 2014. *Cyber Warfare.* Amsterdam: Elsevier.

Arzheimer, K., 2009. Contextual factors and the extreme right vote in Western Europe, 1980–2002. *American Journal of Political Science*, 53(2), pp. 259–275.

Athique, A., 2013. *Digital Media and Society. An Introduction.* Cambridge: Polity.

Bach, D. & Newman, A. L., 2010. Transgovernmental networks and domestic policy convergence: Evidence from insider trading regulation. *International Organization*, 64(3), pp. 505–528.

BBC News, 2014. *North Korea berates Obama over the interview release.* [Online] Available at: www.bbc.co.uk/news/world-asia-30608179 [Accessed 21 11 2020].

BBC News, 2017. *Ukraine power cut 'was cyber-attack'.* [Online] Available at: www.bbc.co.uk/news/technology-38573074 [Accessed 21 11 2020].

Bélanger, J. J. et al., 2019. Passion and moral disengagement: Different pathways to political activism. *Journal of Personality*, 87, pp. 1234–1249.

Bin He, M. P., Zhang, Z. & Chen-Chuan Chang, K., 2007. Accessing the deep web. *Communications of the ACM*, 50(5), pp. 94–101.

Bowen, J. & Purkis, J., 2018. Introduction: Why anarchism still matters. In: *Changing Anarchism.* Manchester: Manchester University Press, pp. 1–20.

Bowman-Grieve, L., 2015. Cyberterrorism and moral panics. A reflection on the discourse of cyberterrorism. In: *Terrorism Online. Politics, Law and Technology.* Abingdon: Routledge, pp. 98–118.

Braha, D., 2012. Global civil unrest: Contagion, self-organisation, and prediction. *PloS One*, 7(10) e48596.

Brownlee, K., 2013. *Civil disobedience.* [Online] Available at: https://plato.stanford.edu/entries/civil-disobedience/ [Accessed 08 11 2020].

Bull, H., 1977. *The Anarchical Society: A Study of Order in World Politics.* London: Macmillan.

Byman, D. & Kreps, S. E., 2010. Agents of destruction? Applying principal agent analysis to state-sponsored terrorism. *International Studies Perspective*, 11, pp. 1–18.

Chang, K. C.-C. & Cho, J., 2006. Accessing the web: From search to integration. In *Proceedings of the 2006 ACM SIGMOD International Conference on Management of Data*. New York: Association for Computing Machinery, pp. 804–805.

Chmiel, A. et al., 2011. Collective emotions online and their influence on community life. *PloS One*, 6(7), e22207.

Cimpanu, C., 2021. *Microsoft links Serv-U zero day attacks to Chinese hacking group.* [Online] Available at: https://therecord.media/microsoft-links-serv-u-zero-day-atta cks-to-chinese-hacking-group/ [Accessed 14 07 2021].

CIS, 2021. *Election security spotlight – The Surface Web, Dark Web, and Deep Web.* [Online] Available at: www.cisecurity.org/spotlight/cybersecurity-spotlight-the-surface-web-dark-web-and-deep-web/ [Accessed 07 08 2021].

Clayton, D. M., 2018. Black lives matter and the civil rights movement: A comparative analysis of two social movements in the United States. *Journal of Black Studies*, 49(5), pp. 118–480.

Clough, J., 2015. *Principles of Cybercrime.* 2 ed. Cambridge: Cambridge University Press.

Croon, A., 1999. *Making Sense of Cyberspace. A Question of Being-With Information Technology.* Newcastle: University of Northumbria, pp. 1–9.

Cullen, P. J. & Reichborn-Kjennerud, E., 2017. *MCDC Countering Hybrid Warfare Project: Understanding Hybrid Warfare.* Norway: MCDC.

Delmas, C. & Brownlee, K., 2021. *Civil disobedience.* [Online] Available at: https:// plato.stanford.edu/cgi-bin/encyclopedia/archinfo.cgi?entry=civil-disobedience [Accessed 10 07 2021].

Doffman, Z., 2021. *Yes, telegram really is 'dangerous' for you.* [Online] Available at: www. forbes.com/sites/zakdoffman/2021/04/22/forget-whatsapp-new-telegram-warning-for-millions-of-windows-10-users/?sh=4f53fe578575 [Accessed 11 07 2021].

ENISA, 2020. *Web-based attacks. From January 2019 to April 2020.* [Online] Available at: www.enisa.europa.eu/publications/web-based-attacks [Accessed 18 11 2021].

Europol, 2019. *Internet Organised Crime Threat Assessment (IOCTA) 2018.* The Hague: Europol.

Europol, 2020. *The Internet Organised Crime Threat Assessment (IOCTA).* The Hague: Europol.

Faizan, M. & Khan, R. A., 2019. Exploring and analysing the dark Web: A new alchemy. *First Monday*, 24(5–6). https://doi.org/10.5210/fm.v24i5.9473.

Fearon, J. & Laitin, D., 2003. Ethnicity, insurgency and civil war. *American Political Science Review*, 97(1), pp. 75–86.

Fiala, A., 2017. *Anarchism.* [Online] Available at: https://plato.stanford.edu/entries/ anarchism/?utm_source=rss&utm_medium=rss [Accessed 08 11 2020].

Friedman, O., 2018. *Russian 'Hybrid Warfare'. Resurgence and Politicisation.* Oxford: Oxford University Press.

Gálik, S. & Tolnaiová, S. G., 2019. Cyberspace as a new existential dimension of man. Location: IntechOpen.

Ganor, B., 2010. Defining terrorism: Is one man's terrorist another man's freedom fighter? *Police Practice and Research*, 3(4), pp. 287–304.

Gillespie, A. A., 2019. *Cybercrime. Key Issues and Debate.* 2 ed. Abingdon: Routledge.

Gohel, H. A., 2014. Looking back at the evolution of the internet. *CSI Communications-Knowledge Digest for IT Community*, 38(6), pp. 23–26.

Grey, C. S., 2006. *Another Bloody Century*. London: Phoenix.

Grustniy, L., 2021. *Darknet, dark web, deep web, and surface web – What's the difference?* [Online] Available at: www.kaspersky.co.uk/blog/deep-web-dark-web-darknet-surface-web-difference/22254/ [Accessed 07 08 2021].

Hamilton, A., 2017. *Interview: Telegram and terror: How data encryption shapes our lives.* [Online] 13. 06.2017. Available at: www.digit.fyi/whatsapp-telegram-terror/ [Accessed 19 11 20210].

Hanna, K. T., Ferguson, K. & Rosencrance, L., 2021. *Cyberwarfare*. [Online] Available at: https://searchsecurity.techtarget.com/definition/cyberwarfare [Accessed 11 07 2021].

Hautala, L., 2016. *We're fighting an invisible war – In cyberspace.* [Online] Available at: www.cnet.com/news/were-fighting-an-invisible-war-in-cyberspace/ [Accessed 21 11 2020].

Hoffmann, F. G., 2009. Hybrid threats: Reconceptualising the evolving character of modern conflict. *Strategic Forum*, 4, pp. 1–8.

Hoffmann, F. G., 2010. 'Hybrid threats': Neither omnipotent not unbeatable. *Oris*, 54(3), pp. 441–455.

Hofman, O., 2021. *Turning telegram toxic: 'ToxicEye' RAT is the latest to use telegram for command & control.* [Online] Available at: https://blog.checkpoint.com/2021/04/22/turning-telegram-toxic-new-toxiceye-rat-is-the-latest-to-use-telegram-for-command-control/ [Accessed 11 07 2021].

Holt, T., Bossler, A. M. & Siegfried-Spellar, K. C., 2018. *Cybercrime and Digital Forensics. An Introduction.* 2 ed. Abingdon: Ruthledge.

Holt, T. J. & Bossler, A. M., 2016. *Cybercrime in Progress. Theory and Prevention of Technology-Enabled Offenses.* London: Routledge.

IT Governance, 2021. *Types of cyber threats in 2021.* [Online] Available at: www.itgovernance.co.uk/cyber-threats [Accessed 11 07 2021].

Jakobi, A. P., 2020. *Crime, Security and Global Politics. An Introduction to Global Crime Governance.* London: Macmillan.

Jentzsch, C., Kalyvas, S. N. & Schubiger, L. I., 2015. Militias in civil wars. *Journal of Conflict Resolution*, 59(5), pp. 755–769.

Jordan, J. & Taylor, P. A., 2004. *Hacktivism and Cyberwards. Rebels with a Cause?* Abingdon: Routledge.

Kalyvas, S. N., 2006. *The Logic of Violence in Civil Wars.* Cambridge: Cambridge University Press.

Kalyvas, S. N., 2008. Ethnic defection in civil war. *Comparative Political Studies*, 41(8), pp. 1043–1068.

Kalyvas, S. N. & Balcells, L., 2010. International system and technologies of rebellion: How the end of the cold war shaped internal conflict. *American Political Science Review*, 104(3), pp. 415–429.

Kaspersky, 2021. *What are web threats?* [Online] Available at: www.kaspersky.com/resource-center/threats/web [Accessed 11 07 2021].

Kiras, J. D., 2009. Irregular warfare: Terrorism and insurgency. In: *Strategy in the Contemporary World: An Introduction to Strategic Studies.* Oxford: Oxford University Press, pp. 185–207.

Kiras, J. D., 2019. Irregular warfare: Terrorism and insurgency. In: *Strategy in the Contemporary World.* 6 ed. Oxford: Oxford University Press, pp. 183–201.

Kshetri, N., 2014. *Cybersecurity and International Relations: The U.S. Engagement with China and Russia.* Greensboro: Proc. FLACO-ISA Joint Conference.

Lavorgna, A., 2020. *Cybercrimes. Critical Issues in a Global Context*. London: Macmillian.

Leddy, B., 2021, *Double extortion ransomware*. [Online] Available at: www.darktrace.com/en/blog/double-extortion-ransomware/ [Accessed 18 11 2021].

Lenard, P. T., 2020. *How Should Democracies Fight Terrorism?* Cambridge: Polity Press.

Li, X., 2013. Hacktivism and the first amendment: Drawing the line between cyber protests and crime. *Harvard Journal of Law and Technology*, 27(1), pp. 302–330.

Macdonald, S. & Mair, D., 2015. Terrorisms online. A new strategic environment. In: *Terrorism Online*. Abingdon: Routledge, pp. 22–46.

Manjikian, M., 2021. *Introduction to Cyber Politics and Policy*. London: Sage.

Manning, P. K., 2006. Case studies of American anti-terrorism. In: *Democracy, Society and the Governance of Security*. Cambridge: Cambridge University Press, pp. 52–85.

Martin, G. & Prager, F., 2019. *Terrorism. An International Perspective*. London: Sage.

Mendrez, R. & Kazymirskyi, N., 2021. *Diving deeper into the Kaseya VSA attack: REvil returns and other hackers are riding their coattails*. [Online] Available at: www.trustwave.com/en-us/resources/blogs/spiderlabs-blog/diving-deeper-into-the-kaseya-vsa-attack-revil-returns-and-other-hackers-are-riding-their-coattails/ [Accessed 07 07 2021].

Merrin, W., 2018. *Digital War*. Abingdon: Routledge.

Mimecast, 2021. *The danger of web security threats*. [Online] Available at: www.mimecast.com/content/web-security-threats/ [Accessed 11 07 2021].

Molloy, D. & Tidy, J., 2020. *George Floyd: Anonymous hackers re-emerge amid US unrest*. [Online] Available at: www.bbc.co.uk/news/technology-52879000 [Accessed 11 07 2021].

Mudde, C., 2007. *Populist Radical Right Parties*. Cambridge: Cambridge University Press.

Mumford, A., 2013a. *Proxy Warfare*. Cambridge: Polity Press.

Mumford, A., 2013b. Proxy warfare and the future of conflict. *The RUSI Journal*, 2, pp. 40–46.

Munk, T., 2018. Policing virtual spaces: Public and private online challenges in a legal perspective. In: *Comparative Policing from a Legal Perspective*. Cheltenham: Edward Elgar, pp. 228–254.

Munk, T. H., 2015. *Cyber-security in the European Region: Anticipatory Governance and Practices*. Manchester: The University of Manchester.

Najžer, B., 2020. *The Hybrid Age. International Security in the Era of Hybrid Warfare*. London: I. B. Tauris.

NCSC, 2016. *How cyber attacks work*. [Online] Available at: www.ncsc.gov.uk/information/how-cyber-attacks-work [Accessed 10 07 2021].

Nolas, S.-M., Varvantakis, C. & Aruldoss, V., 2017. Political activism across the life course. *Contemporary Social Science*, 12(1–2), pp. 1–12.

Norman, K. L., 2017. *Cyberpsychology. An Introduction to Human-Computer Interaction*. 2 ed. Cambridge: Cambridge University Press.

Norris, P., 2009. Political activism: New challenges, new opportunities. In: *The Oxford Handbook of Comparative Politics*. Draft ed. Oxford: Oxford University Press, pp. 628–652.

Parker, J. & Kremling, A. M. S., 2017. *Cyberspace, Cybersecurity, and Cybercrime*. Thousand Oaks: Sage Publications, Inc.

Paytoncular, C. E., 2021. *U.S. to treat cyber attacks with same urgency as terrorism.* [Online] Available at: www.teiss.co.uk/u-s-to-treat-cyber-attacks-with-same-urgency-as-terrorism/ [Accessed 10 07 2021].

Perera, D., 2015. *Foundation of 'dark web' steps into the light.* [Online] Available at: www.politico.com/story/2015/10/foundation-of-dark-web-steps-into-the-light-215027 [Accessed 27 07 2020].

Porche III, I. R., 2019. *Fighting and winning the undeclared cyber war.* [Online] Available at: www.rand.org/blog/2019/06/fighting-and-winning-the-undeclared-cyber-war.html [Accessed 21 11 2020].

Pratt, M. K., 2021. *Cyber attack.* [Online] Available at: https://searchsecurity.techtarget.com/definition/cyber-attack [Accessed 04 07 2021].

Puyvelde, D. V. & Brantly, A. F., 2019. *Cybersecurity. Politics, Governance and Conflicts in Cyberspace.* 1 ed. Cambridge: Polity Press.

Ranger, S., 2018. *What is cyberwar? Everything you need to know about the frightening future of digital conflict.* [Online] Available at: www.zdnet.com/article/cyberwar-a-guide-to-the-frightening-future-of-online-conflict/ [Accessed 11 07 2021].

Ropolyi, L., 2013. *Philosophy of the Internet. A Discourse on the Nature of the Internet.* Budapest: Eötvös Loránd Tudományegyetem.

Sang-Hun, C., 2014. *North Korea warns U.S. over film mocking its leader.* [Online] Available at: www.nytimes.com/2014/06/26/world/asia/north-korea-warns-us-over-film-parody.html [Accessed 21 11 2020].

Sayer, A., 2011. *Why Things Matter to People: Social Science, Values and Ethical Life.* Cambridge: Cambridge University Press.

Schafer, S., 1969. *Theories in Criminology: Past and Present Philosophies of the Crime Problem.* New York: Random House.

Schafer, S., 1971. The concept of the political criminal. *Journal of Criminal Law and Criminology,* 62(3), pp. 380–387.

Scheffler, S., 2006. Is terrorism morally distinctive? *Journal of Political Philosophy,* 14(1), pp. 1–17.

Scheuerman, W. E., 2018. *Civil Disobedience.* Cambridge: Polity Press.

Secureworks, 2021. *SUPERNOVA web shell deployment linked to SPIRAL threat group.* [Online] Available at: www.secureworks.com/blog/supernova-web-shell-deployment-linked-to-spiral-threat-group#:~:text=SPIRAL%20threat%20group's%20SUPERNOVA%20deployment,deliver%20the%20SUPERNOVA%20web%20shell. [Accessed 14 07 2021].

Sharma, A., 2021. *The state of the dark web: Insights from the underground.* [Online] Available at: www.csoonline.com/article/3601686/the-state-of-the-dark-web-insights-from-the-underground.html [Accessed 11 07 2021].

Siapera, E., 2018. *Understanding New Media.* 2 ed. London: Sage.

Sitkoff, H., 2008. *The Struggle for Black Equality.* Farrar (New York): Straus & Giroux.

Sliwinski, M., 2016. *The evolution of activism: From the streets to social media.* [Online] Available at: https://web.archive.org/web/20160130020535/http://lawstreetmedia.com/issues/politics/evolution-activism-streets-social-media/ [Accessed 06 08 2021].

Snow, D. A., Soule, S. A. & Kriesi, H., 2004. *Mapping the Terrain: The Blackwell Companion to Social Movements.* Oxford: Blackwell Publishing Ltd.

Tindall, D. B., Kay, F. M., Zuberi, D. M. & Bates, K. L., 2008. Urban and community studies. *Encyclopedia of Violence, Peace, & Conflict,* 2, pp. 2224–2244.

TOR, 2020. *Browse privately. Explore freely.* [Online] Available at: www.torproject.org/ [Accessed 27 07 2020].

Townshend, C., 2002. *Terrorism. A Very Short Introduction.* Oxford: Oxford University Press.

Trend Micro, 2015. *Hacktivism 101: A brief history and timeline of notable incidents.* [Online] Available at: www.trendmicro.com/vinfo/pl/security/news/cyber-attacks/hacktivism-101-a-brief-history-of-notable-incidents [Accessed 22 11 2020].

US DoD, 2008. *An Organised Movement Aimed at the Overthrow of a Constituted Government Through Use of Subversion and Armed Conflict.* Virginia: DoD.

Varma, Y. R. C. S., 2018. *CISO guide: Surface Web, Deep Web and Dark Web – Are they different?* [Online] Available at: www.cisoplatform.com/profiles/blogs/surface-web-deep-web-and-dark-web-are-they-different [Accessed 07 08 2021].

Von Clausewitz, C., 1997. *On War.* London: Wordsworth.

Wallance, P., 2016. *The Psychology of the Internet.* 2 ed. Cambridge: Cambridge University Press.

Wilkinson, P., 2011. *Terrorism Versus Democracy. The Liberal State Response.* 3 ed. Abingdon: Routledge.

Williams, P. D., 2008. War. In: *Security Studies. An Introduction.* Abingdon: Routledge, pp. 151–170.

Wittel, A., 2015. *What is anarchism all about?* [Online] Available at: https://theconversation.com/what-is-anarchism-all-about-50373 [Accessed 06 08 2021].

Yar, M. & Steinmetz, K. F., 2019. *Cybercrime and Society.* 3 ed. London: Sage.

Zetter, K., 2016. *Inside the Cunning, unprecedented hack of Ukraine's power grind.* [Online] Available at: www.wired.com/2016/03/inside-cunning-unprecedented-hack-ukraines-power-grid/ [Accessed 26 08 2020].

3 Cyber Attacks, Means, and Methods

Introduction

The online environment creates an architecture that offers numerous opportunities for politically motivated actors to launch attacks that exploit computer technologies, devices, and networks. The technological development opens up new avenues allowing the attackers to enter and manoeuvre undetected, often for a long time before they are discovered and the vulnerabilities used are patched. The frequency and severity of these attacks have reached a level that cannot be recreated in the offline environment. The previous chapter outlined the different actors linked to politically motivated attacks to generate a comprehensive understanding of the different groups' motivations. This chapter aims to define how the attacks are conducted and the tools available to the attackers. Finally, this chapter offers insight into various means and methods used by the actors.

Cyber-dependent and Cyber-enabled Attacks

Politically motivated cyber actors have several means available for their activities, and these have been extended over the years. The attackers are capitalising on modern technologies and the lack of security. Therefore, these actors continually develop their modus operandi to exploit computer technologies, systems, and networks to fulfil their political agenda. Some attacks mirror offline crime, but there is a difference in the scope and the reach. Whereas other attacks are innovative and can only be conducted in online environments. These constitute a new way of attacking propelled by constant technological development. The attack types fall into two categories, cyber-dependent and cyber-enabled attacks deriving from the cybercrime typologies (Holt & Bossler, 2016; McGuire & Dowling, 2013; Rokven et al., 2018).

Previously, politically motivated actors were considered in the realm of either cyberwar or cyberterrorism. Yet, the scope has been extended significantly to cover states, terrorists, state-sponsored hacking groups, or state-supported groups and actors outside the state sphere, where online activism or hacktivism are emerging. These groups are using the same means and

DOI: 10.4324/9781003126676-3

Table 3.1 Cyber-dependent and cyber-enabled attacks

Typology	Characteristic	Examples
Cyber-dependent attacks	New types of crime These attacks are **dependent** on the online environment and cannot be replicated in the offline environments	Malware, ransomware, APTs, supply-chain attacks, DoS and DDoS attacks, etc.
Cyber-enabled attacks	Mirrors offline crimes The online environment **enables** these attacks, and they can be replicated in the offline environment	Espionage, surveillance, disinformation, doxxing, defacement and trolling, etc.

Source: UK CPS (2019).

methods, and they all are linked to a political motivation, but the actions and the groups are considered differently. Therefore, it is crucial to consider the motivation behind these groups and individuals to categorise the attack.

Cyber-dependent attacks are those crimes that can only be committed using information and communication technology (ICT) devices. In this context, the device becomes both the tool for committing the crime and the actual target, i.e. developing and propagating malware for financial gain, hacking to steal, damage, alter, or destroy data, computer systems or networks – or particular online activities. These can, for example, be developing and circulating malware, hacking, stealing sensitive personal or industrial data, attacking using denial-of-service (DoS) or distributed denial-of-service (DDoS) attacks to overflood web pages or mailboxes with requests to face financial or reputational damage (Clough, 2015, p. 11; Europol, 2020, p. 14; HM Government, 2016, p. 17; Munk, 2018, p. 235; Rokven, et al., 2018, p. 28; UK CPS, 2019). Hackers are central to developing these new attack forms as well as hacking into systems.

Cyber-enabled attacks are those crimes that mirror crimes committed in an offline environment, where the Internet and cyberspace create opportunities to offend on an unprecedented scale. By using ICTs to conduct attacks, it is possible to reach out to a broader number of targets using computers, networks, or other forms of ICT (Clough, 2015, p. 11; Munk, 2018, p. 235; Rokven et al., 2018, p. 28; UK CPS, 2019).

Politically Motivated Cyber-dependent and Cyber-enabled Attacks

The different types of cybercrime, dependent or enabled by the online environment, can be separated into three areas depending on the offender's motivation. These are personal cybercrime, financial cybercrime, and political cybercrime. The motivation is the drive behind the actions; however, this is not necessarily a clear-cut distinction. For example, the attackers can be involved in a politically motivated campaign and benefit financially from the attack. Alternatively, the motivation can predominately be personal, but the target is political. This makes it difficult to make a precise classification of the attackers. Many attacks are originating from Russia, China, North Korea, Iran, and other places. Countries like the US and Israel are also involved in large-scale cyberwarfare campaigns. However, threats are also emerging from other countries and regions as well as domestically. New regional cybercrime hotspots are also beginning to threaten South Asia and West Africa, which creates a growing concern (HM Government, 2016, p. 17).

The aim and motivation behind the attacks can be multifold, but they are mostly linked to damage, distorting or destroying data or networks (UK CPS, 2019). Several different means and methods are being used. Hostile takeovers or extortion, such as ransomware, are methods that are rapidly increasing. These attack forms have proven effective, and politically motivated actors have adopted them, tricking victims into downloading innocent-looking software to enable access. The software used encrypts the data on the computer or server, preventing the targets from accessing the systems unless they pay a ransom (Europol, 2020; Jeffray, 2014, p. 5).

There is some confusion about the typology used to separate these two areas. A cyber-dependent crime could be an organised cyber attack using malicious software or malware, such as a virus, a worm, a Trojan horse, or a logic bomb to carry out the attack. However, the categorisation is not straightforward in determining whether this is a personal cybercrime, a financial cybercrime, or a politically motivated crime. The attack could be politically motivated carried out against financial institutions because of the business cases. However, it could also be that the political group needed money to finance their other activities. Is this a financial attack, or is it politically motivated? For example, in terms of attributing an attacker, it is nearly impossible to identify whether an attack originates from a military unit, an independent hacker or an organised crime group. All these would use the same means and methods. Of course, all of them could have been involved in the same attack (Klimburg, 2009, 2011, pp. 41–42; Munk, 2015, p. 49).

Hacking and Hackers

There has been a shift in the targets of cyber attacks. The motivation for attacks is not necessarily linked to targeting the public sector, the government, or the establishment; businesses, corporations, groups, and individuals are equally targeted by the politically motivated groups and individuals. Hacking does not have a single comprehensive definition. Instead, it covers several different activities. The phrase 'hacking' covers both those who write the codes and those exploiting them. The people involved in these two processes have different goals. Nevertheless, both groups' means and methods are linked to problem-solving techniques (Erickson, 2008, p. 10).

It is essential to consider the actual impact of the hack and all the impacts associated with the primary behaviour. The impact of the actions goes beyond the actual hack. For states, groups, companies, and individual users, there are financial losses related. However, there might also be long-term effects, such as get the system up running again or actual damage to physical or virtual assets. Hacks that modify, alter, or subvert security protocols are illegal in most jurisdictions (UK CPS, 2019). Hacking can also be used to obtain information or access computer systems and other protected computer technologies or networks to further an illegal act (Holt et al., 2018, p. 69). The actual hack does not necessarily introduce anything new to the systems, but it enables the hackers to derive everything from the hosts' protocols and procedures. Often the hack is deployed to understand how the system operated, and the hacker experiment with different manipulations linked to the system's initial programming and interconnected devices (Gunkel, 2018, p. 6).

New vulnerabilities have appeared, allowing hackers to develop tools and pathways that follow new technologies. Most hackers are still involved in the process, but their activities have been diversified to fulfil a demand from less technical skilled groups and individuals. Beyond the actual hacking, some hackers are developing and selling hacking software solutions on the Dark Web, which makes it easy for less technical skilled hackers to access computer systems and networks illegally. Hackers are developing advanced hacking tools, for example, botnet, control server infrastructure, remote access tools, malware creation and obfuscation services, source-code writing services, and targeted exploitation toolkits available on various underground markets (An, 2017; Palmer, 2019).

Hackers

Ludlow claimed in 1996 that the word 'hackers' had a twofold meaning:

> Originally, a hacker was someone who liked to hack computer code (i.e., write programs) or, in some cases, hack electronic hardware (i.e., design and build hardware). Thanks to the news media, 'hacker' has also come to have a negative connotation, usually meaning those who illicitly hack their way into other people's computer systems. Some folks have tried to preserve the original (good) sense of 'hacker' by introducing the term cracker to cover cases of electronic trespassers. However, like all attempts to fight lexical drift, their efforts have failed.
>
> (Ludlow, 1996, p. 125)

As Ludlow argued, hackers are perceived negatively, but hackers can also be individuals who enable technologies to be used in new innovative ways for legitimate and illegitimate activities (Gunkel, 2018, pp. 3–4; Holt et al., 2018, pp. 69, 678). The term 'cracking' is a more accurate term for describing illegal access to computer systems (hacking) for criminal purposes by misusing computer systems. The word 'cracking' is a combination of 'criminal' and 'hacker'. However, strangely enough, this term has never really been adopted as a typology to describe the criminal intent behind the hack (Moore, 2011, p. 19). Instead, hacker and hacking are the preferred words to describe both legal and illegal intrusions into computer systems.

In the early days of the Internet, the hackers from both groups (legal and illegal) needed to understand programming to conduct the hacks. Compared with offline typologies, a hack is different from random violence or a simple form of vandalism. Hacking is a calculated and very precise incision into computer systems, programme, or networks. This practice was codified into the unofficial hacker commandments stating that "thou shalt not destroy" (Gunkel, 2018, pp. 6–7). Although these hackers were deeply involved in exploring computer systems and networks, they argued that they did it to learn, discover, and freely share their findings with a broader audience. Damaging computer systems and networks were considered unethical and incompetent (Yar & Steinmetz, 2019, p. 53). The hacker commandment demonstrates the key element of hacking associated with the pride of those with superior computer skills. The hackers did not aim to do anything unauthorised to damage or destroy. In the early days of computing, hacking merely described someone skilled in developing creative, sophisticated, and practical solutions to computer problems (Gillespie, 2019, p. 28; Kirwan & Power, 2013, p. 53; Yar & Steinmetz, 2019, p. 53).

WHITE, GREY, AND BLACK HAT HACKERS

The time has changed, and hacking is no longer seen as something ethical. Instead, the term 'hackers' is overshadowed by the notion of illegal activities. Hackers use all available means and methods to access, steal, damage, destroy, or circulate information. Hackers are divided into three different overall categories. These are white hat hackers, grey hat hackers, and black hat hackers. Of course, those engaged with the early development of hacking did not call themselves criminals, crackers, computer intruders, computer trespassers, or something similar awkward. Instead, the word 'hackers' is widely accepted despite attempts to make this more detailed by introducing under-categories, such as newbies, scripts kiddies, hacker-taggers, microserfs, cyberterrorists, and hacktivists (Kirwan & Power, 2013, pp. 55–57). See Table 3.2.

In a simple explanation of a complex area, white hat hackers are traditionally ethical hackers or pen-testers commonly associated with hackers employed by companies or states to seek vulnerabilities in systems to make them more secure by filling the gaps. White hat hackers are using hacking techniques to test various security measures following ethics, processes, and practices established by the owner of the networks and systems (Gillespie, 2019, p. 29; Kirwan & Power, 2013, p. 54; Poppy, 2019). The white hat hackers' practices are predominately linked to cybersecurity and building up resilience,

Table 3.2 Hacker typologies

Typology	Actions	Motivations
White hat hacker	Traditionally ethical hackers or pen-testers Employed by companies or states to find vulnerabilities in systems to make them more secure Ethical, licenced hackers.	Using illegal practices but not considered as unauthorised access Conducted under the supervision of the owner of systems and networks Following ethics, processes, and practices established
Grey hat hacker	Accessing computer systems and networks unauthorised No intention of damage and destroy	Using illegal practices Conducted for own gratification: curiosity and improve reputation in the hacking community Practices are illegal and linked to unauthorised access to computer systems and networks
Black hat hacker	Accessing computer systems and networks unauthorised Intention to exploit computer systems and networks	Using illegal practices Conducted to steal, destroy or damage for their gain Some will try to gain a monetary award afterwards (bug bounty) by notifying the online users about the issue

Sources: Gillespie (2019, p. 29); Kirwan & Power (2013, p. 54); Moore (2011, pp. 24–25); Poppy (2019).

and patching vulnerabilities. The grey hat hackers are slightly different, and they are operating in a grey zone. The activities of the grey hat hackers are associated with the early hackers driven by a curiosity about what they can find and what they can access. However, these practices are still illegal and linked to unauthorised access to computer systems and networks (Gillespie, 2019, p. 29; Kirwan & Power, 2013, p. 54; Moore, 2011, p. 25). Finally, the black hat hackers intend to access systems and networks unauthorised to exploit information or software. Their activities are overly malicious hackers, with the primary goal to steal, destroy, or damage files, servers, or websites (Gillespie, 2019, p. 29; Moore, 2011, p. 24).

Hackers can, in some situations, be understood as information terrorism. The black hat hackers are feared for their powers to access computer systems undetected. In the sense of politically motivated hackers, the black hat hackers are using their powers against governmental bureaucracies and international capital and regimes. Whereas in other situations, the hackers are not aiming to destroy or amend existing systems, programmes, or networks. Instead, the hackers aim to beat the machine in an ongoing trial of human strengths vs computer technologies (Green, 2001, p. 177).

Not all politically motivated groups have the necessary skills for carrying out attacks, but there are ready-made solutions. Since the mid-1990s, many political actors have enabled their activities by using tools and techniques developed by hackers. The mobilisation of these means and methods has developed in different directions (Yar & Steinmetz, 2019). Groups and individual hackers are involved in political cyber attacks despite not being a part of the political grouping. These hackers operating from a purely financial motivation are spreading their services to also including politically motivated areas.

HfH groups and individuals engage in these activities for personal or economic gain regardless of the customers' motivation. For example, they are seeking profits by selling their hacking skills and software on the Dark Web. Europol (2020) raised concerns about current trends, such as crime-as-a-service (CaaS), influencing various attack types. Cybercriminals develop and use prolific malware as a commodity for others to use. Widespread collaboration between hackers enables them to share infrastructure, services, and compromised credentials (Europol, 2020). They might also profit from their botnets and DoS/DDoS attack services for hire against either state, corporations, or groups by leveraging their infrastructure to facilitate attack (Holt & Bossler, 2016; Holt et al., 2018, p. 385). HfH customises the hacking service to enable individual or group attacks based on a specified agreement between the service provider and the customer. This service type adds another layer to the actors and the practices developed to carry out politically motivated large-scale attacks (McNemar, 2020).

The HfH group behind the Dark Basin campaign in 2017 pursued powerful actors who may not have sophisticated cybersecurity resources. The Dark Basin's operations targeted thousands of individual groups and industries with links to the political environments. This form of custom-made attacks opens up for an increase in the numbers of political attacks conducted against political entities in all sectors of society spanning from politics, advocacy, and government to global commerce (Muncaster, 2020; Murphy & Shubber, 2020; Scott-Railton et al., 2020). Another group, Bahamut (2020), has been involved in numerous highly sophisticated attacks and disinformation campaigns against government officials, leading industry, non-governmental organisations (NGOs), and individuals. Despite the range of targets and attacks, a notable lack of discernible pattern or unifying motive indicates that the group is likely an HfH mercenary. The group operates above average and has shown exceptional attention to detail, and the hackers surveil their target over a long time (BlackBerry, 2020; Coker, 2020; Palmer, 2020; Sheridan, 2020; Teiss, 2020).

Politically Motivated Attacks

A cyber attack in the traditional sense can be defined as "an assault launched by cybercriminals using one or more computers against a single or multiple computers or networks" (Check Point, 2020). A cyber attack is a malicious and unauthorised attempt to breach the information system of another individual or organisation with the intent of causing damage. Generally, the attacker aims to gain benefits from accessing the victim's network. For example, to disable, disrupt, destroy computer systems, or alter, delete, manipulate, or steal the data (Check Point, 2020; CISCO, 2021; Pratt, 2021). Although various attack tools are available to buy on the Dark Web, attacks against critical infrastructure (CI) require an understanding of the systems' target, preparations, and reconnaissance to exploit new vulnerabilities in systems. It is believed that future attacks would be conducted by compromising the development and engineering phase of industrial systems to embed hidden vulnerabilities only known to them (Europol, 2019, p. 21).

Cyberspace and the Internet provide online offenders with global resources for moving data and information around and finding safe havens for conducting cybercrimes and attacks. Communications are routed through multiple jurisdictions, and the online environment offers anonymity for the users. This signifies that the different cyber offences are challenging to prevent, detect, and investigate. It is increasingly easy to cover up an identity, take on a fake identity or hide behind VPNs or the Dark Web. Portability and transferability of devices and data make it difficult to trace the offenders as data can be stored on various portable devices, cloud storage, and the Internet (Clough, 2015, pp. 7–9; Gillespie, 2019, p. 13; Munk, 2018). The politically motivated attackers are progressively targeting governmental entities, units, and businesses with close ties to the state or CIs. Although governmental targets are on the agenda, the impact of attacks against a wider group of targets demonstrates the vulnerabilities in contemporary societies. Financial institutions, businesses and corporations, cybersecurity companies and units, academic institutions, research labs, Internet service providers (ISPs), tech companies, and social media businesses all have a role to play to understand, analyse, and respond to the constant changing behaviours, technologies, and online trends and to help to secure various online platforms and computer technologies.

According to Specops Software (2020), the US has been the target of substantial cyber attacks over the last 14 years compared with other countries (Brasseur, 2020; Specops, 2020). The attacks conducted include attacks on government agencies, defence, and high-tech companies. The US has experienced 156 significant cyber attacks between May 2006 and June 2020. In the second place, the UK has 47 attacks included on this list. The Labour Party's digital platform experience two DDoS attacks during the general election campaign in 2019 (Walker & Hern, 2019; Woodcock, 2019). Third on the list is India, which has suffered 23 cyber attacks. Nine attacks recorded in 2020 were against human-rights activists where the malware logged the victims' keystrokes, recorded their audio, and stole personal credentials (Brasseur, 2020; CISI, 2020; Specops, 2020).

Interestingly, the number of states attributed to these attacks is also in the top 20 most attacked counties (Brasseur, 2020). Both Iran and China have been targeted 15 times, Russia has been targeted 8 times, North Korea has suffered 6 significant large-scale attacks (Brasseur, 2020; Specops, 2020). Australia had 16 attacks during the period placing the country as number 6 on the list. Included is the 2020 attack, where sophisticated large-scale cyber attacks targeted government agencies and critical businesses and services (Specops, 2020; Taylor, 2020). On the other end of the top 20 list is North Korea. North Korea has only been targeted five times in contrast to neighbouring South Korea, which suffered from 18 major cyber attacks (Specops, 2020). The data from Secops show that no state is fully resilient towards attacks, and most counties worldwide are involved in attacking other counties (Brasseur, 2020; Specops, 2020).

Attempts from politically motivated groups and individuals, state and non-state actors, penetrating networks for political, diplomatic, technological, commercial, and strategic advances are a growing concern. These groups are principally targeting governments, defence, finance, energy, and telecommunication sectors. The capacity and impact of these actors are varied where the most technologically advanced groups and individuals continue to update their capabilities and methods using encryption and anonymised services to remain covert. State, state-sponsored, and state-supported actors hold the highest level of sophistication in their use of technologies and attack routes. Other non-state actors do not have the same abilities to reach a political end. However, they can archive similar impacts using the necessary tools and techniques because of the low level of cybersecurity imposed by the targets (HM Government, 2016, p. 18).

Essential Cyber Attacks

Historically, large-scale attacks using destructive malware mainly were associated with attacks against states and state-owned CIs. Different means and methods are used to carry out attacks, from stealing and leaking information to malware to DDoS attacks against different CIs. In 2007, the head of Britain's Security Service (MI5), Evans, warned that an increasing number of online threats originated from Russian and China. Evan claimed that:

> A number of countries continue to devote considerable time and energy trying to steal our sensitive technology on civilian and military projects, and trying to obtain political and economic intelligence at our expense. They ... increasingly deploy sophisticated technical attacks, using the Internet to penetrate computer networks.
>
> (CISI, 2020; Fidler & Palmer, 2007; Grant, 2007)

Table 3.3 Significant cyber attacks against CIs

Target	Attack	Attribution
Estonia 2007	DDoS attacks on online services of banks, media outlets, and government bodies	Russia (state-sponsored groups)
Georgia 2008	Combined cyber and kinetic attack DDoS attacks on Georgian government websites, i.e. the president's website	Russia (state-sponsored groups)
Iran 2010	The Stuxnet worm attacked numerous centrifuges in Iran's Natanz uranium enrichment facility and caused physical destruction on the equipment controlled by the infected computers	The US and Israel (state actors)
WannaCry 2017	Ransomware attacks brought down numerous computer systems worldwide	North Korea (state-sponsored groups)
NotPetya 2017	Ransomware attacks brought down numerous computer systems worldwide	Russia (state-sponsored groups)

Sources: McAfee (2020); McGuinness (2017); Smith (2014); Ransomware Task Force (2021).

Over the years, several significant attacks have made headlines worldwide and enhanced people's knowledge of the powers of these attacks. However, also security actors have increasingly reacted to these attacks.

DDOS ATTACK: ESTONIA

The Estonian cyber attack in 2007 was a wake-up call, and it showcased the impact of cyber powers. European security institutions, governments, and private companies realised that there were considerable consequences to developing an advanced information society. This attack called for strengthening cybersecurity, regulation, and awareness is national and transnational and cross-sectoral (European Commission (EC), 2008, p. 2; EC, 2013; McGuinness, 2017; Roxana, 2013, p. 12; Tikk, 2011, p. 119). In Estonia, hackers closely linked to Russia blocked websites and froze the entire Internet infrastructure, i.e. banks, governmental activities, official documents, and email accounts (Archer, 2014, p. 611; BBC News, 2007; McGuinness, 2017). The attack was an international revelation because it exploited the vulnerabilities in the digital society with a significant impact on the population. Similarly, Georgia suffered a large-scale cyber attack during the 2008 conflict where pro-Russian hackers launched a DDoS attack towards Georgian websites. The attack was coordinated with the military invention during the Russo-Georgian war. The Russian hackers played an essential role in bringing down the network system, albeit without the same significant media coverage as the Estonia attack (Archer, 2014, p. 612; Siapera, 2018, p. 121).

Although there have been other large-scale cyber attacks in the following years, the Estonia cyber attack stands out as a powerful attack and a starting point for considering cybersecurity and protection of CIs. After the attack on Estonia in 2007, the speaker of the Estonian parliament said:

> When I look at a nuclear explosion and the explosion that happened in our country in May, I see the same thing.
>
> (Munk, 2015, p. 176; Poulsen, 2007)

State, state-sponsored, and state-supported actors are increasingly engaged in online attacks by developing and deploying offensive cyber capabilities targeting crucial infrastructures and services. Although destructive attacks are relatively limited, the numbers are rising (HM Government, 2016, p. 18).

MALWARE: STUXNET

In 2010, the International Atomic Energy Agency visited the uranium enrichment plant in Natanz, Iran. At an early stage, the inspectors noticed failures in the centrifuges used to enrich the uranium gas. Later, a cybersecurity company from Belarus found malicious files on one of the systems. These files led to the discovery of what is now the first digital weapon, the Stuxnet worm. The worm was dissimilar to existing worms as it did not hijack the computers or stealing information from them. Instead, the aim was to cause physical destruction on equipment controlled by the infected computers (Zetter, 2014).

The worm was based on an unprecedentedly masterful and robust malicious code that attacked in three phases. First, the worm attacked Microsoft Windows machines by replicating itself. Second, the worm targeted Siemens control systems, especially those controlling the Iranian uranium enrichment project's centrifuges damaging 1,000 centrifuges and delaying the project. Finally, the worm compromised programmable logic controllers allowing the attackers to spy on industrial systems and damage the fast-spinning centrifuges (Kushner, 2013; Ranger, 2018, p. 45). The size and the sophistication of the worm led experts to believe that it could only be developed with the sponsorship of a state. The US and Israel allegedly developed the worm, yet, this attribution remains unconfirmed (Kushner, 2013; Ranger, 2018, p. 45). The Stuxnet worm added a new dimension to cyberweapons by showing the powers of tailored malware and how they can simultaneously attack the physical and virtual world. The worm has been used as a base for other weaponised malware, such as Duqu, Flame, and Gauss. In 2012, the US cooperation, Chevron, admitted that Stuxnet had spread across its machines. This confirmation highlighted that the worm cannot be contained to its original target but works through machines based on its code (Kushner, 2013; McAfee, 2020).

Ransomware attacks developed significantly from the mid-2010s and onwards. There are constant news reports about politically motivated attacks and new challenges for governments, law enforcement, and cybersecurity actors to enhance resilience and preparedness proactively. Issues are related to detection and prosecuting the attacker operating in the interconnected online environment. High-profile ransomware attacks in 2017 pressured governments, corporations, and businesses, which was first perceived as financial cybercrime, but later the attacks were attributed to state-sponsored groups in North Korea and Russia. WannaCry and NotPetya attacks in 2017 demonstrated the long social damages that there could be related to ransomware attacks.

WannaCry   The WannaCry cyber attack in 2017 had a detrimental effect. The attack was classified as 'the worst attack' targeting numerous public and private entities. The WannaCry attack caused panic, systems went down, and data were lost. The ransomware propagated through the systems like a worm infecting new computers by automatically sending itself across the networks. Therefore, the malware was not tied up to infected files or links to spread (DigWatch, 2017; Hern, 2017a; Whittaker, 2019). Interestingly, the ransomware was routed through old computer systems using an outdated version of Microsoft Windows, the Windows SMB protocol. The attackers targeted weaknesses in the systems by using an exploit initially developed by the US National Security Agency (NSA). The NSA backdoor DoublePulsar created a persistent backdoor for the attackers to deliver the EternalBlue exploit. Two months before the attack, Microsoft released a patch to protect the users' systems. However, numerous individuals and organisations did not regularly update their operating systems, which exposed them to the ransomware (Kaspersky, 2021; Whittaker, 2019).

The ransomware spread through the online environment encrypting more than 230,000 computers in 150 countries within one day. Public and private entities were attacked in Russia, the US, the UK, Germany, Spain, France, South Korea, China, Japan, Indonesia, India, Australia, etc. (BBC News, 2017). The attackers charged the victims to obtain the decryption code allowing them access to the hijacked data (Latto, 2021; Whittaker, 2019). The WannaCry ransomware had a significant impact worldwide, and it is estimated that the attack caused 4 billion dollars in losses worldwide (Kaspersky, 2021). One of the victims of this attack was the UK National Healthcare Service (NHS). The National Audit Office (NAO) said that 19,500 medical appointments were cancelled, computers were locked, and 600 GP surgeries. Moreover, five hospitals were forced to divert their ambulances elsewhere. The NAO heavily criticised the NHS for its lack of cybersecurity. The NAO stated that the WannaCry attack was relatively unsophisticated, and it could have been prevented if the NHS had followed basic information technology (IT) security practices (Hern, 2017a). The WannaCry ransomware continues to spread and infect targets that have not updated the system. Two years after the attack, approximately 1.7 million Internet-connected endpoints were still vulnerable to the EternalBlue exploit, with most of these devices in the US (Whittaker, 2019).

NotPetya The NotPetya ransomware attack followed shortly afterwards. The NotPetya attack had a financial impact that has exceeded 10 billion dollars (InfoTransec, 2021; Ransomware Task Force, 2021, p. 17). Although the attack appeared to be financially motivated, the means and method used covered state-sponsored actors. The attack started in Ukraine, where computer systems in airports, bus stations, railways, postal services were infected and hostage by the attackers. Automated teller machines, (ATM), payment systems, and the radiation monitors at Chernobyl were shut down, leaving the workers manually monitoring the radiation levels. The virus was designed to spread and reach factories in locations far away from where the attack originated, i.e. Tasmania (Ransomware Task Force, 2021). The attack affected the pharmaceutical company Merck and its production of critical vaccines. The company reported the highest loss at 870 million dollars. FedEx followed this by reporting a loss of 400 million dollars. The attack affected the French construction company Saint-Gobain. The construction company reported a loss of 384 million dollars (InfoTransec, 2021; Ransomware Task Force, 2021). The Danish international shipping company Mærsk shut down their entire network in response to the attack, leading to an accumulated loss of 300 million dollars. The loss was linked to severe business disruption and reinstallment of 4,000 servers and 45,000 workstations. This was a huge wake-up call to the industry, and security experts were alerted by the impact of the ransomware attack (InfoTransec, 2021). Other parties affected showed that the attack impacted ordinary life on the lower level. For example, doctors in Virginia and Pennsylvania were unable to access patient records and prescription systems.

Two years after the attack, railway and shipping systems are not fully restored. Packages have been lost, and senior citizens have continued to miss their pension payments as the attack wiped out their records (InfoTransec, 2021; Ransomware Task Force, 2021, p. 17). The UK, US, Canada, Australia, and New Zealand all attributed the attack to actors from Russia, and they linked the attack to Russia's ongoing conflict with Ukraine (InfoTransec, 2021). These two attacks were eye-openers for governments and businesses equal to the Estonia attack in 2007.

Since 2018, attacks are rapidly expanding beyond nation-states, and several private sector companies are fearing both the growing number of ransomware attacks and destructive cyber attacks. The destructive cyber attacks are linked to sabotage, permanently damaging data and systems by erasing company data. This type of destructive attack doubled during the first six months of 2019, where 50% of the targets were within the manufacturing sector (Europol, 2020, p. 17). Microsoft revealed in 2018 that the company had detected nearly

800 cyber attacks in the past year targeting think tanks, NGOs, and other global political organisations, with the majority of attacks originating in Iran, North Korea, and Russia (CSIS, 2020).

Attack Types and Targets

Following the SolarWind attack by the end of 2020, hackers affiliated with Russia gained access to computer systems belonging to multiple US government departments, including the US Treasury and Commerce, in a lengthy supply-chain attack campaign. The victims of this attack included customers of 425 of the US Fortune 500 group, 10 top US accounting companies, the US military, the Pentagon, the State Department, and hundreds of universities and colleges globally (Constantin, 2021). Significant attacks in the first half of 2021 include powerful attacks against CI and ICTs. These attacks demonstrate the diversity in attack targets and attribution. See Table 3.4.

Hackers with close links to the Chinese government are attributed for targeting Microsoft's enterprise email software to steal data from over 30,000 global organisations. Among the targets in this attack are governmental agencies, policy think tanks, legislative bodies, law companies, defence contractors, defence contractors, and infectious disease researchers (BBC News, 2021b; KrebsOnSecurity, 2021). Two state-sponsored hacking groups targeted organisations across the US and Europe, and one of the groups has close ties to the Chinese governments. The two groups exploited vulnerabilities in a VPN service to attack defence contractors (Johnson, 2021). However, not all attacks have been attributed to any groups. The European Commission announced that they and other European Union (EU) organisations were attacked simultaneously (Paganini, 2021). The Belgian parliament suffered a significant DDoS attack, which disabled the ISP used by Belgium's government. This attack impacted more than 200 organisations and resulted in the cancellation of multiple parliamentary meetings (Montalbano, 2021). The Norwegian green energy technology company Volue was targeted by a ransomware attack, which resulted in the shutdown of water and water treatment facilities in 200 municipalities. This ransomware attack affected approximately 85% of the Norwegian population (CSIS, 2020; Kovacs, 2021).

In the year 2021 the Western states were targeted in a wave of ransomware attacks. Attacks have been launched against governmental entities and agencies, governmental contractors, CI, and services significantly impacted. Ransomware attacks are now considered a national security threat. The attack on the US-based Colonial Pipeline substantially impacted ordinary citizens on the East Coast (Afifi-Sabet, 2021; Associated Press, 2021a; CSIS, 2020). This attack is attributed to the Russia state-supported RaaS group DarkSide. The Avaddon ransomware also targeted various sectors across states, such as Australia, Belgium, Brazil, Canada, China, France, Germany, India, the UK, the US, and others. The targeted industries include academia, airlines, constriction entities, energy equipment, financial services, transportation,

Table 3.4 Selected attacks in the first half of 2021

Attribution	Attacks	Targets
Hezbollah hackers	Breached telecom companies, ISPs for intelligence gathering and data theft	The U.S, the U.K, Egypt, Israel, Lebanon, Jordan, Saudi Arabia, the UAE, and the Palestine Authority
Indian hackers	Online espionage Targeted more than 150 individuals Among the targets were Pakistan's Atomic Energy Commission, the Pakistan Air Force, Kashmir election officials	Pakistan, Kazakhstan, and India
Iranian hackers	Gained control of a server in Amsterdam. This server was used to launch attacks against political opposition	The Netherlands, Germany, Sweden, and India
Iranian hackers	Espionage based on spearphishing attacking governmental entities, academia, and the tourist industry	Azerbaijan, Bahrain, Israel, Saudi Arabia, and the UAE
Russian hackers	A multiday DDoS attack against the websites of the state's security services	Ukraine
Russian hackers	Compromise the government's file sharing systems	Ukraine
Russian hackers	Briefly gained control over the websites belonging to the National Atomic Energy Agency and Health Ministry The hackers used the access to spread false alerts of a non-existent radioactive threat	Poland
Russian hackers	Attempted a cyber attack attempt targeting social media accounts belonging to Bundestag members from the CDU, CSU and SPD governing parties and 31 members of the federal parliaments	Germany

Sources: Associated Press (2021b); Cimpanu (2021b, 2021c); CSIS (2020); Fitsanakis (2021); Mehrotra (2021); Peretz & Thek (2021); Reuters (2021).

governments, health services, IT, law enforcement, manufacturing, etc. This attack demonstrates that all public and private sectors in various states can become a target (CSIS, 2020). The Health Service Executive (HSE), Ireland's national health service, suffered a ransomware attack attributed to a Russian state-supported cybercrime group using the Conti RaaS (Palmer, 2021). This attack was followed by a ransomware attack on the world largest meat processing company, JBS. The attack was launched towards the US and Australian meat plants and resulted in shutting down the factories. Also this attack is attributed to a Russian state-sponsored RaaS group REvil (BBC News, 2021a; CSIS, 2020; Lerman, 2021). The REvil ransomware group also conducted a large-scale zero-day supply-chain attack exploiting a vulnerability in Kaseya VSA software against multiple-managed service providers and their customers. Hundreds of companies, including a railway, pharmacy chain, and the Swedish Coop grocery chain, were directly hit by the attack, with more than 36,000 companies indirectly affected (Moyer, 2021; Osbourne, 2021).

Attack Means and Methods

Attacks against information systems are growing concerns globally. These are potential targets for politically motivated groups and individuals launching attacks against parts of the important CI (EC, 2013, p. 1). According to the EU (2013) these large-scale cyber attacks can have significant economic impact on the targets. For example, cyber attacks can interrupt information systems and communication, can cause loss or alteration of commercially important confidential information or other types of data. CI, CNI, CII, ICTs are considered particularly vulnerable to such attacks due to their increased dependence on the functioning and availability of information systems and often limited resources for enhancing their cybersecurity (EU, 2013, p. 1). New ways of carrying out attack campaigns have emerged to undermine trust and create uncertainties, such as coordinated political trolling, spreading dis-, mis-, and malinformation, as well as DDoS attacks, espionage, or ransomware attacks. States and state-sponsored groups have significant cyber capabilities to target governments, businesses, and individuals. Yet, non-state actors also use their cyber powers to launch attacks to show their political stance, i.e. hacktivism and online civil disobedience.

New means and methods have emerged that can be used against several targets or allow the attackers to access the systems and stay operational for a long time. Some attack forms are sophisticated, such as APTs, brute force, zero-day, and supply-chain attacks. However, new ways of using legitimate tools have also emerged, such as overloading web pages with images and information without using DDoS tools. These attacks are straightforward, and no computing skills are required. However, the new attack form requires a level of organisation to enable several actors to conduct simple pre-determined tasks simultaneously. These attacks challenge the current understanding of cyber attacks and the preferred means and methods. Table 3.5 covers several contemporary means used by politically motivated actors.

These attacks are widely used and provide the concern stops of the contemporary cyber attacks used by state and non-state actors.

Table 3.5 Key attack means and methods

Type	Characteristics
Malware	An umbrella term for different types of malicious software deployed to attack computer systems, devices, and networks
Ransomware	A form of malware that prevents or limits victims from accessing their system until a ransom is paid
Data compromise	Illegally accessing individual user credentials or accessing large databases with potentially sensitive information
Denial-of-service (DoS)	An attack that overflood a server with traffic until the targeted website or resource is unavailable
Distributed-denial-of-service (DDoS)	A DoS attack that are using multiple computers or machines to overflood a targeted website of resource
Botnets	A collection of internet-connected devices infected by malware to allow hackers to take control over them
Defacements	Any unauthorised modification of web pages, which included additions, removals, or alterations of existing content
Espionage	A process of obtaining information that usually is hidden to the public using technical means (hacking)
APTs	A prolonged and targeted attack where the hacker gain access to the computer systems and networks and remains undetected for a long period
Zero-day vulnerability/exploit	An attack that exposes an unpatched software security flaw known to the software vendor
Brute force attack	An attack that uses trial and error to guess login info, encryption keys, or find a hidden web page by working through all possible combinations
Supply-chain attack	A cyber attack that is targeting less secure elements in a supply chain to damage an organisation

Sources: Akamai (2021); CIS (2021); Europol (2020a); Fortinet (2021); Fruhlinger (2020); Holt et al. (2018, p. 73); M15 (2021); Norton (2020); Rosencrance (2020).

Malware

Malware is an umbrella term covering diverse types of malicious software deployed to attack computer systems, devices, and networks. Malware is designed to target specific computers, systems, or networks (Holt et al., 2018, p. 73). Malware can be viruses where the online users actively perform a task to release the virus into the system. For example, by clicking on a link or opening an attachment. Malware can also be a more sophisticated work as it can replicate and transmit itself without any activities from the online user. Trojan horses are malware concealed as something else which looks like a legit function or website. However, the malware is being launched into the system from the host. These can be coded to transmit information back (spyware), or they can be set to destruct at a particular time (Logic bomb) (Lavorgna, 2020,

p. 62). The actors are using different means and measures to load the malware into the systems.

For example is the Stuxnet attack (2010), which was launched using malware (McAfee, 2020). Another example is the Group of 20 (G20) Summit in 2011, where an email containing a PDF document with an embedded malware-targeted French governmental computers. In total, 150 of the French Finance Ministry's computers were infected by the malware (Sword, 2016). Researchers from Cisco Talos (2019) has also uncovered a large number of politically charged malware campaigns, distributing ransomware, remote access Trojans (RATs) using a variety of political themes or names of prominent politicians to trick the victims into downloading the malware, such as the former US President Trump, Russia's President Putin, and North Korean ruler Kim Jong-un (O'Donnell, 2019).

Ransomware

Ransomware is a form of malware that prevents or limits victims from accessing their system. This malware either locks the system's screen or files upon the ransom payment (Fruhlinger, 2020; Trend Micro, 2021b). Users are shown instructions for how to pay a fee to get the decryption key. The costs can range from a few hundred dollars to thousands, payable to cybercriminals in Bitcoin. This method has been used in state-sponsored attacks where weaponised ransomware has destroyed data, i.e. WannaCry and the NotPetya attacks in 2017 (Hern, 2017b). The standard hacking tool used to inject the malware can be phishing emails to trick online users into handing over passwords or sensitive data. This move allows the attacker access to the computer systems and networks (Ranger, 2018, p. 43). The surge in ransomware attacks in 2020 and 2021 has changed the perception of these attacks. Previously, the attacks have been perceived as financial cybercrime and managed in isolation, but it is now considered a national security threat/terrorism. The change is based on the groups constantly targeting CIs and the impact these attacks have on society (Associated Press, 2021a; Shaban et al., 2021).

Data Compromises and Data Breaches

After ransomware, data compromises and data breaches are a growing threat. These attacks are mostly linked to illegally obtaining sensitive data using phishing, data breaches, and information-gathering malware (Europol, 2020). A data breach happens when the entity responsible for securing the data suffers a security incident that results in a breach of confidentiality, availability, or integrity. A data breach is based on authorised access to computer systems or networks, where the attacks obtain or disclose sensitive, confidential, or otherwise protected data (Hanna et al., 2021; Trend Micro, 2021a). Data compromises and breaches can, for example, occur in relation to ransomware groups' data extortion before the ransomware is injected into the system. These attacks can also be linked to espionage campaigns where data are obtained during the attack. However, this method is not limited to ransomware groups and their double or triple extortion schemes. An example of a data breach is the attacks during the 2016 US presidential election. The Democratic National Committee (DNC) and the Democratic Congressional Campaign Committee (DCCC) were hacked by Russian state-sponsored groups. The group used techniques such as spearphishing, RATs, implants, and C2 servers, which are traditionally associated with the financial types of cybercrime (BBC News, 2016b; Green & Ng, 2020). Later, WikiLeaks uploaded thousands of emails onto the Internet from the DNC hack concerned Clinton's presidential campaign (BBC News, 2016a; Mafli, 2017).

DoS/DDoS Attacks

Various actors widely use DoS and DDoS as they do not require a high level of computer knowledge. DoS is conducted to overflood Internet websites or with a large amount of data that consume all the resources of the target computer. This attack form overloads the system until the target computer or system crashes. The goal for the attackers is not to access the system but to prevent other users from accessing it. DoS attacks have been further developed with DDoS as technological development has enabled the systems to manage a more substantial amount of data (Moore, 2011, pp. 39–40). DDoS are linked to cyber attacks against several actors, agencies, and online users by sending multiple repeated messages to servers housing online content to overload these servers and disrupt their performance (Attrill, 2015, p. 269). The difference between these two denials of service techniques is that DDoS is more potent by sending multiple requests simultaneously (Holt et al., 2018, p. 669). These types can cause both economic damages and reputational damage to the victim. The attackers aim to take down the system or network and send a strong signal to the target and similar commodities as part of mission fear. The DoS/DDoS attacks show off the attackers cyber capabilities and create uncertainties about their other tools and abilities to attack (Office of the National Counterintelligence Executive, 2011, p. i). Attacks can cause significant losses loss when customers cannot access web pages or services. The tactic is also used where the bot master blackmails the owners into paying a ransom to stop the attack – or it can be used to distract IT personal while they carry out a more damaging attack against the entity (Holt et al., 2018, p. 142).

DOS/DDOS ATTACKS AND THE USE OF BOTNETS

Politically motivated actors are also deploying botnets designed to infect and gain control of numerous personal computers. The botnets allow cybercriminals to harvest identities and carry off many tasks. The botnet connects an army of zombie computers infected with a malicious code designed to access a target. The cybercriminal will activate the master zombie computers to attack at a time. The process begins when the master zombie computers send attack commands to the slave computers in the botnet. The process overfloods the victim's computer system for some time. However, the process can be repeated until the victim can patch the vulnerabilities in the systems (Lavorgna, 2020, p. 61). The problems regarding botnets are the unknown number of computers involved in the attacks, making it nearly impossible to locate the people behind the attacks. The botnets are helpful to generate a large-scale attack, which affects information systems, causes considerable damage, disrupts the data transmission, and causes financial costs or loss of personal data (EC, 2013, p. 3; Munk, 2015, p. 51). Although the 2016 Mirai attack is not attributed to any political actors, it is still a powerful attack. It demonstrated the powers of botnets by interlinking a large number of insecure IoT devices such as everyday things like digital cameras, printers, and digital video recorder (DVR) players where the factory settings have not been changed. This cyber attack brought down a large part of the American Internet in a coordinated DDoS attack towards DYN, a company controlling a large amount of the Internet's domain system infrastructure. This attack prevented access to companies such as Twitter, the Guardian, Netflix, Reddit, and CNN (Antonakakis et al., 2017, p. 1063; Munk, 2018, p. 235; Woolf, 2016).

Defacements

Website defacement is an unauthorised modification of web pages. This includes the addition, removal, or alteration of existing content (CIS, 2021). Attackers compromise a website or web server and replace or alter the hosted website information by posting their messages. Unskilled actors primarily focus on website defacements due to the low sophistication needed (CIS, 2021; Europol, 2021; Trend Micro, 2021c). These actors are using automated applications to test vulnerabilities of websites, i.e. SQL injection attacks. The attack are then launched against unpatched or misconfigured web pages or systems (CIS, 2021). The defacement of public and private websites belonging to governments, corporations, and businesses are increasing. Although the case numbers are lower than the other attack forms, they are common (Europol, 2021). This attack form can act as a DoS attack by preventing access to information. Moreover, the attack form is used to post graphic images or information to shock the reader and disrupt and damage the target's reputation (CIS, 2021; Trend Micro, 2021c).

Defacements have for a long time been used by hacktivist groups. Other less cyber-sophisticated state-sponsored hackers have also embraced this attack form. For example, in 2009 and 2010, the Iranian Cyber Army hacked into Twitter, launching a political message on Iranian opposition supporters on the social media platform (Arthur, 2009). In 2010, the group disrupted the Chinese search engine Baidu, which commands 60% of the Chinese market. On Baidu, the attacker directed to online uses to a web page which had an

Iranian political message: "This site has been hacked by the Iranian Cyber Army" next to a picture of the Iranian flag (BBC News, 2010; Branigan, 2010). This attack was partly repeated in an attack against Saudi Aramco in 2012, where the Shamoon malware wiped out thousands of Saudi Aramco computers' hard drives, leaving behind a picture of a burning American flag on the screens (Munk, 2015, p. 179; The Economist, 2014).

Espionage

Cyberespionage is an attack form conducted against a competitive company or governmental entity. The overarching goal is to gather sensitive or classified data, or secrets, where information is obtained to give the attacker a competitive advantage over the target (Crowdstrike, 2021; Gillis, 2021a). Cyberespionage is often referred to as APTs. These attacks are part of cyberwarfare where one nation-state launch the attack against another. Using APTs, that attacker can remain undetected for an extended period. However, these attacks are often complicated and expensive to conduct, but they are equally difficult to detect (Crowdstrike, 2021; Gillis, 2021a). The emerging level of sophistication associated with these attacks opens up the possibility of coordinated and advanced attacks that have a significant disruptive impact on several modern-day services, i.e. operation of the electricity grid, disturbance to financial markets, and interference in primary elections (Crowdstrike, 2021). States and state-sponsored actors are developing various programmes to access information from other states. However, tools are accessible on the Dark Web for less skilled actors where market spaces and carding forums are trading software and skills (HM Government, 2016, p. 18).

APTs

APTs are a reasonably new attack form that requires a high level of computing knowledge of the attackers. APTs are a prolonged and targeted attack where the intruder gets access to the computer systems and networks and remains undetected there for an extended period. These attacks are aimed at organisations, for example, national defence, manufacturing, and financial institutions, by accessing the intellectual property, military plans, and other security data from governments (Rosencrance, 2020). To enable hackers to remain in the system without being discovered, they continuously rewriting malicious code to avoid detection and other advanced evasion methods. Some of these techniques are so complex that they require full-time administrators to maintain the compromised access to systems and software. The attacks are developed in different phrases. First, the attackers need to access the target (Belding, 2019; Rouse, 2020). The groups use advanced attack methods such as exploits of zero-day vulnerabilities, targeted spearphishing, and social engineering (Crowdstrike, 2021). These methods enable the hackers to get a foothold inside the computer systems and networks. When they are inside, the attackers create backdoors to move around or later enter the system (Belding, 2019; Kaspersky, 2021; Rouse, 2020).

Zero-day Attacks

Accessing zero-day vulnerabilities are another tool widely used by hackers. The zero-day vulnerabilities are bugs, flaws, weaknesses in software, hardware, or firmware that the developer has not discovered or patched. Exploiting the zero-day vulnerabilities allows the attackers access to or control over systems. These flaws are particularly useful as nothing stops attackers from misusing this access until the pathway is patched (FireEye, 2021; Ranger, 2018, p. 44; Trend Micro, 2019). The zero-day vulnerabilities can be a result of improper computer or security configurations and programming errors. Hackers write codes targeting specific security weaknesses which are being released using a zero-day exploit to compromise or change the behaviour of a computer system (Norton, 2020). These attack forms are rarely discovered until later; it can take months or years before the target becomes aware of the vulnerability (FireEye, 2021). There is a growing trade in zero-day exploits that allow attackers to sidestep security procedures. It is believed that states are stockpiling zero-day exploits to be used in espionage or as a cyberweapon. Zero-day exploits were an essential part of the Stuxnet cyberweapon to access the facilities. Compared with conventional weapons, zero-day exploits are reusable, and when discovered, the exploits can be analysed and reused by the original target (Ranger, 2018, p. 44).

Zero-day exploit malware can take many forms. The malware can be designed to steal data, allow hackers to take unauthorised control over the computer systems or networks, install other malware corrupting files, or access contact lists to send spam messages – or install spyware to steal sensitive information (Norton, 2020). In 2021, threat actors used LinkedIn to send messages with malicious links to governmental officials in Western states. Google attributed four zero-day exploits to Russian SVR hackers to attack Google Chrome, Internet Explorer, and Safari for iOS users. Three of these are linked to commercial surveillance vendors arming state-sponsored hackers, and one is linked directly to a Russian APT group (Cimpanu, 2021a; Gatlan, 2021).

Brute Force Attacks

A brute force attack is using excessive forceful attempts to access the computer systems. This attack form is usually introduced in the early stages of a cyber kill chain during the reconnaissance and infiltration states where the attackers need a point of entry (Peters, 2021; Swinhoe, 2020). The attack forms are repeatedly linked to a trial-and-error process and systematically submitting usernames and passwords to guess login info, encryption keys, or find a hidden web page that will enable access. The attackers are working through numerous combinations to find the correct usernames, passwords, passphrases, and personal identification numbers (PINs). The attackers let the computers do the work using a script or bot to try different combinations. Automated tools are also developed to enable less computer-skilled attackers to conduct these attacks (Kaspersky, 2021; Peters, 2021; Swinhoe, 2020).

Supply-chain Attacks

A supply-chain attack occurs when the hacker accesses the computer system through an outside partner or provider with access to the system (Korolov, 2021). The supply chain is based on a network of all individuals, organisations, resources, activities, and technologies. The attackers target the weak points in a supply chain in order to succeed. The critical element is that the attackers exploit the trust that a company or organisation has in third-party vendors (Gillis, 2021b). Supply-chain attacks are an increasingly common form of hacking. This attack type is based on a technique in which an attacker injects a malicious code or a malicious component into trusted software or hardware. By compromising a single supplier, the attacker can hijack the distribution systems to turn any application, software, or physical equipment into Trojan horses. With one well-placed intrusion, the attacker creates a route into the networks of a supplier's customers, and thereby, they can attack a large number of victims linked to the supply chain (Greenberg, 2021).

This attack form is challenging to manage, as demonstrated in 2020. It was revealed that Russian state-sponsored attackers hacked into the software company SolarWinds and injected the malicious code into Orion's IT management tool. This allowed access to approximately 18,000 customers' networks worldwide using the Orion tool, including multiple US governmental departments, including the US Treasure and Commerce (Constantin, 2021; Greenberg, 2021; Korolov, 2021). The risks associated with a supply-chain attack are high, and new tools are constantly developing. There is a going awareness of the threats deriving from this attack type. However, the attackers have more resources and tools available, which create the perfect storm (Korolov, 2021).

Conclusion

This chapter provides an understanding of hackers and hacking, which have developed significantly from the early days of computing, where their curiosity drove hackers. Cyber attacks are not following one particular pathway; there are numerous means and methods developed and used. The attack routes are constantly changing, and the attackers exploit new techniques, making the attacks challenging to prevent and detect. At present, hacking underpins most elements of cyber attacks, and this area is constantly developing with new computer technologies and innovative attack forms. Some of the actors have considerable technical skills, but it is not a requirement. Hacking software and HfH are commodities on the Dark Web. This chapter has highlighted some of the most used hacking tools. However, these only represent a snapshot of the most used attack forms.

References

Afifi-Sabet, K., 2021. *Ransomware operators in turmoil after Colonial Pipeline backlash.* [Online] Available at: www.itpro.co.uk/security/ransomware/359558/ransomware-operators-in-turmoil-after-colonial-pipeline-backlash [Accessed 28 06 2021].

Akamai, 2021. *What is a botnet attack?* [Online] Available at: www.akamai.com/uk/en/resources/what-is-a-botnet.jsp [Accessed 03 08 2021].

An, A., 2017. *Chinese cybercriminals develop lucrative hacking services.* [Online] Available at: www.mcafee.com/blogs/mcafee-labs/chinese-cybercriminals-develop-lucrative-hacking-services/ [Accessed 14 08 2020].

Antonakakis, M. et al., 2017. *Understanding the Mirai Botnet.* Vancouver: USENIX.

Archer, E. M., 2014. Crossing the Rubicon: Understanding cyber-terrorism in a European context. *The European Legacy,* 19(5), pp. 606–621.

Arthur, C., 2009. *Twitter hack by 'Iranian Cyber Army' is really just misdirection.* [Online] Available at: www.theguardian.com/technology/blog/2009/dec/18/twitter-hack-iranian-cyber-army-dns-mowjcamp [Accessed 09 07 2021].

Associated Press, 2021a. *Colonial Pipeline confirms it paid $4.4m ransom to hacker gang after attack.* [Online] Available at: www.theguardian.com/technology/2021/may/19/colonial-pipeline-cyber-attack-ransom [Accessed 24 06 2021].

Associated Press, 2021b. *Polish state websites hacked and used to spread false info.* [Online] Available at: www.securityweek.com/polish-state-websites-hacked-and-used-spread-false-info [Accessed 04 07 2021].

Attrill, A., 2015, *Cyberpsychology* (Ed.) Oxford: Oxford University Press.

BBC News, 2007. *Estonia hit by 'Moscow Cyber War' world.* [Online] Available at: http://news.bbc.co.uk/1/hi/world/europe/6665145.stm [Accessed 13 08 2020].

BBC News, 2010. *Baidu hacked by 'Iranian cyber army'.* [Online] Available at: http://news.bbc.co.uk/1/hi/technology/8453718.stm [Accessed 09 07 2021].

BBC News, 2016a. *18 revelations from Wikileaks' hacked Clinton emails.* [Online] Available at: www.bbc.co.uk/news/world-us-canada-37639370 [Accessed 09 07 2021].

BBC News, 2016b. *Clinton campaign 'hacked' along with other Democratic groups.* [Online] Available at: www.bbc.co.uk/news/election-us-2016-36927523 [Accessed 09 07 2021].

BBC News, 2017. *Ransomware cyber-attack: Who has been hardest hit?* [Online] Available at: www.bbc.co.uk/news/world-39919249 [Accessed 13 07 2021].

BBC News, 2021a. *JBS: FBI says Russia-linked group hacked meat supplier.* [Online] Available at: www.bbc.co.uk/news/world-us-canada-57338896 [Accessed 28 06 2021].

BBC News, 2021b. *Microsoft accuses China over email cyber-attacks.* [Online] Available at: www.bbc.co.uk/news/business-56261516 [Accessed 04 07 2021].

Belding, G., 2019. *Malware spotlight: What is APT?* [Online] Available at: https://resources.infosecinstitute.com/malware-spotlight-what-is-apt/#gref [Accessed 29 08 2020].

BlackBerry, 2020. *BlackBerry uncovers massive hack-for-hire group targeting governments, businesses, human rights groups and influential individuals.* [Online]

Available at: www.blackberry.com/us/en/company/newsroom/press-releases/2020/ blackberry-uncovers-massive-hack-for-hire-group-targeting-governments-businesses-human-rights-groups-and-influential-individuals [Accessed 21 03 2021].

Branigan, T., 2010. *'Iranian' hackers paralyse Chinese search engine Baidu.* [Online] Available at: www.theguardian.com/technology/2010/jan/12/iranian-hackers-chinese-search-engine [Accessed 09 07 2021].

Brasseur, K., 2020. *Study: U.S. largest target for 'significant' cyber-attacks.* [Online] Available at: www.complianceweek.com/cyber-security/study-us-largest-target-for-significant-cyber-attacks/29180.article [Accessed 03 10 2020].

Check Point, 2020. *What is a cyber attack?* [Online] Available at: www.checkpoint. com/cyber-hub/cyber-security/what-is-cyber-attack/ [Accessed 12 08 2020].

Cimpanu, C., 2021a. *Google: Three recent zero-days have been used against Armenian targets.* [Online] Available at: https://therecord.media/google-three-recent-zero-days-have-been-used-against-armenian-targets/ [Accessed 15 07 2021].

Cimpanu, C., 2021b. *Hezbollah's cyber unit hacked into telecoms and ISPs.* [Online] Available at: www.zdnet.com/article/hezbollahs-cyber-unit-hacked-into-telecoms-and-isps/ [Accessed 04 07 2021].

Cimpanu, C., 2021c. *Ukraine reports cyber-attack on government document management system.* [Online] Available at: www.zdnet.com/article/ukraine-reports-cyber-attack-on-government-document-management-system/ [Accessed 04 07 2021].

CIS, 2021. *Election security spotlight – Website defacements.* [Online] Available at: www.cisecurity.org/spotlight/cybersecurity-spotlight-website-defacements/ [Accessed 06 07 2021].

CISCO, 2021. *Definition of cyber attacks.* [Online] Available at: www.cisco.com/c/en_uk/products/security/common-cyberattacks.html [Accessed 04 07 2021].

CISI, 2020. *Significant cyber incidents since 2006.* [Online] Available at: https:// csis-website-prod.s3.amazonaws.com/s3fs-public/200727_Cyber_Attacks.pdf [Accessed 26 08 2020].

Clough, J., 2015. *Principles of Cybercrime.* 2 ed. Cambridge: Cambridge University Press.

Coker, J., 2020. *Cyber-espionage group BAHAMUT responsible for "Staggering" number of attacks.* [Online] Available at: www.infosecurity-magazine.com/news/ cyber-espionage-bahamut-staggering/ [Accessed 27 03 2021].

Constantin, L., 2021. *SolarWinds attack explained: And why it was so hard to detect.* [Online] Available at: www.csoonline.com/article/3601508/solarwinds-supply-chain-attack-explained-why-organizations-were-not-prepared.html [Accessed 05 07 2021].

Crowdstrike, 2021. *What is cyber espironage?* [Online] Available at: www. crowdstrike.com/cybersecurity-101/cyberattacks/cyber-espionage/#:~:text=Cyber %20espionage%2C%20or%20cyber%20spying,competitive%20advantage %20or%20political%20reasons [Accessed 06 07 2021].

CSIS, 2020. *Significant cyber incidents.* [Online] Available at: www.csis.org/programs/ technology-policy-program/significant-cyber-incidents [Accessed 26 08 2020].

DigWatch, 2017. *WannaCry: The ransomware cyber attack explained.* [Online] Available at: https://dig.watch/trends/wannacry [Accessed 13 07 2021].

EU, 2013, Directive 2013/40/EU of the European Parliament and the Council of 12 August 2013 on attacks against information systems replacing Council Framework decision 2005/222/JHA. Official Journal of the European Union. L 218/8.

14.8.2013. [Online] Available at: https://eur-lex.europa.eu/legal-content/EN/TXT/HTML/?uri=CELEX:32013L0040 [Accessed 16 11 20210]

European Commission, 2008. *Article 12 of the Council Framework Decision of 24 February 2005 on Attacks against Information Systems.* Brussels: EUR-Lex.

European Commission, 2013. *Directive 2013/40/EU of the European Parliament and of the Council of 12 August 2013 on attacks against information systems and replacing Council Framework Decision 2005/222/JHA.* [Online] Available at: https://eur-lex.europa.eu/legal-content/EN/ALL/?uri=CELEX%3A32013L0040 [Accessed 12 08 2020].

Erickson, J., 2008. *Hacking: The Art of Exploitation.* 2 ed. San Francisco: William Pollock.

Europol, 2019. *Internet Organised Crime Threat Assessment (IOCTA) 2018.* The Hague: Europol.

Europol, 2020. *The Internet Organised Crime Threat Assessment (IOCTA).* The Hague: Europol.

Europol, 2021. *Other threats – Website defacement.* [Online] Available at: www.europol.europa.eu/iocta/2016/data-breach.html [Accessed 06 07 2021].

Fidler, S. & Palmer, M., 2007. *MI5 warns banks of Chinese hackers.* [Online] Available at: www.ft.com/content/b3e357b8-9fa3-11dc-8031-0000779fd2ac [Accessed 26 08 2020].

FireEye, 2021. *What is a zero-day exploit?* [Online] Available at: www.fireeye.com/current-threats/what-is-a-zero-day-exploit.html [Accessed 07 07 2021].

Fitsanakis, J., 2021. *Iran spies on dissidents via web server based in Holland, registered in Cyprus.* [Online] Available at: https://intelnews.org/2021/02/19/01-2959/ [Accessed 04 07 2021].

Fortinet, 2021. *DoS vs. DDoS.* [Online] Available at: www.fortinet.com/resources/cyberglossary/dos-vs-ddos [Accessed 03 08 2021].

Fruhlinger, J., 2020. *Ransomware explained: How it works and how to remove it.* [Online] Available at: www.csoonline.com/article/3236183/what-is-ransomware-how-it-works-and-how-to-remove-it.html [Accessed 06 07 2021].

Gatlan, S., 2021. *Google: Russian SVR hackers targeted LinkedIn users with Safari.* [Online] Available at: www.bleepingcomputer.com/news/security/google-russian-svr-hackers-targeted-linkedin-users-with-safari-zero-day/ [Accessed 15 07 2021].

Gillespie, A. A., 2019. *Cybercrime. Key Issues and Debate.* 2 ed. Abingdon: Routledge.

Gillis, A. S., 2021a. *Cyber espionage.* [Online] Available at: https://searchsecurity.techtarget.com/definition/cyber-espionage [Accessed 06 07 2021].

Gillis, A. S., 2021b. *Supply chain attack.* [Online] Available at: https://searchsecurity.techtarget.com/definition/supply-chain-attack [Accessed 07 07 2021].

Grant, I., 2007. *Spies greater threat than terrorists to infosecurity.* [Online] Available at: www.computerweekly.com/news/2240084153/Spies-greater-threat-than-terrorists-to-infosecurity [Accessed 26 08 2020].

Green, A. & Ng, C., 2020. *When a cyber attack is a political weapon.* [Online] Available at: www.varonis.com/blog/when-a-cyber-attack-is-a-political-weapon/ [Accessed 09 07 2021].

Green, L., 2001. *Communication, Technology and Society.* London: Sage.

Greenberg, A., 2021. *Hacker Lexicon: What is a supply chain attack?* [Online] Available at: www.wired.com/story/hacker-lexicon-what-is-a-supply-chain-attack/ [Accessed 07 07 2021].

Gunkel, D. J., 2018. *Hacking Cyberspace.* New York: Routledge.

Hanna, K. T., Ferguson, K. & Beaver, K., 2021. *Data breaches.* [Online] Available at: https://searchsecurity.techtarget.com/definition/data-breach [Accessed 06 07 2021].

Hern, A., 2017a. *NHS could have avoided WannaCry hack with 'basic IT security', says report.* [Online] Available at: www.theguardian.com/technology/2017/oct/27/nhs-could-have-avoided-wannacry-hack-basic-it-security-national-audit-office [Accessed 13 07 2021].

Hern, A., 2017b. *WannaCry, Petya, NotPetya: How ransomware hit the big time in 2017.* [Online] Available at: www.theguardian.com/technology/2017/dec/30/wannacry-petya-notpetya-ransomware [Accessed 29 08 2020].

HM Government, 2016. *The UK National Cyber Security Strategy 2016–2021.* London: GOV.UK.

Holt, T. J. & Bossler, A. M., 2016. *Cybercrime in Progress. Theory and Prevention of Technology-Enabled Offenses.* London: Routledge.

Holt, T. J., Bossler, A. M. & Siegfried-Spellar, K. C., 2018. *Cybercrime and Digital Forensics. An Introduction.* 2 ed. Abingdon: Routledge.

InfoTransec, 2021. *The impacts of NotPetya ransomware: What you need to know.* [Online] Available at: https://infotransec.com/news/the-impacts-of-notpetya-ransomware-what-you-need-to-know/ [Accessed 12 06 2021].

Jeffray, C., 2014. *The Threat of Cyber-Crime to the UK.* London: Royal United Services Institute.

Johnson, D. B., 2021. *Hackers exploit unpatched vulnerabilities, zero day to attack governments and contractors.* [Online] Available at: www.scmagazine.com/home/security-news/apts-cyberespionage/hackers-exploit-unpatched-vulnerabilities-zero-day-to-attack-governments-and-contractors/ [Accessed 05 07 2021].

Kaspersky, 2021. *What is WannaCry ransomware?* [Online] Available at: www.kaspersky.co.uk/resource-center/threats/ransomware-wannacry [Accessed 13 07 2021].

Kirwan, G. & Power, A., 2013. *Cybercrime. The Psychology of Online Offenders.* Cambridge: Cambridge University Press.

Klimburg, A., 2009. *Cyber-attacken als Warnung. Wer hat die Website des US-Präsidenten lahmgelegt? [Cyber-attacks as a warning, where has the webpage paralyzed the US president?].* [Online] Available at: www.diepresse.com/493918/cyber-attacken-als-warnung [Accessed 02 07 2020].

Klimburg, A., 2011. Mobilising cyber power. *Survival: Global Politics and Strategy,* 53(1), pp. 41–60.

Korolov, M., 2021. *Supply chain attacks show why you should be wary of third-party providers.* [Online] Available at: www.csoonline.com/article/3191947/supply-chain-attacks-show-why-you-should-be-wary-of-third-party-providers.html [Accessed 07 07 2021].

Kovacs, E., 2021. *Green energy company Volue hit by ransomware.* [Online] Available at: www.securityweek.com/green-energy-company-volue-hit-ransomware [Accessed 05 07 2021].

KrebsOnSecurity, 2021. *At least 30,000 U.S. organizations newly hacked via holes in Microsoft's email software.* [Online] Available at: https://krebsonsecurity.com/2021/03/at-least-30000-u-s-organizations-newly-hacked-via-holes-in-microsofts-email-software/ [Accessed 04 07 2021].

Kushner, D., 2013. *The real story of Stuxnet.* [Online] Available at: https://spectrum.ieee.org/telecom/security/the-real-story-of-stuxnet [Accessed 13 07 2021].

Latto, N., 2021. *What is WannaCry?* [Online] Available at: www.avast.com/c-wannacry [Accessed 13 07 2021].

Lavorgna, A., 2020. *Cybercrimes. Critical Issues in a Global Context.* London: Macmillan.

Lerman, R., 2021. *JBS paid $11 million in ransom after hackers shut down meat plants.* [Online] Available at: www.washingtonpost.com/technology/2021/06/09/jbs-11-million-ransom/ [Accessed 28 06 2021].

Ludlow, P., 1996. *High Noon on the Electronic Frontier: Conceptual Issues in Cyberspace.* Cambridge: MIT Press.

M15, 2021. *Counter-espionage.* [Online] Available at: www.mi5.gov.uk/counter-espionage [Accessed 06 07 2021].

Mafli, K., 2017. *Hillary's email data breach taught us all the wrong lesson.* [Online] Available at: https://info.townsendsecurity.com/hillarys-email-data-breach-taught-us-all-the-wrong-lessons [Accessed 09 07 2021].

McAfee, 2020. *What is Stuxnet?* [Online] Available at: www.mcafee.com/enterprise/en-gb/security-awareness/ransomware/what-is-stuxnet.html#:~:text=Stuxnet%20is%20a%20computer%20worm,used%20to%20automate%20machine%20processes [Accessed 26 08 2020].

McGuinness, D., 2017. *How a cyber attack transformed Estonia.* [Online] Available at: www.bbc.co.uk/news/39655415 [Accessed 13 08 2020].

McGuire, M. & Dowling, S., 2013. *McGuire, M., & Dowling, S. (2013). Cyber Crime: A Review of the Evidence. London: Home.* London: Home Office.

McNemar, D., 2020. *An overview of the unethical services offered on the darknet.* [Online] Available at: www.binarydefense.com/hackers-for-hire-an-overview-of-the-unethical-services-offered-on-the-darknet/#:~:text=But%2C%20are%20you%20aware%20of,necessarily%20hard%20to%20find%2C%20either [Accessed 27 03 2021].

Mehrotra, K., 2021. *Indian cyber-espionage effort targets election, energy officials.* [Online] Available at: www.bloomberg.com/news/articles/2021-02-11/indian-cyber-espionage-effort-targets-election-energy-officia [Accessed 04 07 2021].

Montalbano, E., 2021. *Massive DDoS attack disrupts Belgium parliament.* [Online] Available at: https://threatpost.com/ddos-disrupts-belgium/165911/ [Accessed 13 06 2021].

Moore, R., 2011. *Cybercrime. Investigating High-Technology Computer Crime.* 2 ed. Abingdon: Routledge.

Moyer, E., 2021. *Ransomware attack on Kaseya, a software firm, threatens businesses worldwide.* [Online] Available at: www.cnet.com/news/ransomware-attack-on-kaseya-a-software-firm-threatens-businesses-worldwide/ [Accessed 06 07 2021].

Muncaster, P., 2020. *Dark Basin: Researchers uncover major hack-for-hire group.* [Online] Available at: www.infosecurity-magazine.com/news/dark-basin-researchers-major/ [Accessed 22 11 2020].

Munk, T., 2018. Policing virtual spaces: Public and private online challenges in a legal perspective. In: *Comparative Policing from a Legal Perspective.* Cheltenham: Edward Elgar, pp. 228–254.

Munk, T. H., 2015. *Cyber-security in the European region: Anticipatory governance and practices.* [Online] Available at: www.escholar.manchester.ac.uk/api/datastream?publicationPid=uk-ac-man-scw:266937&datastreamId=FULL-TEXT.PDF [Accessed 12 08 2020].

Murphy, P. & Shubber, K., 2020. *Hackers for hire 'targeted hundreds of institutions'.* [Online] Available at: www.ft.com/content/315aceba-935a-4e70-83c4-1d1fd7cf939b [Accessed 22 11 2020].

Norton, 2020. *Zero-day vulnerability: What it is, and how it works.* [Online] Available at: https://us.norton.com/internetsecurity-emerging-threats-how-do-zero-day-vuln erabilities-work-30sectech.html [Accessed 06 09 2020].

O'Donnell, L., 2019. *Trump, Putin and politics name-dropped to peddle malware.* [Online] Available at: https://threatpost.com/trump-putin-and-politics-name-drop ped-to-peddle-malware/149884/ [Accessed 09 07 2021].

Office of the National Counterintelligence Executive, 2011. *Foreign spies stealing US economic secrets in cyberspace.* [Online] Available at: https://bit.ly/3x7Rowv [Accessed 05 09 2020].

Osbourne, C., 2021. *Kaseya ransomware attack: What you need to know.* [Online] Available at: www.zdnet.com/article/kaseya-ransomware-supply-chain-attack- what-you-need-to-know/ [Accessed 06 07 2021].

Paganini, P., 2021. *European Commission and other institutions were hit by a major cyber-attack.* [Online] Available at: https://securityaffairs.co/wordpress/116441/hacking/ european-commission-institutions-cyberattack.html [Accessed 05 07 2021].

Palmer, D., 2019. *Enterprise under attack: Dark Web cyber criminals sell hacking tools aimed at business.* [Online] Available at: www.zdnet.com/article/enterprise-under- attack-dark-web-cyber-criminals-sell-hacking-tools-aimed-at-business/ [Accessed 13 08 2020].

Palmer, D., 2020. *This stealthy hacker-for-hire group is using phishing, malicious apps and zero-day attacks against its victims.* [Online] Available at: www.zdnet.com/ article/this-stealthy-hacker-for-hire-group-is-using-phishing-malicious-apps-and- zero-day-attacks-against-its-victims/ [Accessed 27 03 2021].

Palmer, D., 2021. *Ransomware: Ireland's health service remains 'significantly' disrupted weeks after attack.* [Online] Available at: www.zdnet.com/article/ransomware- irelands-health-service-is-still-significantly-disrupted-weeks-after-attack/ [Accessed 19 06 2021].

Peretz, A. & Thek, E., 2021. *Earth Vetala – Muddy water continues to target organisations in the Middle East.* [Online] Available at: www.trendmicro.com/en_ us/research/21/c/earth-vetala---muddywater-continues-to-target-organizations-in- t.html [Accessed 04 07 2021].

Peters, J., 2021. *What is a brute force attack?* [Online] Available at: www.varonis.com/ blog/brute-force-attack/ [Accessed 18 11 2021].

Poppy, J., 2019. *The hacker's economy.* [Online] Available at: www.bulletproof.co.uk/ blog/the-hackers-economy [Accessed 13 08 2020].

Poulsen, K., 2007. *"Cyber-war" and Estonia's panic attack.* [Online] Available at: www. wired.com/2007/08/cyber-war-and-e/ [Accessed 09 09 2020].

Pratt, M. K., 2021. *Cyber attack.* [Online] Available at: https://searchsecurity.techtar get.com/definition/cyber-attack [Accessed 04 07 2021].

Ranger, S., 2018. What is cyberwar? Everything you need to know about the frightening future of digital. In: ZDNet & TechRepublic, ed. *Cyberwar and the Future of Cybersecurity.* San Francisco: CBS Interactive Inc, pp. 36–51.

Ransomware Task Force, 2021. *Combatting Ransomware. A Comprehensive Framework for Action: Key Recommendations from the Ransomware Task Force.* San Francisco Bay Area: Institute for Security and Technology.

Reuters, 2021. *Russian hackers target German parliament again - Der Spiegel.* [Online] Available at: www.reuters.com/article/uk-germany-politics-cyber-idAFKBN2BI25P [Accessed 04 07 2021].

Rokven, J. J., Weijters, G., Beerthuizen, M. G. & Laan, A. M. v. d., 2018. Juvenile delinquency in the virtual world: Similarities and differences between cyber-enabled, cyber-dependent and offline delinquents in the Netherlands. *International Journal of Cyber Criminology*, 12(1), pp. 27–46.

Rosencrance, L., 2020. *Advanced persistent threat (APT).* [Online] Available at: https://searchsecurity.techtarget.com/definition/advanced-persistent-threat-APT [Accessed 06 07 2021].

Rouse, M., 2020. *Advanced persistent threat (APT).* [Online] Available at: https://searchsecurity.techtarget.com/definition/advanced-persistent-threat-APT [Accessed 29 08 2020].

Roxana, R., 2013. Power technology and powerful technologies: The dynamics of global governmentality in the cyberspace. In: *Cyber Space and International Relations: Theory, Prospects and Challenges.* Berlin: Springer-Verlag, pp. 3–20.

Scott-Railton, J. et al., 2020. *Dark Basin. Uncovering a massive hack-for-hire operation.* [Online] Available at: https://citizenlab.ca/2020/06/dark-basin-uncovering-a-massive-hack-for-hire-operation/ [Accessed 13 08 2020].

Shaban, H., Nakashima, E. & Lerman, R., 2021. *JBS, world's biggest meat supplier, says its systems are coming back online after cyberattack shut down plants in U.S.* [Online] Available at: www.washingtonpost.com/business/2021/06/01/jbs-cyberattack-meat-supply-chain/ [Accessed 28 06 2021].

Sheridan, K., 2020. *'Bahamut' threat group targets government & industry in Middle East.* [Online] Available at: www.darkreading.com/threat-intelligence/-bahamut-threat-group-targets-government-industry-in-middle-east [Accessed 03 08 2021].

Siapera, E., 2018. *Understanding New Media.* 2 ed. London: Sage.

Smith, D. J., 2014. *Russian cyber strategy and the war against Georgia.* [Online] Available at: www.atlanticcouncil.org/blogs/natosource/russian-cyber-policy-and-the-war-against-georgia/ [Accessed 09 08 2021].

Specops, 2020. *The countries experiencing the most 'significant' cyber-attacks.* [Online] Available at: https://specopssoft.com/blog/countries-experiencing-significant-cyber-attacks/ [Accessed 03 10 2020].

Swinhoe, D., 2020. Brute-force attacks explained, and why are they on the rise [Online] Available at: www.csoonline.com/article/3563352/brute-force-attacks-explained-and-why-they-are-on-the-rise.html [Accessed 18 11 2021].

Sword, A., 2016. *Cybergate: 5 major political cyber attacks.* [Online] Available at: https://techmonitor.ai/techonology/cybersecurity/cybergate-5-major-political-cyber-attacks-4973433 [Accessed 16 11 2021].

Taylor, J., 2020. *Australian cyber attack not 'sophisticated' – Just a wake-up call for businesses, experts say.* [Online] Available at: www.theguardian.com/technology/2020/jun/19/australian-cyber-attack-not-sophisticated-just-a-wake-up-call-for-businesses-experts-say [Accessed 04 07 2021].

Teiss, 2020. *Massive "Hack-For-Hire" group targeting governments, businesses, human rights groups and influential individuals uncovered.* [Online] Available at: www.teiss.co.uk/massive-hack-for-hire-group-targeting-governments-businesses-human-rights-groups-and-influential-individuals-uncovered/ [Accessed 21 03 2021].

The Economist, 2014. *Defending the digital frontier.* [Online] Available at: www.economist.com/special-report/2014/07/10/defending-the-digital-frontier [Accessed 12 08 2020].

Tikk, E., 2011. Ten rules for cyber security. *Survival: Global Politics and Strategy,* 53(3), pp. 119–132.

Trend Micro, 2019. *Security 101: Zero-day vulnerabilities and exploits.* [Online] Available at: www.trendmicro.com/vinfo/us/security/news/vulnerabilities-and-exploits/security-101-zero-day-vulnerabilities-and-exploits [Accessed 06 09 2020].

Trend Micro, 2021a. *Data breaches.* [Online] Available at: www.trendmicro.com/vinfo/us/security/definition/data-breach [Accessed 06 07 2021].

Trend Micro, 2021b. *Ransomware.* [Online] Available at: www.trendmicro.com/vinfo/us/security/definition/ransomware [Accessed 06 07 2021].

Trend Micro, 2021c. *Website defacement.* [Online] Available at: www.trendmicro.com/vinfo/us/security/definition/website-defacement [Accessed 06 07 2021].

UK CPS, 2019. *Cybercrime – prosecution guidance.* [Online] Available at: www.cps.gov.uk/legal-guidance/cybercrime-prosecution-guidance [Accessed 08 08 2020].

Walker, P. & Hern, A., 2019. *Labour suffers second cyber-attack in two days.* [Online] Available at: www.theguardian.com/politics/2019/nov/12/labour-reveals-large-scale-cyber-attack-on-digital-platforms [Accessed 04 07 2021].

Whittaker, Z., 2019. *Two years after WannaCry, a million computers remain at risk.* [Online] Available at: https://techcrunch.com/2019/05/12/wannacry-two-years-on/ [Accessed 13 07 2021].

Woodcock, A., 2019. *Labour says it has suffered a 'sophisticated and large scale cyber-attack' on its digital platforms.* [Online] Available at: www.independent.co.uk/news/uk/politics/labour-cyber-attack-online-today-jeremy-corbyn-latest-a9199426.html [Accessed 04 07 2021].

Woolf, N., 2016. *DDoS attack that disrupted internet was largest of its kind in history, experts say.* [Online] Available at: www.theguardian.com/technology/2016/oct/26/ddos-attack-dyn-mirai-botnet [Accessed 09 08 2020].

Yar, M. & Steinmetz, K. F., 2019. *Cybercrime and Society.* 3 ed. London: Sage.

Zetter, K., 2014. *An unprecedented look at Stuxnet, the world's first digital weapon.* [Online] Available at: www.wired.com/2014/11/countdown-to-zero-day-stuxnet/ [Accessed 13 07 2021].

4 Cybersecurity and Strategies

Introduction

This chapter follows the previous two chapters to conceptualise politically motivated cyber attacks. This chapter creates a theoretical framework to provide an insight into current cybersecurity issues and strategies developed to manage the threats. Risk, nodal governance, and complexity are essential areas to understand the current cybersecurity framework. This chapter includes international, regional, and national security strategies. Key international actors have developed several cybersecurity strategies, covering essential national, regional, and international approaches. This section highlights the diversity and the similarities in developing cybersecurity strategies as well as the challenges.

Risk Management

The nature of protecting various CI forms and structures means that governance is centred around means of calculation, imagining worst-case scenarios to prepare for possible scenarios and mitigate the attack afterwards. The different governing authorities or agencies involved in the process have different knowledge and techniques useful for enhancing the security level (Dean, 2010, p. 18; Munk, 2015, pp. 64–65).

Public and private cybersecurity actors respond to the constant developing risks by qualifying and prioritising risks in the decision-making procedure. Risk, as a concept, is linked to the assumption that the risks cannot be abolished, and 100% security cannot be archived. Instead, risk needs to be recognised and managed before mutating into actual threats. The usefulness of risk management is that it enables actors to assess and classify the risks and impose possible solutions to enhance the security level. Moreover, it enables actors to consider possible outcomes if the risks are not managed or only partly managed (NCSC, 2020). Integrated into the different procedures are cyber assessments to identify what might compromise computer systems and networks – this is also an attempt to identify how severe these risks might be (IT Governance, 2020)

DOI: 10.4324/9781003126676-4

Risk management is based on 'not-yet' events by simulating precautionary actions against imagined attack types. Future events are anticipated from speculative risk scenarios to avoid the unwanted consequences of events. However, there is no guarantee that these imagined risks will materialise; it is more a way of categorising something that 'might happen'. Beck (1992) has defined risks as "a systematic way of dealing with hazards and insecurities induced and introduced by modernisation itself" (p. 260). In this context, risks in society derive from a boomerang effect where the producers of risks also are exposed to them. This boomerang effect is linked to the use of computer systems and technologies in everyday life. Online users benefit from the extended online connectivity for communications, exchanges, searches, work, etc. The same computer systems and technologies can also be turned into powerful weapons that can be used against online users. Beck's notion of risk is linked to globalisation, where states and private actors face an equal uniform set of non-quantifiable, uncontrolled risks on multiple levels. Geographical risks are hard to measure and manage, as security problems in one place tend to affect other areas, and risky events can happen anywhere (Munk, 2015, pp. 76–77). These are the core elements of Rumsfeld's speech from 2003 that illustrates the complexity, uncertainty, and unpredictability of risk assessment:

> The message is that there are no 'knowns'. There is a thing we know that we know. There are known unknowns. That is to say, there are things that we now know we don't know. But there are also unknown unknowns. There are things we don't know we don't know.
>
> (Logan, 2009; NATO, 2002)

The 'unknown unknowns' are featuring heavily in cybersecurity assessment processes. Attackers and politically motivated actors are constantly exploring new ways to attack. These attacks can be conducted using known means, new methods using existing means, or by developing innovative and detrimental means. For example, an attack can suddenly emerge, which no one had predicted, such as Gen-Z/K-pop's actions in 2020 (Alexander, 2020; Bedingfield, 2020).

Risk assessment and management trigger an imaginative outset where scenarios and responses are predicted without knowing if they would be used or correctly designed in accordance with the perceived risks. Recognition of potential targets can enhance the cybersecurity level. Past knowledge about the attackers, their grouping, and their attack modus operandi would be added to the assessments. According to the UK NCSC (2015), not engaging in cybersecurity is no longer an option. Preventing, detecting, or disrupting cyber attacks at an early point in the process limit the impact and the potential reputational damage afterwards (NCSC, 2015). It is important to recognise limitations in knowledge. Understanding past vulnerabilities and attack forms do not indicate that this understanding can be transferred to all new attacks. There are constant insecurities about whether these means and methods would be used again or whether attack forms have developed further. These uncertainties call for a complex cybersecurity strategy framework and tactics that consider and implement proactive processes where the attack predictability and likelihood are calculated and assessed.

Resilience and Preparedness

Included in anticipatory governance forms are resilience building and preparedness. Both areas are linked to imminent threats and foreseeable threats – as well as potential risks related to the development of computer technologies and networks. For example, cyber attacks are a security risk and attacks would be conducted based on various political motivations. However, it is uncertain how and when it would happen – and which entities would be the target. Both resilience and preparedness are preconditions and responses to threats. Resilience is linked to the ability to imagine increasingly uncertain and traumatic futures, where measures are imposed that can adapt and respond to uncertain situations (Munk, 2015, p. 84; O'Malley, 2012, p. 6). To manage cybersecurity, it is vital to have a system of foresight analysing alternative future scenarios by monitoring prospective events, prompt warnings to alert actors about potential consequences.

By using different proactive and reactive techniques and assessing future risks based on past knowledge, it is possible to secure potential targets and attack routes. Areas to include in the risk assessment are malware types, CI, CNI, CII, and ICT vulnerabilities, the Internet architecture, platforms, and devices and online user behaviours (Goldsmith, 2008; Munk, 2015, p. 90; Sandin, 1999, p. 892). In terms of CIs, it has been established that all the areas incorporated within this umbrella term are particularly vulnerable. Resilience is closely linked to proactive security to either prevent an attack or make it difficult for attackers to enter. This increases the likelihood of discovering the attack before it can cause significant damage to the system or society.

Cybersecurity and governance of cyberthreats are based on an understanding of the interaction of political, social, and economic resilience and human adaptability based on the complexity of the differentiated systems and technologies, i.e. self-organisation, functional diversity, and non-linear behaviours (Joseph, 2013, p. 2; Munk, 2015, p. 86). This also means that cybersecurity and resilience are not static but constant processing of assessing and responding to new means and methods developed by the threat actors.

The WannaCry ransomware attack in 2017 on the UK National Healthcare Service (NHS) displayed the importance of constantly assessing computer systems and security maintenance to enhance resilience. In 2014, the UK Department of Health and the Cabinet warned NHS trusts about the security level. The department stated it was essential to develop resilience plans and move away from using old software. Before the attack, NHS Digital conducted an on-site cybersecurity assessment. Out of 23 health trusts, 88 were assessed, and none of these trusts passed the tests. However, the agency did not have the power to take remedial actions despite security concerns (Hern, 2017; Syal, 2018).

Protect, detect, respond, and recover are areas largely incorporated in all cybersecurity strategies. In 2013, US President Obama issued an Executive Order (EO) 13636 to improve CI cybersecurity. The Order instructed the US National Institutes of Standards and Technology (NIST) to work with relevant stakeholders to develop a voluntary framework based on existing standards, guidelines, and practices to reduce the cyber risks to CI (NIST, 2020). The European Union (EU) created its cybersecurity strategy around similar areas. The 2020 EU Cybersecurity Strategy goes beyond traditional cyber policies and compliance by including three key areas: resilience and technological sovereignty; the ability to prevent, deter, and respond to cyber attacks; and, finally, increased focus on teamwork (Van Impe, 2021).

Prevent, detect, and respond cover both physical and cybersecurity. Traditionally, cybersecurity has been introduced to prevent a successful adversary attack. However, that is not possible unless other mechanisms are used in conjunction with preparedness plans. The stage after an attack has been launched also needs to be taken into account. Preparedness plans are introduced to detect attacks that are progressing and minimise the damage caused by these attacks. It is a crucial feature in cybersecurity that victims can restore the systems and networks quickly and effectively afterwards to ensure continuality, especially CI attackers were services and structures unpinning vital areas of society. These risks are expected to be mitigated where services and structures continue with limited or no disruption to the users. Lessons learned from responses are included in a continuous cybersecurity loop where the experiences are factored into future preparedness plans (Bayuk, et al., 2012, p. 2; Munk, 2015, p. 90).

Cybersecurity and Nodal Governance

Cybersecurity and nodal governance forms are created on a multistakeholder structure involving transnational and cross-sectoral organisations, groups, and individuals beyond the actual object. In terms of CIs, several stakeholder groups and individuals are involved in running and maintaining the services. The management structure is linked to a fragmented and differentiated security construction where security should be multilayered. The actual anticipatory governance structure aims to be proactive by including several actors working together in different nodes, ad hoc or permanent (Munk, 2015, pp. 64–65). The nodal governance is the overarching foundation for perceiving, managing, and responding to the online dangers before they develop further. The cybersecurity responses need to mirror the attack types. In the current environment, the attackers can deploy a wide range of cyberweapons. There might be crossovers between the means and methods used, combining several tactics in one attack. For example, the attackers might target the supply chain by combining brute force to enter with APTs for a persistent presence within the system to spy on the target and steal intellectual property over a long period (Skopik, 2017, p. 194).

The multistakeholder approach can best explain the organisation of cybersecurity and the management of CI resources. Preventing cyber attacks requires a coordinated response with several actors working across traditional divisions, i.e. national and international, public and private. The different collaborative nodes are situated in complex institutions, organisations, and apparatuses involving state and non-state actors. For example, the structure of the network can include regulatory state bodies, international institutions and agencies, self-regulating bodies of industry, and corporations governing numerous quasi-autonomous initiatives within the security apparatus (Lentzos & Rose, 2009, pp. 233–234; Miller & Rose, 2008, p. 55; Munk, 2015, p. 65).

Individual organisations or security agencies might develop plans to coordinate their responses. At present, politically motivated cyber attacks are launched against public and private entities. Therefore, the focus is on coordinated cooperation across all communities of interest (Bayuk et al., 2012, p. 38). Threat intelligence communities and cybersecurity nodes are embracing the concept of standardised and automated information exchange, including actors with similar profiles and technical infrastructures. Pooling resources and exchanging knowledge are essential parts of cybersecurity. Despite this, the different nodes are inherently closed by being restricted by specific criteria or invitations (Skopik, 2017, p. 187). When assessing the different areas, such as cyberwar and warfare, cyberterrorism, and other political cyber attacks, it is evident that attack groups and actions are assessed in isolation.

Transnational cooperation is one of the cooperation types which influence governance structure in cybersecurity. The global aspect included in online communications and interconnectivity is present on all levels. All types of illegal online activities and attacks can originate outside the national jurisdiction and create challenges to managing the risks. The main obstacles to efficiently managing these areas derive from:

> [J]udicinary limits, insufficient intelligence gathering/sharing capabilities, technical difficulties, disparate investigative and forensic capacities, lack of trained staff, and inconsistent cooperation with other stakeholders involved in cybersecurity.
>
> (EC, 2012, p. 3)

The cross-sectoral element is equally important as public and private entities, computer systems, devices, and networks are interlinked on an unprecedented scale. All the actors involved are facing the same level of online risks. Cross-sectoral cooperation has obtained a central position based on a particular relationship between the state and private security actors. This implies that governance derives from the mobilising exchange of knowledge, capacity, and resources of various organisations, groupings, and individuals. Everyone can become the target for politically motivated actors, and this risk encourages public and private actors to participate and take responsibility for security within their interest domain (Munk, 2015, p. 127).

Public and private actors' brings together a diverse range of resources, capabilities, priorities, and perspectives that sometimes compete or are incompatible. The two sets of actors are aligned on the tactical level to develop efficient cybersecurity solutions. By maximising their collective resources, it is possible to create practical and sustainable security solutions (Germano, 2014, p. 1). For example, regulators, private cybersecurity actors, supply-chain actors, and customers have practical knowledge for managing the area and understanding the impact of attacks (Crawford & Lister, 2004, p. 21; Dupont, 2006; Johnson, 1992; Munk, 2015, p. 68). This nodal security structure has resulted in an extended hybrid formation that is neither public nor private. In terms of CI areas, cybersecurity collaborations often include the actual partners involved in the daily running of these services and structures.

Collaborative Networks

Collaborative networks are expanding beyond the traditional regulatory framework where numerous actors facilitate information sharing and establish standards of practice and performance. Several actors experience the same types of risk, and their operations are interlinked. Therefore, it is beneficial for all actors to collaborate in nodes to enhance security. Learning from each other, pooling resources together and developing functional responses are positive outcomes. However, these collaborative hybrid structures become very complex and challenging to manage. There is, therefore, a risk of vital information about cybersecurity getting lost or duplicated along the communication line.

Closer collaborations have been developed based on the cybersecurity strategy areas: prevent, detect, respond, and recover. Important global security actors and agencies have created platforms for transnational and cross-sectoral cooperation. The international police cooperation, Interpol, collaborates with states and private cybersecurity partners to share up-to-date knowledge about threats, trends, and risks. The shared data create cyber intelligence to support states in developing preventive strategies to manage current and future threats (Interpol, 2020). In 2000, The US Federal Bureau of Investigation (FBI) created an Internet Crime Complaint Centre (IC3) to provide a reliable and convenient reporting mechanism for suspected Internet facilitate crimes (FBI, 2021). The European police cooperation, Europol, established European Cybercrime Centre (EC3) in 2013 to strengthen cybersecurity and police cooperation aiming to improve responses and facilitate cooperation between the member states. This agency includes prevention and stakeholder management, strategy and development, forensics, and cyber intelligence (Europol, 2020).

Complexity Theory

Cybersecurity collaborations can be linked to various systems incorporated in the complexity theory. Complexity theory enhances understanding of how systems like CIs, the Internet, corporations and actors, and the economy appear, develop, and grow. Additionally, the theory aims to understand how complex relationships and interactions among the members enable collective behaviours (Sammut-Bonnici, 2015, p. 1). There are substantial internal and external complexities included in the different cybersecurity collaborations. The nodes consist of multi-identities, redefinition of public and private entities, and eroding boundaries between public and private actors. Complex non-linear systems consist of several similar, independent and interdependent actors and entities that constantly communicate. The actors need to adapt to new situations to address the cyber risks and create order in the chaotic systems. Still, the organisation of the nodes is based on spontaneous self-organisation within the system to ensure adaptiveness. To ensure that the groups function, some local rules are developed within the collaboration. These rules apply to all actors, but they should not be created in a way that ruins flexibility. Finally, it is essential that the actors can develop together within the collaboration (Erkoçak & Açıkalın, 2013).

Complexity theory is helpful to understand how systems develop from chaotic situations. For example, organisations and agency formations are complex and organic structures, and each actor acts autonomously within the system, driven by their self-interest and establishment. However, each entity involves several self-organising components of employees, business units, resources, and stakeholders. This flexibility is paramount in a technological environment that is continuously exposed by hackers and politically motivated actors (Sammut-Bonnici, 2015, p. 1). None of the actors has the same structure, nor do they face the same risks. Therefore, it is impossible to address the risks and responses like-for-like – or develop strategies that cover all the risks. However, the complexity is also linked to the way attacks are carried out and the type of the targets. Cyber-physical attacks are significantly different from pure cyber attacks. Cyber-physical attacks are traditionally linked to compromise devices and domains' safety or physical integrity. In comparison, the pure cyber attacks are predominately linked to threats against cybersecurity, such as the confidentiality, integrity, and availability of devices (Liu et al., 2017).

Game Theory

Just as the attacking groups follow a strategy and an incitement to pursue a political agenda by launching attacks, the cybersecurity actors are also developing international, national, and organisational strategies to respond to the growing number of cyber risks. The different strategic positions are linked to game theory and the payoff that can be archived by weighing up the costs and the benefits. The outcome of these calculations is essential for both

Table 4.1 Strategic games

Type	Game	Actions
Decision-making under risk	Based on the inherent uncertainties linked with the consequences of actions, i.e. taking chances calculated together with the probabilities of occurrence Other decision-makers are perceived as non-strategic fixed targets	The right choices yield the greatest expected return The expected return can be monetary, enhanced security, psychological, or physical satisfaction
Game-theoretic decision-making	Based on actors pursuing their own goals while considering their existing knowledge of adversaries, i.e. a knowledge game to predict future movements based on past known behaviours and possible changes Other decision-makers are not fixed targets, but the situation and actions can continually develop and change	An ongoing circle of assessments and predictions and multiple directions and possibilities Closely linked to the current cyber-risk assessments and worst-case scenarios, i.e. known knowns, known unknowns, or unknown unknowns

Source: Niou & Ordeshook (2015, pp. 2–3).

groups and their decision-making: what would generate the best payoff (Niou & Ordeshook, 2015, pp. 2–3).

There are two game theories that is important to understand the strategies that underpins cybersecurity. The first direction is 'decision-making under risks', and the second direction is 'game-theoretical decision making'.

Strategic Positions and Payoff

The way CIs are organised and interlinked in large and distributed systems creates a complicated network of actors. These different systems are targets for attacks. At the same time, they are facing many security challenges that require a robust and flexible strategic foundation (Liu et al., 2017, p. 13). The games are developed to predict the outcome of attacks, strategic moves and priorities in collaboration, counterattack measures, and enhance general resilience and preparedness. Therefore, the security actors constantly calculate the cost and benefit to get a positive strategic payoff.

The actors in the cyber attack game are individual entities, and the decision-making is entwined with each game move. It is crucial to notice that each of the actors (players) discerns the actions of the other participants in the strategic game. The decision-making strategy predicts the potential behaviour of the opponent, the move, and the payoff. The payoff is the amount of satisfaction each actor archive from the game; these can be both positive and negative – and the payoff is made known by the end of the game (Patil et al., 2018, pp. 12987–12988).

In cybersecurity, many games can be considered stimulation to enhance the payoffs for the individual players. Some cybersecurity actors will be involved to enhance their position, where other actors focus on the group. Other cybersecurity actors engage in a lengthy tit-for-tat game with their opponents. Additionally to the actors' strategic positions, some games are ongoing and develop over time. Whereas other games are linked to one particular problem, and the game is over when the strategic position is stated. These games can be linked back to the complexity theory, where the strategies are developed in a non-linear way as the actors and the problems they face cannot be easily compared.

Actors have different levels of knowledge and self-interest. Resources, skills, and problems are not always levelled and comparable. These inconsistencies in the knowledge and application make the actual management of cybersecurity difficult. Interpol's Secretary General Stock (2021) has called for all police agencies to form a global collaboration with industry partners to prevent the increasing number of ransomware attacks. Stock suggested that global police forces should develop the same international collaboration structure used to fight terrorism, human trafficking, and organised crime to prevent and disrupt ransomware attackers. The online threats have reached a level where it is impossible for one actor or sector to manage the risks alone. The magnitude and the likelihood of these attacks call for collective responses to improve the cybersecurity level across sectors. The different responses to the risks should make it more risky and costly for the attackers to launch ransomware attacks. Thereby, the attackers' payoff will be reduced (Interpol, 2021).

The Game

Two opponents can play the game, where one actor is the attacker, and the other is the defender. The attacker makes malicious entries into the system to threaten the current security level by seeking out vulnerabilities. The strategies of the attackers can go in multiple directions. For example, they can span from a single action to a sequence of interlinked activities or be directed towards an ultimate goal. The defender in this game would be the opponents responsible for applying cybersecurity based on defence techniques to secure the ICs from malicious attacks. To counter possible attacks, the defender has prepared several strategies to monitor and protect computer systems, devices, networks, and physical assets. Each successful attack is a negative payoff for the cybersecurity actors. Depending on the actors involved, the payoff can be preventing or not preventing an attack. An example, North Korean hackers attempted in 2020 on attacking Israeli defence manufacturers. The payoff was negative for the North Korean hackers as the Israeli defence successfully stopped the attack (CSIS, 2020). By contrast, an Iranian hacking group successfully targeted significant US companies and governmental agencies by exploiting vulnerabilities in high-end network equipment. In this attack, the hacking group created backdoors for other groups to use, and that move is a negative payoff for the cybersecurity actors (CSIS, 2020).

The strategic game can also involve two actors developing strategies or agreements; the payoff is the level of success in the negotiations. There has been made several attempts of developing global cybercrime conventions or agreements on conduct in cyberspace; most of these negotiations have failed, so some of the actors might have perceived that outcome as a success whereas others see it as failure depending on the starting point and what has been offered during the negotiations. Attempts have been made within the United Nations (UN), but these have failed. For example, Russia and China have blocked UN attempts in 2010 of creating an international cybercrime treaty. The discussions ended as Russia, China, and several developing countries disagreed with the US, Canada, the UK, and the EU regarding national sovereignty and human rights (Masters, 2010; Munk, 2018, p. 240). In 2010, Russia proposed a cybercrime treaty at the Twelfth UN Crime Congress, but the negotiations stalled because of disagreements on complicated national sovereignty and online rights (Ballard, 2010; Masters, 2010; Walker, 2019). Again, the status quo is upheld with no change in the strategic position or the payoff.

Contrary to traditional approaches, the outcome of game theory is linked to both the actions of the current player and the other players in the game. Therefore, this approach is extremely accessible and flexible. In cybersecurity, this flexibility is paramount as the dependencies and development of computer technology and networks are both increasing and transforming (Kakkad et al., 2019, p. 681). In the game, all players are considered to be instrumentally rational. However, the utility is subjective and is linked to the perceived outcome for the individual actors. The game does not imply that the actors will succeed and obtain their shared objectives. These actors might receive an outcome different from what they expected. All the available strategic game models are based on the assumption that the actors primarily use past knowledge, interpreted in the present time, to decide future outcomes. It might be that the actors are not fully informed about the current situation. Therefore, the actors base their strategy on limited information or misinformation (Zagare, 2019, p. 47). The actors might not have relevant or complete information about their opponents/attacker, but they can draw into other types of knowledge to develop a strategy.

International, Regional, and National Cybersecurity Strategies

Developing strategies to manage large-scale cyber attacks is about consequences interlinked with the payoff of the actions taken. The different means included are based on a categorisation of their level of appropriateness to archive success. Therefore, the strategy's effect is not directly linked to the nature of the means used but the consequences of using this mean to reach the desired end (Cilluffo & Clark, 2015, p. 10; Grey, 2013). There are obstacles to developing strategies as actors need to consider protecting the state sovereignty, national security concerns, and perceptions of the risks based on the states' societal, cultural, and legal background. Finally, there are issues with the general weakness of the implementation of the strategies. States and other actors are reluctant to engage with immediate or long-term cooperation if they do not directly gain from it. Not being engaged in the collaborations can also be the desired outcome and a positive payoff. States and security actors can benefit from unregulated cyberspace, where norms, processes, and practices are underdeveloped. The most technically advanced states can use cyberspace to their advantage on others' expenses (Jakobi, 2020, p. 216).

International Institutional Frameworks

UNITED NATIONS

The UN has increasingly focused on ICT-related issues for almost two decades, driven by positive benefits and malicious purposes deriving from the increased dependency on ICTs. The international system includes a series of built-in safety mechanisms that enable mitigating existing and new emerging threats. Different areas are priorities within this organisation, such as developing norms and standard behaviour and confidence and capacity-building in responding to online threats (UNIDIR, 2017, pp. 1–2). However, only a limited number of regulatory initiatives have progressed; yet, the progress has been slow due to geopolitics and different states' priorities.

In 2018, the UN General Assembly set up two separate groups to study international law and norms concerning cyberspace due to the deadlock of developing this area. A UN Resolution 73/27 was proposed by states, including Russia, to create the Open-Ended Working Group (OEWG). Another group of states, including Australia, France, Germany, the UK, the US, supported another proposal advocating to continue the existing Group of Governmental Experts (GGE) (Achten, 2019; EU Cyber Direct, 2020; Peters, 2019; UN, 2019). These two groups are now working in parallel.

The GGE and the OEWG groups aim to address cyber norms, confidence-building, and issues surrounding the implementation of international laws to cyberspace (Achten, 2019; Geneva Internet Platform, 2020; Walker, 2019,

Table 4.2 Working groups

Name	Group
The OEWG	All interested parties within the UN
The GGE	A working group of 25 selected member states

Sources: Geneva Internet Platform (2020); Walker (2019, p. 2).

p. 2). Both groups' discussion is founded on the substantive UN GGE reports from 2009/2010, 2012/2013, and 2014/2015. Essential outcomes from these discussions are fed into the new framework. For example, the 2012/2013 report confirmed that international law could be applied to the ICT environment, such as the UN Charter. Additionally, the 2014/2015 GGE report included separate section norms, rules, and principles for states' responsible behaviour (Achten, 2019; Schmitt, 2021; UN, 2010, 2013, 2015a). This means that both groups are based on previous agreements about the applicability of existing international laws in cyberspace and compliance with the prohibition of force, respect territorial sovereignty and independence. Also, the principles for settling disputes using peaceful means should be included in the discussion. The 2014/2015 report highlighted that Article 51 of the UN Charter, the right to self-defence, can be invoked if a cyber attack or a large-scale cyber attack can be classified as an armed attack. Yet, the classification of an armed attack remains disputed (UN, 2015a, 2020; Wolter, 2014).

THE GGE REPORTING

In 2014, a UN-level GGE group agreed on an essential set of recommendations of norms, rules, and principles of acceptable behaviour in cyberspace. The establishment of this expert group was a stepping stone to create global cooperation and progress a universal legal framework that removes the previous lack of clarity about these areas (Achten, 2019; Walker, 2019, p. 10; Wolter, 2014).

The GGE's 2021 report is considered essential, replacing the 2016–2017 GGE group, which failed in producing an agreed report within the time frame. The group disagreed on areas such as the right to self-defence and international humanitarian law (Schmitt, 2021; UN GGE, 2021). Given the geopolitical climate, it is not surprising that there are tensions internally within the group. Experts from 25 states were appointed. Most of them were selected because of their equitable geographical location. In contrast, six experts were from the five permanent Security Council member states which continuously disagree over cyber issues, i.e. China and Russia vs the US, the UK, and France (Schmitt, 2021; UN GGE, 2021). However, 2020 and 2021 stands out because of the exceptionally high number of politically motivated cyber attacks. Frequent and severe hostile cyber operations have targeted GGE's members' national states, i.e. persistent election interference, espionage, APTs, and ransomware attacks on CIs. The new report acknowledged that international humanitarian law applies to cyber operations in armed conflicts. However, there are disagreements about how international law can govern cyber operations (Schmitt, 2021).

THE OEWG REPORTING

According to the published 2021 report, all the sessions was based on substantive, interactive exchanges among the participating states and representatives from civil society, the private sector, academia and the technical community (Gold, 2021; UN OEWG, 2021). In terms of cyberthreats, some states expressed worries regarding developing or using ICT capabilities for purposes inconsistent with the UN objective of maintaining international peace and security. Other state representatives highlighted concerns that the ICT environment could encourage unilateral measures rather than settle disputes according to the UN objectives. The group also raised concerns that the development and use of ICT capabilities for military purposes would undermine international peace and security, how states used cyber capabilities, stockpiling of vulnerabilities, and lack of transparency. Other issues were rained in the forum, such as the lack of defined processes for disclosure, the exploitation of harmful hidden functions, and the integrity of global ICT supply chains and data security. It was argued that these actions could lead to reduction or disruption of connectivity, unintended escalation or action that would harm third parties. Some states also noted that the lack of clarity regarding the responsibilities of the private sector constituted a specific concern (Achten, 2019; UN OEWG, 2021).

Despite scepticism and tensions between international actors, the UN member states endorsed the 2021 OEWG group's report. The report included recommendations for improving peace and security in cyberspace. Although the report is not legally binding or cover groundbreaking content, it is still exceptional; this is the first time all states have agreed on international cybersecurity (Gold, 2021; O'Sullivan, 2021; UN OEWG, 2021).

OTHER UN COLLABORATIONS TO DEVELOP CYBERSECURITY

Developing processes and practices within the UN framework is complicated. There are persisting disagreements between the member states on applying existing international law rules to the online environment. Some states have been slow in implementing the recommended norms of state behaviour. They lack the capabilities and resources to adopt the recommended norms and confidence-building, such as establishing national structures and mechanisms required to enhance security and respond to the different cyber risks. There is also a lack of awareness of the various normative processes developed within and outside the UN framework to enhance peace and security. The continuing distrust among states and various stakeholders spills over to the cybersecurity framework, undermining the development of global cybersecurity strategies (UNIDIR, 2017, p. 2).

China, Russia, Tajikistan, and Uzbekistan submitted in September 2011 a 'Draft Convention on International Information Security' at the 69th session of the UN General Assembly. Although the draft was rejected, it created the foundation for a new proposal, the International Code of Conduct for Information Security. This proposal was forwarded by six Shanghai Cooperation Organisation (SCO) members in 2015 (McKune, 2015; Munk, 2018; Rõigas, 2015; UN, 2015b). The revised code did not have any significant changes to the first rejected proposal. Unsurprisingly, the code did not find global support.

Regional Approaches

Several regional approaches and strategies have been developed in a regional framework. All these are important to enhance cybersecurity and address the constantly developing threats.

Table 4.3 outlines some of the key perspectives and initiatives launched in a regional context.

Table 4.3 Key regional perspectives on cybersecurity

Actors	Initiatives	Areas
The NATO	Recognised that cyberthreats are becoming more frequent, complex, destructive, and coercive. Developed several responses As a part of NATO's core tasks, the organisation develops its cyber defence following international laws	Adopted processes and practices to develop strong and resilience cyber defences Measures align with collective defence, crisis management, and cooperative security
The CoE	Developed the only international Cybercrime Convention from 2001: The Convention on Cybercrime (CETS No.185), also known as the Budapest Convention Developed through cooperation between a large group of actors	It does not set out a framework for cybersecurity Provides a legal instrument for collaborating, developing, and harmonising national measures, processes, and practices
The EU	Developed a legislative framework and cybersecurity strategies from an early stage. Already in 2003, cybersecurity was included in the European Security Strategy	Initiatives have been launched to address the growing number of threats developing in cyberspace CI protection, resilience, and preparedness are incorporated in strategies
The OAS	Initiatives have been launched since the adoption of the General Assembly resolution AG/RES.2004. Provides a multidimensional and multidisciplinary approach to creating a culture of cybersecurity	Initiatives have been launched to securing cyberspace and protecting computer devices, systems and networks

(continued)

Table 4.3 Cont.

Actors	Initiatives	Areas
The AU	Initiatives have been launched to manage the damage caused by online attacks since the AU Convention on Cybersecurity, and Personal Data Protection (AUCCPDP) (The Malabo Convention) was launched in 2011	Initiatives are aiming to patch gaps in the legislative and regulatory cybersecurity framework. Lacking slightly behind in recognising new types of offences and adopting amendments to existing legislation
The ASEAN	Reinforced in 2012 that the region's need to intensify regional cooperation concerning securing ICTs. The need for cybersecurity is on the agenda in the Asia-Pacific region	Struggles to create a unified framework for the region No developed cybersecurity strategy. But non-binding initiatives and plans have been developed to progress a more robust framework in the region
The SCO	In 2009, the member states of the SCO agreed to develop a legal and organisational foundation for collaboration	This cooperative framework does also include cybersecurity

Sources: AU (2016, p. 3); CoE (2020b); EC, CoEU (2009); Juneidi (2002); NATO (2020a); OAS (2004a); SCO (2009); UNIDIR (2019, 2020a).

THE NATO CYBERSECURITY INITIATIVES

NATO member states adopted the Alliance's first defence policy in 2008. This adoption led to cyber defences becoming a core part of the collective defence. To keep the Alliance at the forefront of the constantly changing cyberthreat landscape and uphold a robust cyber defence, NATO adopted in 2014 an enhanced policy and action plan, which was further amended in 2017. The 2014 policy incorporated cyber defence into the Alliance's core tasks of collective defence, affirmed that international law applies to cyberspace, set out a plan for further NATO and its allies' cyber capabilities, and established closer links to industry (NATO, 2021). Importantly, NATO recognised already in 2014 that a cyber attack could trigger the Alliance's collective defense clause (Article 5) of NATO's founding treaty: The North Atlantic Treaty (known as the Washington Treaty) (Brent, 2019; NATO, 1949).

NATO's cybersecurity strategy is established by a framework covering Cyber-Development, Cyber-Democracy, and Cyber-Defense (Efthymiopoulos, 2019, p. 3). In 2016, the organisation reaffirmed the defensive mandate for developing effective defences in cyberspace similar to those applicable to air, land, and sea. The adoption of the Cyber Defence Pledge (2016) creates responsibilities for the member states in accordance with the

Washington Treaty Article 3 to resist armed attack. As a matter of priority, the member states are required to enhance their cyber defence of CNIs and networks according to the allied security and collective defence (Brent, 2019; NATO, 1949, 2016, 2020b).

In 2016, the member states agreed on prioritising their national networks and infrastructure, which also induced cyber education capabilities; mutual training and exercises; information sharing; and mutual assistance in preventing, mitigating, and recovering cyber attacks. One of the biggest challenges for the Alliance is to recognise the private industry and the civilian government's involvement. The threat arising from cyberspace cannot purely be managed by military means, and the attackers are not necessarily state actors (Brent, 2019; NATO, 2020a).

The NATO Cooperative Cyber Defence Centre of Excellence (CCDCOE) Within the Alliance, the NATO CCDCOE has been launched as an international and interdisciplinary cyber defence hub providing research, training, and exercises in four essential areas, i.e. technology, strategy, operations, and law (CCDCOE, 2020b). The centre supports the member states and NATO with cyber defence expertise and foster collaborations between like-minded nations, researchers, analysts, and educators from military, governmental, academic, and industrial entities (CCDCOE, 2020a). An example of collaboration between multiple stakeholders is included in the Tallinn Manual on International Law Applicable to Cyberwarfare (2013). The first Tallinn manual addressed the most severe cyber operations. Included in the manual are those cyber operations violating the prohibition of the use of force, entitling states to exercise their right of self-defence, or occurring during armed conflict (NATO CCDCOE, 2013). The second Tallinn manual was published in 2017. This edition expands the influencing first manual's coverage of international law governing cyber operations to legal regimes in peacetime (NATO CCDCOE, 2017). Both manuals have provided a blueprint for understanding cyberwarfare and enabling decision-making and strategies.

THE COUNCIL OF EUROPE (COE)'S CONVENTION ON CYBERCRIME

The CoE's Convention on Cybercrime 2001 is the only binding international instrument that serves as a guideline for signatory states in developing a comprehensive framework in a national context against cybercrime. The main objective is to pursue a standard criminal policy to protect society against cybercrime by developing and adopting appropriate legislation (CoE, 2001a, 2020a).

The overarching aims of the Convention are to harmonise the domestic criminal substantive law elements of offences and connected provisions in cybercrime. The Convention provides a framework for national criminal procedural law powers useful for carrying out investigations and prosecutions (CoE, 2001b). Although the Convention is broadly formulated and useful in developing cybersecurity plans and legislation in the signatory states, the Convention is based on criminal cybercrimes from the late 1990s. The areas and typologies in the Convention are linked to the threat level and knowledge in 2001. However, the typology is not fully applicable as cybercrime and attack have been expanded and new means and methods have been developed. Instead, the new criminal activities are covered by national criminal law. However, they lack the same level of harmonisation as those included in the Convention (Schjolberg & Ghernaouti-Hélie, 2009, p. ii).

THE EU: CYBERSECURITY INITIATIVES

The different initiatives launched by the EU create a comprehensive framework to manage cybercrime attacks and cybersecurity. In 2010, the European Commission introduced the EU Internal Security Strategy in Action to provide a shared agenda for the member states and the EU institutions, agencies, and other actors. The 2013 Cybersecurity Strategy of the EU clarified essential principles that should guide the member states in establishing their national cybersecurity plans (EC/HREUFASP, 2013). The EU Cyber Defence Policy Framework (2014) established priority areas for cyber defences and clarified the actors' roles (CoEU, 2014; UNIDIR, 2020e). Over the years, initiatives have been launched to counter cybercrime, strengthen a judiciary network, cooperate between different actors, develop best practices, and support investigations and cybercrime prosecution (EC, CoEU, 2016, 2017, 2020a). One of the most important initiatives is adopting the EU Cybersecurity Act in 2019, which introduces the EU-wide certification. The act upgrades the European Agency for Network and Information Security (ENISA) by expanding the mandate to cement its role in the framework (EC, CoEU, 2018a, 2020d). By implementing this initiative, the EU expressed a willingness to continue developing and implement voluntary, non-binding norms, rules, and principles for responsible state behaviour online within the UN framework and other international forums (EC, 2018; EC, CoEU, 2019a). While this initiative progressed through the institutional framework, the Council adopted a conclusion to share and support the EU Digital Strategy implementation. The conclusions on malicious cyber activities aim to ensure global, open, free, stable, and secure cyberspace. The conclusions also expressed grave concerns about the increasing activities of malicious actors (EC, CoEU, 2020a, 2020d).

These initiatives were supported by the High Representative of the EU (2020b) forwarding a declaration on behalf of the EU. This declaration highlighted the states to respect the rules-based order in cyberspace. This declaration also urged actors to end malicious cyber activities, including the theft of intellectual property. The declaration also included a call for closer international cooperation to enhance cybersecurity and stability (EC, CoEU, 2019a, 2019b). Due to the COVID-19 pandemic, this declaration was expanded to include malicious cyber activities exploiting the global pandemic. Since the pandemic started, phishing and malware, scanning, and DDoS attacks have been detected, and some have been launched against CIs (EC, CoEU, 2020b). However, numerous initiatives are launched within the EU framework, but it is difficult to get a comprehensive overview of the different actors, rules, and initiatives. Hopefully, the new cybersecurity framework will create a coherent framework interlinking with different areas and topics. Moreover, the initiatives launched take time to get through the whole EU system. Bureaucratic processes hinder quick response to the constantly changing cyberthreats.

The Cyber Diplomatic Toolbox   The EU is focusing on the increasing number of large-scale cyber attacks. Large-scale cyber attacks are not new to the EU, as legislation has already been introduced to criminalise the area. However, attacks, such as the WannaCry and NotPetya attacks in 2017, have increased the focus on these actions (EC, CoEU, 2018b, 2019c). In 2019, the Council established a framework for imposing targeted restrictive measures to deter and respond to the growing external cyberthreats to the EU and/or its member states. The EU has launched initiatives such as the EU's Cyber Diplomatic Toolbox covering cooperation, conflict prevention, and threat mitigation. The toolbox also includes means to deter and influence possible aggressors' behaviour (CoEU, 2019, p. 2; EC, CoEU, 2019c).

The Council's framework for sanctions marks a new direction for the EU. The Cyber Diplomatic Toolbox permits sanctions on persons or entities responsible for attacks, attempting or supporting attacks against entities within the EU (EC, CoEU, 2018b, 2019c). In 2020, the EU imposed the first sanctions against six individuals and three entities involved in various cyber attacks. These sanctions include travel bans and assets freeze. Moreover, EU persons and entities are prohibited from making funds available to the people or entities included in the ban (EC, CoEU, 2020a, 2020c).

THE ORGANISATION OF AMERICAN STATES (OAS): CYBERSECURITY INITIATIVES

The Comprehensive Inter-American Strategy to Combat Threats to Cybersecurity (2004) provides a multidimensional and multidisciplinary approach to creating a culture of cybersecurity. The strategy includes the Inter-American Committee against Terrorism (CICTE), Inter-American Telecommunication Commission (CITEL), Meeting of Ministers of Justice or Other Ministers or Attorneys General of Americans (REMJA) (OAS, 2004a, 200b; UNIDIR, 2020c).

OAS' cybersecurity programme covers three pillars: policy development, capacity development, i.e. training and cyber exercises, and research and outreach (OAS, 2020). Like other initiatives launched, this cybersecurity programme aims to develop tools to prevent, identify, respond, and recover from possible cyber attacks. Moreover, the agenda promotes the development of processes and practices to improve information sharing, cooperation, and robust, effective, and timely coordination among the different cybersecurity actors on national, regional, and international levels. Finally, the programme aims to increase access to knowledge about the threat and cybersecurity by the public, private, and civil society stakeholders and Internet users (OAS, 2020). Compared with the European region, this regional framework is developing, and more engagement from all actors is needed to lift the level of cybersecurity in the region.

The OAS' Cybersecurity Strategy also focuses on developing public–private partnerships and collaborations, bringing together the efforts and expertise of CICTE, CITEL, and REMJA to protect CIs and ICTs. Within the strategy, there is an understanding that creating and progressing various public–private partnerships can enhance resilience and preparedness. One aims to increase training, education, and awareness within privately owned and privately operated CNIs. The strategy also fuels the capabilities to identify, evaluate, and stimulate the adoption of technical standards, best practices, and processes to advance information security during the online transmission, i.e. the Internet and communication networks (OAS, 2004a).

THE AFRICAN UNION (AU): CYBERSECURITY INITIATIVES

Various measures have been developed with AU as the drive for change. The AU Convention on Cybersecurity and Personal Data Protection (AUCCPDP) (The Malabo Convention) was drafted in 2011 with mixed reviews about the text and the slow progress on the ratification implementations. Critics claimed that the Convention was drafted too vaguely and flawed. Moreover, it was problematic that the management structure depended on broad cooperation among all the states, leaving the AU trailing behind its counterparts in other regions (Dalton et al., 2017, p. 117). Nevertheless, the Convention marks the beginning of a commitment to developing cybersecurity strategies despite not being sufficient to manage the threats (AU, 2016; Dalton et al., 2017, p. 114; UNIDIR, 2019).

In 2016, the African Ministers for Communication and ICTs agreed to develop a comprehensive approach to cybersecurity and cybercrime in Africa to address the flaws in the AUCCPDP Convention (AU, 2016; UNIDIR, 2019). In 2019, the AU's Peace and Security Council adopted a Communique on Mitigating the Threats of Cyber Security to Peace and Security in Africa to ensure that the region develops cyber strategies, norms, and practices. Several areas are identified in the Communique to enhance resilience and preparedness towards the growing number of threats, such as engaging in regular cybersecurity risks assessment, investing in cybersecurity and education, developing multilayered approaches, and encouraging various collaborations and partnerships. Moreover, it aims to create synergies and enhance national, regional, and continental cybersecurity coordination, harmonising laws and providing legal assistance in cybercrime cases (AU, 2019; UNIDIR, 2019).

The Internet Society's Survey on Policy Issues in Asia-Pacific (2018) listed cybersecurity as the top Internet policy concern. Cybersecurity is still a developing issue in the region, and the disparate level of cybersecurity showing a visible gap between the states' engagement to develop national cybersecurity strategies (Thinyane & Christine, 2020, p. 8). Association of Southeast Asian Nations (ASEAN) is facing issues in pulling together a unifying framework. The ASEAN Inter-Parliamentary Assembly has only limited powers compared with its European counterpart, the EU (A.T. Kearney, 2018, p. 8).

The statement of the Ministers of Foreign Affairs on Cooperation on Ensuring Cyber Security (2012) highlighted that member states should promote further consideration of strategies to manage the emerging ICTs threats, and these initiatives should be consistent with international law and basic principles; they should engage in dialogue regarding confidence-building, stability, and risk reduction to address the increasing uses of ICTs. This dialogue should include a debate on the use of ICTs in conflicts. Moreover, the statement aimed to enhance cooperation in developing a cybersecurity culture. In line with other regions, ASEAN should also focus on developing an ASEAN Regional Forum (ARF) work plan to secure ICTs. This work plan should focus on practical cooperation, confidence-building, setting corresponding goals, implementing a time frame, and develop common terms and conditions relevant to the use of ICTs (ARF, 2012; UNIDIR, 2020a).

In 2015, ARF also outlined a 2015 ARF Working Plan on Security of Information Communication Technologies to promote a peaceful, secure, open, and cooperative ICT environment. This plan also aimed to prevent conflicts and crises by increasing the trust and confidence between the member states. Central to the work plan is promoting transparency; increasing and intensifying confidence-building; and reducing the risks of misperception, miscalculation, conflict escalations, and tensions. The work plan is based on a desire to develop regional capacities to respond to criminal and terrorist use of ICT, especially after the WannaCry attacks, where several victims were in the South Asia and Pacific areas. The region has also been targeted by North Korean state-sponsored group's cryptocurrency raising activities (Kono, 2021). This should be archived through improved coordination and coordinated responses (ARF, 2015; UNIDIR, 2020a). In 2017, the ASEAN cyber capacity programme was introduced to strengthen the regional ability to respond to constant cyberthreats by developing cyber policies, legislation, strategy development, and incident response (UNIDIR, 2020a).

International Cooperation   The Singapore-funded ASEAN cyber capacity-building programme (ACCP) supports and improves cyber capacities across ASEAN member states (EU Cyber Direct, 2017). Within this programme, ASEAN-Singapore (2019) has established the Singapore-ASEAN Cybersecurity Centre of Excellence (ASCCE) merged cyber diplomacy with operation issues like incident response and information sharing (Cheok, 2017; Heinl, 2019; UNIDIR, 2020a). The centre is another step in the right direction to enhance state cooperation and develop a unified ASEAN perspective for improving cybersecurity. Hopefully, the ASCCE will address the current limitations in ASEAN. For example, the low coordination of enhancing the cyber capacity-building in the region (Heinl, 2019).

Other Cybersecurity Collaborations in the Region   Outside ASEAN, other organisations have been formed to promote various areas. China, Kazakhstan, Kyrgyzstan, Russia, Tajikistan, and Uzbekistan agreed to coordinate and implement necessary joint measures to protect international information security as a part of the SCO collaboration. The states work towards a system for joint monitoring and response to threats. More importantly, the states decided on elaborating joint measures to develop provisions of the international law to limit the use of information weapons threatening defence capacity, national security, and public safety (SCO, 2009; UNIDIR, 2020f).

The Asia-Pacific area is vast. Therefore, it is not surprising that several organisations have developed in the region, promoting cybersecurity among members. This is a positive development, but the lack of organisations covering the region is also its weakness. However, this region also includes three complicated cybersecurity actors, Russia, China, and the US. Each with strong aspirations to be leading in cybersecurity and online military defence. These three states are already struggling reaching agreements within the UN framework on cybersecurity because of their internal disagreements. This results in an unequal level of cybersecurity in the Asia-Pacific region. Enhancing cybersecurity should be at the forefront of all the states as it provides the best payoff. However, the tensions between the prominent cybersecurity actors in this collaboration are resulting in fragmented approaches.

National Cybersecurity Strategies

THE UNITED KINGDOM (THE UK)

The UK published its first National Cyber Security Strategy in 2011. The strategy aimed to increase the UK's cybersecurity and resilience against cyber attacks and protect online interests. The strategy should also create open, vibrant, and stable cyberspace supporting open societies (HM Government, 2015, p. 40). Money was allocated to the Government Communications Headquarters (GCHQ) to detect and analyse cyberthreats and pre-empt attacks and trace the cybercriminals behind the attacks. Under the GCHQ, a new National Cyber Crime Centre (NCCC) was established as a focal point for companies' advice (HM Government, 2015, pp. 40–41). The second National Cyber Security Strategy 2016–2021 set out the government's plans to make the UK more secure and resilient in cyberspace (GOV.UK, 2016; HM Government, 2016, p. 9; UNIDIR, 2020g). The UK government launched a Call for Evidence (2019) to gain insight into managing the cyber risks. This result highlighted that there still are a wide range of inabilities within organisations that create obstacles for enhancing security. The Evidence Call also identified a lack of commercial rationale or business drivers necessary to prioritise and invest in cyber risk management. The digital environment within organisations was too complicated and insecure. Two other obstacles were directed towards the government's management of cyber risks. There is a lack of incentives to support organisations in enhancing online protection, and the imposed regulation was insufficient to compel organisations to introduce adequate cyber risks management (GOV.UK, 2020).

The following UK National Cybersecurity strategy would be published by the end of 2021. Based on the 2016–2021 cybersecurity review, trends like more significant reliance on digital networks and systems, rapid technological changes, a more comprehensive range of adversaries, and competing visions for the future of the Internet are areas that need to be addressed (Cabinet Office, 2020).

THE UNITED STATES OF AMERICA (THE US)

The US has developed several strategies on the federal level. The US introduced its first policy in 2003. This strategy has been replaced several times as the strategy runs for five years before being replaced with an updated version addressing current cyberthreats. The strategies provide the department with a framework to "keep pace with the evolving cyber risk landscape by reducing vulnerabilities and building resilience; countering malicious actors in cyberspace; responding to incidents; and making the cyber ecosystem more secure and resilient" (US DHS, 2019).

The Comprehensive National Cybersecurity Initiative (CNCI) was developed and implemented by the White House in 2009 after an evaluation by US President Obama's Cyberspace Policy Review. This initiative was initially launched in 2008 by US President Bush (NSPD-54/HSPD-23). The cybersecurity strategy encompasses 12 initiatives within three overarching goals. These goals are to establish a front line of defence, enable the US to defend against the full spectrum of threats, and, finally, strengthen cybersecurity for the future (EOPUS, 2009; UNIDIR, 2020h; US DHS, 2011a). The US President Obama determined that the CNCI and its associated activities should be developed and integrated into a broader and updated version of the national US cybersecurity strategy (The White House, 2009).

The Department of Homeland Security (DHS) has a prominent role in this framework, including cooperating with the owners and operators of CI and essential resources (CIKRs), including private, state, or municipality-owned entities. The aim is to help these entities bolster their cybersecurity preparedness, risk assessment and mitigation, and incident response capabilities (UNIDIR, 2020h; US DHS, 2011b). The department got its mandate extended by its cybersecurity strategy from 2018 to 2023. By 2023, the aim is to improve the national cybersecurity risk management plan that increases security and resilience across networks and CI. The aim is to decrease illicit cyber activity and improve responses to cyber incidents by developing a more secure and reliable cyber ecosystem (US DHS, 2018). The US strategies are built on a multistakeholder approach using transparent, bottom-up, consensus-driven processes, enabling governments, the private sector, civil society, academia, and the technical community to participate as equal partners on state, federal, and international levels (The White House, 2018, pp. 25–26).

The US Cybersecurity Strategy 2018–2023   The latest national cybersecurity strategy was introduced in 2018 to secure federal networks and information (The White House, 2018). The strategy identifies the need to protect CI and pursue malicious cyber actors. The core part of the strategy covers areas such as ensuring that various actors and agencies are deploying layered defence; improving information sharing and sensing; building secure government networks; responding to the challenges and opportunities of the cyber era to determine future prosperity and security; improving attribution, accountability, and response; enhancing cyber tools and expertise; and, finally, improving the integration and agility between government bodies (UNIDIR, 2020i). All of these are key areas to strengthen in the current climate where online threats are increasing, and multistakeholder approaches, resilience, and preparedness are critical factors for enhancing cybersecurity.

The 2018–2023 cybersecurity strategy has been criticised for being overly optimistic about US domination worldwide. First, the cybersecurity strategy claims that the US will maintain leadership in developing emerging technologies. Of course, emerging technologies are vital for the US' economic and military development. However, the world leadership is contested by China and its ambitious 'Made in China 2025 plan' where the state also aims to become a world leader. Coats, the Director of National Intelligence, made it clear in 2019 that the US was losing the game concerning emerging technology as innovations that drive military and economic combativeness are emerging outside the US. The second claim is that the US would preserve peace through cyberspace strength and encourage other states to adhere to global cyber norms. However, as already outlined above, contrary to the US, China and Russia are active in developing cyber norms and propose international agreements within international institutions, such as the UN (Zegart, 2019).

The US Department of Defence Cyber Strategy 2018   The US Department of Defence's (DoD) strategy from 2018 replaces the 2015 strategy. The strategy's overall aim is to ensure strategic competition in cyberspace and defend civilian assets that enable US military advantages (US DoD, 2018). The defence strategy priorities the challenge of 'great power competition', such as Russia China. Therefore, the DoD recognises that to counter the threats from US' competitions long-term and coordinated campaigns of malicious attacks, i.e. political, economic, and military, it is vital to enable attacks forwards. This strategy normalised military cyberspace activity by integrating operations across physical domains and reinforces the need to act preventatively to eliminating the threats before they damage US' national interests (Cronk, 2020; US DoD, 2018).

THE PEOPLE'S REPUBLIC OF CHINA (CHINA)

China has promoted its own national 'China solution' to global cyber governance by launching a strategy paper (2017) emphasising its doctrine of 'cyber sovereignty' (ASPI, 2017, p. 31). The core element of China's cybersecurity approach is to safeguard its sovereignty, security, and development. The focus on state sovereignty in cyberspace contrasts with the US model of multistakeholder Internet governance (ASPI, 2017, p. 31). China and the US disagree on crucial issues as their values and governance models are entirely different, i.e. cyber sovereignty vs multistakeholder approach (Rosenbach & Chong, 2019). China aspires to build a community of 'common destiny' in cyberspace with these overarching purposes. The cybersecurity strategy includes protecting CII, shared responsibility for the government, businesses, and civil society (Thinyane & Christine, 2020, p. 36).

China's main cybersecurity strategies are linked to the International Strategy of Cooperation on Cyberspace developed by the Ministry of Foreign Affairs and the Cyberspace Administration of China. The strategy identifies four basic principles: peace, sovereignty, shared governance, and shared benefits. The strategy aims are safeguard sovereignty and security, a system of international rules, fair Internet governance, rights and interest of citizens, cooperation, and a platform for cyber cultural exchange (Ministry of Foreign Affairs of the People's Republic of China, 2015; UNIDIR, 2020b). Additionally, China has adopted a Cyberspace Security Strategy (2016) under the Office of the Central Cyberspace Affairs Commission (CAC), setting out state's position and propositions on cyberspace development and security to establish China's leading role as a cyber power (UNIDIR, 2020b; USITO, 2016). Finally, the state has developed a China's Military Strategy under the Ministry of National Defence covering outer space and cyberspace (English. Gov.CN, 2015; UNIDIR, 2020b). This strategy aims to enhance the state's cyber capabilities, capacities, responses to manage major cyber crises, protect the national network and information security, and maintain national security and social stability (English.Gov.CN, 2015).

THE RUSSIAN FEDERATION (RUSSIA)

Like the countries above, Russia has developed its national cybersecurity strategic framework. However, it does not consist of one overarching strategy but several doctrines that constitute the strategy. It is possible to trace back the first initiatives regarding cybersecurity to a joint session of Russia's Security Council and the State Council in 2003. This session reformulated the Russian policy on critical infrastructure protection (CIP) after President Putin raised questions about formulating a new policy towards objects critical to national security and protection from human-made, natural and terrorist threats. The first principle of this strategy was documented in the 2006 presidential strategy (Pursiainen, 2020; Pynnöniemi & Busygina, 2013).

The Russian Information Security Doctrine from 2008 shares the governmental policy on information security. It is setting out the national interest of the Federation about information security (ITU, 2008). The 2000 doctrine provided a broad definition of the information sphere, which was further codified in the 2016 doctrine (Lilly & Cheravitch, 2020). The new doctrine was launched to ensure strategic deterrence and prevent military conflicts using information technologies. The doctrine also upgraded military information systems that used various troops, formations, and bodies (Lilly & Cheravitch, 2020; The Ministry of Foreign Affairs of the Russian Federation, 2016; UNIDIR, 2020d). The first significant initiative launched by Russia is the State Programme: Information Society, 2011–2020. The framework was implemented in 2010, and it has been amended in 2014 and 2019. It is now extended until 2024. This programme includes six sub-programmes where cybersecurity is interlinked with vital areas covering information and communication technologies, infrastructures, etc. (The Russian Government, 2012; UNIDIR, 2020d).

In 2013, a presidential decree was issued to create a state system for detecting, preventing, and eliminating the consequences of computer attacks on vital information resources. This decree conferred authority to the Federal Security Service (FSB), including interaction with privately owned information resources. Despite the short text, the decree was a starting point for a comprehensive CII policy (Pursiainen, 2020; UNIDIR, 2020d). Threats such as information weapons for military and political purposes, terrorism, and interference in internal matters and crimes were also identified and included in the strategy (UNIDIR, 2020d).

The 2017–2030 Strategy for the Development of the Information Society in Russia defines goals, aims, and measures within domestic and foreign policy. The strategy aims to develop the information society, form the national digital economy, ensure national interests, and implement strategic national priorities (UNIDIR, 2020e). The strategy acknowledges Russia's vulnerabilities as the state is behind other states in developing its information technologies. Therefore, the strategy calls for several new measures to be implemented between 2017 and 2030 (Sukhankin, 2017). Russia failed to fulfil the goals outlined in the 2008–2015 Strategy, and questions have been raised whether the strategy would meet the aims and objectives of this very ambitious strategy within the time frame. However, the approved strategy is vague about the expected results, and there is an absence of performance indicators included in the previous strategy (Sukhankin, 2017).

Conclusion

With a constantly changing threat landscape, the response needs to follow the exact directions. Therefore, it is essential to assess the risks and develop a response accordingly. There is no linear solution to the issues as numerous actors are involved in various cooperations. Cybersecurity and anticipatory governance are currently implemented in a complex nodal system with multiple actors, various strategies, and dynamics, which must be flexible to adhere to constantly changing risks. The flexibility enables the actors to adjust to the constantly changing technological environment and various types of ecosystems. The strategic positions and cost impositions are essential to consider when developing proactive and reactive responses. Numerous cybersecurity strategies have been developed, and the different states or cooperations have different perspectives. However, one of the most significant issues is the lack of an international framework for dealing with the attacks.

References

A.T. Kearney, 2018. *Cybersecurity in ASEAN: An urgent call to action.* [Online] Available at: www.kearney.com/documents/20152/989824/Cybersecurity+in+ ASEAN.pdf/2e0fb55c-8a50-b1e3-4954-2c5c573dd121 [Accessed 14 07 2021].

Achten, N., 2019. *New U.N. debate on cybersecurity in the context of international security.* [Online] Available at: www.lawfareblog.com/new-un-debate-cybersecurity-context-international-security [Accessed 07 11 2020].

Alexander, J., 2020. *K-pop stans overwhelm app after Dallas police ask for videos of protesters.* [Online] Available at: www.theverge.com/2020/6/1/21277423/k-pop-dallas-pd-iwatch-app-flood-review-bomb-surveillance-protests-george-floyd [Accessed 01 04 2021].

ARF, 2012. *ASEAN regional forum statement by the ministers of foreign affairs on cooperation in ensuring cyber security.* [Online] Available at: http://aseanregionalfo rum.asean.org/wp-content/uploads/2019/01/ARF-Statement-on-Cooperation-in-Ensuring-Cyber-Security.pdf [Accessed 21 12 2020].

ARF, 2015. *2015 ASEAN regional forum work plan on security of and in the use of information and communication technologies.* [Online] Available at: https://cil.nus.edu. sg/wp-content/uploads/2019/02/2015-ARF-WP-on-ICT-Security.pdf [Accessed 22 12 2020].

ASPI, 2017. *Cyber Maturity in the Asia-Pacific Region 2017.* Barton, ACT: The Australian Strategic Policy Institute.

AU, 2016. *A global approach on cybersecurity and cybercrime in Africa.* [Online] Available at: https://au.int/sites/default/files/newsevents/workingdocuments/31357-wd-a_common_african_approach_on_cybersecurity_and_cybercrime_en_final_ web_site_.pdf [Accessed 19 12 2020].

AU, 2019. *Communique. Peace and security council 850th meeting.* [Online] Available at: https://archives.au.int/bitstream/handle/123456789/6336/850th%20Meeting%20 of%20the%20AUPSC%20on%20Cyber%20Security%2020%20May%202019_ E%20.pdf?sequence=1&isAllowed=y [Accessed 19 12 2020].

Ballard, M., 2010. *UN rejects international cybercrime treaty.* [Online] Available at: www.computerweekly.com/news/1280092617/UN-rejects-international-cybercrime-treaty [Accessed 07 12 2020].

Bayuk, J. L. et al., 2012. *Cyber Security. Policy Guidebook.* Hoboken: John Wiley & Sons Inc.

Beck, U., 1992. *Risk Society. Towards a New Modernity.* London: Sage.

Bedingfield, W., 2020. *How K-pop stans became an activist force to be reckoned with.* [Online] Available at: www.wired.com/story/how-k-pop-stans-became-an-activist-force-to-be-reckoned-with/ [Accessed 30 03 2021].

Brent, L., 2019. *NATO's role in cyberspace.* [Online] Available at: www.nato.int/docu/review/articles/2019/02/12/natos-role-in-cyberspace/index.html [Accessed 16 12 2020].

Cabinet Office, 2020. *National cyber security strategy 2016–2021. Progress report.* [Online] Available at: https://assets.publishing.service.gov.uk/government/uploads/system/uploads/attachment_data/file/937702/6.6788_CO_National-Cyber-Security-Strategy-2016-2021_WEB3.pdf [Accessed 14 07 2021].

CCDCOE, 2020a. *About us.* [Online] Available at: https://ccdcoe.org/about-us/ [Accessed 16 12 2020].

CCDCOE, 2020b. *The NATO Cooperative Cyber Defence Centre of Excellence is a multinational and interdisciplinary cyber defence hub.* [Online] Available at: https://ccdcoe.org/ [Accessed 16 12 2020].

Cheok, J., 2017. *Singapore to launch S$10m ASEAN programme to fund cybersecurity efforts.* [Online] Available at: www.businesstimes.com.sg/government-economy/singapore-to-launch-s10m-asean-programme-to-fund-cybersecurity-efforts [Accessed 14 07 2021].

Cilluffo, F. J. & Clark, J. R., 2015. Building a Conceptual Framework for Cyber's Effect on National Security. *Journal of Information Warfare,* 15(2), pp. 1-16.

CoE, 2001a. *Details of treaty no. 185.* [Online] Available at: www.coe.int/en/web/conventions/full-list/-/conventions/treaty/185[Accessed 16 12 2020].

CoE, 2001b. *European treaty series no. 185. Explanatory report to the convention on cybercrime.* [Online] Available at: https://rm.coe.int/16800cce5b [Accessed 17 12 2020].

CoE, 2020a. *Budapest convention and related standards.* [Online] Available at: www.coe.int/en/web/cybercrime/the-budapest-convention [Accessed 16 12 2020].

CoE, 2020b. *Convention on cybercrime.* [Online] Available at: www.europewatchdog.info/en/international-treaties/treaties_and_monitoring/cybercrime/ [Accessed 17 12 2020].

CoEU, 2014, EU Cyber Defence Policy Framework [Online]. Available at: www.europarl.europa.eu/meetdocs/2014_2019/documents/sede/dv/sede160315eucyberdefencepolicyframework_/sede160315eucyberdefencepolicyframework_en.pdf 9 [Accessed 18 11 2021].

CoEU, 2019. *Council Decision concerning restrictive measures against cyber-attacks threatening the union or its member states.* [Online] Available at: https://data.consilium.europa.eu/doc/document/ST-7299-2019-INIT/en/pdf [Accessed 17 12 2020].

Crawford, A. & Lister, S., 2004. *The Extended Policing Family: Visible Patrols in Residential Areas.* York: Joseph Rowntree Foundation.

Cronk, T. M., 2020. *OD's cyber strategy of past year outlined before Congress.* [Online] Available at: www.defense.gov/Explore/News/Article/Article/2103843/dods-cyber-strategy-of-past-year-outlined-before-congress/ [Accessed 14 07 2021].

CSIS, 2020. *Significant cyber incidents.* [Online] Available at: www.csis.org/programs/technology-policy-program/significant-cyber-incidents [Accessed 26 08 2020].

Dalton, W., Vuuren, J. J. v. & Westcott, J., 2017. Building cybersecurity resilience in Africa. In: *Proceedings of the 12th International Conference on Cyber Warfare and Security.* Dayton: AFIT, pp. 112–120.

Dean, M., 2010. *Governmentality. Power and Rule in Modern Society.* London: Sage.

Dupont, B., 2006. Power struggles in the field of security: Implications for democratic transformation. In: *Democracy, Society and the Governance of Security.* Cambridge: Cambridge University Press, pp. 86–100.

EC, 2012. *Tackling crime in our digital age: Establishing a European cybercrime centre.* [Online] Available at: https://eur-lex.europa.eu/LexUriServ/LexUriServ.do?uri=COM:2012:0140:FIN:EN:PDF [Accessed 19 08 2020].

EC, 2018. *Conclusions.* [Online] Available at: https://data.consilium.europa.eu/doc/document/ST-13-2018-INIT/en/pdf [Accessed 17 12 2020].

EC, CoEU, 2009. *European Security Strategy: A Secure Europe in a Better World.* Brussels: European Union.

EC, CoEU, 2016. *Fight against criminal activities in cyberspace: Council agrees on practical measures and next steps.* [Online] Available at: www.consilium.europa.eu/en/press/press-releases/2016/06/09/criminal-activities-cyberspace/ [Accessed 16 12 2020].

EC, CoEU, 2017. *Cybersecurity: EU institutions strengthen cooperation to counter cyber-attacks.* [Online] Available at: www.consilium.europa.eu/en/press/press-releases/2017/12/20/cybersecurity-eu-institutions-strengthen-cooperation-to-counter-cyber-attacks/ [Accessed 16 12 2020].

EC, CoEU, 2018a. *EU to become more cyber-proof as Council backs deal on common certification and beefed-up agency.* [Online] Available at: www.consilium.europa.eu/en/press/press-releases/2018/12/19/eu-to-become-more-cyber-proof-as-council-backs-deal-on-common-certification-and-beefed-up-agency/ [Accessed 16 12 2020].

EC, CoEU, 2018b. *Response to malicious cyber activities: Council adopts conclusions.* [Online] Available at: www.consilium.europa.eu/en/press/press-releases/2018/04/16/malicious-cyber-activities-council-adopts-conclusions/ [Accessed 17 12 2020].

EC, CoEU, 2019a. *Cyber-attacks: Council is now able to impose sanctions.* [Online] Available at: www.consilium.europa.eu/en/press/press-releases/2019/05/17/cyber-attacks-council-is-now-able-to-impose-sanctions/ [Accessed 17 12 2020].

EC, CoEU, 2019b. *Declaration by the High Representative on behalf of the EU on respect for the rules-based order in cyberspace.* [Online] Available at: www.consilium.europa.eu/en/press/press-releases/2019/04/12/declaration-by-the-high-representative-on-behalf-of-the-eu-on-respect-for-the-rules-based-order-in-cyberspace/ [Accessed 17 12 2020].

EC, CoEU, 2020a. *Cybersecurity in Europe: Stronger rules and better protection.* [Online] Available at: www.consilium.europa.eu/en/policies/cybersecurity/#[Accessed 16 12 2020].

EC, CoEU, 2020b. *Declaration by the High Representative Josep Borrell, on behalf of the European Union, on malicious cyber activities exploiting the coronavirus pandemic.* [Online] Available at: www.consilium.europa.eu/en/press/press-releases/2020/04/30/declaration-by-the-high-representative-josep-borrell-on-behalf-of-the-european-union-on-malicious-cyber-activities-exploiting-the-coronavirus-pandemic/ [Accessed 13 07 2021].

EC, CoEU, 2020c. *EU imposes the first ever sanctions against cyber-attacks.* [Online] Available at: www.consilium.europa.eu/en/press/press-releases/2020/07/30/eu-imposes-the-first-ever-sanctions-against-cyber-attacks/ [Accessed 17 12 2020].

EC, CoEU, 2020d. *Shaping Europe's digital future – Council adopts conclusions.* [Online] Available at: www.consilium.europa.eu/en/press/press-releases/2020/06/09/shaping-europe-s-digital-future-council-adopts-conclusions/ [Accessed 17 12 2020].

EC/HREUFASP, 2013. *Cybersecurity strategy of the European Union: An open, safe and secure cyberspace.* [Online] Available at: https://ec.europa.eu/home-affairs/sites/homeaffairs/files/e-library/documents/policies/organized-crime-and-human-trafficking/cybercrime/docs/join_2013_1_en.pdf [Accessed 21 12 2020].

Efthymiopoulos, M. P., 2019. A cyber-security framework for development, defense and innovation at NATO. *Journal of Innovation and Entrepreneurship,* 8(12), pp. 1–26.

English.Gov.CN, 2015. *China's military strategy.* [Online] Available at: http://english.www.gov.cn/archive/white_paper/2015/05/27/content_281475115610833.ht [Accessed 20 12 2020].

EOPUS, 2009. *The comprehensive national cybersecurity initiative.* [Online] Available at: https://obamawhitehouse.archives.gov/sites/default/files/cybersecurity.pdf [Accessed 20 12 2020].

Erkoçak, E. & Açıkalın, Ş. N., 2013. Complexity theory in public administration and metagovernance. In: *Chaos, Complexity and Leadership.* Chams: Springer, pp. 73–84.

EU Cyber Direct, 2017. *ASEAN cyber capacity program (ACCP).* [Online] Available at: https://eucyberdirect.eu/content_knowledge_hu/asean-cyber-capacity-program-accp/ [Accessed 14 07 2021].

EU Cyber Direct, 2020. *Background note.* [Online] Available at: https://eucyberdirect.eu/wp-content/uploads/2020/06/backgroundnote.pdf [Accessed 07 12 2020].

Europol, 2020. *European Cybercrime Centre (EC3).* [Online] Available at: www.europol.europa.eu/about-europol/european-cybercrime-centre-ec3[Accessed 19 08 2020].

FBI, 2021. *Internet crime report 2020.* [Online] Available at: www.ic3.gov/Media/PDF/AnnualReport/2020_IC3Report.pdf [Accessed 12 07 2021].

Geneva Internet Platform, 2020. *UN GGE and OEWG.* [Online] Available at: https://dig.watch/processes/un-gge [Accessed 07 12 2020].

Germano, J. H., 2014. *Cybersecurity Partnership: A New Era of Public-Private Collaboration.* New York: NYC School of Law.

Gold, J., 2021. *Unexpectedly, All UN countries agreed on a cybersecurity report. So what?* [Online] Available at: www.cfr.org/blog/unexpectedly-all-un-countries-agreed-cybersecurity-report-so-what [Accessed 21 07 2021].

Goldsmith, A., 2008. The Governance of Terror: Precautionary Logic and Counterterrorist Law Reform after September 11. *Law & Policy,* 30(2), pp. 141–167.

GOV.UK, 2016. *The UK cyber security strategy 2011–2016: Annual report.* [Online] Available at: www.gov.uk/government/publications/the-uk-cyber-security-strategy-2011-2016-annual-report [Accessed 21 12 2020].

GOV.UK, 2020. *Cyber security incentives & regulation review: Summary of responses to the call for evidence.* [Online] Available at: www.gov.uk/government/publications/cyber-security-incentives-regulation-review-government-response-to-the-call-for-evidence/cyber-security-incentives-regulation-review-summary-of-responses-to-the-call-for-evidence [Accessed 21 12 2020].

Grey, C. S., 2013. *Making strategic sense of cyber power: Why the sky is not calling.*
[Online] Available at: https://publications.armywarcollege.edu/pubs/2219.pdf
[Accessed 21 11 2020].

Heinl, C., 2019. *An ASEAN way of cybersecurity.* [Online] Available at: www.
policyforum.net/an-asean-way-of-cybersecurity/ [Accessed 14 07 2021].

Hern, A., 2017. *NHS could have avoided WannaCry hack with 'basic IT security',
says report.* [Online] Available at: www.theguardian.com/technology/2017/oct/27/
nhs-could-have-avoided-wannacry-hack-basic-it-security-national-audit-office
[Accessed 13 07 2021].

HM Government, 2015. *National Security Strategy and Strategic Defence and Security
Review 2015. A Secure and Prosperous United Kingdom.* London: HM Government.

HM Government, 2016. *The UK national cyber security strategy 2016–2021.* [Online]
Available at: https://assets.publishing.service.gov.uk/government/uploads/system/
uploads/attachment_data/file/567242/national_cyber_security_strategy_2016.pdf
[Accessed 21 12 2020].

Interpol, 2020. *Cybercrime threat response.* [Online] Available at: www.interpol.int/en/
Crimes/Cybercrime/Cybercrime-threat-response [Accessed 19 08 2020].

Interpol, 2021. *Immediate action required to avoid ransomware pandemic – INTERPOL.*
[Online] Available at: www.interpol.int/News-and-Events/News/2021/Immediate-
action-required-to-avoid-Ransomware-pandemic-INTERPOL?s=09[Accessed   13
07 2021].

IT Governance, 2020. *Cyber risk management service.* [Online] Available at: www.
itgovernance.co.uk/cyber-security-risk-management [Accessed 02 11 2020].

ITU, 2008. *Information security doctrine of the Russian Federation.* [Online] Available
at: www.itu.int/en/ITU-D/Cybersecurity/Documents/National_Strategies_
Repository/Russia_2000.pdf [Accessed 21 12 2020].

Jakobi, A. P., 2020. *Crime, Security and Global Politics. An Introduction to Global
Crime Governance.* London: Macmillan.

Johnson, 1992. *The Rebirth of Private Policing.* London: Routledge.

Joseph, J., 2013. Resilience in the UK and French security strategy: An Anglo-Saxon
bias? *Politics,* 33(4), pp. 253–264.

Juneidi, S. J., 2002. *Council of Europe Convention on Cyber Crime.* Samos: University
of Aegean.

Kakkad, V., Shah, H., Patel, R. & Doshi, N., 2019. A comparative study of applications
of game theory in cyber security and cloud computing. *Procedia Computer Science,*
155, pp. 680–685.

Kono, K., 2021. *ASEAN cyber developments: Centre of excellence for Singapore, cybercrime convention for the Philippines, and an open-ended working group for everyone.*
[Online] Available at: https://bit.ly/3DJiDzS [Accessed 14 07 2021].

Lentzos, F. & Rose, N., 2009. Governing insecurity: Contingency planning, protection,
resilience. *Economy and Society,* 38(2), pp. 230–254.

Lilly, B. & Cheravitch, J., 2020. The past, present, and future of Russia's cyber strategy
and forces. In: *20/20 Vision: The Next Decade.* Tallinn: NATO CCDCOE, pp.
129–155.

Liu, X., Zhang, J. & Zhu, P., 2017. Modeling cyber-physical attacks based on probabilistic colored Petri nets and mixed-strategy game theory. *International Journal of
Critical Infrastructure Protection,* 16, pp. 13–25.

Logan, D. C., 2009. Known knowns, known unknowns, unknown unknowns and the
propagation of scientific enquiry. *Journal of Experimental Botany,* 60(3), pp. 712–714.

Masters, G., 2010. *Global cybercrime treaty rejected at U.N.* [Online] Available at: www.scmagazine.com/home/security-news/global-cybercrime-treaty-rejected-at-u-n/ [Accessed 07 12 2020].

McKune, S., 2015. *An analysis of the international code of conduct for information security.* [Online] Available at: https://citizenlab.ca/2015/09/international-code-of-conduct/

Miller, P. & Rose, N., 2008. *Governing the Present.* Cambridge: Polity Press.

Ministry of Foreign Affairs of the People's Republic of China, 2015. *International Strategy of Cooperation on Cyberspace.* [Online] Available at: www.fmprc.gov.cn/mfa_eng/wjb_663304/zzjg_663340/jks_665232/kjlc_665236/qtwt_665250/t1442390.shtml [Accessed 20 12 2020].

Munk, T., 2018. Policing virtual spaces: Public and private online challenges in a legal perspective. In: Monica den Boer, ed. *Comparative Policing from a Legal Perspective.* Cheltenham: Edward Elgar, pp. 228–254.

Munk, T. H., 2015. *Cyber-security in the European region: Anticipatory governance and practices.* [Online] Available at: www.escholar.manchester.ac.uk/api/datastream?publicationPid=uk-ac-man-scw:266937&datastreamId=FULL-TEXT.PDF [Accessed 12 08 2020].

NATO CCDCOE, 2013. *Tallinn Manual on the International Law Applicable to Cyber Warfare.* 1 ed. Cambridge: Cambridge University Press.

NATO CCDCOE, 2017. *Tallinn Manual 2.0 on the International Law Applicable to Cyber Operations.* 2 ed. Cambridge: Cambridge University Press.

NATO, 1949. *The North Atlantic Treaty.* [Online] Available at: www.nato.int/cps/en/natolive/official_texts_17120.htm [Accessed 16 12 2020].

NATO, 2002. *Press conference by US secretary of defence, Donald Rumsfeld.* [Online] Available at: www.nato.int/docu/speech/2002/s020606g.htm [Accessed 04 11 2020].

NATO, 2016. *Cyber defence pledge.* [Online] Available at: www.nato.int/cps/en/natohq/official_texts_133177.htm [Accessed 13 07 2021].

NATO, 2020a. *Cyber defence.* [Online] Available at: www.nato.int/cps/en/natohq/topics_78170.htm [Accessed 16 12 2020].

NATO, 2020b. *Resilience and article 3.* [Online] Available at: www.nato.int/cps/en/natohq/topics_132722.htm [Accessed 16 12 2020].

NATO, 2021. *Cyber defence.* [Online] Available at: www.nato.int/cps/en/natohq/topics_78170.htm [Accessed 13 07 2021].

NCSC, 2015. *Reducing your exposure to cyber attack.* [Online] Available at: www.ncsc.gov.uk/information/reducing-your-exposure-to-cyber-attack [Accessed 09 07 2021].

NCSC, 2020. *Risk management guidance.* [Online] Available at: www.ncsc.gov.uk/collection/risk-management-collection/essential-topics/fundamentals [Accessed 03 11 2020].

Niou, E. & Ordeshook, P., 2015. *Strategy and Politics.* Abingdon: Routledge.

NIST, 2020. *Cyberspace.* [Online] Available at: https://csrc.nist.gov/glossary/term/cyberspace [Accessed 13 06 2020].

OAS, 2004a. *A comprehensive inter-American cybersecurity strategy: A multidimentional and multidisciplinary approach to creating a culture of cybersecurity.* [Online] Available at: https://bit.ly/3FGO2Uk [Accessed 19 12 2020].

OAS, 2004b. *Proceedings volume I.* [Online] Available at: www.oas.org/en/council/ag/resdec/ [Accessed 19 12 2020].

OAS, 2020. *Cybersecurity program.* [Online] Available at: www.oas.org/en/sms/cicte/prog-cybersecurity.asp [Accessed 19 12 2020].

O'Malley, P., 2012. Security after risk: Security strategies for governing extreme uncertainty. *Current Issues in Criminal Justice,* 23(5), pp. 5–15.

O'Sullivan, K., 2021. *UN makes critical progress on cybersecurity.* [Online] Available at: https://blogs.microsoft.com/on-the-issues/2021/03/29/un-working-group-cybersecurity-report/ [Accessed 13 07 2021].

Patil, A. P., Bharath, S. & Annigeri, N. M., 2018. Applications of game theory for cyber security system: A survey. *International Journal of Applied Engineering Research,* 13(17), pp. 12987–12990.

Peters, A., 2019. *Russia and China are trying to set the U.N.'s rules on cybercrime.* [Online] Available at: https://foreignpolicy.com/2019/09/16/russia-and-china-are-trying-to-set-the-u-n-s-rules-on-cybercrime/ [Accessed 07 12 2020].

Pursiainen, C., 2020. Russia's critical infrastructure policy: What do we know about it? *European Journal for Security Research,* 6(1), pp. 21–38.

Pynnöniemi, K. & Busygina, I., 2013. Critical infrastructure protection and Russia's hybrid regime. *European Security,* 22(4), pp. 559–575.

Rõigas, H., 2015. *An updated draft of the code of conduct distributed in the United Nations – What's new?* [Online] Available at: https://ccdcoe.org/incyder-articles/an-updated-draft-of-the-code-of-conduct-distributed-in-the-united-nations-whats-new/ [Accessed 07 12 2020].

Rosenbach, E. & Chong, S. M., 2019. *Governing cyberspace: State control vs. the multistakeholder model.* [Online] Available at: www.belfercenter.org/publication/governing-cyberspace-state-control-vs-multistakeholder-model [Accessed 14 07 2021].

Sammut-Bonnici, T., 2015. *Complexity theory.* [Online] Available at: www.researchgate.net/publication/272353040[Accessed 04 11 2020].

Sandin, P., 1999. Dimensions of the precautionary principle. Appendix II: Various formulations of the precautionary principle. *Human and Ecological Risk Assessment: An International Journal,* 5(5), pp. 889–907.

Schjolberg, S. & Ghernaouti-Hélie, S., 2009. *A Global Protocol on Cybersecurity and Cybercrime.* Oslo: Cybercrimedata.

Schmitt, M. (2013). *Tallinn Manual on the International Law Applicable to Cyber Warfare.* Cambridge: Cambridge University Press.

Schmitt, M. (2017). *Tallinn Manual 2.0 on the International Law Applicable to Cyber Operations* (2nd ed.). Cambridge: Cambridge University Press.

Schmitt, M., 2021. *The sixth United Nations GGE and international law in cyberspace.* [Online] Available at: www.justsecurity.org/76864/the-sixth-united-nations-gge-and-international-law-in-cyberspace/ [Accessed 13 07 2021].

SCO, 2009. *Agreement on cooperation in ensuring international information security between the member states of the Shanghai Cooperation Organization.* [Online] Available at: https://bit.ly/3cGEPyI [Accessed 20 12 2020].

Skopik, F., 2017. *Collaborative Cyber Threat Intelligence.* London: Auerback Publications (T&F).

Sukhankin, S., 2017. *Russia adopts new strategy for development of information society.* [Online] Available at: https://jamestown.org/program/russia-adopts-new-strategy-development-information-society/. [Accessed 21 12 2020].

Syal, R., 2018. *Every NHS trust tested for cybersecurity has failed, officials admit.* [Online] Available at: www.theguardian.com/technology/2018/feb/05/every-nhs-trust-tested-for-cyber-security-has-failed-officials-admit [Accessed 13 07 2021].

·

The Ministry of Foreign Affairs of the Russian Federation, 2016. *Doctrine of information security of the Russian Federation.* [Online] Available at: www.mid.ru/en/foreign_policy/official_documents/-/asset_publisher/CptICkB6BZ29/content/id/2563163. [Accessed 21 12 2020].

The Russian Government, 2012. *State programme: Information Society, 2011–2020.* [Online] Available at: http://government.ru/en/docs/3369/ [Accessed 21 12 2020].

The White House, 2009. *The comprehensive national cybersecurity initiative.* [Online] Available at: https://obamawhitehouse.archives.gov/issues/foreign-policy/cybersecurity/national-initiative [Accessed 14 07 2021].

The White House, 2018. *The national cyber strategy of the United States of America.* [Online] Available at: www.whitehouse.gov/wp-content/uploads/2018/09/National-Cyber-Strategy.pdf [Accessed 21 08 2020].

Thinyane, M. & Christine, D., 2020. *Cyber Resilience in Asia-Pacific – A Review of National Cybersecurity Strategies.* Macau: United Nations University.

US DHS, 2011a. *Fact sheet: Preventing and defending against cyber attacks.* [Online] Available at: www.dhs.gov/news/2011/10/18/preventing-and-defending-against-cyber-attacks [Accessed 20 12 2020].

US DHS, 2011b. *Preventing and defending against cyber attacks.* [Online] Available at:www.dhs.gov/xlibrary/assets/preventing-and-defending-against-cyber-attacks-october-2011.pdf [Accessed 20 12 2020].

US DHS, 2018. *U.S. Department of Homeland Security Cybersecurity Strategy.* [Online] Available at: www.dhs.gov/sites/default/files/publications/DHS-Cybersecurity-Strategy_1.pdf [Accessed 21 08 2020].

US DHS, 2019. *DHS cybersecurity strategy.* [Online] Available at: www.dhs.gov/publication/dhs-cybersecurity-strategy [Accessed 21 08 2020].

US DoD, 2018. *Summary. Department of Defence. Cyber Strategy 2018.* Washington, DC: Department of Defence.

UN, 2010. *Group of governmental experts on developments in the field of information and telecommunications in the context of international security.* [Online] Available at: https://undocs.org/A/65/201 [Accessed 07 12 2020].

UN, 2013. *Group of governmental experts on developments in the field of information and telecommunications in the context of international security.* [Online] Available at: https://undocs.org/A/68/98 [Accessed 07 12 2020].

UN, 2015a. *Group of governmental experts on developments in the field of information and telecommunications in the context of international security.* [Online] Available at: https://undocs.org/A/70/174 [Accessed 07 12 2020].

UN, 2015b. *Letter dated 9 January 2015 from the permanent representatives of China, Kazakhstan, Kyrgyzstan, the Russian Federation, Tajikistan and Uzbekistan to the United Nations addressed to the Secretary-General.* [Online] Available at: https://digitallibrary.un.org/record/786846?ln=en [Accessed 07 12 2020].

UN, 2019. *Countering the use of information and communications technologies for criminal purposes.* [Online] Available at: https://undocs.org/en/A/RES/73/187 [Accessed 07 12 2020].

UN, 2020. *UN Charter.* [Online] Available at: www.un.org/en/sections/un-charter/un-charter-full-text/ [Accessed 07 12 2020].

UN GGE, 2021. *Report of the Group of Governmental Experts on Advancing Responsible State.* New York: UN.

UNIDIR, 2017. *The United Nations, Cyberspace and International Peace and Security. Responding to Complexity in the 21st Century.* New York: The United Nations Institute for Disarmament Research.

UNIDIR, 2019. *African Union.* [Online] Available at: https://unidir.org/cpp/en/organi zations/africanunion [Accessed 17 12 2020].

UNIDIR, 2020a. *Association of Southeast Asian Nations (ASEAN).* [Online] Available at: https://unidir.org/cpp/en/organizations/associationofsoutheastasian nations [Accessed 21 12 2020].

UNIDIR, 2020b. *China.* [Online] Available at: https://unidir.org/cpp/en/states/china [Accessed 20 12 2020].

UNIDIR, 2020c. *Organization of American States (OAS).* [Online] Available at: https://bit.ly/3DJXi9n [Accessed 19 12 2020].

UNIDIR, 2020d. *Russian Federation.* [Online] Available at: https://unidir.org/cpp/en/ states/russianfederation [Accessed 21 12 2020].

UNIDIR, 2020e. *Russian Federation. Cybersecurity strategy.* [Online] Available at: https://bit.ly/3cGQE8g [Accessed 21 08 2020].

UNIDIR, 2020f. *Shanghai Cooperation Organisation (SCO).* [Online] Available at: https://bit.ly/3CNWK14 [Accessed 20 12 2020].

UNIDIR, 2020g. *United Kingdom of Great Britain and Northern Ireland.* [Online] Available at: https://unidir.org/cpp/en/states/unitedkingdomofgreatbritainandnort hernireland [Accessed 21 12 2020].

UNIDIR, 2020h. *United States of America.* [Online] Available at: https://unidir.org/ cpp/en/states/unitedstatesofamerica [Accessed 20 12 2020].

UNIDIR, 2020i. *United States of America. Cybersecurity policy.* [Online] Available at: https://unidir.org/cpp/en/states/unitedstatesofamerica [Accessed 21 04 2020].

UN OEWG, 2021. *Open-ended working group on developments in the field of infor- mation and telecommunications in the context of international security.* [Online] Available at: https://front.un-arm.org/wp-content/uploads/2021/03/Chairs-Summ ary-A-AC.290-2021-CRP.3-technical-reissue.pdf [Accessed 13 07 2021].

USITO, 2016. *China publishes first national cybersecurity strategy.* [Online] Available at: www.usito.org/news/china-publishes-first-national-cybersecurity-strategy [Accessed 14 07 2021].

Van Impe, K., 2021. *Cyber resilience strategy changes you should know in the EU's digital decade.* [Online] Available at: https://securityintelligence.com/articles/cyber- resilience-strategy-changes-european-union/ [Accessed 13 07 2021].

Walker, S., 2019. *Cyber-insecurities. A Guide to the UN Cybercrime Debate.* Geneva: Global Initiative Against Transnational Organized Crime.

Wolter, D., 2014. *The UN takes a big step forward on cybersecurity.* [Online] Available at: www.armscontrol.org/act/2013-09/un-takes-big-step-forward-cybersecurity [Accessed 07 12 2020].

Zagare, F. C., 2019. *Game Theory and Security Studies.* Oxford: Oxford University Press.

Zegart, A., 2019. *America's Misbegotten Cyber Strategy.* [Online] Available at: www. theatlantic.com/ideas/archive/2019/02/trumps-national-cyber-strategy-overly-opti- mistic/581839/ [Accessed 20 12 2020].

5 Cyberwar and Warfare
State and State-sponsored Attacks

Introduction

Although most states worldwide have developed cyber capacities and capacities for deterrence and defence, there are a growing number of incidents where states are directly attacking foreign public and private entities. However, these attacks are low-key events launched below the threshold of cyberwar, which makes them problematic to manage. States are increasingly relying on state-supported actors to conduct the attack. This use of proxies removes the state from the actions where these groups act independently but under the directions of the state. States claim that they adhere to international law. At the same time, they are using a tactic not covered by the international framework. There is a legislative lacuna regarding the protection of vital assets, online users, and behaviours that is exploited by states. Therefore, this chapter will online the essential parts of international law and apply them to the online actors and actions. The chapter focuses on a selection of states which are constantly engaged in online attacks, i.e. China, North Korea, Russia and the US. The main discussions are centred around motivations, the actors and the means and methods used. These three areas will be linked to the current cybersecurity framework and the lack of legislation to manage the area.

Conceptualising War and Warfare

For years, cyberwarfare or information warfare has been considered an exaggerated threat unlikely to cause impact beyond the time-limited attack. However, this stance has changed substantially from an abstract idea to a core element of modern warfare. States and military units have adopted cyberwar and warfare as a core strategy for future wars and ongoing disputes where control, attack and defences are instrumental. Several attacks are linked to espionage or disrupting CIs using sophisticated techniques or zero-day exploits (Shaikh, 2014). Strategic targets in cyberwar and warfare are to attack privately owned and publicly operated platforms and services where the impact on the civil population is severe, i.e. businesses, corporations, groups, and individuals. These attacks can be part of espionage, an act of warfare,

DOI: 10.4324/9781003126676-5

or retaliation. CIs act as a pathway to attack and targetolitically motivated adversaries (Zittrain, 2017, p. 300).

Modern war and warfare are regulated through a set of international laws. Violence and attacks are not necessarily interlinked. However, violence is common in all types of war and warfare situations, where the intensity differs depending on the type of conflict and the weapons used. Moreover, the violence used in these situations is also linked to the existing regulation (Jakobi, 2020, p. 136). The basic framework of cyberwar and warfare is mainly developed during the last century as a part of conventional warfare, and some key documents are still useful for assessing state-based cyber attacks. The Charter of the UN (1945), the NATO Treaty (1949), the Geneva Conventions (1949), the Geneva Protocol I (1977) were introduced to protect victims in international conflicts. At the same time, the Hauge Conventions included the laws and customs of war (Hauge II, 1899; Hauge IV, 1907).

Additionally, the Convention on Prohibitions or Restrictions on the Use of Certain Conventional Weapons (1980) covers weapons that might be considered excessively Injurious or has indiscriminate effects (UN, 2020; NATO, 1949; ICRC, 1949; ICRC, 1977; ICRC, 1907; UN, 1980). The laws apply to military activities and operations to prevent unnecessary suffering and destruction in wars (Westby, 2011, p. 84). Concerning cyberwarfare, special attention should be drawn to civilians. In cyber conflicts, these civilians are individual online users, businesses, and civil society as a whole. This includes entities with no links to governmental actors or the actual conflict. They should have the same protection as civilians in conventional warfare.

Offline War and Warfare Definitions

JUS AD BELLUM

The fundamental rule in the use of force in war and warfare is the prohibition of the threat or use of force included in article 2(4) of the UN Charter (Gray, 2004, pp. 5, 29). Concerning Jus ad Bellum, the principle is founded primarily in Articles 2(3)–(4) and Chapter VII of the UN Charter, stating that all member states should settle international disputes by peaceful means to avoid that international peace and security is endangered (Article 3). According to this principle, member states should refrain from threats or use force against other states' territorial integrity or political independence (Article 4) (Morris, 2019, pp. 117–118). Included in the concept of Jus ad Bellum are just cause, legitimate authority, right intervention, last resort (necessity), proportionality, and the prospect of success. For example, a sovereign authority can wage war, but there must be a just cause for war, such as self-defence or enforcing human rights. The principle also states that all peaceful means for resolving a dispute should be exhausted before taking action. Moreover, it should be considered that it is likely that the actions taken would be successful (Hough, 2008, p. 39; Finlay, 2019, p. 28; Westby, 2011, p. 84).

JUS IN BELLO

Jus in Bello has two principal subdivisions. These are generally named 'Geneva law' and 'Hague law' to recognise the principal treaty series they founded. The Geneva laws regulate the protection of the victims in armed conflicts. Currently, the Geneva laws are based on the four 1949 Geneva Conventions covering (I) wounded and sick on land; (II) wounded, sick, and shipwrecked at sea; (III) prisoners of war; and (IV) civilians (ICRC, 1949). Additionally, Article 48 of the 1977 Protocol I to the Geneva Conventions of 1949 set out the basic rules:

> [T]he Parties to the conflict shall at all times distinguish between the civilian population and combatants and between civilian objects and military objectives and accordingly shall direct their operations only against military objectives.
>
> (ICRC, 1977)

This is an important principle as it is directly applicable to the online environment (Dinstein, 2012). Unfortunately, little attention is given to online users about cyberwarfare and ongoing online conflicts involving state and state-sponsored actors. Online users of all ages suffer unnecessarily and disproportional from a large-scale attack against CIs due to the disruption, the damage, the espionage, and the theft of personal data from these activities, the risks of becoming a victim, and uncertainties associated with these types of attacks. Therefore, rules to protect online users who are not a part of the cyber conflicts should be prioritised

The Hauge laws regulate the methods and means employed in war and warfare. These include control on types of weapons, usage, tactics, and the general conduct of hostilities. The Hague laws are based on the Hague Conventions of 1899 and 1907 in conjunction with the 1977 Additional Protocol III to the Geneva Conventions (ICRC, 1899; ICRC, 1907; ICRC, 1977). This protocol includes methods and means of warfare and discrimination in bombardment (Morris, 2019, p. 171). Military targets are those, that by nature, location, purpose or use, effectively contribute to an enemy's military capabilities, which can be totally or partially destroyed or neutralised during the attack to enhance legitimate military objectives. In the Geneva Conventions, protected targets are outlined, such as hospitals, transportation of wounded or sick, religious or cultural areas, or safety zones. There are limitations to this provision; if these targets are exploited for military purposes, they might become legitimate military targets (Westby, 2011; ICRC, 1949). Yet, it is significant that attacks are launched towards CI online systems and networks, with no links to military purposes.

The different worst-case scenarios are weighed up against each other. For example, the wrong of non-resistance should be greater than the wrong of fighting. The payload should be considered together with means and methods. Especially, if the method enacted deliberately killing people who otherwise are immune from attacks. In this context, it is essential to consider whether the harms inflected are unnecessary for pursuing the military objective, are disproportionate to the goal/values, or the military activities are less likely to satisfy the criteria of Jus in Bellum regarding immunity. The principles incorporated in Jus in Bello states that the measures used need to be proportionate to the wrong being rectified. Therefore, these means should not be introduced beyond what is necessary, and they should not be used as retributions (Hough, 2008, p. 39; Finlay, 2019, p. 28; Westby, 2011, pp. 84–85).

International Law and Cyberspace

The UN Charter, the Geneva Conventions, the Hauge Conventions, and the NATO Treaty are silent about cyber conflict and online attacks as a part of an ongoing conflict. Although the UN Charter and the NATO Treaty include territorial integrity, armed force, air, land or sea forces, and armed attacks, no amendments have been adopted to cover cyberspace. Therefore, online military conflicts are not directly covered by international law (UN, 2020; ICRC, 1949; ICRC, 1899; ICRC, 1907; ICRC, 1977; NATO, 1949; Westby, 2011, p. 86).

The frequency, scale, and impact of cyber attacks are escalating. The states have embraced the online environment to conduct different types of attacks depending on their overall strategies. There is not only one technique, one target type, or one pathway to take. The online environment provides an incredible number of possibilities for attacking. Because of the increased use of proxies acting on behalf of states or in close cooperation, the role of these actors should be established. The critical point is how the state uses these state-sponsored actors to create a buffer between the state and the target. This use of proxies enables the state to overcome the different prohibitions in international law and custom. NATO has highlighted that state and state-sponsored attacks present an imminent challenge as these attacks can substantially impact cyberspace or the physical domain. However, state and state-sponsored groups' activities are different from other politically motivated actors as the cyber attacks conducted require a high level of detailed knowledge, skills, and abilities. Developing and conducting these attacks requires substantial financial and organisational resources. It is unlikely that other actors than states and their proxies have the funds to meet this threshold (Davis, 2019, p. 2).

The Estonia attack in 2007 was a wake-up call, and cybersecurity strategies have been widely developed to manage cyber defence against attacks and enhance the resilience and preparedness level. Nevertheless, very little has been done to develop cyberwarfare conventions to regulate online conduct, weapons, protection of particular targets and civilians (online users). There is a legislative lacuna regarding cyber weapons and the groups involved in cyberwar and warfare. These areas should be regulated under the Hauge

Conventions. Additionally, there is a call for broader protection of CIs to prevent unnecessary damage, harm, and suffering. These provisions should ensure that essential communication routes, entities, services, and networks are constantly operational.

The first Tallinn Manual 1.0 (2013) covers the laws applicable to armed conflicts, whereas the second Tallin Manual 2.0 (2017) covers a broader scope, including cyber operations in and outside an armed conflict. However, the two manuals do not outline a doctrine (Schmitt, 2013; Schmitt, 2017). They only provide an attempt on applying international law to cyberspace at the time they were drafted. The Tallinn Manual 1.0 has removed the uncertainty regarding the nature of cyberwar operations by extending customary international law to cyber conflicts. The Tallinn Manual recognises that the use of force regardless of means violates customary international law. However, the manual also states that a cyber attack must not rise to the level of an armed attack, and the manual does not rule out cyber attacks as illegal (The Cyber Diplomat, 2019; NATO CCDCOE, 2013; NATO CCDCOE, 2017; Seker, 2020).

Cyberwar and Warfare

For military operations, technological development has sharply increased the combat capabilities for troops. By selectively targeting the adversary's computer systems, networks, infrastructure, and services of military and civilian actors, it is possible to terminate a conflict before deploying kinetic combat operations (Barletta et al., 2011, p. 75). Yet, it does not mean that there is no impact beyond the computer systems and networks. The harmfulness and frequency of attacks can have far-reaching potential. Attacks can impose considerable online damage, as well as extensive physical damage. The contagious element of persistent and sustained cyber attacks creates a pathway for various political actors to engage in asymmetric cyberwarfare (Barletta et al., 2011). Businesses, governments, and utilities are increasingly dependent on computer systems, networks, and the Internet. This makes these areas attractive pathways for state and state-sponsored actors. Cyberwarfare offers state actors and governments several possibilities to weaken their opponents. These actors weigh up their strategic possibilities by using cyber attacks often, but on a level that does not trigger an actual war (Simmons, 2011; Kshetri, 2014, p. 5).

STATE-SPONSORED GROUPS

Outside the core areas of the state, non-state actors are included in war and warfare. Instead of entering a war conflict alone, a state might hire help from non-state actors to get the job done (Salehyan, 2010, p. 494). The conventions are straightforward; only lawful combatants authorised by a governmental authority can engage in the hostilities. However, irregular forces can still be engaged, but that should happen under the command of state actors. There are clear rules for this person-in-command. The state actors should be recognisable from a distance, carry arms openly, and conduct operations in accordance with the law of wars conventions (Westby, 2011, p. 84). However, a tactic used by states is to empower rebel organisations or para-militant groups as substitutes. By doing so, the state circumvents the international requirements included in Jus ad Bellum and Jus in Bello by distancing themselves from the attacking groups (Salehyan, 2010, p. 494). Empowering non-state actors have clear benefits for the military units. Non-state actors are cheaper, act faster, and the rule of wars does not bind them. The state actors can also complement their political agenda using non-state actors in joint military operations (Salehyan, 2010, p. 494).

The justification for using state-sponsored groups goes in two directions. First, it is cost-effective as the proxies do not require much support. Often, it is enough to give the hackers a target list with vectors, and then, they work their way through the list autonomously. This process distances the state even further from the actions. The hackers can be mobilised quickly, and they can also easily be disbanded when their skills are no longer needed. Often, the state-affiliated or sponsored actors are aligned with the state's political, commercial, or military interests. The primary motive for state-sponsored activities is to destabilise the political and financial balance to promote their own goals (Pratley, 2015; Goud, 2019). Second, proxies create a buffer between the attack and the state, where the hackers create a distance to the state apparatus to cause confusion about the attack.

Various types of irregular cyber forces should be made illegal. The attacker can be an insider, a lone hacker, a rough actor, an organised criminal, a terrorist, or a national state. It is a difficult task to track and trade the attackers and criminal activities. Often, it is impossible to attribute the attack to a particular individual, group, or state. Moreover, this buffer ensures that investigations into attacks rarely create the direct link between the target, attack route, state, governmental networks, or Internet protocol (IP) addresses (Connell & Vogler, 2016, p. 9).

Contrary to the rules of war, the attackers or the people involved in the attack do not wear distinctive emblems. They cannot be identified from a distance. Even skilled researchers and investigators can struggle to find the attacker, the origin of the attack, and the attack's motivation. Often attacks are attributed to known hackers, known groups' motivation, and an identifiable means and method, rather than a clean-cut identification (Westby, 2011, p. 90). State-sponsored attacks have proven very rewarding and can be conducted at relatively low cost/low risk. The likelihood of gaining clear evidence sufficient to link the attacker to an even and a state is extremely low. Moreover, there is a high success rate associated with these operations. States that have used this practice have increased their capabilities significantly, whereas the states not using this strategy are left behind (Pratley, 2015).

Motivation and Actors

Cyberwar can be broadly understood as a war fought in cyberspace by targeting ICTS. The exact definition of cyberwar is still undefined. The global reliance on CI, CNIs, CIIs, and ICTs demonstrates that cyber conflicts' potential scope and reach can be linked to the national state's security and economic well-being (Touré, 2011, p. 7). The innovations and new areas included in modern cyberwar and attacks are often perceived as 'risk-free' hi-tech 'clean war' of 'surgical' strikes and minimised casualties (Merrin, 2018, p. 42). Cyberwar and warfare are not very different from conventional warfare on land, sea, or air. Direct cyber-warfare has the same dangers as conventional offline war, where a conflict quickly can escalate. Therefore, there is an incitement to have minor low-level, but well-executed, attacks that do not disrupt the global or geopolitical order (Kshetri, 2014; Parker & Kremling, 2017, p. 113; Barletta et al., 2011). China, North Korea, Russia, and the US are increasingly involved in cyberwar and warfare, building up capacities and capabilities on multiple levels. However, these states have different motivations to be involved in cyber attacks. Cyber attacks are also intricately linked to cybersecurity, so the states are engaged on multiple levels: offensive actions on adversaries' virtual territory and cyber-defence of their own and allied's virtual space. All actors use a hybrid method, including state actors and state-sponsored actors, to conduct the operations on behalf of the state.

China

Over the years, Chinese state and state-sponsored actors have developed sophisticated means and methods for conducting cyber attacks. Many of these cyberactivities are conducted over a long time following the state strategy for political and economic growth. One of the means used is persistent advance threats against CI structures and services of public and private entities. Due to zero-day exploits, the threat actors can stay within the computer systems and networks for a long time until the vulnerabilities are patched.

China has capitalised on cyberspace's interconnectivity to make the state superior to other states worldwide. China was previously regarded as a second-tier cyberpower. However, the state has aggressively and consistently pursued its strategic goals of enhancing its cybercapacities and competencies to become one of the world's leading cyberactors. The Chinese Communist Party uses its cyberstrategy to prioritise computer science and technology education to create a consistent talent pipeline for cybermilitary operations (Hlevek, 2020). The Chinese warfare strategies are based on the two areas. First, the strategies incorporate modern People's War tactic. Second, they also incorporate the ancient 36 Stratagems by Sun Tzu by focusing on deceptive knowledge-based warfare tactics and an asymmetrical advantage over its enemies (Burrow, 2013, p. 10).

Table 5.1 shows the main Chinese state actors and their responsibilities.

Table 5.1 Chinese actors

State actors	Responsibilities
The General Staff Department. Second Department	Covers general military intelligence, HUMINT, and overhead imagery
The Third Department (Technical Department)	Covers SIGINT and cyber espionage
The Fourth Department (Electronic Countermeasures and Radar Department)	Covers elements of computer espionage and electronic intelligence (ELINT)

Source: US Gov (2016).

China possesses substantial cyber attack capabilities and presents a growing threat due to China's cyberpursuits and proliferation of related technologies (DNI, 2021, p. 8). China's leaders have recognised that technological development has created new challenges to the government's ability to regulate and control it. Therefore, the government has created new institutions, legislations, and policies to manage hardware, software, data flows, and information within its borders, changing the landscape for foreign and domestic ICT companies and internet users (Sacks, 2020). China's strategies mirror the states complex hierarchies, command structures, and various defence units. Similar to Russia, the governance of cyberspace can be perceived as a global existential competition between China's political system and the Western world (Raud, 2016).

The Chinese PM Xi Jinping launched in 2015 the 'Made in China 2025' strategic plan. The 'Made in China' plan aims to gain parity with the US in ten key industries, including biomedicine, robotics, space technology, cloud computing, and artificial intelligence. China has used illegally obtained information from cyber attacks to improve its military capabilities and develop new technologies. Moreover, the information has been utilised to enhance the state's abilities for competing on the global market and support commercial companies in becoming global players (Hlevek, 2020).

China has a substantial professional community linked to espionage, demonstrating capabilities to infiltrate national commercial entities over the years. The targets are chosen per their abilities to benefit the defence industry and high-tech communities (USCC, 2019). The Chinese governmental actors employ tactics to influence lawmakers and public opinion to develop policies favourable to China's strategic goals (FBI, 2021).

CYBER UNITS

Chinese hackers linked to the Chinese's People's Liberation Army are involved in a large-scale campaign stealing large amounts of data from Western governments' computer systems (Lemos, 2011; Martin, 2011). There is a vast number of groups involved in these operations known under different names. Some of the most well-known groups are outlined in the Table 5.2.

Several state-sponsored cyber units with close ties to the Chinese military have emerged over the years. APT and Tactic, Techniques, and Procedures (TTP) groups have succeeded in building up China's cybercapabilities during the past two decades. Two of the most know APT groups are outlined below in Table 5.3.

Table 5.2 Chinese state units

State Units	Responsibilities	Aliases
Unit 61398	Specialised in computer network operations that compromise several information systems	Linked to aliases such as UglyGorilla, KandyGoo, and WinXYHappy
Unit 61486	Specialised in cyber attacks on American, Japanese, and European corporations focused on satellite and communications technologies	Linked to aliases such as Putter Panda
Unit 78020	Collect intelligence from political and military sources to advance China's interests in the South China Sea	Linked to aliases, such as Naikon
Unit 61419	Conduct cyber-espionage campaigns against multiple antivirus companies	Linked to aliases, such as Tick Group APT
Unit 69010	Conduct year-long cyberespionage attacks to collect military intelligence from states. Has mainly targeted India in relation to border tensions between China and India	Linked to aliases, such as RedFoxtrot

Sources: Cimpany (2021z); Wilson (2021); Paganini (2021a); Mimoso (2015); Kovacs (2017); Insikt group (2021).

Table 5.3 Chinese state-supported groups

Name	Characteristics	Aliases
APT40	Targeted shipbuilding, maritime and engineering entities, governmental and academic institutions, either placed or close ties to states bordering the South China Sea. Constantly upgrading and developing their attack forms to undertake new strategic activities	Using several aliases, such as TEMP.Periscope, TEMP. Jumper and Leviathan
APT41	Founded under the Winniti umbrella, and it is considered highly agile and persistent. Conducted operations against healthcare, high-tech companies, pharmaceutical, telecommunication, retail, education and video game industries, etc.	Using several aliases, such as Zhang Xuguang, Wolfzhi, Barium, Winnti, Wicked Panda, Wicked Spider, TG-2633, Bronze Atlas, Red Kelpie, Blackfly

Sources: Hlevek (2020); Henderson et al. (2018); Plan et al. (2019); MITRE ATT&CK (2020c); FireEye (2019); US DoJ (2020c); Eddy (2019).

North Korea

Where China is pursuing a strategy to enhance the powers of the state, the Democratic People's Republic of Korea's (North Korea) national cyber objectives are different. The state aims to ensure the regime's survival, displaying powers and its position in the international environments and maintaining its domestic control. North Korea has been accused of being behind numerous cyber attacks, causing disruption and financial damage on an unprecedented level.

The impact of WannaCry demonstrates that the state is no longer a secondary cyberpower, and it is using the cyberdomain to display its capabilities and capacities (BBC News, 2017n). For over a decade, the regime has been widely involved in espionage campaigns against the South-Korean defence industrial base (Parsons & Bureau, 2020; Bartlett, 2020). The state-sponsored Lazarus group is instrumental for the online activities operating with different subunits. The proxies create a buffer between the state and the activities. However, all use of the Internet and cyber education of citizens are highly controlled by the state. Therefore, it is likely that Lazarus and other APT groups act under the state's authority (Bartlett, 2020).

The engagement in cyberwarfare has been pursued despite the state's diplomatic and economic situation. The North Korean leader, Kim Jong-un, believes that cyberwarfare is an all-purpose tool that guarantees North Korea striking capabilities and nuclear weapons. The all-purpose weapon has been adapted and deployed against North Korea's adversaries by launching ransomware attacks, destroying computer systems, and espionage (Ji Young et al., 2019, p. 1; Casear, 2021). The strategies of cyberwarfare are not surprising due to the payoff for the state. Developing cyber capabilities and capacities can be done to low cost and high effect. North Korea has risen significantly in the online war game despite limited powers and a relatively isolated position. The state has developed its asymmetric military powers by enlisting elite soldiers with considerable computer skills. At the same time, as developing an internal structure with a large group of cybersoldiers, the state minimises Internet dependencies internally within its territory. North Korea claims to have 6,000 cyberspecialist engaged in cyber attacks, and 19–20 percentages of the military budget are used on these activities (Ji Young et al., 2019, p. 3; Park et al., 2016, p. 88).

North Korea has developed an internal domestic intranet for its citizens, the Ministry of People's Security, the Ministry of State Security (MSS), and the military. The unclassified intranet, Kwangmyong, has around 50,000 users connected to 3,700 organisations using this separate online communication platform. Having such tight control over the online environment makes the state less vulnerable to attacks from other states (Park et al., 2016, pp. 87–88). North Korea is profoundly controlling the access and the use of the Internet. Like China, The North Korean leader believes that open access to information would harm the regime (Ji Young et al., 2019, p. 3). Therefore, there are only a limited number of citizens who can access the Internet beyond the elite hacking units.

Table 5.4 North Korean state units

State actors	Foundation	Responsibilities
The Ministry of State Security (MSS)	North Korea's core counterintelligence service It acts independently of the North Korean Government by reporting directly to Kim Jong-Un	The MSS' cyber missions cover investigating cases of domestic espionage and conducting overseas counterespionage activities as a part of North Korea's foreign missions
The Reconnaissance General Bureau (RGB)	North Korea's primary foreign intelligence bureau	This Bureau has established units within the Ministry of People's Armed Forces to collect strategic and tactical intelligence

Sources: Global Security (2021); US DoD (2018a).

CYBER UNITS

North Korea's cyber programme is hydra-headed. The state has pursued alternative revenues by conducting several financially motivated attacks from bank heists, ransomware attacks, and stealing cryptocurrencies from online exchanges. According to the UN, funds stolen by the North-Korean state-sponsored hackers are used to finance the state, including the Korean People's Army's weapon and nuclear program (Casear, 2021; Parsons & Bureau, 2020; Nichols, 2019). For example, between 2015 and 2016, APT38, the Lazarus group, launched a wave of attacks over the SWIFT banking network, which generated 80 million dollars in hard currency (TrendMicro, 2018; Vijayan, 2021; Parsons & Bureau, 2020).

Within RGB, hackers are trained to attack for political and financial gains aligning with the state strategy. The RGB department consists of six bureaus with compartmented functions. These include operations, reconnaissance, technology and cyber capabilities, overseas intelligence, inter-Korean talks, and service support (US DoD, 2018a, p. 20; Casear, 2021). In 2013, the Korean Leader, Kim Jong-un, praised the hackers working in the unit by calling them the "brave RGB", and "warriors … for the construction of a strong and prosperous nation" (Casear, 2021). The RGB was formed in 2009, and it is supposed to counter the US Directorate of National Intelligence. The RGB formed Office 91 as the headquarter for hacking operations (Park, 2016).

Within the structure of Office 91, Unit 110 and Bureau 121 are operational. Despite limited Internet capacity in North Korea, Bureau 121 is an elite cyberwarfare unit believed to be behind several cyber attacks. Bureau 121 is the primary office tasked with disruptive cyberoperations. For example, the unit is tasked with infiltrating computer networks, hacking, and extort foreign intelligence, deploying viruses (Global Security, 2021; Ji Young et al., 2019, pp. 5–6). Bureau 121 is considered to be responsible for the 2014

Sony Entertainment hack (Global Security, 2021). Table 5.5. shows the four subunits within the RGB.

The North Korean state-sponsored APT37 and APT38 groups are well-known worldwide. Although both APTs have links to the Lazarus group, the actual operations are distinct. Lazarus is associated with attacks attributed to groups dubbed HIDDEN COBRA, Guardian of Peace, Nickel Academy, and Zinc (MITRE ATT&CK, 2020d). HIDDEN COBRA, for example, is notorious for its capabilities to target and compromise a range of victims; some intrusions have resulted in the exfiltration of data while others have been disruptive (CISA, 2017). See Table 5.6.

Table 5.5 RGB subunits

Actors	Name	Responsibilities
Unit 110	The Technology Reconnaissance Team	This unit is used to carry out attacks and engage in clandestine operations
Unit 35	The Central Party's Investigation Team	The unit covers internal security functions and external offensive cyber capabilities
Unit 121	The North Korean People's Army Joint Chiefs Cyberwarfare unit	This unit's overall task is to disable South Korea's military command and communication networks during the armed conflict between the two states
Unit 205	The Enemy Secret Department Cyber Psychology Warfare	This unit is specialised in cyber elements of information warfare

Sources: Global Security (2021); Park (2016).

Table 5.6 North Korean state-sponsored groups

Actor	Characteristics	Aliases
APT37	Primarily, but not exclusively, targeted victims in South Korea The group has also conducted separate attacks on targets worldwide The focus on South Korea has enabled the group to keep a low profile compared with other parts of Lazerus' operations	Linked to aliases, such as ScarCruft, Reaper, Group123, TEMP.Reaper
APT38	Primarily financially motivated threat group supported by the regime This group mainly target financial institutions and banks This group has been attributed for attacking more than 16 organisations within at least 13 counties since 2013	Linked to aliases, such as Bluenoroff, TEMP. Hermit

Sources: Greenberg (2018); Marchuk (2020); Rouse (2020); MITRE ATT&CK (2020b); FireEye (2018b); FireEye (2018a, pp. 3–4).

Russia

Russia has developed a Cold War mentality believing in hostile ideologies and actors surrounding its territory. The tactic is more aggressive about following the state's foreign politics, military strategic, and current events, influencing how it is perceived internally and externally. This indicates that Russia is less likely to restrain its strategies or operations online or offline (Manjikian, 2021, p. 291). Russia uses cyberspace as an asymmetric means to engage with Western states that dominate other sectors, such as economic and military. In contrast to China, Russia deliberately utilises cyberoperations to project its powers by creating chaos and uncertainties (Puyvelde & Brantly, 2019, p. 83). Yet, Russia shares the aspiration with China about becoming a dominant world power online and offline. This aspiration is the drive along with protecting the state's interests and reputation.

The state has a slightly imprecise definition of information warfare and information security. Russia does generally not refer to this as cyber or cyberwarfare. Instead, the state, similar to China, is using 'information' when conceptualising online operations. This means that their activities cover a far-reaching spectrum of information warfare (informatsionnaya voyna) (Connell & Vogler, 2016, p. 2; Lilly & Cheravitch, 2020, p. 3). Nevertheless, information security is a component of information warfare covering two areas: the technical and psychological or cognitive elements. These two areas cover a large mixture of different technical tools and systems to conduct attacks, as well as a strategy of cognitively influencing populations and decision-makers of the conflicting state to erode their willingness to fight and their decision-making structures and processes (Lilly & Cheravitch, 2020, pp. 133–134; Connell & Vogler, 2016, p. 3).

Russia's cyberoperations are not conducted in a strategic vacuum. The operations are enabled by broader geopolitical considerations with close links to the military's institutional culture, intelligence, and political leadership, build on evolution from the immediate post-Soviet period to the contemporary leadership. Russia is engaged in an evolving asymmetric interstate competition conducted just below the threshold for an all-out conflict (Lilly & Cheravitch, 2020, p. 130). It is recognised that the state has been involved in cyber attacks for more than 20 years. During that time, Russia's military and political leadership have fundamentally changed its concept of warfare and incorporated cyberoperations in the strategies (Westby, 2020; Lilly & Cheravitch, 2020, p. 129). According to the Military Doctrine of the Russian Federation (2010), an essential feature in modern warfare is the early implementation of information warfare measures to archive political objectives without mobilising military force. As a result, Information warfare becomes a legitimate tool in peace and war (Connell & Vogler, 2016, p. 6).

Russian is primarily using state-sponsored and state-supported groups (organised cybercrime groups). These groups' activities feed into the overall

Table 5.7 Russian state units

Actor	Responsibilities	Liked to state-sponsored groups
The Main Centre for Special Technologies of the Main Directorate of the General Staff of the Armed Forces of the Russian Federation (GU/GRU) GTsST 74455	GTsST 74455 has been attributed to cyber attacks that created external threats to Western states and allied	Linked to groups, such as Sandworm Team, BlackEnergy Group, Voodoo Bear, Quedagh, Olympic Destroyer and telebots
The 85th Main Centre for Special Services of the Main Directorate of the General Staff of the Armed Forces of the Russian Federation (GU/GRU) GTsSS 26165	GTsSS 26165 has been behind major cyber attacks and threatening numerous entities worldwide	Linked to groups, such as APT28, Fancy Bear, Sofacy Group, Pawn Storm and Strontium

Sources: Corfield (2020); CoEU (2019a, p. 15); FireEye (2017); Shead (2020); NCSC (2018).

strategy by supplementing the state's skills, conducting cyber attacks on a global scale, and interfering in domestic issues in various nation-states (Scroxton, 2020a). State-sponsored actors like Fancy Bear, Pawn Storm, Sofacy, Sednit, Tsar Team, and Strontium have been active for a long time. Like REvil and DarkSide, new state-supported groups have developed capabilities to attack foreign public and private entities as a part of their ransomware campaigns (Scroxton, 2020a; Otto, 2021; Abrams, 2021c).

CYBER UNITS

The Russian Military Intelligence Unit, GRU, is presumed to be the master-mind behind many cyber attacks targeting political institutions, businesses, media, and sport. Predominately, the unit is using state-sponsored actors to carry out the online attacks. The Main Directorate of the General Staff of the Armed Forces of the Russian Federation (abbreviated GU) has replaced the Main Intelligence Directorate. Although the name has changed, this unit is still known by its previous abbreviation GRU (Faulconbridge, 2018; Reuters, 2009; Hodge, 2020). The overall aim of the Main Directorate is to supply intelligence to the President and the Government as well as to ensure the state's military, economic, and technological security. GRU is an aggressive and well-funded organisation with direct access to and support from President Putin. It is considered a principal Russian cyberagency, and it enjoyed the rights and freedoms linked to the support given by state authorities (Faulconbridge, 2018). President Putin has publicly called this unit legendary and praised the officers' patriotism (Hodge, 2020).

The two central cyber units are GTsST 74455 and GTsSS 26165, which have demonstrated their capabilities and capacities to carry out numerous cyber attacks against public and private entities at a high pace. The Soviet-era KGB agency has been divided into two central Intelligence and security services: the Foreign Intelligence Service (SVR) and the Federal Security Service (FSB) (Faulconbridge, 2018; Reuters, 2009). See Table 5.7.

Over the years, the units have conducted several high-profile attacks with a limited level of operational security and secrecy. A part of the operations of the units is to create uncertainties about their capabilities and capacities. The publicity the groups are getting is a part of the game to establish Russia as a leading cyberpower (NCSC, 2018; US Congress, 2021). Several state-sponsored actors are used as a part of the Russian strategy. The most well-known groups are APT28 and APT29:

Table 5.8 Russian state-sponsored groups

Actor	Characteristics	Aliases
ATP28	The group's espionage activities include targeting governments and militaries; defence attaches, media entities, and dissidents and opponents of the current Russian Government	Linked to aliases, such as Fancy Bear, SNAKEMACKEREL, Swallowtail, Group 74, Pawn Storm, Sofacy Group, and Sednit
	The group has been linked to attacks against Eastern Europe and former Soviet states, including several attacks on Ukraine and Georgia. It has also been active in targeting NATO, the EU member states and various US defence contractors	
ATP29	The group is known for a series of cyber-espionage operations responsible for attacks against high-profile individuals	Linked to aliases, such as Cozy Bear, Dark Halo, StellarParticle, NOBELIUM, UNC2452, YTTRIUM, EuroAPT, the Dukes, CozyDukes and OfficeMonkeys
	The group has predominately been linked to political entities since 2010, i.e. attacks compromising governmental and diplomatic organisations, think-thanks, healthcare services and energy organisations in Europe and the US to obtain intelligence	
	Cozy Bear is the most well-known due to the state-sponsored attacks during the US Presidential Election in 2016	

Sources: Rouse (2020); MITRE ATT&CK (2021a); FireEye (2017); Shead (2020); Johnson (2015); Westby (2020).

The US

The number of attacks the US is subjected to from foreign actors has prompted a new perspective on cyber responses. However, the US is equally involved in attacks on other countries' critical infrastructure utilising the powers of actors like the US Cyber Command (USCYBERCOM), the NSA, the US Central Intelligence Agency (CIA). The CIA was issued a secret order in 2018, giving the agency a White House approval for conducting offensive cyberoperations against states such as Russia, China, Iran, and North Korea. Since the order was signed, the CIA has reportedly been behind a large number of attacks (Cimpanu, 2020n; Ray, 2020; Dorfman et al., 2020).

Currently, the US is undergoing a resounding policy shift on cyber conflict with profound implications for national security and the future of the Internet. The US DoD and the USCYBERCOM stated in 2019 that the US cyberforces are in a persistent engagement with its adversaries. Therefore, the tactic has changed to 'defend forward' to continuously contesting enemies in their virtual space, according to the DoD's Cyber Strategy 2018. The argument for this expansion of the persistent engagement stance is that more offensive tools are needed to match the powers of the attackers. This means the operations should be extended beyond the DoD's networks (Healey, 2019; US DoD, 2018d).

The US is engaged in strategic competitions with China and Russia, which requires additional strategic capabilities and capacities (US DoD, 2018d). Parts of US President Trump's administration were very vocal about these changes. Security advisor Bolton argued that the military needed to respond offensive and defend by imposing costs on the adversaries. Vice-President Pence stated that the days have gone where the US should allow adversaries to attack the US with impunity (Healey, 2019). One of the arguments for developing the 2018 DoD strategy was that increasing costs to adversaries would change the current situation. Investing in the US' situational awareness about its opponents' behaviour and capabilities would be a game-changer. Disrupting the attack infrastructures would decrease the payoff related to attackers' ability to operate; thereby, the strategy will increase costs on the adversaries and decrease the willingness of being involved in online operations (US DoD, 2018b; Borghard, 2020b).

To ensure that the US strategic goals are met, the military's ability to engage in cyberwarfare is a fundamental requirement. The main point for protecting and securing the US is to deter aggression, such as cyber attacks. Therefore, the DoD aims to enhance its capabilities to defend internal and external military networks, systems, and information from malicious attacks. Other areas, such as privately owned and operated CIs, need to be protected, despite being outside DoD's domain. The strategic goal is also to supply integrated cyber capabilities to support operations and developed contingency plans. Also, DoD should work closely with its allies and partners to strengthen cyber capacity, expand combined operations, and increase bidirection information sharing (US DoD, 2018b).

The US recognised early that cyberwarfare was a possibility. Therefore, USCYBERCOM was established in 2009 and became operational in 2010. This department is a part of the US National Security Agency (NSA) and the US DoD. USCYBERCOM contributes to the US' national strategic deterrence by preparing, operate and collaborate with various combatant commands, services, departments, allies, and industries. As a part of the operational structure, USCYBERCOM works closely with Defense Information Systems Agency (DISA), the NSA, and the rest of the Intelligence Community it is missions (USCYBERCOM, 2018, p. 7).

USCYBERCOM is a sub-section of the US Strategic Command. It comprises elements from each military service, i.e. the Air Force's 24th Air Force, the Navy's 10th fleet, the 2nd Army, and the Marine Corps Cyberspace Command. The Command has 133 teams that are divided into three areas: The Cyber Protection Forces, the National Mission Forces, and the Combat Mission Forces. See Table 5.9.

The US President Trump issued new powers to Cyber Command in 2018 in a security classified document: National Security Presidential Memoranda 13. This document gives USCYBERCOM far more flexibility to conduct offensive online operations without presidential approval (Sanger & Perlroth, 2019). Therefore, security of online systems and proactive monitoring of the election were prioritiesed.

The command has undertaken the tasks of defending vital systems and imposing costs on adversaries. Simultaneously, the command supported the US government and allied partners in performing their missions effectively (USCYBERCOM, 2018; Lopez, 2020; US DoD, 2018b; Borghard, 2020a). USCYBERCOM and NSA are collaborating to identify, mitigate, and respond to illegal intrusions. For example, these two institutions have worked together to investigate the SolarWinds attack in 2020 (USCYBERCOM, 2021).

Table 5.9 US state units

1. Actor	2. Responsibilities
3. A Cyber Protection Forces	Established to augment traditional defensive measures and defend the Department of Defence's networks
4. The National Mission Forces	Established to defend the US and its interests against cyber threats
5. The Combat Mission Forces	Established to integrate cyber operations into operational plans

Source: Heginbotham et al. (2015, pp. 277–278).

Table 5.10 US subunits

Actors	Characteristics	Responsibilities
The NSA	Tailored Access Operations (TAO) An elite hacker unit specialising in gaining undetected access to	An in-house hacking unit is known as Provides intelligence support to military operations through Signal intelligence Conducting actions spanning from infiltrating systems to zero-day vulnerabilities and website malware injections
The CIA	Has been active in developing hacking tools and stockpiling exploits 2018: Approval for conducting own offensive cyber operations alongside official operations (NSPM 13)	In 2001, the CIA gained political and budgetary powers, which enabled the agency to develop a hacking unit under the Centre for Cyber Intelligence The unit had produced more than a thousand hacking systems, trojans, viruses, and malware

Sources: WikiLeak (2017); NSA. CSS (2021); Zetter (2016); Lewis (2014); McCarthy (2020).

Together with the NSA, the US Central Intelligence Agency (CIA) is also engaged in online actions. See Table 5.10.

Means and Methods: Deterrence and Defence

States agree that international law applies to activities in cyberspace, including the principles of sovereignty and non-intervention. However, the interpretation of these rules differs. This has created legal uncertainties. Some states prefer this as it allows more room for their actions. Moreover, they believe that stricter rules could be damaging for pursuing their interest in cyberspace. Adhering to rules is essential for state actions, and a clear legal base would clarify how and when to engage in cyber operations and when it is possible to make assertions if other states break the rules (Moynihan, 2019, p. 4). States are using cyberspace to alter the balance of information and gain advantages in the long-term cyber competition. The complexity of having various cybersecurity frameworks developed regionally and nationally creates an unbalanced level of rules, participants, and responses. The current game plan for states includes cyber espionage, destruction, and retaliation within broad coercive campaigns and crisis bargains. Through these attacks, the actors signal their capacities or determine their rivals' abilities and resolve to attack (Jensen et al., 2020).

Interference in Democratic Processes

The UN Charter Article 2 states that all member states should refrain in their international relations from using threats or force against the territorial integrity or political independence of any state or in any actions incompatible with the purpose of the UN (UN, 2020). The increasing number of cyber interferences in elections should be seen in conjunction with the prohibition of intervention into other states' internal or external affairs (Tallinn Manual, Rule 66) (NATO CCDCOE, 2013; Schmitt, 2020). In this area, two principles are deriving from customary law. First, the cyberoperation must affect another state's internal or external affairs. Second, the operation should be coercive (Schmitt, 2020).

Russia has a long history of meddling in democratic elections. The online environment has provided the state with unprecedented opportunities to use this tactic. The state has tried to influence politics in former Soviet states since the collapse of the Soviet Union. In 2014, Russia began targeting states beyond the Eastern bloc, combining misinformation campaigns with cyber attacks (Tennis, 2020). Russia considers the US–European partnership as being an obstacle for the state becoming a political and military power that dominates or controls its neighbours in Europe (Holcomb, 2020). Several attacks against political events, entities, and institutions have been attributed to GTsSS 261665 and the state-sponsored group APT28. Russia hackers attacked the Polish electoral commissions' webpage, undermining public confidence. Again in 2020, Polish politicians were attacked (Cerulus, 2021b; AP, 2014). An attack was launched against the German Federal Parliament (Deutscher Bundestag) in 2015 (Tennis, 2020; BBC News, 2016gg). In France, the presidential candidate Marcon's campaign *En Marche!* was attacked in the 2017 election. Leaked documents using the hashtag #Macrongate were circulated (Tennis, 2020; Holcomb, 2020). The UK also suffered a cyber attack against its voter registration web page regarding the Brexit referendum in 2016 (Tennis, 2020; Intelligence and Security Committee of Parliament, 2020, p. 14; BBC News, 2017h). In 2020, Norway attributed Russia to a cyber attack against the Norwegian Parliament, calling the attack a serious and wilful provocation. As a part of the Russian strategy, the Russian Embassy launched a verbal counter-attack on Norway and other Western states, stating that numerous attacks are being launched against Russian Internet resources. However, being a target in the past does not automatically give Russia the right indiscriminately to blame the states' authorities assumed to be behind them without providing evidence (BBC News, 2020bb).

The Russian interference in the US Presidential election in 2016 brought these tactics to the world's attention. Russian state-sponsored hackers are attributed for the attacks on the Democratic National Committee's private email servers. The subsequent release of these emails on WikiLeaks and mass media profoundly damaged Hillary Clinton's presidential campaign. Although the attacks are attributed to the state-sponsored groups, Guccifer 2.0 and Fancy Bear, there are clear links to Russia (Lavorgna, 2020, p. 176; Manjikian, 2021, p. 245). After the US Presidential election in 2016, it is more apparent how Russia is trying to interfere with democratic elections by combining cyberoperations with hack-and-dump practices and misinformation using proxies to distance the state from the attacks (Puyvelde & Brantly, 2019, p. 84). During the 2020 election, the Russian state-sponsored hackers targeted political parties in the US and Europe. Other states are also attacking elections. Chinese groups targeted individuals within the Biden campaign during the 2020 US Presidential Election campaign. Iranian hackers attempted to breach the online accounts of President Trump's campaign staff. Additionally, hackers attacked political consultants, think tanks, and groups outside the two campaigns, such as the German Marshall Fund and Stimson Center, promoting international cooperation (Starks, 2020).

Attacks on CIs

There are many examples of CIs being targeted over the years, which have significantly impacted the civil population and private businesses. The effectiveness of norms regulating and protecting CI from cyber attacks is questionable. Attacking these services, spanning from water to financial industries, the civil populations would suffer the most from attack. In the Geneva Convention VI, protection of the civil population (Art, 15, 16, 18) is established. The Hauge Conventions highlights that states should respect the neutrality of another state. Therefore, they cannot transmit any attacks through their CIs (ICRC, 1899; ICRC, 1907; Westby, 2011, p. 90).

Table 5.11 Examples of attacks impacting the population

Attacks	Impact
The attacks on power plants in Ukraine (2015–2016) left the population without power for a short period	Had a significantly impact on the civil population with a clear link to hybrid warfare
The Stuxnet attack (2010) against Iran's nuclear facilities	Could potentially have affected the civil population
CIA's hacking tool Vault-7 had been used in recent operations targeting at least 40 organisations across 16 states, such as companies, universities, and governmental institutions and agencies	Impacted numerous entities and people not involved in a political conflict has been targeted
The WannaCry and Not Petya (2017) ransomware attacks disturbed governments, businesses, and online users worldwide	Impacted numerous entities and online users were directly and indirectly affected by this attack without links to governmental entities
The SolarWinds attack (2020) is an attack against numerous military and non-military entities	Impacted numerous entities and online users were directly and indirectly affected by this attack without links to governmental entities

Sources: Ranger (2018); Coble (2020a); BBC News, (2020ii); Paganini (2020b); Paganini (2020d); Mutsuo & Hirofumi (2017); CoEU (2019a); Hern (2017).

Attacks against CIs, such as power plants, can be deployed through an overload of the systems. Most states are interdependent on transnational systems, often owned or run by private actors. Additionally, they supply other countries with power, and the attack will affect beyond the intended target. Allowing countries to conduct cyber attacks that could transit over several state's networks without their knowledge is largely incompatible with the codification of norms included in the law of wars (Westby, 2011, p. 90).

Until rules and practices have been developed to limit the impact on civil society, planning and conducting operations in cyberspace should be assessed in conjunction with Geneva Convention, Protocol 1, Articles 48–59, which outlines provisions regarding civilians' protection. In the Convention, everyone who is not a member of the armed force is classified as a civilian. Civilians should not be objects of attacks or subjected to any acts designed to spread terror or to indiscriminate attacks that are not directed at a specific object (Art 51). Attacks targeting the population for acts of revenge is prohibited (Art 52), or attacks targeting object indispensable to the survival of the civil population (Art 54), work or installation contain dangerous elements that can release of dangerous forces and consequent cause severe losses among the civil population, i.e. dams, power plants, and nuclear facilities (Art 56). The Convention also highlights that constant care needs to be taken to protect the civilian population (Art 57). The planners of an attack should take all necessary precautions to ensure that the object of an attack is not civilians or civilian objects – or that the targets are not subjected to special protections. Therefore, the military attack planners must take all possible precautions to avoid or minimise all related activities that can cause civilian life loss (Art 57). Finally, it is prohibited to attack non-defended localities where no military operations occur, or no military personnel are located (Art 59) (Westby, 2011; ICRC, 1977).

ATTACKS ON HEALTHCARE FACILITIES

Healthcare, services, supplies, facilities, organisations, and research are vulnerable to attacks from state and state-sponsored actors. Although these areas are recognised in international law, the growing number of cyber attacks against these areas also demonstrates a lack of recognition of international law. The Geneva Convention IV (1949) clearly protects civilians in times of war (ICRC, 1949; Stilgherrian, 2020). Civilian hospitals organised to care for the wounded and the sick, the infirm and maternity cases, should under no circumstances be an object of attacks. Instead, hospitals should be respected and protected by the parties to the conflict (Art 18). Moreover, the Convention states that all parties in a conflict should provide all civilian hospitals with certificates that show their status. They should also ensure that buildings are not used for any purposes that deprive them of this protection. The personnel engaged in the search for, removal, transporting, and careering of these protected groups shall also be protected (Art 20). Transportation and the medical supply line are equally protected (Art 23) (ICRC, 1949; Stilgherrian,

2020). However, the states behind the online attacks have not declared war; they use proxies for low-level conflict attacks operating below the threshold of warfare. These areas are, therefore, not protected by the Geneva Convention, but that does not mean that international practices should not be respected in peacetime. The COVID-19 pandemic is a problem worldwide, and this should prompt an incitement for developing rules, practices, and processes protecting healthcare organisations, facilities, and populations.

The impact of COVID-19 did not foster closer cooperation or a cease-fire in dealing with cyberwarfare. Instead, the pandemic turned into a societal, economic, and military race to develop the vaccine first and protect own populations. The North Korean regime has continuously denied being involved in attacks on healthcare organisations and entities involved in developing a COVID-19 vaccine. Nevertheless, North Korea has been attributed for being involved in ongoing hacking campaigns aimed at defence companies, media organisations, and COVID-19 related targets, i.e. vaccine scientists and pharmaceutical companies (Paganini, 2020c). Due to the North Korean political situation, getting access to information about the vaccine is beneficial to the state. The Lazarus group is affiliated with the cyber attack against pharmaceutical company AstraZeneca. In 2020, AstraZeneca was targeted in a campaign that bore the hallmark of an attack originating from the North Korean regime. The attackers used malware-infected phishing emails forwarded to AstraZeneca's workforce (Goud, 2020; Stubbs, 2020; Davis, 2020). It is a well-known tactic by posing as recruiters on popular social network platforms and instant messaging applications, such as LinkedIn and WhatsApp. This method enabled the attackers to approach AstraZeneca employees with fake job offers as an attack vector (Paganini, 2020c).

In 2020, the Canadian Communication Security Establishment (CSE), the US DHS, US CISA and NSA, the UK NCSC revealed that Russian state-sponsored actors from the APT28 group, the Dukes/Cozy Bear, had operated on behalf of the Russian Intelligence Services by targeting organisations involved in national and international COVID-19 responses (NCSC, 2020). Microsoft (2020) detected cyber attacks from three nation-state actors targeting seven prominent companies directly involved in the research and treatment of COVID-19. These targets include leading pharmaceutical companies and vaccine researchers in Canada, France, India, South Korea, and the US. A Russian state-sponsored actor, Strontium, was attributed to these attacks. Two other actors affiliated with North Korea, Zinc and Cerium, were also involved in the cyber attacks against these targets (Burt, 2020). North Korea has been able to leverage its cyberpowers along with China and Russia during a pandemic. The state has reportedly been attacking funds from the pharmaceutical companies working on the COVID-19 vaccines, and they have also targeted national COVID-19 relief funds (Bartlett, 2020; Anon., 2020).

The search for a vaccine has become a state matter, and there is fierce competition between actors to get access to information that can restore normality and protect populations. In 2020, Kaspersky's research team published information about two APT incidents, a publicly unidentified Ministry of Health body and a pharmaceutical company attributed to the Lazarus group from North Korea (Knowles, 2020). Pfizer/BioNTech claimed in December 2020 that documents regarding developing a COVID-19 vaccine at the European Medicine Agency (EMA) were unlawfully accessed in a cyber attack (Stubbs, 2020a,b). The documents regarding a regulatory submission for the COVID-19 candidate, BNT162b2, were stored on the EMA server. Researchers at IMB's X-Force security unit revealed that the COVID-19 supply chain elements were under persistent attack by a state-sponsored group. This attack was active since September 2020, targeting organisations linked to the cold chain that ensures the vaccine is preserved in a temperature-controlled environment during transportation (Scroxton, 2020c; Stilgherrian, 2020). The lack of online protection is visible. According to the laws of war, the sick and the wounded should have superior protection, and so should other health issues, as all countries worldwide are facing the same challenge during the pandemic.

Espionage

International governmental espionage is primarily allowed. However, the problem is that cyber espionage and cyber attacks require computer and networks intrusion, which is illegal. Additionally, the increase in governmental spying on private companies cannot be justified in the same way. It creates an unhealthy level of competition when economic state powers are based on state practices of spying (Barletta et al., 2011, p. 81). The US has accused China of intellectual property theft and forced technology transfer from US companies to Chinese state units. Trade has become a part of the cyber-conflict between the two actors (Parsons & Raff, 2020; Office of the United States Trade Representative, 2018). During his presidency, US President Trump argued that he wanted to stop the "unfair transfers of American technology and intellectual property to China" as well as protect American jobs (BBC News, 2018pp; Schneider-Petsinger et al., 2019, p. 2). However, the measures imposed did not have the expected payoff. The initiative was launched to protect American interests and prevent state-owned Chines enterprises from collaborating with American companies. Instead, the tech industry was divided into separate US-centric and China-centric markets, forcing tech companies to rethink their organisations and structures to serve these two global supply networks by adding cost complexity to operations (Waters, 2019).

Although China is still behind in developing its components, the Chinese government has allocated funding to the tech industry with its state-owned enterprises and the states' provincial and private equity funds. Based on previous successes, Chinese companies continue to develop their skills within espionage and large-scale attacks to access information and steal intellectual properties that they cannot develop or buy (Swanson & Kang, 2020). The former US Assistant Attorney General for the National Security, Demers, argued in 2020 that China's cyberthreats are persistent, well-organised, and well-resourced and supported by intelligence officers within the Chinese MSS (Cimpanu, 2020e). Therefore, it is likely that China increased its efforts to collect foreign data legally and illegally to support the goals outlined in the 'Made in China' plan and associated strategies to make China a leading global technological superpower by 2049 (US DHS, 2020, p. 2). However, while the US increases its verbal attacks and the negative narrative, China increases its online operations.

It is not only China that engages in long-term cyber espionage. The Chinese cyber-security company, Qihoo 360, reported that the US had conducted an 11-year long campaign against China throughout most of the 2010s. These cyber attacks have targeted vital areas, such as aerospace, science and research institutions, the oil industry, governmental institutions, and Internet companies, predominately targeting Chinese provinces Beijing, Guangdong, and Zhejiang. This long-term attack was attributed to the CIA's National Clandestine Service (NCS). According to the Chinese cybersecurity company, the hacking group APT-C-39 used CIA-exclusive cyberweapons, Fluxwire and Grasshopper, to attack China. These activities are also associated with the NSA (Coble, 2020; Paganini, 2020b; Doffman, 2020; Janofsky, 2021; 360 Core Security, 2020). Later in 2019, China's National Computer Network Emergency Response Team (CNCERT) report suggested that the US attacks were escalating. The report highlights two key findings. First, the report claims that the US is the primary over-seas cyber adversary to China. The US servers have been used to employ viruses and conduct botnet attacks against Chinese computer systems and assess. Attacks with links to the US have increased by 90.8% within one year. Second, US IP addresses are instrumental in conducting these attacks. 3,325 US IP addresses were identified in these attacks, which infected 3,607 Chinese websites in 2018 (Lindsey, 2019; Heginbotham et al., 2015, p. 278; Goud, 2019; Janofsky, 2021)

THE SOLARWINDS ATTACK

Both 2020 and 2021 have been years when large-scale cyber attacks have been discovered based on illegal exploits by state-sponsored hackers. The SolarWinds attacks detected by the end of 2020, dubbed SUNBURST, are one of the most significant attacks so far against a company's supply chain targeting several government agencies and companies. In 2020, hackers inserted malicious code into a network management product, Onion, from SolarWinds, an IT provider whose client list includes 300,000 institutions. Approximately, 18,000 of these institutions were exposed to downloading a legitimate update from SolarWinds between March and June 2020. This download enabled the hackers to access the entire network. Paradoxically, such download was carried out to keep the cyber defence updated. This update allowed the attackers to harvest data and insert vulnerabilities in the systems for a long time before it was detected.

Cybersecurity experts and the US government have linked the attack to hackers affiliated with the Russian Government, although the authorities have denied responsibility (Brustein, 2020; BBC News, 2020ii; Schneier, 2020; Bertand & Desiderio, 2020). It is assumed that Cozy Bear hackers, in collaboration with SVR, were behind the SolarWinds attack (Schneier, 2020) (Rash, 2020). The SVR hackers followed a standard playbook scheme to create persistent access, even if the original vulnerability was patched. The tactic made it possible for the hackers to move around in the system by compromising other systems and accounts and then exfiltrate data. This attack form is a lengthy process requiring a high level of patience from the attackers, but this patience weights up the actual outcome of the hack (Schneier, 2020; BBC News, 2020mm).

THE MICROSOFT EXCHANGE ATTACK

Another important attack was detected in the aftermath of the SolarWinds attack. The Microsoft Exchange hack was identified at the beginning of 2021. This widespread breach enabled attackers to access approximately 30,000 US-based organisations (Vincent, 2021; KrebsOnSecurity, 2021). The attack targeted a vast number of small businesses, towns, cities, and local governments by an unusually aggressive Chinese espionage group by exploiting four newly discovered Microsoft Exchange Server email software flaws. The system access provided the attackers with total remote control over the affected systems (KrebsOnSecurity, 2021). The attack was initially attributed to Hafnium, a hacking group affiliated with China, against many industry sectors, including infectious disease researchers, law companies, educational institutions, defence contractors, policy think tanks, and NGOs. (Vincent, 2021; KrebsOnSecurity, 2021). Despite being closely associated with China, Hafnium used a web of virtual private servers (VPS) placed in the US to cover its actual location (Osborne, 2021).

RESPONDING TO SOLARWIND

The SolarWind attack has raised questions about the US ability to enhance resilience and preparedness toward this type of supply-chain attack against numerous targets. The assumption is that there are no purely technical solutions to these cyber attacks on the national level. It is possible to patch vulnerabilities, but the problem does not disappear as attackers will identify other weaknesses to access computer systems. Public–private collaboration is needed to increase the protection against these attacks before and after a hack. The SolarWinds attack has demonstrated again that both public and private entities share the weaknesses in the systems, and the digital environments are far too complex for individual actors to monitor and manage in isolation. Individual users rely on governmental actors and companies to do this (Brustein, 2020).

The attack has revealed a large number of vulnerabilities in the US system. The US has one of the most extensive and aggressive intelligence services in the world. The NSA's budget is one of the largest that leverage the US position worldwide by controlling large parts of the Internet and associated tech companies. Therefore, it concerns when such a major attack can go undetected for a long time on the NSA and the USCYBERCOM's watch (Schneier, 2020). Attacks, such as the SolarWinds, have clearly shown that the US government and private actors have underinvested in cybersecurity. An effective defence strategy should be built on a collective effort, but state agencies and companies are often unprepared. Therefore, they are left defenceless when these large-scale attacks are carried out (Kolbe, 2020). The attack demonstrates weaknesses in strategies, resilience, and preparedness on multiple levels. It is not only about developing rules and regulations; it is equally important to developing cybersecurity within the organisations to maintain cybersecurity.

Strategies and the Game

With no legislative global cyberwarfare framework in place, the use of cyberspace for attacks reveals a borderless environment for the states to act within. States are using cyberspace to alter the balance of information and gain advantages in the long-term cyber competition. The complexity of various cybersecurity frameworks developed regionally and nationally creates an unbalanced level of rules, participants, and responses. The current game plan for states includes cyber espionage as a broader coercive campaign and crisis bargain. Through these attacks, the actors signal their capacities or determine their rivals' capabilities and resolve (Jensen et al., 2020). Considering the actual issues in the light of game theory, recent cyber attacks have shown that the vision of persistent engagement calls for preventively imposing costs on adversaries to sharpen competition (Valeriano, 2020; Jensen et al., 2020). Imposing costs are included in a layered cyber deterrence strategy to influence the decision-making procedures (US Cyberspace Solarium Commission, 2020). Yet, the costs imposed do not have a level that outweighs the actual benefit from the operations. The payoff of a successful attack is too high for attacking states to have any deterrence effect in the absence of international rules in this area (Valeriano, 2020; US Cyberspace Solarium Commission, 2020).

Cybersecurity

As the attacks are not restricted to actors within national borders, it is essential to add an entanglement strategy to leverage international institutions, regulatory bodies, and international law, bringing together partners, allies, and international organisations to share information and facilitate global actions that isolate and prosecute state officials and cybercriminals linked to these cyber attacks. In the layered cybersecurity strategy, states must increase cooperation with the private sectors, harmonise legislation, and create cybersecurity incentives on multiple levels. These areas are already included in various regional and national cybersecurity strategies, processes, and practices. However, this can be strengthened even further. The next step to enhance cybersecurity concerning large-scale cyber attacks is collecting and standardising data, conducting tests and validations to create a more function anticipatory governance structure (Jensen et al., 2020; Munk, 2015). Even with constantly ongoing online conflicts, the response should not be solely linked to deterrence or defence. States should be prepared to use diplomacy and communicate to prevent an escalation of operational conflicts. It is essential to consider various types of proactive and reactive responses on multiple levels. If states are not prepared to engage in this and accept restrictions on their own capabilities and capacities, they cannot expect other states will limit their attack strategies (Kolbe, 2020).

With the laws of war, most states agree on some common principles to create order in cyberspace. If these were not generally followed, the issues would be much worse than seen at this stage. However, it is time to address the complexity of managing politically motivated attacks that constantly develop new technological innovations, capabilities, and capacities. Although it is generally acknowledged that cyber attacks on CIs are not legitimate weapons of attack – nor are they acceptable during kinetic wars where the analogy is made to biological and chemical weapons – they are still the primary target (Barletta et al., 2011, p. 81).

Although many of the SolarWind targets are state institutions or military entities, the majority are not. Therefore, there is a violation of the use of force in an armed conflict and the principle of distinction. The use of state-sponsored actors to attack might be a strategic move by state actors to circumvent international law. However, the same move also impacts the state-sponsored actors as they are removed from the protection provided to military combatants in armed conflict. Thereby, these state-sponsored actors can be prosecuted under national law in the victim state (Hathaway et al., 2012, p. 854).

Cyber Defence

PERSISTENT ENGAGEMENT AND DEFEND FORWARD

The US has developed its strategy from persistent engagement to defend forward. The argument is that persistent engagement is a strategic prescription based on an analysis of adversaries' behaviour in cyberspace. However, the continuous attacks have become normalised, and therefore, a new strategic position is needed. A defend forward concept is considered a useful replacement for persistent engagement as part of layered cyber deterrence (US DoD,

2018b). The argument is that the US, for too long, has been held back in this defensive strategy. In contrast, cyber-capable nations have escalated their actions worldwide, which not only have had a significant impact on the targets, but these actions have undermined the US as a cyberpower (Devanny, 2021, p. 6).

The concept of 'defend forward' includes several proactive measures, such as anticipatory processes and practices to observing, pursuing, and countering adversaries' operations. The strategic position should be included imposing costs in the day-to-day competition to disrupt and defeat the constant malicious cyber campaigns, deter future campaigns, and reinforce favourable international norms of behaviour by using all national instruments available (Borghard, 2020b; Valeriano, 2020). Yet, this strategy cannot stand alone. It needs to be linked to costs and diplomacy, and internationally developed norms and behaviours in cyberspace. There should also be a requirement for more engagement by private actors to enhance cybersecurity.

US' DEFEND FORWARD

The US has used the defend forward strategy in responding to the attacks originating from Russia. However, it is difficult to see how successful this strategy is as the frequency of attacks is escalating and society's impact becomes more prominent. The current stance by Western states offers little incitement to change the balance between cost–benefit calculations. Moreover, this tactic did not impact the tactical or operational level, as Russian actors conducted a large-scale supply-chain exploit in 2020. The SolarWind attack is considered a prominent cyber attack targeting various public and private entities, not only in the US but worldwide (Jensen et al., 2020). However, the SolarWinds attack in 2020 has shown that the US approach is somehow ineffective as large-scale cyber attacks continue to emerge (Schneier, 2020)

Under customary law of countermeasures, an attacking state that violates its obligations not to intervene in another sovereign state can be met with lawful countermeasures from the victim state. That customary law also applies to harmful cyber attacks, and the countermeasures might go beyond passive defence. However, the active defence still needs to meet the requirements of necessity and proportionality (Hathaway et al., 2012, p. 858; Kramer & Rodihan, 2020). The defend forward strategy was used to stop the Russian Internet Research Agency's activities concerning the 2018 US midway election and the period before the US Presidential election in 2020.

According to USCYBERCOM, Russia used the 2018 mid-term election as a 'warm-up' for the 2020 US Presidential Election. To secure these elections, USCYBERCOM worked closely with the defence teams from the Department of Homeland Security (DHS), the FBI, and industry sectors with knowledge about previous Russian hacker attacks (The Washington Post, 2019). The new powers included in the defend forward strategy allowed USCYBERCOM and the NSA to conduct attacks on adversaries' territorial space. In 2018, US

President Trump confirmed that the US was behind a covert cyber attack 2018 against the Russian Research Agency. The Russian Research Agency is a troll farm believed to orchestrate online attacks against the 2016 US Presidential election and the 2018 mid-terms elections (Bohn, 2018; Nakashima, 2019; Kolbe, 2020).

In 2019, the US claimed that it had conducted offensive operations against Russian infrastructure. The attack was launched in response to Russia's cyber intrusions into a US energy grind (Carroll, 2019; Kolbe, 2020). The details about an impending attack were surprisingly announced via mass media, telling openly that malware had been injected into a Russian power grid. This malware could turn off electricity supply to homes, hospitals, and schools with short notice. Despite the public announcement, the actual operation was kept on a need-to-know basis, include the information provided to President Trump. This announcement is open to interpretation; was there malware included, or was it a part of a tit-for-tat strategy, or was the malware discovered and the US tried to act proactively to manage the situation? (Carroll, 2019). The rationale behind these operations is not always a matter of strategic deterrence or part of the customary law of countermeasures. The tactic is also deployed to sow confusion about capabilities and capacities.

NATO'S APPROACH

Inspired by the US strategy, NATO has also acknowledged that the alliance needs an approach combining deterrence and defence to deliver proactive and continuous responses to the growing risks emerging from threat actors, such as China and Russia. Both states are engaged in online, hybrid warfare attacks where Russian activities involve intrusion into CIs, manipulating elections, and blocking NATO military capabilities. China is engaged in cyber espionage, intellectual property theft related to sensitive technologies, industries, and CIs closely aligned to the objectives in the 'Made in China' plan. To counter the attack against the European and North American states, the alliance should develop and implement a resilience cybersecurity architecture for the organisation, member states, and significant CIs. It is also recognised that NATO should coordinate with its members to develop a more active cyber defence. Finally, it is believed that NATO should be central in coordinating a strategy of persistent engagement to reduce Russian and Chinese cyberactivities. However, NATO remains a defensive alliance and waits to respond to cyber incidents. Yet, the alliance aims to improve the intelligence-gathering level about opponents capabilities, provide early warnings of impending attacks, and enable rapid counter-cyber responses and information sharing with targeted owners and operations while reducing the adversaries access to national information and data (Borghard, 2020b; Kramer & Rodihan, 2020; Davis, 2019). As NATO has been targeted over a long period, offensive actions are justified, and inaction is more dangerous (Kramer & Rodihan, 2020). However, it is a balancing act as a more active NATO in cyberspace can be considered a provocation by Russia. So far, NATO has used its cyber intelligence norm to pevent an escalation and misinterpretation of actions. According to NATO, building up offensive powers does not equal preparing for military actions (Jacobsen, 2021).

Including Cost-impositions

Considering the actual issues in the light of game theory, recent cyber attacks show that the vision of persistent engagement calls for preventively imposing costs on adversaries to sharpen competition (Valeriano, 2020; Jensen et al., 2020). Imposing costs are included in a layered cyber deterrence strategy where states are trying to influence adversaries decision-making procedures (US Cyberspace Solarium Commission, 2020). Unfortunately, at this stage, the cost of these attacks does not outweigh the actual benefit from the operations. The payoff of a successful attack is too high for attacking states to have any deterrence effect in the absence of international rules (Valeriano, 2020; US Cyberspace Solarium Commission, 2020). States are also becoming more willing to attribute attacks to other states. The number of public attributions has increased significantly. There is also a growing tendency for states to work together in the investigation and later the public attribution of attacks (Moynihan, 2019, p. 4). Despite the importance of attributions in international law to establish facts and circumstances to enable the affected states to execute their rights and obligations, it does not include any legal consequences of the attacks. So far, there are no developed international standards for producing sufficient evidence for wrongdoing. The use of state-sponsored actors adds to the complexity, as no rule is developed in relation to their actions online. These are likely to fall under national rather than international law (Katagiri, 2021, p. 3).

Since the cyber attack on the UK Defence Science and Technology Laboratory, while investigating the Salisbury biological terror attacks and the UK. has been more active in attribute attacks to Russia (GOV.UK, 2020; Intelligence and Security Committee of Parliament, 2020; Scroxton, 2020d). The Intelligence and Security Committee (ISC) had recommended that the UK leverages its diplomatic relationship and assign blame to Russia to gain support from the international in community to find ways to retaliate or prevent cyber attacks (Intelligence and Security Committee of Parliament, 2020; Scroxton, 2020a). Public naming and shaming can have an indirect economic effect where private and public actors might refrain from investing in states or reconsider collaborations due to the state's cyber record. Cyber attacks are often the precursor to an actual war, but the state becomes even more vulnerable when prioritising offensive defence rather than a multi-layered strategy. Therefore, there needs to be a shift in using the offensive-dominant strategies to escalate the tit-for-tat game. Yet, it would indicate that states have to refrain from using exploits to spy on other states (Schneier, 2020)

THE EU SANCTIONS

In 2020, as a part of the EU's cyber diplomacy toolbox, the Council imposed the first restrictive measures against six individuals (Chinese and Russian individuals) and three entities (two Russian and one North-Korean entities) attributed to being involved in various cyber attacks, such as the attacks against the Organisation for the Prohibition of Chemical Weapons (OPCW), and the WannaCry, NotPetya, and Operation Cloud Hopper attacks. These sanctions are added to the list of people involved in attacks with chemical weapons, i.e. the UK Salisbury attack conducted in early 2018. In 2020, a hacking group and individuals from Russia were attributed to the cyber attack against the German Bundestag in 2015 which was also added to the Cyber Sanction List (Simmons + Simmons, 2020; Dumortier et al., 2020; EC, CoEU, 2020). The sanctions can only be imposed against non-state actors, such as natural or legal persons, other entities, or bodies different from a State. These sanctions include both the travel ban and assets freeze. They also prohibit EU individuals and entities from making funds available to those on the sanction list (EC, CoEU, 2020; Dumortier et al., 2020; Botek, 2021).

Sanctions can be seen as an option to enhance the costs of being involved; both the actual sanctions and the public naming and shaming can have a deterrent and dissuasive effect. However, there are limitations to these measures developed by the EU. In practice, the option to impose sanctions has a limited effect beyond the signal they send to a broader audience. Often, the attacks are conducted on behalf of the state, so they have a limited effect on the state's decision-making process. However, the penalties set out in the EU Directives on Attacks against Information Systems 2013 could be applied towards the state-sponsored actors that might have a deterrent effect depending on the state's ties to the attacker (Dumortier et al., 2020; EU, 2013).

THE US INDICTMENTS AND ARREST WARRANTS

In 2018, the US indicted seven Russians associated with APT 28 (Fancy Bear) for their involvement in persistent and sophisticated cyber attacks affecting US persons, corporations, and international organisations. The US argued that these Russian citizens' campaigns from 2014 to at least 2018 had a strategic interest in the Russian Government (Westby, 2020). In 2020, the US DoJ announced criminal charges against six Russian military intelligence officers employed by GRU. These officers have been linked to the Sandworm. VoodooBear's cyberactivities, i.e. the 2018 Olympic Winter Games and the 2018 attack against the UK's Defence Science and Technology Laboratory (GOV.UK, 2020; Borger, 2020). The US DoJ also opened three indictments against the Chinese APT41 group members in 2020. DoJ brought charges against five Chinese nationals and two Malaysians for a widespread series of network intrusions. The APT41's activities have been linked to a Chinese company known as Chengdu 404 Network Technology. This company is believed to operate at the command of the Chinese MSS. The indictments covered intrusions across over 100 victim organisations in several countries (Hlevek, 2020; US DOJ, 2020).

ATTRIBUTION AFTER THE SOLARWIND ATTACK

The US President Biden signed in 2021 an executive order imposing sanctions on Russia after several malicious cyber attacks against the US and its allied. These sanctions included the attackers behind the 2020 SolarWind attack formally attributed to the Russian state-sponsored APT29 (Cosy Bear) (Scroxton, 2021b). The sanctions also include 32 individuals believed to have participated in government efforts to influence the 2020 election and Russian private-sector cybersecurity firms for their work supporting government efforts (Brandom, 2021). The Russian spokesperson Peskov reacted to the sanctions by stating that Russia would retaliate against the new sanctions. "The principle of reciprocity applies ... to best ensure our own interests" (Roth, 2021).

ATTRIBUTION AFTER THE MICROSOFT EXCHANGE ATTACK

After the Microsoft Exchange attack in 2021, the US and a broad coalition of allies, the EU, NATO, UK, Australia, Japan, New Zealand, and Canada, have accused the Chinese Government of hiring hackers to attack the West. The states and institutions increased the rhetoric by claiming that China has action maliciously and irresponsible. The US has also issued a public warning about the conduct of China. The NSA, CISA, and the FBI all consider China poses a serious threat to the US and its allies in its pursuit of strategic military and economic objectives by using state-sponsored actors to target political, economic, military, and educational entities (The White House, 2021h; CISA, 2021). Concerns have been raised whether this hack signifies a change from targeted espionage to damaging raid-like attacks, which means China is changing its cyber behaviour (BBC News, 2021j).

The US government claimed that the Chinese authorities paid hackers using the so-called HfH method. Thereby, China has fostered an ecosystem of criminal hackers operating on the political and criminal levels. According to the US, the Chinese MSS uses criminal contract hackers to conduct unsanctioned cyberoperations globally, also non-political attacks (Vincent, 2021; The White House, 2021h; Holland & Chiacu, 2021; Holland & Chiacu, 2021). The EU and the UK NCSC supported these claims by highlighting that some of APT40's attacks were conducted against maritime industries and naval defence contractors in the US and Europe, whereas APT31 were involved in attacks on the governmental entities, i.e. the attack on the Finnish Parliament in 2020 (Vincent, 2021; CoEU, 2021; NCSC, 2020).

These direct attributions to China follow a string of political disagreements between the US and China over trade, the military, the South Chinese Sea, democracy activists in Hong Kong, and Uyghurs in the Xinjiang region

(Holland & Chiacu, 2021). Although the Western states call out to end this practice, the US has not imposed sanctions on China similar to the economic sanctions given to Russia after the SolarWind attack in 2020 (Vincent, 2021; Brandom, 2021). However, the US DoD announced criminal charges against four named MSS hackers for being involved in year-long global cyber campaigns against foreign governments and entities in key sectors (Vincent, 2021; US DoJ, 2021). China reacted to these accusations by the US and its allied by stating that the state condemned all forms of cybercrime, and these claims were fabricated and unreasonable (BBC News, 2021j). The strong rhetoric used by the US and its allies makes it difficult for them to use proxies for politically motivated cyber attacks against China and other states. It will backfire if China and Russia can provide evidence of these states using the same means and methods. China fuelled the verbal conflict by highlighting the attacks conducted by the US, which China argues conduct the most significant number of cyber attacks (Janofsky, 2021). The active Chinese defence is linked to Mao's strategy: "[W]e will not attack unless we are attacked, but we will surely counter-attack if attacked" (China Ministry of National Defense, 2015; APRS, 2019). Therefore, it is unlikely that the public attributions of China's involvement in the Microsoft Exchange hack will end the conflict; it is more likely to increase because of this.

Conclusion

In cyberwar and warfare, states are operating below the threshold of international law by using proxies to conduct the attacks. The normless area facilitates these actions where the frequency of attacks increases and society is more severely impacted. Different strategies are developed to manage the attacks and defence. However, the lack of international rules and norms for politically motivated activities in cyberspace has a detrimental effect beyond the original scope of the attacks. The protection of CIs, private businesses, and online users is circumvented to archive states' overall aim. Despite international pressure, the attacking state's payoff is too high, and the initiative to stop these practices does not incite changes.

References

360 Core Security, 2020. *The CIA Hacking Group (APT-C-39) conducts cyber-espionage operation on China's critical industries for 11 Years.* [Online] Available at: https://blogs.360.cn/post/APT-C-39_CIA_EN.html [Accessed 20 07 2021].

Abrams, L., 2021c. *REvil ransomware hits US nuclear weapons contractor.* [Online] Available at: www.bleepingcomputer.com/news/security/revil-ransomware-hits-us-nuclear-weapons-contractor/ [Accessed 27 06 2021].

Anon., 2020. *Global Covid-19 Related Phishing Campaign by North Korean Operatives Lazarus Group exposed by Cyfirma Researchers.* [Online] Available at: www.cyfirma.com/early-warning/global-covid-19-related-phishing-campaign-by-north-korean-operatives-lazarus-group-exposed-by-cyfirma-researchers/ [Accessed 21 07 2021].

AP, 2014. *Polish election commission website hacked.* [Online] Available at: https://apn ews.com/article/5aba677736f6448ab0a33740bb057499 [Accessed 17 07 2021].

APRS, 2019. *Chapter five: China's cyber power in a new era.* London:IISS.

Barletta, G. A., Barletta, W. A. & Tsygichko, V. N., 2011. Cyber conflict. In: *The Quest for Cyber Peace.* Geneva: ITU, pp. 53–65.

Bartlett, J., 2020. *Why is North Korea so good at cybercrime?* [Online] Available at: https://thediplomat.com/2020/11/why-is-north-korea-so-good-at-cybercrime/ [Accessed 21 07 2021].

BBC News, 2016gg. *Russia 'was behind German parliament hack'.* [Online] Available at: www.bbc.co.uk/news/technology-36284447 [Accessed 17 07 2021].

BBC News, 2017h. *Brexit vote site may have been attacked, MPs say in report.* [Online] Available at: www.bbc.co.uk/news/uk-politics-39564289 [Accessed 17 07 2021].

BBC News, 2017n. *Cyber-attack: US and UK blame North Korea for WannaCry.* [Online] Available at: www.bbc.co.uk/news/world-us-canada-42407488 [Accessed 28 08 2020].

BBC News, 2018pp. *US-China trade row: What has happened so far?.* [Online] Available at: www.bbc.co.uk/news/business-44529600[Accessed 05 09 2020].

BBC News, 2020bb. *Norway blames Russia for cyber-attack on parliament.* [Online] Available at: www.bbc.co.uk/news/world-europe-54518106 [Accessed 22 07 2021].

BBC News, 2020ii. *SolarWinds: Hacked firm issues urgent security fix.* [Online] Available at: www.bbc.co.uk/news/technology-55442732 [Accessed 26 12 2020].

BBC News, 2020mm. *US cyber-attack: Around 50 firms 'genuinely impacted' by massive breach.* [Online] Available at: www.bbc.co.uk/news/world-us-canada-55386947 [Accessed 26 12 2020].

BBC News, 2021j. *China says Microsoft hacking accusations fabricated by US and allies.* [Online] Available at: www.bbc.co.uk/news/world-asia-china-57898147 [Accessed 20 07 2021].

Bertand, N. & Desiderio, A., 2020. *How suspected Russian hackers outed their massive cyberattack.* [Online] Available at: www.politico.com/amp/news/2020/12/16/ russian-hackers-fireeye-cyberattack-447226 [Accessed 26 12 2020].

Bohn, K., 2018. *Trump confirms US conducted cyberattacks against Russia in 2018.* [Online] Available at: https://edition.cnn.com/2020/07/10/politics/donald-trump-us-russia-cyberattack/index.html [Accessed 30 08 2020].

Borger, J., 2020. *Russian cyber-attack spree shows what unrestrained internet warfare looks like.* [Online] Available at: www.theguardian.com/technology/2020/oct/19/ russian-hackers-cyber-attack-spree-tactics?CMP=Share_AndroidApp_Other [Accessed 01 01 2021].

Borghard, E., 2020a. *Cyber command's role in election defense: Important, but not a panacea.* [Online] Available at: www.lawfareblog.com/cyber-commands-role-election-defense-important-not-panacea [Accessed 17 07 2021].

Borghard, E. D., 2020b. *Operationalizing defend forward: how the concept works to change adversary behavior.* [Online] Available at: www.lawfareblog.com/ operationalizing-defend-forward-how-concept-works-change-adversary-behavior [Accessed 27 12 2020].

Borghard, E. D. & Lonergan, S. W., 2020. *To defend forward, the U.S. must strengthen the cyber mission force.* [Online] Available at: www.lawfareblog.com/defend-forward-us-must-strengthen-cyber-mission-force [Accessed 27 12 2020].

Botek, A., 2021. *European Union establishes a sanction regime for cyber-attacks.* [Online] Available at: https://ccdcoe.org/library/publications/european-union-esta blishes-a-sanction-regime-for-cyber-attacks/ [Accessed 07 01 2021].

Brandom, R., 2021. *US institutes new Russia sanctions in response to SolarWinds hack.* [Online] Available at: www.theverge.com/2021/4/15/22385371/russia-sanctions-solarwinds-biden-white-house-putin-hack [Accessed 19 07 2021].

Brustein, J., 2020. *Relentless hacking is turning all of us into data nihilists.* [Online] Available at: www.bloomberg.com/news/articles/2020-12-24/solarwinds-hack-is-the-latest-to-affirm-our-data-nihilism [Accessed 26 12 2020].

Burrow, B. P., 2013. *Engaging the Nation's critical infrastructure sector to deter cyber threats.* [Online] Available at: www.hsdl.org/?view&did=812044 [Accessed 16 07 2021].

Burt, T., 2020. *Cyberattacks targeting health care must stop.* [Online] Available at: https://blogs.microsoft.com/on-the-issues/2020/11/13/health-care-cyberattacks-covid-19-paris-peace-forum/ [Accessed 03 01 2021].

Carroll, O., 2019. *US cyber attack: Did America really try to override the Russian power grid?.* [Online] Available at: www.independent.co.uk/news/world/europe/us-cyber-attack-russia-power-grid-war-kremlin-a8964506.html [Accessed 30 08 2020].

Casear, E., 2021. *The incredible rise of North Korea's hacking army.* [Online] Available at: www.newyorker.com/magazine/2021/04/26/the-incredible-rise-of-north-koreas-hacking-army [Accessed 15 07 2021].

Cerulus, L., 2021b. *Polish politicians hit by 'large-scale' cyberattack, Russia blamed.* [Online] Available at: www.politico.eu/article/polish-politics-hit-with-by-cyberattack/ [Accessed 18 07 2021].

China Ministry of National Defense, 2015. *2015 White paper: China's military strategy.* Available at: http://english.www.gov.cn/archive/white_paper/2015/05/27/content_281475115610833.htm (Acessed 19 11 2021).

Cimpanu, C., 2020e. *FBI is investigating more than 1,000 cases of Chinese theft of US technology.* [Online] Available at: www.zdnet.com/article/fbi-is-investigating-more-than-1000-cases-of-chinese-theft-of-us-technology/ [Accessed 06 09 2020].

Cimpanu, C., 2020n. *Report: CIA received more offensive hacking powers in 2018.* [Online] Available at: www.zdnet.com/article/report-cia-received-more-offensive-hacking-powers-in-2018/ [Accessed 17 07 2021].

Cimpany, C., 2021z. *Sprawling cyber-espionage campaign linked to Chinese military unit.* [Online] Available at: https://therecord.media/sprawling-cyber-espionage-campaign-linked-to-chinese-military-unit/ [Accessed 16 07 2021].

CISA, 2017. *Alert (TA17-164A). HIDDEN COBRA – North Korea's DDoS Botnet infrastructure.* [Online] Available at: https://us-cert.cisa.gov/ncas/alerts/TA17-164A [Accessed 30 08 2020].

CISA, 2021. *Alert (AA21-200B). Chinese state-sponsored cyber operations: observed TTPs.* [Online] Available at: https://us-cert.cisa.gov/ncas/alerts/aa21-200b [Accessed 19 07 2021].

Coble, S., 2020. *CIA accused of mounting 11-year cyber-attack against China.* [Online] Available at: www.infosecurity-magazine.com/news/qihoo-accuses-cia-of-cyber/ [Accessed 07 09 2020].

CoEU, 2019a. *Council Decision (CFSP) 2019/797 of 17 May 2019 concerning restrictive measures against cyber-attacks threatening the Union or its Member States.* [Online] Available at: https://eur-lex.europa.eu/legal-content/EN/TXT/PDF/?uri=CELEX:02019D0797-20201124&from=EN [Accessed 17 07 2021].

CoEU, 2019b. *Council decision concerning restrictive measures against cyber-attacks threatening the union or its member states.* [Online] Available at: https://data.consilium.europa.eu/doc/document/ST-7299-2019-INIT/en/pdf [Accessed 17 12 2020].

CoEU, 2021. *China: Declaration by the High Representative on behalf of the European Union urging Chinese authorities to take action against malicious cyber activities undertaken from its territory.* [Online] Available at: www.consilium.europa.eu/ en/press/press-releases/2021/07/19/declaration-by-the-high-representative-on-behalf-of-the-eu-urging-china-to-take-action-against-malicious-cyber-activities-undertaken-from-its-territory/pdf [Accessed 17 07 2021].

Connell, M. & Vogler, S., 2016. *Russia's approach to cyber.* [Online] Available at: https:// apps.dtic.mil/sti/pdfs/AD1019062.pdf [Accessed 16 07 2021].

Corfield, G., 2020. *GRU won't believe it: UK and US call out Russia for cyber-attacks on Georgia last year.* [Online] Available at: www.theregister.com/2020/02/20/apt28_ hacked_georgia_uk_us_declaration/ [Accessed 20 07 2021].

Davis, J., 2020. *AstraZeneca targeted by nation-state actors via phishing attacks, Malware.* [Online] Available at: https://healthitsecurity.com/news/astrazeneca-targe ted-by-nation-state-actors-via-phishing-attacks-malware [Accessed 07 01 2021].

Davis, S., 2019. *Nato in the cyber age: Strengthening security & defence, stabilising deterrence,* Brussels: NATO Parliamentary Assembly.

Devanny, J., 2021. 'Madman Theory' or 'Persistent Engagement'? Thecoherence of US Cyber Strategy under Trump. *Journal of Applied Security Research* [online].

Dinstein, Y., 2012. The principle of distinction and cyber war in International Armed Conflicts. *Journal of Conflict & Security Law*, 17(2), pp. 261–277.

DNI, 2021. *Annual Threat Assessment of the US Intelligence Community*, Washington DC: Office of the Director of National Intelligence.

Doffman, Z., 2020. *CIA hackers accused of 11-year attack in New Chinese Cyber Report: This is what's behind it.* [Online] Available at: www.forbes.com/sites/ zakdoffman/2020/03/03/new-chinese-cyber-report-just-accused-cia-of-11-year-attack-this-is-whats-behind-the-report/?sh=11bb2ec457e6 [Accessed 19 07 2021].

Dorfman, Z., McLaughlin, K. Z. J. & Naylor, S. D., 2020. *Exclusive: Secret Trump order gives CIA more powers to launch cyberattacks.* [Online] Available at: https:// news.yahoo.com/secret-trump-order-gives-cia-more-powers-to-launch-cyberatta cks-090015219.html?guccounter=1 [Accessed 17 07 2021].

Dumortier, F., Papakonstantionou, V. & Hert, P. d., 2020. *EU sanctions against cyber-attacks and defense rights: Wanna Cry?.* [Online] Available at: https://europeanlawb log.eu/2020/09/28/eu-sanctions-against-cyber-attacks-imposed-and-defense-rights-wanna-cry/ [Accessed 07 01 2021].

EC, CoEU, 2020. *EU imposes the first ever sanctions against cyber-attacks.* [Online] Available at: www.consilium.europa.eu/en/press/press-releases/2020/07/30/eu-imposes-the-first-ever-sanctions-against-cyber-attacks/ [Accessed 17 12 2020].

Eddy, M., 2019. *APT41 is not your usual Chinese hacker group.* [Online] Available at: https://uk.pcmag.com/news/121996/apt41-is-not-your-usual-chinese-hacker-group [Accessed 17 07 2021].

EU, 2013. *Directive 2013/40/EU of the European Parliament and of the Council of 12 August 2013 on attacks against information systems and replacing Council Framework Decision 2005/222/JHA.* [Online] Available at: https://eur-lex.europa.eu/legal-cont ent/EN/TXT/PDF/?uri=CELEX:32013L0040&from=EN [Accessed 15 03 2018].

Faulconbridge, G., 2018. *What is Russia's GRU military intelligence agency?.* [Online] Available at: www.reuters.com/article/us-britain-russia-gru-factbox/what-is-russias-gru-military-intelligence-agency-idUSKCN1MF1VK [Accessed 17 07 2021].

FBI, 2021. *The China threat.* [Online] Available at: www.fbi.gov/investigate/counter-intelligence/the-china-threat [Accessed 17 07 2021].

Finlay, C., 2019. *Is Just War Possible?.* Cambridge: Polity Press.

FireEye, 2017. *APT28: At the Centre of the Storm,* Milpitas: FireEye.

FireEye, 2018a. *APT38. Unusual Suspects,* Milpitas: FireEye.

FireEye, 2018b. *APT37 (Reaper) The Overlooked North Korean Actor,* Milpitas: FireEye.

FireEye, 2019. *Double Dragon. APT41, A Dural Espironage And Cyber Crime Operation,* Milpitas: FireEye.

Global Security, 2021. *Reconnaissance general bureau.* [Online] Available at: www.globalsecurity.org/intell/world/dprk/rb.htm [Accessed 17 07 2021].

Goud, N., 2019. *China to strongly retaliate US cyber attacks.* [Online] Available at: www.cybersecurity-insiders.com/china-to-strongly-retaliate-us-cyber-attacks/ [Accessed 02 01 2021].

Goud, N., 2020. *Cyber attack on AstraZeneca COVID-19 vaccine research.* [Online] Available at: www.cybersecurity-insiders.com/cyber-attack-on-astrazeneca-covid-19-vaccine-research/ [Accessed 08 01 2021].

GOV.UK, 2020. *UK exposes series of Russian cyber attacks against Olympic and Paralympic Games.* [Online] Available at: www.gov.uk/government/news/uk-exposes-series-of-russian-cyber-attacks-against-olympic-and-paralympic-games [Accessed 01 01 2021].

Gray, C., 2004. *Interenational Law and the Use of Force.* 2 ed. Oxford: Oxford University Press.

Greenberg, A., 2018. *The toolset of an elite North Korean hacker group on the rise.* [Online] Available at: www.wired.com/story/north-korean-hacker-group-apt37/ [Accessed 18 07 2021].

Hathaway, O. A. et al., 2012. The Law of cyber-attack. *California Law Review,* 08, 100(4), pp. 817–885.

Healey, J., 2019. The implications of persistent (and permanent) engagement in cyberspace. *Journal of Cybersecurity,* 5(1).

Heginbotham, E. et al., 2015. Scorecard 9: U.S. and Chinese cyberwarfare capabilities. In: R. Corporation, ed. *The U.S.-China Military Scorecard. Forces, Geography, and the Evolving Balance of Power, 1996–2017.* s.l.:JESTOR, pp. 259–284.

Henderson, S. et al., 2018. *Chinese Espionage Group TEMP.periscope targets Cambodia ahead of July 2018 elections and reveals broad operations globally.* [Online] Available at: www.fireeye.com/blog/threat-research/2018/07/chinese-espionage-group-targets-cambodia-ahead-of-elections.html [Accessed 02 01 2021].

Hern, A., 2017. *WannaCry, Petya, NotPetya: how ransomware hit the big time in 2017.* [Online] Available at: www.theguardian.com/technology/2017/dec/30/wannacry-petya-notpetya-ransomware [Accessed 29 08 2020].

Hlevek, A., 2020. *China cyber attacks: The current threat landscape.* [Online] Available at: https://securityboulevard.com/2020/12/china-cyber-attacks-the-current-threat-landscape/ [Accessed 02 01 2021].

Hodge, N., 2020. *Russia's GRU: Spy agency known for brazenness back in the headlines.* [Online] Available at: https://edition.cnn.com/2020/06/29/europe/russia-afghanistan-gru-analysis-intl/index.html [Accessed 17 07 2021].

Holcomb, F., 2020. *Countering Russian and Chinese cyber-aggression. Prospects for transatlantic cooperation.* [Online] Available at: https://cepa.org/countering-russia-and-chinese-cyber-aggression/ [Accessed 19 07 2021].

Holland, S. & Chiacu, D., 2021. *US and allies accuse China of global hacking spree.* [Online] Available at: www.reuters.com/technology/us-allies-accuse-china-global-cyber-hacking-campaign-2021-07-19/ [Accessed 19 07 2021].

Hough, P., 2008. *Understanding global security.* 2 ed. Abingdon: Routledge.

ICRC, 1899. *Convention (II) with respect to the Laws and Customs of War on Land and its annex: Regulations concerning the Laws and Customs of War on Land. The Hague, 29 July 1899.* [Online] Available at: https://ihl-databases.icrc.org/ihl/ INTRO/150 [Accessed 28 12 2020].

ICRC, 1907. *Convention (IV) respecting the Laws and Customs of War on Land and its annex: Regulations concerning the Laws and Customs of War on Land. The Hague, 18 October 1907.* [Online] Available at: https://ihl-databases.icrc.org/ihl/INTRO/ 195 [Accessed 28 12 2020].

ICRC, 1949. *The Geneva Conventions of 12 August 1949.* [Online] Available at: www. icrc.org/en/doc/assets/files/publications/icrc-002-0173.pdf [Accessed 29 12 2020].

ICRC, 1977. *Protocol additional to the Geneva Conventions of 12 August 1949, and relating to the protection of victims of International Armed Conflicts (Protocol I), 8 June 1977.* [Online] Available at: https://ihl-databases.icrc.org/ihl/INTRO/470 [Accessed 29 12 2020].

Insikt group, 2021. *China's PLA Unit 61419 Purchasing Foreign Antivirus Products, Likely for Exploitation.* [Online] Available at: www.recordedfuture.com/china-pla-unit-purchasing-antivirus-exploitation/ [Accessed 24 07 2021].

Intelligence and Security Committee of Parliament, 2020. *Russia,* London: House of Commons.

Jacobsen, J. T., 2021. Cyber offense in NATO: challenges and opportunities. *International Affairs*, 05, pp. 703–720.

Jakobi, A. P., 2020. *Crime, security and global politics. An introduction to global crime governance.* London: Macmillan.

Janofsky, A., 2021. *China accuses US of launching cyberattacks, denies Microsoft Exchange hack.* [Online] Available at: https://therecord.media/china-accuses-us-of-launching-cyberattacks-denies-microsoft-exchange-hack/ [Accessed 20 07 2021].

Jensen, B., Valeriano, B. & Montgomery, M., 2020. *The strategic implications of SolarWinds.* [Online] Available at: www.lawfareblog.com/strategic-implications-solarwinds [Accessed 26 12 2020].

Ji Young, K., Jong In, L. & Kyoung Gon, K., 2019. The all-purpose sword: North Korea's cyber operations and strategies. In: *Silent Battle.* Tallinn: NATO CCD COE, pp. 143–162.

Johnson, A. L., 2015. *"Forkmeiamfamous": Seaduke, latest weapon in the Duke armory.* [Online] Available at: https://bit.ly/30SO7VS [Accessed 28 12 2020].

Katagiri, N., 2021. Why international law and norms do little in preventing non-state cyber attacks. *Journal of Cybersecurity*, 18(2), pp. 1–9.

Knowles, C., 2020. *Kaspersky discovers COVID-19 research related cyber threats.* [Online] Available at: https://securitybrief.eu/story/kaspersky-discovers-covid-19-research-related-cyber-threats [Accessed 02 01 2021].

Kolbe, P. R., 2020. *With hacking, the United States needs to stop playing the victim.* [Online] Available at: www.nytimes.com/2020/12/23/opinion/russia-united-states-hack.html?smid=em-share [Accessed 01 01 2021].

Kovacs, E., 2017. *Cyber spies targeting U.S. Defense, tech firms linked to China's PLA: Report.* [Online] Available at: www.securityweek.com/cyber-spies-targeting-us-defense-tech-firms-linked-chinas-pla-report [Accessed 17 07 2021].

Kramer, F. D. & Rodihan, L. S. C., 2020. *NATO needs continuous responses in cyberspace.* [Online] Available at: www.atlanticcouncil.org/blogs/new-atlanticist/nato-needs-continuous-responses-in-cyberspace/ [Accessed 23 07 2021].

KrebsOnSecurity, 2021. *At Least 30,000 U.S. Organizations newly hacked via holes in Microsoft's email software.* [Online] Available at: https://krebsonsecurity.com/2021/03/at-least-30000-u-s-organizations-newly-hacked-via-holes-in-microsofts-email-software/ [Accessed 19 07 2021].

Kshetri, N., 2014. *Cybersecurity and International relations: The U.S. engagement with China and Russia,* Greensboro: s.n.

Lavorgna, A., 2020. *Cybercrimes. Critical issues in a global context.* London: Macmillian.

Lemos, R., 2011. *'Byzantine Hades' shows China's cyber chops.* [Online] Available at: www.csoonline.com/article/2128120/-byzantine-hades--shows-china-s-cyber-chops.html [Accessed 29 08 2020].

Lewis, N., 2014. *NSA TAO: What tailored access operations unit means for enterprises.* [Online] Available at: https://searchsecurity.techtarget.com/tip/NSA-TAO-What-Tailored-Access-Operations-unit-means-for-enterprises [Accessed 19 07 2021].

Lilly, B. & Cheravitch, J., 2020. The past, present, and future of Russia's cyber strategy and forces. In: 12th International Conference on Cyber Conflict. T. Jančárková, L. Lindström, M. Signoretti, I. Tolga, G. Visky (eds.). *20/20 Vision: The Next Decade.* Tallin: NATO CCDCOE Publications, pp. 129–156.

Lindsey, N., 2019. *New CNCERT report shows most cyber attacks on China originate from United States.* [Online] Available at: www.cpomagazine.com/cyber-security/new-cncert-report-shows-most-cyber-attacks-on-china-originate-from-united-states/ [Accessed 07 09 2020].

Lopez, T., 2020. *For 2020 election, threat is bigger than Russia.* [Online] Available at: www.defense.gov/Explore/News/Article/Article/2306001/for-2020-election-threat-is-bigger-than-russia/ [Accessed 17 07 2021].

Manjikian, M., 2021. *Introduction to cyber politics and policy.* London: Sage.

Marchuk, V., 2020. *APT37.* [Online] Available at: https://attack.mitre.org/groups/G0067/ [Accessed 29 08 2020].

Martin, A., 2011. *Report: China spying extensively on U.S. Government and companies.* [Online] Available at: www.theatlantic.com/international/archive/2011/04/report-china-spying-extensively-us-government-companies/349657/ [Accessed 29 08 2020].

McCarthy, K., 2020. *Report: CIA runs secret cyberwar with little oversight after Trump gave the OK, say US government officials.* [Online] Available at: www.theregister.com/2020/07/16/cia_secret_cyberwar/ [Accessed 24 07 2021].

Merrin, W., 2018. *Digital War.* Abingdon: Routledge.

Mimoso, M., 2015. *Naikon APT group tied to China's PLA Unit 78020.* [Online] Available at: https://threatpost.com/naikon-apt-group-tied-to-chinas-pla-unit-78020/114798/ [Accessed 17 07 2021].

MITRE ATT&CK, 2021a. *APT28.* [Online] Available at: https://attack.mitre.org/groups/G0007/ [Accessed 17 07 2021].

MITRE ATT&CK, 2020b. *APT38.* [Online] Available at: https://attack.mitre.org/groups/G0082/ [Accessed 18 07 2021].

MITRE ATT&CK, 2020c. *APT41.* [Online] Available at: https://attack.mitre.org/groups/G0096/ [Accessed 06 09 2020].

MITRE ATT&CK, 2020d. *Lazarus group.* [Online] Available at: https://attack.mitre.org/groups/G0032/ [Accessed 30 08 2020].

Morris, J., 2019. Law, politics, and the use of force. In: *Strategy in Contemporary World.* 6 ed. Oxford: Oxford University Press, pp. 66–91.

Moynihan, H., 2019. *The Application of International Law to State Cyberattacks Sovereignty and Non-intervention,* London: Chatham House.

Munk, T. H., 2015. *Cyber-security in the European Region: Anticipatory Governance and Practices.* [Online] Available at: www.escholar.manchester.ac.uk/api/datastream?publicationPid=uk-ac-man-scw:266937&datastreamId=FULL-TEXT.PDF [Accessed 12 08 2020].

Mutsuo, N. & Hirofumi, U., 2017. An analysis of the actual status of recent cyberattacks on critical infrastructures. *NEC Technical Journal,* 12(7).

Nakashima, E., 2019. *U.S. Cyber Command operation disrupted Internet access of Russian troll factory on day of 2018 midterms.* [Online] Available at: www.washingtonpost.com/world/national-security/us-cyber-command-operation-disrupted-internet-access-of-russian-troll-factory-on-day-of-2018-midterms/2019/02/26/1827fc9e-36d6-11e9-af5b-b51b7ff322e9_story.html| [Accessed 01 01 2021].

NATO CCDCOE, 2013. *Tallinn Manual on the International Law Applicable to Cyber Warfare.* 1 ed. Cambridge: Cambridge University Press.

NATO CCDCOE, 2017. *Tallinn Manual 2.0 on the International Law Applicable to Cyber Operations.* 2 ed. Cambridge: Cambridge University Press.

NATO, 1949. *The North Atlantic Treaty.* [Online] Available at: www.nato.int/cps/en/natolive/official_texts_17120.htm [Accessed 16 12 2020].

NCSC, 2018. *Reckless campaign of cyber attacks by Russian military intelligence service exposed.* [Online] Available at: www.ncsc.gov.uk/news/reckless-campaign-cyber-attacks-russian-military-intelligence-service-exposed&xid=25657,157000 23,15700124,15700149,15700186,15700191,15700201,15700214 [Accessed 04 10 2020].

NCSC, 2020. *UK and allies expose Russian attacks on coronavirus vaccine development.* [Online] Available at: www.ncsc.gov.uk/news/uk-and-allies-expose-russian-attacks-on-coronavirus-vaccine-development [Accessed 01 01 2021].

Nichols, M., 2019. *North Korea took $2 billion in cyberattacks to fund weapons program: U.N. report.* [Online] Available at: www.reuters.com/article/us-northkorea-cyber-un-idUSKCN1UV1ZX [Accessed 05 08 2021].

NSA. CSS, 2021. *Support to the military.* [Online] Available at: www.nsa.gov/what-we-do/support-the-military/ [Accessed 17 07 2021].

Office of the United States Trade Representative, 2018. *Findings of the investigation into China's acts, policies, and practices related to technology transfer, intellectual property, and innovation under section 301 of the Trade Act of 1974,* Washington DC: Office of the United States Trade Representative.

Osborne, C., 2021. *Everything you need to know about the Microsoft Exchange Server hack.* [Online] Available at: www.zdnet.com/article/everything-you-need-to-know-about-microsoft-exchange-server-hack/ [Accessed 19 07 2021].

Otto, G., 2021. *Here's what we know about DarkSide ransomware.* [Online] Available at: https://intel471.com/blog/darkside-ransomware-colonial-pipeline-attack[Accessed 28 06 2021].

Paganini, P., 2021a. *Chinese PLA Unit 61419 suspected to have purchased AVs for cyber-espionage.* [Online] Available at: https://securityaffairs.co/wordpress/117608/cyber-warfare-2/pla-unit-61419.html [Accessed 17 07 2021].

Paganini, P., 2020b. *CIA hacking unit APT-C-39 hit China since 2008.* [Online] Available at: https://securityaffairs.co/wordpress/98885/apt/cia-hacking-china.html [Accessed 02 01 2021].

Paganini, P., 2020c. *North Korean hackers allegedly behind cyberattacks on AstraZeneca.* [Online] Available at: https://securityaffairs.co/wordpress/111569/cyber-warfare-2/astrazeneca-north-korea-hackers.html [Accessed 26 12 2020].

Paganini, P., 2020d. *Millions of devices could be hacked exploiting flaws targeted by tools stolen from FireEye.* [Online] Available at: https://securityaffairs.co/wordpress/112588/hacking/fireeye-tools-exploits.html [Accessed 26 12 2020].

Park, D., 2016. *North Korea cyber attacks: A new asymmetrical military strategy.* [Online] Available at: https://jsis.washington.edu/news/north-korea-cyber-attacks-new-asymmetrical-military-strategy/ [Accessed 17 07 2021].

Parker, J. & Kremling, A. M. S., 2017. *Cyberspace, cybersecurity, and cybercrime.* Thousand Oaks: SagePublications, Inc.

Park, J., Rowe, N. & Cisneros, M., 2016. South Korea's options in responding to North Korean cyberattacks. *Journal of Information Warfare*, 15(4), pp. 86–99.

Parsons, E. & Bureau, H., 2020. *Understanding the cyber threat from North Korea.* [Online] Available at: www.f-secure.com/en/consulting/our-thinking/understanding-the-cyber-threat-from-north-korea [Accessed 31 08 2020].

Parsons, E. & Raff, M., 2020. *Understanding the cyber threat from China.* [Online] Available at: www.f-secure.com/en/consulting/our-thinking/understanding-the-cyber-threat-from-china [Accessed 05 09 2020].

Plan, F. et al., 2019. *APT40: Examining a China-nexus espionage actor.* [Online] Available at: www.fireeye.com/blog/threat-research/2019/03/apt40-examining-a-china-nexus-espionage-actor.html [Accessed 02 01 2021].

Pratley, P., 2015. *State-sponsored Cyber Attacks.* [Online] Available at: www.f-secure.com/gb-en/consulting/our-thinking/state-sponsored-cyber-attacks [Accessed 23 07 2021].

Puyvelde, D. V. & Brantly, A. F., 2019. *Cybersecurity. Politics, governance and conflicts in cyberspace.* 1 ed. Cambridge: Polity Press.

Ranger, S., 2018. What is cyberwar? Everything you need to know about the frightening future of digital conflict, ZDNET. accessed 14/9/19 (December 2018). https://www.zdnet.com/article/cyberwar-a-guide-to-the-frightening-future-of-online-conflict/ (Accessed 18 11 2021).

Rash, W., 2020. *Why the Russian breach of the government affects you.* [Online] Available at: www.forbes.com/sites/waynerash/2020/12/24/why-the-russian-breach-of-the-government-affects-you/?sh=1f7ffcd01dc8 [Accessed 26 12 2020].

Raud, M., 2016. *China and cyber: Attitudes, strategies, organisation,* Tallinn: NATO CCD COE.

Ray, S., 2020. *Report: CIA conducted cyber attacks against Iran, Russia after secret trump order in 2018.* [Online] Available at: www.forbes.com/sites/siladityaray/2020/07/15/report-cia-conducted-cyber-attacks-against-iran-russia-after-secret-trump-order-in-2018/#4ff442054600 [Accessed 27 08 2020].

Reuters, 2009. *FACTBOX: Five facts about Russian military intelligence.* [Online] Available at: www.reuters.com/article/worldNews/idUSTRE53N3K820090424 [Accessed 17 07 2021].

Roth, A., 2021. *Biden to unveil Russia sanctions over SolarWinds hack and election meddling.* [Online] Available at: www.theguardian.com/us-news/2021/apr/14/biden-set-to-sanction-russian-officials-over-massive-solarwinds-hack [Accessed 25 07 2021].

Rouse, M., 2020. *Advanced persistent threat (APT).* [Online] Available at: https://searchsecurity.techtarget.com/definition/advanced-persistent-threat-APT [Accessed 29 08 2020].

Sacks, S., 2020. *China's emerging cyber governance system.* [Online] Available at: www.csis.org/chinas-emerging-cyber-governance-system [Accessed 21 08 2020].

Salehyan, I., 2010. The delegation of war to rebel organizations. *Journal of Conflict Resolution,* 54(3), pp. 493–515.

Sanger, D. E. & Perlroth, N., 2019. *U.S. escalates online attacks on Russia's power grid.* [Online] Available at: www.nytimes.com/2019/06/15/us/politics/trump-cyber-russia-grid.html [Accessed 30 08 2020].

Schmitt, M. (2013). *Tallinn Manual on the International Law Applicable to Cyber Warfare.* Cambridge: Cambridge University Press.

Schmitt, M. (2017). *Tallinn Manual 2.0 on the International Law Applicable to Cyber Operations (2nd ed.).* Cambridge: Cambridge University Press.

Schmitt, M., 2020. *Foreign cyber interference in elections: An international law primer, Part I.* [Online] Available at: www.ejiltalk.org/foreign-cyber-interference-in-elections-an-international-law-primer-part-i/ [Accessed 25 07 2021].

Schneider-Petsinger, M., Wang, J., Jie, Y. & Crabtree, J., 2019. *US–China strategic competition. The quest for global technological leadership*, London: Chatham house.

Schneier, B., 2020. *The US has suffered a massive cyberbreach. It's hard to overstate how bad it is.* [Online] Available at: www.theguardian.com/commentisfree/2020/dec/23/cyber-attack-us-security-protocols?CMP=Share_AndroidApp_Other [Accessed 26 12 2020].

Scroxton, A., 2020a. *Russia report reveals long-running cyber warfare campaign against UK.* [Online] Available at: www.computerweekly.com/news/252486422/Russia-Report-reveals-long-running-cyber-warfare-campaign-against-UK [Accessed 01 01 2020].

Scroxton, A., 2021b. *Biden sanctions Russia over SolarWinds cyber attacks.* [Online] Available at: www.computerweekly.com/news/252499384/Biden-sanctions-Russia-over-SolarWinds-cyber-attacks [Accessed 25 07 2021].

Scroxton, A., 2020c. *Data on Pfizer/BioNTech Covid-19 vaccine stolen in cyber attack.* [Online] Available at: www.computerweekly.com/news/252493445/Data-on-Pfizer-BioNTech-Covid-19-vaccine-stolen-in-cyber-attack [Accessed 03 01 2021].

Scroxton, A., 2020d. *Russia report reveals long-running cyber warfare campaign against UK.* [Online] Available at: www.computerweekly.com/news/252486422/Russia-Report-reveals-long-running-cyber-warfare-campaign-against-UK [Accessed 04 10 2020].

Seker, E., 2020. *Tallinn manual — International law to cyberspace.* [Online] Available at: https://medium.com/digital-diplomacy/tallinn-manual-international-law-to-cyberspace-fc2304ebcd93 [Accessed 15 07 2021].

Shaikh, S. A., 2014. *Cyber-espionage is more difficult to pin to a state than spying in the physical world.* [Online] Available at: https://theconversation.com/cyber-espionage-is-more-difficult-to-pin-to-a-state-than-spying-in-the-physical-world-32977 [Accessed 21 07 2021].

Shead, S., 2020. *Russia's fancy bear and cozy bear hacking groups are under the spotlight.* [Online] Available at: www.cnbc.com/2020/07/17/fancy-bear-cozy-bear-russia.html [Accessed 30 08 2020].

Simmons + Simmons, 2020. *The European fight against cybercriminals: 'cyber sanctions'.* [Online] Available at: www.simmons-simmons.com/en/publications/ckh6ccivq1229095252uglboa/the-european-fight-against-cybercriminals-cyber-sanctions- [Accessed 07 01 2021].

Simmons, B. A., 2011. International studies in the global information age. *International Studies Quarterly,* 55(3), pp. 589–599.

Starks, T., 2020. *Russia, China and Iran trying to hack presidential race, Microsoft says*. [Online] Available at: www.politico.com/news/2020/09/10/russia-china-iran-cyberhack-2020-election-411853 [Accessed 27 12 2020].

Stilgherrian, 2020. *Cyber attacks on COVID-19 vaccine production are not quite a war crime*. [Online] Available at: www.zdnet.com/google-amp/article/cyber-attacks-on-covid-19-vaccine-production-are-not-quite-a-war-crime/ [Accessed 03 01 2021].

Stubbs, J., 2020a. *Exclusive: Suspected North Korean hackers targeted COVID vaccine maker AstraZeneca - sources*. [Online] Available at: www.reuters.com/article/uk-healthcare-coronavirus-astrazeneca-no/exclusive-suspected-north-korean-hackers-targeted-covid-vaccine-maker-astrazeneca-sources-idUKKBN28719Y [Accessed 08 01 2021].

Stubbs, J., 2020b. *Hackers steal Pfizer/BioNTech COVID-19 vaccine data in Europe, companies say*. [Online] Available at: https://uk.mobile.reuters.com/article/amp/idUKKBN28J2Q7 [Accessed 03 01 2021].

Swanson, A. & Kang, C., 2020. *Trump's China deal creates collateral damage for tech firms*. [Online] Available at: www.nytimes.com/2020/01/20/business/economy/trump-us-china-deal-micron-trade-war.html [Accessed 05 09 2020].

Tennis, M., 2020. *Russia ramps up global elections interference: Lessons for the United States*. [Online] Available at: www.csis.org/blogs/technology-policy-blog/russia-ramps-global-elections-interference-lessons-united-states [Accessed 17 07 2021].

The Cyber Diplomat, 2019. *Tallinn manual — A brief review of the international law applicable to cyber operation*. [Online] Available at: https://medium.com/@cyberdiplomacy/tallinn-manual-a-brief-review-of-the-international-law-applicable-to-cyber-operations-5643c886d9e2 [Accessed 15 07 2021].

The Washington Post, 2019. *The Cybersecurity 202: Here's how the military's hacking arm is gearing up to protect the 2020 election*. [Online] Available at: www.washingtonpost.com/news/powerpost/paloma/the-cybersecurity-202/2019/05/08/the-cybersecurity-202-here-s-how-the-military-s-hacking-arm-is-gearing-up-to-protect-the-2020-election/5cd23177a7a0a46cfe152c7e/ [Accessed 04 10 2020].

The White House, 2021h. *The United States, joined by allies and partners, attributes malicious cyber activity and irresponsible state behavior to the people's Republic of China*. [Online] Available at: www.whitehouse.gov/briefing-room/statements-releases/2021/07/19/the-united-states-joined-by-allies-and-partners-attributes-malicious-cyber-activity-and-irresponsible-state-behavior-to-the-peoples-republic-of-china/ [Accessed 19 07 2021].

Touré, H. I., 2011. Cyberspace and the threat of cyberwar. In: ITU, ed. *The Quest for Cyber Peace*. Geneva: ITU, pp. 7–13.

TrendMicro, 2018. *A look into the Lazarus Group's operations*. [Online] Available at: www.trendmicro.com/vinfo/us/security/news/cybercrime-and-digital-threats/a-look-into-the-lazarus-groups-operations [Accessed 30 08 2020].

US Congress, 2021. *Russian cyber units*. [Online] Available at: https://crsreports.congress.gov/product/pdf/IF/IF11718 [Accessed 17 07 2021].

US Cyberspace Solarium Commission, 2020. *The United States of America cyberspace solarium commission,* s.l.: The United States of America Cyberspace Solarium Commission.

US DHS, 2020. *Data security business advisorys*. [Online] Available at: www.dhs.gov/sites/default/files/publications/20_1222_data-security-business-advisory.pdf [Accessed 26 12 2020].

US DoD, 2018a. *Military and Security Developments Involving the Democratice People's Republic of Korea.* [Online] Available at: https://fas.org/irp/world/dprk/dod-2017.pdf [Accessed 17 07 2021].

US DoD, 2018b. *Summary. Department of defence. cyber strategy 2018,* Washington DC: The Department of Defence.

US DoJ, 2020. *Seven International Cyber Defendants, Including "Apt41" Actors, Charged In Connection With Computer Intrusion Campaigns Against More Than 100 Victims Globally.* [Online] Available at: www.justice.gov/opa/pr/seven-international-cyber-defendants-including-apt41-actors-charged-connection-computer [Accessed 17 07 2021].

US DoJ, 2021. *Four Chinese nationals working with the Ministry of State Security charged with global computer intrusion campaign targeting intellectual property and confidential business information, including infectious disease research.* [Online] Available at: www.justice.gov/opa/pr/four-chinese-nationals-working-ministry-state-security-charged-global-computer-intrusion [Accessed 19 07 2021].

US Gov, 2016. *China's intelligence service and espionage operations.* [Online] Available at: www.uscc.gov/sites/default/files/transcripts/June%2009,%202016%20Hearing%20Transcript.pdf [Accessed 17 07 2021].

UN, 1980. *The convention on prohibitions or restrictions on the use of certain conventional weapons which may be deemed to be excessively injurious or to have indiscriminate effects.* [Online] Available at: https://treaties.un.org/Pages/ViewDetails.aspx?src=TREATY&mtdsg_no=XXVI-2&chapter=26&lang=en[Accessed 28 12 2020].

UN, 2020. *UN Charter.* [Online] Available at: www.un.org/en/sections/un-charter/un-charter-full-text/ [Accessed 07 12 2020].

USCC, 2019. *Chinese intelligence services and espionage threats to the United States.* [Online] Available at: https://bit.ly/3nOW1IA [Accessed 17 07 2021].

USCYBERCOM, 2018. *Achieve and maintain cyberspace superiority. Command vision for US cyber command,* s.l.: United States Cyber Command.

USCYBERCOM, 2021. *Our history.* [Online] Available at: www.cybercom.mil/About/History/ [Accessed 17 07 2021].

Valeriano, B., 2020. *Cost imposition is the point: Understanding U.S. cyber operations and the strategy behind achieving effects.* [Online] Available at: www.lawfareblog.com/cost-imposition-point-understanding-us-cyber-operations-and-strategy-behind-achieving-effects [Accessed 27 12 2020].

Vijayan, J., 2021. *North Korea's Lazarus group expands to stealing defense secrets.* [Online] Available at: www.darkreading.com/threat-intelligence/north-koreas-lazarus-group-expands-to-stealing-defense-secrets/d/d-id/1340259 [Accessed 17 07 2021].

Vincent, J., 2021. *US and allies accuse Chinese government of masterminding Microsoft Exchange cyberattack.* [Online] Available at: www.theverge.com/2021/7/19/22583251/us-government-blames-china-cyberattacks-microsoft-exchange-hack [Accessed 19 07 2021].

Waters, R., 2019. *How the trade war is damaging the US tech industry.* [Online] Available at: www.ft.com/content/16fa93ba-bf69-11e9-b350-db00d509634e [Accessed 05 09 2020].

Westby, J., 2020. *Russia has carried out 20-years of cyber attacks that call for international response.* [Online] Available at: www.forbes.com/sites/jodywestby/2020/12/20/russia-has-carried-out-20-years-of-cyber-attacks-that-call-for-international-response/?sh=440e91096605 [Accessed 28 12 2020].

Westby, J. R., 2011. A call for geo-cyber stability. In: ITU, ed. *The Quest for Cyber Peace*. Geneva: ITU, pp. 66–76.

WikiLeak, 2017. *Vault 7: CIA hacking tools revealed*. [Online] Available at: https://wikileaks.org/ciav7p1/ [Accessed 19 07 2021].

Wilson, E., 2021. *The inside story on RedFoxtrot: How network traffic analysis revealed ties to Chinese military*. [Online] Available at: www.recordedfuture.com/redfoxtrot-inside-story-network-traffic-analysis/ [Accessed 17 07 2021].

Zetter, K., 2016. *NSA hacker chief explains how to keep him out of your system*. [Online] Available at: www.wired.com/2016/01/nsa-hacker-chief-explains-how-to-keep-him-out-of-your-system/ [Accessed 19 07 2021].

Zittrain, J., 2017. "Netwar": The unwelcome militarization of the. *Bulletin if the Atomic Scientists,* 73(5), pp. 300–304.

6 Cyberterrorism and Ransomware

State-supported Groups

Introduction

In cyberwarfare, the interest is limited to the online space as information warfare, and cyberwarfare is linked to specific targets as a part of an ongoing conflict. In cyberterrorism, there are not the same constraints. Instead, cyberterrorism causes fear to a broader audience, and the actions can potentially harm anyone within the targeted area. This is a constantly developing area and since 2021, the conceptualisation of ransomware attacks has changed which beings these online attacks under the terrorism-umbrella. Therefore, this chapter will predominately focus on ransomware attacks, as the attacks share significant similarities with cyber-terrorism. Chapter 6 will also distinguish between the state-sponsored actors and state-supported actors.

The state-supported groups are closely interlinked with the state and cyberwarfare. In comparison, the state-supported actors act independently but follow the overall state agenda. These are the actors behind the wave of ransomware attacks, and they are often seen as cybercriminals. Currently ransomware groups are perceived as state-supported groups operating with near impunity as long as they are following simple rules; not attacking own citizens, and following they are following the overall strategies of the state in the target selection. The sections in this chapter focus on motivations, the groups, and the means and methods used in the context of cybersecurity strategies.

Conceptualising Terrorism

Cyberterrorism is defined as using computer network tools to shut down CIs, such as energy, transportation, government operations; or the activities are used to coerce or intimidate governments or citizens (Lewis, 2002). The groups are predominately linked to a request for change, spread fear, or support a particular political stance. Defining and differentiating cyberterrorism from politically motivated cyber attacks and groups can be complicated as the different actors share the same means and methods. If a

DOI: 10.4324/9781003126676-6

state sets out the goal, but the groups act independently, the actions are likely to be perceived as cyberwar and warfare (state-sponsored actors). Compared with this definition, the state-supported groups share a common goal with the state. However, they act entirely autonomously in the decision-making process and the operations (state-supported actors). Other groups and activities are considered in relation to cybercrime. These are politically motivated non-state actors operating independently of state actors and state goals, i.e. hacktivism and online.

Offline Terrorism Definitions

There is not developed a universally agreed definition of terrorism and cyberterrorism. Although most states have developed national definitions, there are inconsistencies in applying them to particular incidents. This means that states are left to unilateral defining terrorism as a concept. The definition can change due to the state's interest at a particular time (Marsili, 2019). The definition of terrorism is closely related to the actual perspective on political conflict or disagreement. The perspective "one man's terrorist is another man's freedom fighter" is widely recognised as the core element of failing to develop a comprehensive definition (Carver, 2016, p. 125; Bassiouni, 2001; Ganor, 2002; Kennedy, 1999). These two sides, terrorism versus freedom fighters, depend on the political stance where the conceptualisation may reveal ideological or political bias (Matusitz, 2021).

  Terrorism, in a simple form, can be defined as "politically motivated violence against non-combatants to coerce through fear" (Matusitz, 2021, p. 18; Marks, 2004, p. 107). Walter (1969) created a clear definition of the aim of terrorism by stating that "[t]he proximate aim is to instil terror; the ultimate end is control" (Matusitz, 2021, p. 18; Walter, 1969, p. 13). However, Denning (2000) has a broader definition of terrorism by stating that it is "[t]he unlawful use or threatened use of force or violence by a person or an organised group against people or property with the intention of intimidating or coercing societies or governments, often for ideological or political reasons" (Denning, 2000). The crucial elements are the unpredictability of attacks, and this makes terrorism threatening. Attacks can happen anywhere by striking sensitive targets indiscriminately, cause widespread fear, and make people feel helpless and insecure. This feeling of uncertainty erodes the feeling of security. It is the main drive for people questioning the level of security, the foundation of society, and governments and governmental actors' ability to secure the state and its citizens (Matusitz, 2021, p. 21). The aim of terrorism is not the victims who suffer from the attacks. Instead, the targets are governments, societies, groups of citizens to trigger a reaction or overreaction of fear, repulsion, intimidation, or radicalisation (Cronin, 2003, p. 32).

Table 6.1 International organisations' terrorism definitions

Institution	Definition
UN proposed definition (2005)	Any action constitutes terrorism if it is intended to cause death or serious bodily harm to civilians or non-combatants, with the purpose of intimidating a population or compelling a Government or an international organisation to do or abstain from doing any act (UN, 2005; Costa, 2005, p. 2)
The EU (2017)	...given their nature or context, may seriously damage a country or an international organisation where committed with the aim of: — seriously intimidating a population, or — unduly compelling a Government or international organisation to perform or abstain from performing any act, or — seriously destabilising or destroying the fundamental political, constitutional, economic or social structures of a country or an international organisation (European Parliament, 2015; EU, 2017)
NATO (2019)	The unlawful use or threatened use of force or violence, instilling fear and terror, against individuals or property in an attempt to coerce or intimidate governments or societies, or to gain control over a population, to achieve political, religious, or ideological objectives (NATO, 2019)

Sources: NATO (2019); European Parliament (2015); UN (2005); Costa (2005).

THE LEGISLATIVE FRAMEWORK

On several occasions, the UN has failed to develop an internationally agreed definition of terrorism, making the fight against terrorism more efficient. Yet, more specialised definitions are developed in resolutions and conventions (United Nations, 2021b; European Parliament, 2015). UN Resolution 1566 from 2004 stated that all acts with the purpose of private a state of terror "[u]nder no circumstances justifiable by considerations of a political, philosophical, ideological, racial, ethnic, religious or other similar nature" (European Parliament, 2015; UN, 2004). However, international actors have developed their definitions as outlined in Table 6.1.

Like the definitions above, states have defined terrorism in a national context. Below are selected definitions to enhance the understanding of the concept of terrorism:

Table 6.2 States' terrorism definitions

State	Name	Definition
The United States	The Federal Criminal Code, Title 18 of the United States, Section 2331 of Chapter 113(B), International terrorism	International terrorism is defined as intended activities that "involve violent acts or acts dangerous to human life, which violating criminal laws of the U.S. or any State: (i) to intimidate or coerce a civilian population; (ii) to influence the policy of a government by intimidation or coercion; or (iii) to affect the conduct of a government by mass destruction, assassination, or kidnapping" (US.Gov, 1991)
The United States	Section 802 of the USA PATRIOT Act (Pub. L. No. 107–52). Amendment to Section 2331 of Title 18, United States Code, Domestic terrorism	Domestic terrorism is defined as intended acts dangerous to human life which violates the criminal laws of the United States or of any State: "(i) to intimidate or coerce a civilian population; (ii) to influence the policy of a government by intimidation or coercion; or (iii) to affect the conduct of a government by mass destruction, assassination, or kidnapping" (US Gov, 2001)
The United Kingdom	Terrorism Act 2000, section 1. Amended by Terrorism Act 2006 and Counter-Terrorism Act 2008.	Terrorism is defined as the use of a threat designed to influence the government, or an international governmental organisation, or to intimidate the public or a section of the public. The use of threat is made to advance a political, religious, racial or ideological cause. These actions are: (a) involves serious violence against a person, (b) involves serious damage to property, (c) endangers a person's life, other than that of the person committing the action, (d) creates a serious risk to the health or safety of the public or a section of the public, or (e) is designed seriously to interfere with or seriously to disrupt an electronic system (GOV. UK, 2000)
Russia	2006 Federal Law 36-FZ	Terrorism is defined as "the ideology of violence and the practice of influencing the adoption of a decision by public authorities, local self-government bodies, or international organisations connected with frightening the population and (or) other forms of unlawful violent actions" (European Parliament, 2015)

Table 6.2 Cont.

State	Name	Definition
China	The 2003 Decision on Issues Related to Strengthening Anti-Terrorism Work	Terrorism is defined as "activities that severely endanger society that have the goal of creating terror in society, endangering public security, or threatening state organs and international organisations and which, by the use of violence, sabotage, intimidation, and other methods, cause or are intended to cause human casualties, great loss to property, damage to public infrastructure, and chaos in the social order, as well as activities that incite, finance, or assist the implementation of the above activities" (European Parliament, 2015)

Sources: US Gov (1991); US Gov (2001); GOV.UK (2000); European Parliament (2015).

Cyberterrorism Definitions

Like conventional terrorism, there are no comprehensive and universal recognised definitions of cyberterrorism (Dogrul et al., 2011, p. 31). The first time the term 'cyberterror' appeared was in the mid-eighties. The concept appeared as a vaguely formulated idea at the early stage of developing computer technologies. No one could predict how influential computers networks and devices would be in everyday life (Luiijf, 2014).

Like cybercriminals, adoption of the online environment to reach a broader audience, terrorists, extremists, and activists has embraced the benefit of online operations. Traditional terrorist groups have used the Internet to spread ideas, recruiting and communicating, but the use of virtual spaces, networks, and computer technologies goes beyond these practices. As state actors, non-state actors use the online environment to promote their causes by conducting cyber attacks in various forms. These actions can cause an incredible impact on society when targeting various essential CIs (Halopeau, 2014).

Denning argued (2000) that an attack should result in violence against persons or property or at least cause enough harm to generate fear (Denning, 2000; Weimann, 2004, p. 4). The claim that there should be violence included is problematic. However, there can be significant damage online and offline caused by cyber attacks. It is an outdated presumption that they should be an element of violence and threat of violence in real life for an attack to be classified as cyberterrorism. Therefore, attacks on computing systems and data destruction would not count as violence (Conway, 2014, p. 2). However, with the merger of online and offline life and the increasing use of computer technologies, systems, devices, and networks on multiple levels, that argument

Table 6.3 Cyberterrorism definitions

Name	Definition
Collins (1997)	"The intentional abuse of a digital information system, network, or component toward an end that supports or facilitates a terrorist campaign or action" (Paulose, 2013; Bowman-Grieve, 2015, p. 86; Marsili, 2019)
Denning (2000)	"Unlawful attacks and threats of attack against computers, networks, and the information stored therein when done to intimidate or coerce a government or its people in furtherance of political or social objectives" (Denning, 2000f)
Weimann (2004)	"The use of computer network tools to harm or shut down critical national infrastructures (such as energy, transportation, government operations)" (Weimann, 2004; OSCE, 2013, p. 16)
Ogun (2012)	"Cyberterrorism is generally understood to mean unlawful attacks and threats of attack against computers, networks, and the information stored therein when done to intimidate or coerce a government or its people in furtherance of political or social objectives" (Ogun, 2012; OSCE, 2013, p. 16)

Sources: Denning (2000f); Bowman-Grieve (2015); Paulose (2013); Marsili (2019); Weimann (2004); OSCE (2013); Ogun (2012).

is no longer valid. An online attack on computer systems, technologies, and devices has an equal detrimental political, social, and economic impact as offline violence. A cyber attack might not trigger as many physical causalities as offline attacks. Yet, they can still have a potentially catastrophic impact, such as shutting down a large portion of power plants, cause economies to crash, or populations deprived of essential services (Munk, 2015, p. 176). According to Conway (2014), the definition of cyberterrorism links the convergence of cyberspace and terrorism. This is not the convergence of cyberspace and something big or something bad. If a cyber attack is classified as cyberterrorism, it is likely to be both 'big' and 'bad' (Conway, 2014). However, the critical element is that the attack has a political motive, but it is less important than the attack being conducted through cyberspace or have been linked to the online environment during the process.

THE LEGISLATIVE FRAMEWORK

In the absence of a formal definition, traditional UN terrorism conventions and protocols prohibit terrorism against CI sectors, such as transportation, aviation and maritime, nuclear, and government sectors, which can be transferred to the online environment. The UN recognises an increase in attacks on ICTs by terrorists to commit, incite, recruit, find, or plan terrorist attacks. But the organisation fails to define cyberterrorism (United Nations, 2021a). NATO defines cyber terrorism as "a cyber attack using or exploiting computer or communication networks to cause sufficient destruction or disruption to generate fear or to intimidate a society into an ideological goal" (Marsili, 2019, p. 173). Contrary to conventional terrorism, the actors do not need to be physically present to carry out online terrorist activities. Cyberterrorism makes actions easier for the actors to engage in their actions from a distance (Dogrul et al., 2011, p. 30).

The EU has not developed a cyberterrorism definition but uses the exiting terrorism framework combined with the cybercrime framework. Already in 2011, Europol highlighted that there is a definitional problem regarding the term cyberterrorism. The lack of international consensus creates problems when cyberterrorism is used to describe activities, such as attacks on CI, intellectual property theft, and using computer technologies for circulating propaganda or communication (Munk, 2015, p. 175; Europol, 2012, p. 11). A limited number of states have developed explicit cyberterrorism provisions, but most are transferring the terrorism legislation to the online environment. An example of a definition is incorporated in the US PATRIOT Act 18 USC 2332b's, where cyberterrorism is "acts of terrorism transcending national boundaries", which further references activities and damage defined in the US Computer Fraud and Abuse Act (CFAA) 18 USC 1030a-c (Theohary & Rollins, 2015, p. 9). On the state level, cyberterrorism is defined by the FBI as

[[A]ny] premeditated, politically motivated attack against information, computer systems or computer programs, and data which results in violence against non-combatant targets by sub-national groups or clandestine agents.

(Marsili, 2019, p. 173)

CONCEPTUALISING CYBERTERRORISM

After 9/11, the security and terrorism discourses began to include the idea of cyberterrorism. Using the online environment could create opportunities for terrorist organisations, such as Al Qaeda and the Islamic State of Iraq and Syria (ISIS), to cause significant damage from the distance. This added a new political dimension to terrorism and generated debates about national security, including cyberspace and the online environment (Weimann, 2004). Yet, the significance of the online environment should not be underestimated. The use of the Internet and computer technologies has been instrumental for terrorists' activities on the ground. Although these terrorist organisations have embraced the online environment, they have not engaged in large-scale cyber attacks. Instead, the groups have predominately used cyberspace to spread propaganda, communicate, and recruit new members (Bowman-Grieve, 2015, p. 87; Denning, 2011).

Cyberterrorism can be conducted against a state or/and its citizens on multiple levels. The attacks do not necessarily require a high level of computer capabilities and capacities. Terrorists may use the digital space to advance their agendas by attacking CIs to create offline disruption or damage (Veerasamy, 2020; Cohen, 2014). Compared with cyberwarfare, these attacks are less sophisticated, and there is not the same level of investment made into hardware and software. Hackers with less develop computing skills can easily buy hacking exploits and tutorials online. Investments in toolkits, exploits or hacking software can be weighed against the outcome of online attacks (Cohen, 2014). These attack forms might include well-known means and methods, such as DoS and DDoS attacks or web defacement. Other means and methods are linked to circulating misinformation to a broad audience, hacking to stealing, corrupting, or destroying data. Malware or exploitation of system vulnerabilities can make systems unavailable, disrupt the use of computer systems or networks to disrupt, damage, or destroy the target (Veerasamy, 2020; Cohen, 2014).

Ransomware attacks are becoming a dominant attack form, and until 2021, it was classified as a financial cybercrime (Europol, 2021). However, due to the frequency and the impact of some of these attacks, the US has linked ransomware to terrorism. Other Western states have fallen short of using the terrorism typology. Instead, they have classified ransomware as a national security threat. The attack's origin and the lack of interest from host states to stop the attacks against foreign political institutions, interests, and CI severely impact the civil population. Cyber attack methods are not static, and terrorism classification should be adjusted accordingly to changes in means, methods, and motives. Although the activities of the ransomware groups are not terrorism in the classical sense, the new move to equal the ransomware groups with terrorism opens up for a new interpretation of cyber attacks where the clear political link is missing.

Motivation

Ransomware is malware that encrypts the targets data and holds the information at ransom. The victim is unable to access files, databases, or applications while the data are encrypted. The earliest examples of ransomware were identified in the late 1980s. At that time, payments were sent by ordinary mail. Today, the ransom is paid using cryptocurrency or credit card. During the process, encryption of data inflicts substantial damage and expenses for the target (McAfee, 2021; Malware Bytes, 2021a).

In 1989, the Harvard-trained biologist Popp created the first documented ransomware. This was the AIDS Trojan virus that was distributed to 20,000 infected floppy disks labelled 'AIDS Information – Introductory Diskettes', which locked the user's computer drive. Popp sent the diskettes to AIDS researchers attending the International AIDS conference organised by the World Health Organization. The victims were demanded to send 189 dollars to a post office box owned by the PC Cyborg Corporation to unlock their files. Apart from this attack, ransomware was rarely used until the mid-2000s, when the encryption became more sophisticated. (Lutkevich, 2020; Palmer, 2021b). Today, the attack vectors for ransomware have been expanded to include applications used on IoT and mobile devices. The encryption is becoming more complex, but the attacker does not need sophisticated skills or technological knowledge. Ready-to-use ransomware kits and Ransomware-at-a-Service (RaaS) are easily accessible on the Dark Web. These RaaS features encryption is emerging from collaboration among communities of ransomware developers (Lutkevich, 2020).

Defining Ransomware

In 2020, it was estimated that the cost of ransomware attacks worldwide was approximately 20 billion dollars. This estimation is nearly 75% higher than in 2019. Check Point Research (2021) reported that ransomware attacks increased by 57% in the first half of 2021 compared with the number of attacks in 2020. Between April and March 2021, Check Point Research observed an average of 1,000 organisations every week being impacted by ransomware attacks. This signifies an overall increase of 102% of organisations affected by ransomware attacks in the first five months of 2021 (Check Point, 2021).

THE ATTACK ROUTE

Ransomware is created on past computer worms and viruses, and the recon-struction of these existing malware makes them challenging to manage. The ransomware is malicious software that encrypts files and documents; it can be launched towards single PCs to entire networks, including servers (Chapple, 2021; Palmer, 2021b; Europol, 2020, p. 25). As highlighted in Table 6.4, ransomware attacks deployed against large corporations often have different stages where the threat actors change during the process.

Table 6.4 Ransomware attack route

Step	Action
One	Threat actors access the computer systems by using multiple attack vectors and malware types
Two	The access to the system is subsequently sold to other threat actors, who operate the next phase, i.e. the IT infrastructure mapping, privilege escalation, lateral move, data exfiltration, etc.
Three	The threat actor is now able to finalise the attack by deploying the ransomware

Source: Europol (2020, p. 25).

The attackers use a lateral movement technique, which allows them to install ransomware on numerous computers simultaneously or search for valuable data on networks, such as credit card information stored on servers. The main principle of lateral movement is to gain access privileges. When the hacker has accessed the computer on the network, their goal is to find connection identifiers (credentials) to give them superior rights to conduct the malicious operation (Benazet, 2021).

The key point is that the attackers use the weak points in Internet-facing servers or remote-desktop logins to enter the systems. This access enables the attackers to secretly gain control before launching the encryption tools (Palmer, 2021b). The significant element in some malware, like Maze, is that the malware can be in the victim's server for several months before the attack is executed. Attackers can take their time to reconnaissance online activities and other vulnerabilities. For example, the actors can monitor internal communications to identify critical moments for the deployment of the ransomware where the attack would cause significant issues for the victims, such as merging, selling, and big meetings with customers/sales. By deploying the ransomware before key events, they can put extra pressure on the victims to pay the ransom demand (Europol, 2020, p. 26).

DOUBLE AND TRIPLE-EXTORTIONS

These online attacks pose a significant threat to businesses, organisations, and states, including a growing number of attacks against CI targeting supply chains and third-party services. The ransomware groups are constantly upgrading their business module by including innovative means and measures to their services. The cybercriminals continue their profitable attacks by making them more targeted innovative attack types include a new way of pressuring the victims. A new innovative way is to steal and make extortionary threats to disclose sensitive information by auctioning off victims' data if the ransom demand is not met (Europol, 2020, p. 7; Chapple, 2021). After refusing to pay the ransom forwarded by the Babuk group, the Metropolitan Police Department, the Washington DC, was subjected to an information leak, where numerous sensitive documents, police officers disciplinary files, and intelligence reports were uploaded (Suderman, 2021; Brewster, 2021).

The groups also create pages where they auction off the extorted data. REvil has created a 'Happy Blog' to the action of the data to coercive victims to pay the ransom and name and shame those who do not. The Happy Blog enlists recent victims of the groups' activities, attaching a sample of the stolen data as evidence. REvil also provides the victims with a 'trial' decryption to prove that they can decrypt the data again if they pay (Cluley, 2021; KrebsOnSecurity, 2020).

The victims can either pay the ransom, restore the system using backups, decrypt the files using an available key, or start building up their systems from scratch (Palmer, 2021b). It is now a mainstream practice for ransomware groups to use 'leak sites' to upload sensitive information from the victims who refuse to pay the ransom. This double-extortion tactic puts extra pressure on the targets. The list of ransomware groups using this tactic includes names such as Ako, Avaddon, CLOP, Darkside, DoppelPaymer, Maze, Mespinoza (Pysa), Nefilim, NetWalker, RagnarLocker, REvil (Sodinokibi), and Sekhmet (Cimpanu, 2020a). Some of the groups are small-time operators. However, some of the largest ransomware groups, Maze, DoppelPaymer, REvil, Conti and NetWalker, use this tactic (Cimpanu, 2020a),

Triple-extortions　The creative thinking and complex scenario analysis of double-extortion ransomware attacks have further developed a third-extortion technique. This technique includes third-party victims, company clients, external colleagues, and service providers influenced by the attacks, which are impacted even if they are not directly attacked. These actors are vulnerable to being extorted by affiliation with the original target (Check Point, 2021; Walsh, 2021). The DarkSide group has introduced triple-extortion in its franchise by including a calls service that enables the affiliates to call the victims and pressure them to pay the ransom. This service operated directly from the online platform.

Another innovation is using DDoS attacks against targets to add extra pressure to the ransom negotiations (KrebsOnSecurity, 2021). In 2021, data from the US Financial Services Information Sharing and Analysis Center (FS-ISAC) showed that in 2020, malicious actors had targeted more than 100 financial services companies using ransom DDoS attacks (Hathaway, 2021). In 2021, the REvil (Sodinokibi) ransomware group announced that they had increased their activities. The group has added free two-stage service to their double-extortion scheme, i.e. DDoS attacks and phone calls to victim's business partners and mass media (Check Point, 2021).

Actors

Most ransomware groups are linked to criminal networks. However, various Russian and Chinese groups operate with implicit support from the authorities. In return, some criminal groups are also engaged with the state's intelligence agencies. Subsequently, they are only conducting their ransomware activities outside the state, where they have taken steps to prevent that local companies are affected (Barnes, 2021). The Chinese espionage group ATP27, which has close ties to the Chinese state, has in 2020 moved into financial cybercrime using ransomware to encrypt the servers of gaming companies. ATP27 and Winitti, known as DRBControl, are linked to the Chinese state and operation as state-sponsored and state-support groups depending on the nature of their operations (Zurier, 2021; Muncaster, 2021). Although the attack conducted by the groups is lacking the same level of sophistication as generally observed in state-sponsored operations, there is strong evidence that the means and methods are also used by APT27, known as TG-3390, Emissary Panda, BRONZE UNION, Iron Tiger, and LuckyMouse (Ilascu, 2021).

North-Korea's Lazerus has also successfully crossed over its role as a state elite hacking group to engage with state-supported ransomware operations (Mathews, 2020). The Ukrainian Cl0p group has also been behind attacks against organisations in the US and South Korea. A hacker arrested in Canada is believed to be involved in the ransomware group Netwalker. Yet, the epicentre for the ransomware attacks is linked to Russia and the former Soviet States (Tidy, 2021b).

Russian Groups

The Russian groups have spread ransomware attacks to the extent that the attacks have been sided with terrorism. The fear and uncertainty of these attacks have overshadowed financial cybercrime groups. The Russian groups deliberately focus on targets aboard. Groups from North Korea and China are probably given the same level of protection. However, this is not so obvious as the groups from Russia, who do nothing to hide their origins. The Russian groups operate on their own initiative, but it is difficult to establish whether other groups enjoy the same level of freedom.

The anonymity provided by cyberspace makes it challenging to make a precise attribution to the attackers and where the attack originates. Yet, a definite pattern was observed that created a link between the attack and Russia and the block of former Soviet states. However, the focus is primarily pointing towards Russia as the leading provider of safety for hackers. The evidence is linked to four areas. First, most of the prominent ransomware actors advertise their malicious software products on Russian-speaking Dark Web forums. Second, the groups operate during Moscow business hours, and the activities stop during Russian public holidays. Third, in most cases, the ransomware code contains specific instructions that automatically abort attacks on computer systems based on Russian keyboard configurations. Finally, there are reported a considerably low number of ransomware attacks against targets in Russia or former Soviet states than the number of attacks on Western entities (Tidy, 2021b). The following table contains a non-exclusive list of Russian ransomware groups:

Table 6.5 Outline of ransomware groups

Name	Method	Targets
TrickBot	Observed first time in 2016. One of the most prevalent Trojans distributed through malicious spam emails and Emotet The infected machine on the network will re-infect previously cleaned machines when they rejoin the network	Linked to attacks on banks and financial institutions The monetary demands are set to mirror the victim's ability to pay
Ryuk	Observed first time in 2018. Initial compromise is performed through TrickBot distributed via spam email or Emotet's geo-based download function	Linked to attacks on high-profile organisations likely to pay the ransom demand Attacks tailored to target enterprise environments Uses the double-extortion scheme
Conti	Observed first time in 2020 Shares code with the Ryuk ransomware Use weaponised malicious email links, attachments, or stolen Remote Desktop Protocol (RDP) credentials	Linked to attacks worldwide; a majority of attacks launched against US organisations Uses the double-extortion scheme
DoppelPaymer	Observed first time in 2019 Initially infecting machines with a spam email containing either a malicious link or malicious attachment The then downloads Emotet and Dridex malware into infected systems	Linked to attacks on manufacturing, retail and wholesale, and government Uses the double extortion scheme
REvil (Sodinokib)	Also known as REvil and Sodin Observed the first time in 2019, Uses spam emails, exploit kits, and compromised RDP accounts, exploiting vulnerabilities in Oracle WebLogic	Linked to attacks on transportation, manufacturing, and retail/wholesale Using the double/triple-extortion scheme
Pysa (Mespinoza)	Observed first time in 2019 Uses remote access Trojans (RAT) called ChaChi The code includes obfuscations and persistence with added DNS tunnelling and Port-Forwarding/ Proxy functions	Linked to several attacks in the healthcare industry, finance, IT, non-profit, public sector, food service industries Targeting organisations sensitive to data loss or system downtime Using the double-extortion scheme

(*continued*)

Table 6.5 Cont.

Name	Method	Targets
Maze	Observed first time in 2019 Uses email campaigns, exploit kits, such as Fallout and Spelevo, and hacked RDP services to gain access The Maze group has officially claimed that they have closed the project of attacking	Linked to attacks in manufacturing, legal, financial services, construction, healthcare, technology, retail, and government Targeting primarily US organisations Uses the double extortion scheme
RagnarLocker	First observed in 2019 Uses Internet-exposed remote desktop protocols (RDP) endpoints and compromised managed service providers (MSP) to breach and enter the internal networks	Linked to attacks on the cloud service provider, communication, construction, enterprise software, and travel industries. Uses the double extortion scheme
DarkSide	First observed in 2020 Uses Silent Night botnet (Zloader backdoor) for delivery Does not attack hospitals, hospices, schools, universities, non-profit organisations, or government institutions	Linked to attacks on services, manufacturing, and transportation services Uses the double/triple-extortion scheme Ransomware as a service entity

Sources: HelpNetSecurity (2021); Acronis (2021a); Acronis (2021b); Tavares (2020); Davis (2020); Cimpanu (2020c); Europol (2020); Gatlan (2021); Kennelly et al., (2020); Malwarebytes Labs (2021a); Hanel (2019); Malwarebytes Labs (2021b); Cimpanu (2020b); FBI Flash (2021); Osborne (2021a); Malware Bytes (2021b); The Maritime Executive (2020).

Ransomware-as-a-Service (RaaS)

RaaS is a new model designed to enable an attacker with little knowledge of malware, coding, or cyber attacks to conduct an attack, such as ransomware, to generate a profit (CIS, 2021). The RaaS enterprise enables non-technical criminals to launch ransomware attacks by leasing ransomware variants. The franchised use of ransomware can enable everyone to get the operation up running quickly and affordably. The RaaS groups allow other cybercriminals to lease ransomware variants for operations. However, the methods vary from simple attacks to increasingly sophisticated attacks conducted by technically knowledgeable criminals (Crowdstrike, 2021; Ransomware Task Force, 2021, p. 5).

The RaaS businesses provide a user-friendly service that allows attackers to select their victim, claim a ransom, provide a bitcoin wallet address, and deploy the ransomware attack. The RaaS services, then, take a percentage of the paid ransom (CIS, 2021). The RaaS groups are competitive online. They run marketing campaigns, business websites, videos, white papers and have an active Twitter presence (Crowdstrike, 2021). These forums often require a deposit from the customers, which they will get back if the ransomware does not perform as expected (Europol, 2020; Goodin, 2020). Other more established ransomware groups have already raised the bar by only allowing trusted affiliates into their programs. To be accepted, the customers need to have displayed their capabilities to infect large companies. Moreover, RaaS groups like REvil expels groups that cannot infect large companies or are inactive on the platform for more than a week. (Europol, 2020, p. 27; KrebsOnSecurity, 2021).

DarkSide surfaced in 2020 on Russian language hacking forums. The DarkSide sells malware and hacking services to cybercriminals, who breach companies. The attackers use DarkSide's services to lock up data, progress the ransomware negotiation, and leaking files if the victim does not pay the ransom (Brewster, 2021; Gross, 2021; Bostrup, 2021). DarkSide also promotes services on the Dark Web, where several main Russian-language forums function as both advertising platforms and a facilitator allowing various groups to interact and form partnerships (Gross, 2021; Bostrup, 2021). This group claims that it only targets big companies. It has imposed a form of attack ethics forbidding its affiliates from launching attacks on organisations within several industries, such as healthcare, funeral services, education, the public sector, and non-profits (KrebsOnSecurity, 2021). In 2019, the REvil was identified as behind several high-profile attacks and they increased their activities (KrebsOnSecurity, 2019; KrebsOnSecurity, 2021). REvil has also based its operations on the RaaS business model to conduct operations, recruit affiliates or partners, and spread the malware (Palmer, 2020; BBC News, 2021a).

Means and Methods: Deterrence and Defence

Ransomware is currently the most flourishing criminal industry, which constitutes a risk to individuals' personal and financial security and threatens national security and human life (Ransomware Task Force, 2021, p. 7). A series of uncoordinated attacks have been launched against energy infrastructure, healthcare, and transportation services. A group of attackers' intent to cause chaos could infect several systems online in simultaneous attacks aiming to crippling numerous elements of CI and NCIs (Chapple, 2021). Beyond the economic impact, where the attackers gain monetary reward for their attacks. Attackers also select their target based on their profile and whether the attacks will impact societal, political, and economical.

The targeted institutions and industries lack an adequate level of protection against these attacks. Public institutions and IC services often have irreplaceable data that would have a long-term impact if they were made unavailable. This makes it more likely that the victims would pay the ransom to get the encryption code and restore the computer network (Lutkevich,

2020). However, it is never guaranteed that the encryption code is delivered or that the data are intact. The attack increase in 2020 and 2021 are linked to advanced attacks combining automation with hacking. Due to these complex attacks, it becomes difficult to recover and restore the services (Sophos, 2021).

Ransomware and Terrorism

The overarching question is, are these ransomware attacks merely a part of a criminal enterprise, which sometimes targets public or political institutions. Or can the activities be sidelined with terrorism due to the means and methods used, the target selection, the impact on society? Ransomware is not just about extortion and money. It is an attack form that goes beyond business, government, academic, and geographic boundaries. The attacks have affected the healthcare industry, schools, and higher education, police states, cities, governments, and other vital services (Ransomware Task Force, 2021, p. 3). The attack identified from the state-supported actors involves, for example, espionage where the attackers discover corporate secrets, technologies, and political information. Another helpful tactic is attacking CI, CII, and ICTs of state institutions, departments, or companies. This can severely damage the victims of these practices and diminish their defensive capabilities. These attacks can also be a taster session to check cyber capabilities and the actual cybersecurity level of the victim (Hernández, 2021).

To classify as terrorism, some elements need to be satisfied. An attack needs to be an act of terrorism; it must be a violent act or an act that is dangerous to human life, property, or infrastructure. These elements are included in various terrorism definitions (Patel, 2021). However, recent attacks on CI and other assets differ from the conventional terrorist groups where the attacks are targeting physical assets. These attacks often have a direct impact on ordinary citizens. Yet, this is not necessarily the case with cyberterrorism, but these attacks often have an indirect physical impact. Already in 2013, US President Obama issues an executive order to enhance the protection of CIs, stating that "cyber threat to critical infrastructure continues to grow and represents one of the most serious national security challenges we must confront" (Patel, 2021, p. 29). With the ransomware attacks, the prediction in 2013 has become a reality.

FOR POLITICAL, IDEOLOGICAL, OR RELIGIOUS REASONS

Cyber terrorism is an organic concept, and due to the lack of a clear definition, several different groups can be classified as terrorists. Assumptions derive from the definition that there should be a strong link between ideology and the involvement of terrorism. The actors are seen as acting/driven by a hostile ideology as they carry out the acts. However, terrorism can also be considered when the hostile ideology on the individual level is minimal or absent but the political. This lead to discussions about whether an actor without a cause is, in fact, a terrorist (Holbrook & Horgan, 2019; Crenshaw, 2011, pp. 75–76). Schmid (1988) has argued that:

> Terrorism is an anxiety-inspiring method of repeated violent action, employed by (semi-) clandestine individual, group, or state actors, for idiosyncratic, criminal, or political reasons.
>
> (Schmid & Jongman, 1988, p. 28)

According to this definition, ransomware attacks can be classified as terrorism as there is uncertainty and fear included, and the actions are conducted randomly. Moreover, the activities can be conducted for criminal reasons. Regarding the Russian groups, the activities are only enabled by the acceptance of the state, which also set out the context for launching attacks.

Identifying the politically or ideologically elements in the planning and execution of violence is a factor in classifying the activities as either cyberterrorism or cybercrime. This is important in relation to the legislation and the powers used in the investigation and prosecution (Holbrook & Horgan, 2019, p. 3). In 2021, ransomware attacks have been sidelined with terrorism by US authorities. The impact of the attacks and the fear of these attacks prompted the US DoJ to coordinate the anti-ransomware efforts using the protocols currently used for terrorism. This will also allow the US authorities to take offensive actions against ransomware groups (Walsh, 2021). By making this classification, the actors can use institutional structures, processes, and practices reserved for counter-terrorism activities. Yet, these tools are not available to manage financially motivated cybercrime. The ransomware groups want to be seen as a threat and cause fear to pressure the companies into paying the ransom. However, they might not want Western governments and institutions to develop new processes and practices which limits their activities. Nor do they want law enforcement to trace and ruin their lucrative business (Palmer, 2021a; KrebsOnSecurity, 2021).

The motivation of the ransomware groups is not necessarily political, but they follow the current climate of geopolitics and the directions of the national state. The lack of a clear ideology or political motivation makes this classification problematic but not impossible due to the target selection by the groups. Many terrorists do not have a history of a political, ideological, or religious engagement or practice before being engaged in terrorism. Therefore, it is essential to look at the actual act, its impact on society, and the political link.

ACT OF TERRORISM

Ransomware can be linked to the use of, or a threat designed to influence the government, an international governmental organisation, or intimidate the public or a section of the public (Costa, 2005; UN, 2005). These attacks were previously seen as a nuisance and managed in isolation. But they are now becoming a national security problem and can no longer be managed in isolation (Gura, 2021). Ransomware attacks have reached a significantly dangerous level where ransomware groups paralyse computer networks of essential CIs and services.

These attacks affect the public beyond the original target. For example, various police departments have been targeted by ransomware groups. These attacks have caused a substantially high level of interruption of essential services. Emergency phone lines and services are taken down; important case files are either not accessible or have disappeared (Suderman, 2021). In 2019, a ransomware attack on an unnamed US Maritime Transportation Security Act (MTSA)-regulated facility shut down the service for 30 hours (The Maritime Executive, 2020; Ransomware Task Force, 2021, p. 7). There have also been attacks on public services. Several local councils worldwide have been targeted in attacks. Ransomware groups have attacked significant metro centres like Hackney (London), Tusla, Baltimore, Denver, Knoxville, and New Orleans. In 2021, The City of Liege in Belgium has been attacked. This attack was a warning to the EU after it launched a new Joint Rapid Response Team to manage cyber attacks (Cimpanu, 2021a).

Although ransomware attacks are not actual repeated violent actions, they have the required element of danger. Cyber attacks are not considered as being physical in the same way as conventional terrorism. However, there are physical elements included. Although the attackers are moving around in a nonphysical sphere, cyberspace, they might launch an attack on a physical medium such as a healthcare facility or a power plant. Some of these attacks might not be dangerous in themselves, but they create dangerous situations by stopping access to vital services (Patel, 2021, p. 32). Harm and injury based on ransomware attacks are at risk, as the frequency and the cost of these attacks are growing (Hathaway, 2021). Clearly, attacks on energy grids, nuclear plants, or critical assets could have devastating consequences, including human casualties (Ransomware Task Force, 2021, p. 7).

In February 2020, a ransomware attack on a natural gas pipeline operator shut down the operations for two days (Ransomware Task Force, 2021, p. 8). In 2020, RagnarLocker was behind a ransomware attack against the Portuguese multinational energy company Energias de Portugal (EDP). Stealing or damaging property also falls under the scope of danger if it belongs to a public or private entity and is linked to essential services (Patel, 2021, pp. 32–33). The EDP attack is significant as it affected a company delivering an essential service to 19 countries on four continents with a customer base of more than 11 million households. The ransomware group threatened to leak more than 10TB of sensitive files if the ransom was not paid. These documents include confidential information about billing, contracts, transactions, clients, and partners (Gatlan, 2020; Muncaster, 2020).

The Political Element

The groups do not have the same feature as traditionally actors promoting a particular political stance. These groups are political because they exploit a regulatory vacuum and gain support from national states allowing them to act with near impunity if their activities align with the state's cyber strategy.

RANSOMWARE GROUPS: STATE-SUPPORTED GROUPS

Attacks launched against Western states should be seen in synergy with the state-sponsored actors. The state-sponsored groups are separated by one degree from the state as they act alone under state actors' direction. The state-supported groups are separated by two degrees from the state as they act solely on the group's initiatives within a context defined by the state (Gross, 2021). On the one side, the ransomware groups do not have close ties to the state similar to state-sponsored groups. Usually, ransomware actors are non-state actors with no direct employment by the Staten. On the other side, they are not non-state actors exercising their right to protest. So the challenge is to classify these actors and identify the link to the state. States use various groupings to distance themselves from the activities – or indirectly support the actors as their activities align with the political agenda. Another method deployed by states is to indirectly support the actors, which creates a buffer zone between the state and the actors. This makes it easier for the state to deny involvement if these attacks are detected. The strategy to support or sponsor politically motivated actors is also beneficial in terms of the diplomatic repercussions of the cyber attacks (Hernández, 2021). The ransomware groups are not operating on the request of Russia, but they operate with the tactical acceptance of Russian strategies in terms of target selection (Khurshudyan & Morris, 2021).

THE 'ONE RULE'

The cybercriminals follow their agenda, mixing criminal and political activities with the state's indirect support. The rationale behind the growing number of attacks originating from Russia is the 'one rule' of Russian hacking. The ransomware groups can attack anyone as long as the attack is not launched on friendly soil (Tidy, 2021b; Khurshudyan & Morris, 2021). In return, they are left alone by the state without the risks of prosecution. Because of the high ransom payment, these attacks are financially successful. This tactic creates a vicious circle where the attack form keeps developing and drawing more people into the illegal enterprise (Palmer, 2021a).

There seem to be handshake agreements in place between the ransomware groups and the Russian state. As long as the ransomware groups leave Russia and selected countries alone, they can do whatever they want to and make money the way it suits them (Khurshudyan & Morris, 2021; Lee, 2021; Palmer, 2021a). As a result, the ransomware groups are becoming increasingly bold, showing off their wealth obtained from these ransomware attacks, knowing that tracing, arresting, and prosecuting would not happen within the safe states. The groups can operate freely as long as they play by the 'one rule' (Lee, 2021).

The ransomware codes are evidence that precautions are taken. The ransomware codes are written not to be installed on systems that have Russian-language keyboards, coming from Russian IP addresses, or have installed Russian-language packs to prevent breaking the 'one rule' agreement (Khurshudyan & Morris, 2021). The underlying conditions from the 'one rule' agreements are as follows: leave Russia and Russian interests alone, and when the state needs the hackers, the groups will provide the help (Palmer, 2021a). Groups, such as DarkSide and REvil, are aware of the dangers of breaking the rule. The groups takes precautions to ensure they follow the 'one rule'. For example, they vet business affiliates and customers. They conduct interviews in Russian to seek out potential Western intelligence actors to prevent them from infiltrating the organisations (Khurshudyan & Morris, 2021).

Not all ransomware attacks are linked to state or state interests despite originating from a country well known to be involved in attacks. However, intelligence services likely co-operate with cybercriminals to engage in intelligence gathering. When the US Treasury Department sanctioned the group Evil Corp in late 2019, the department has also claimed that the Russian security service, the FSB, cultivates and co-opts hackers to engage in ransomware attacks (Khurshudyan & Morris, 2021). This loose partnership between groups allows state actors to explore enemies' computer systems by using information from these groups. These groups will forward information they obtain in return for impunity (Gross, 2021).

Russia has rejected the idea that Russia's stance on not investigating attacks on foreign entities has prompted the increase of attacks. In 2016, after Russian hackers were accused of interfering in the US Presidential elections, President Putin hinted at a hands-off approach by stating that the hackers did not break Russian law. This is the same stance the Russian authorities are taking in 2021. The Russian authorities argue that hackers exist anywhere; it is not only a Russian issue. On Russian state television, Putin dismissed claims about Russia's involvement in the attack on the meat plant JBS in 2021 by stating that "Russia does not 'deal with some chicken or beef. This is just ridiculous'". (Khurshudyan & Morris, 2021).

NEAR IMPUNITY

Although these ransomware groups are conducting severe crimes, they also operated with near impunity. They are based in jurisdictions where the public authorities are either unable or unwilling to prosecute them. This problem is intensified by financial systems where attackers can receive the ransomware funds without being traced (Ransomware Task Force, 2021, p. 5). The Russian government has taken the stance that these individuals are not attacking

Russian interests. According to President Putin and Kremlin, Russian law does not have provisions to prosecute these ransomware attacks on foreign soil (Gross, 2021). The actual legislative initiative is within the government and parliament. If the Russian state wanted to deal with the problem, they have the power to do so. Yet, there are other obstacles. Even if Western law enforcement can identify the members behind the ransomware groups, they are unlikely to prosecute them. The Russian constitution protects the ransomware groups if they stay in Russia. According to the constitution, Russian citizens cannot be extradited to prosecution in a foreign country. (Palmer, 2021a).

Attacks on Healthcare Services and Research

Hospitals and other medical centres have been a popular target among ransomware groups: the attacks on these facilities generated fear and uncertainty. Alone, in 2020, the attacks have cost millions of dollars in ransomware and the public from delay in treatment and potential loss of life (Ransomware Task Force, 2021). There are numerous entry points into healthcare networks, making it attractive for threat actors to access hospital computers and networks, deliver payload malware, and steal data (Branch et al., 2019). During the pandemic, these groups targeted vulnerable institutions and threatened patient care and safety using a similar tactic to conventional terrorists. Moreover, the ransomware groups took advantage of the global situations and the fear in society to intimidate and coerce for economic gain (Hathaway, 2021). At the beginning of the COVID-19 pandemic, the Maze ransomware group released a statement on their website claiming that they would not attack healthcare organisations during the pandemic. This was a part of the group's misinformation campaign linked to their activities. The group had already attacked an urgent care centre in Texas and released stolen patient data when the ransom demand was refused. The selected examples in Table 6.6 show the impact ransomware has on the victim and the wider society.

Attacking healthcare services and facilities have been a significant target during the COVID-19 pandemic, which increased the dangers for citizens. The attacks are not only directed towards US services, but they had launched globally. The increase of medical technology and the need to access information online to provide critical care, make appointments, and run the facilities have increased the risks (Branch et al., 2019).

Stealing data or disrupting the use of facilities falls under the scope of terrorism. Stealing data might be dangerous, but it depends on the data type (Patel, 2021, p. 32). However, the threat of double or triple-extortion can determine the victims' decision-making process when weighing up the cost and the consequences. The consequences severely affect the organisation's ability to operate and access essential data to provide essential services. This can force the target to pay the ransom against advice from law enforcement

Table 6.6 Ransomware attack examples

State and targets	Impact	Ransom
The United States University of Vermont Medical Care (2020)	The attack affected 5,000 computers on the hospital's IT network Disrupting several services, i.e. financial systems, radiology services. Medical records were missing, and treatments were recreated from memory. Systems were restored one by one after the attack	Nothing published about a ransom demand or leaks
Germany Duesseldorf University Clinic (2020)	The attack led to gradually failing systems and data access. Unable to provide emergency care. Incoming patients diverted. One patient died after being sent to another facility 30 km away	The attackers withdrew the ransom demand after German police reached out. The hospital has received a decryption key to restore the system
The United Kingdom The Hammersmith Medicine Research Facilities (2020)	Severe attack, but the hospital was able to halt and restore the computer systems within a day	Did not meet the ransom demand. The ransomware group published 2,300 personal historical details of thousands of former patients, dated 8–20 years back
New Zealand Waikato District Health Board (DHB) (2021)	Attack on four hospitals crashed the computer systems and phone lines, causing errors in the payroll system. Elective surgeries and outpatient appointments were cancelled; could not send lab tests electronically. Everything was done manually	Documents have been released onto the Dark Web, including correspondence, medical records, and financial data
France The Villefranche-sur-Saône Hospital Complex and Hospital in Dax-Côte d'Argent (2021)	Two French hospitals attacked, and a third hospital acted pre-emptively. The attack impacted almost all information systems. Patients were transferred to other facilities	A ransom of 50,000 dollars in Bitcoin was demanded. No public information about payment or leaks

Table 6.6 Cont.

State and targets	Impact	Ransom
Ireland **Ireland's Healthcare System (2021)**	The attack paralysed health services for a week. Cutting off the online access to patient records delayed COVID-19 testing. Cancelled medical appointments for radiation treatments, MRIs, gynaecological visits, endoscopies, and other health services	A ransom of 12,999,000 dollars was demanded. The attackers provided unverified decryption tools. But still threatened to publish data

Sources: Perlroth & Satariano (2021); France24 (2021); Livingstone (2021); RNZ (2021); Goodwin (2020); Europol (2020, pp. 27–28); Ransomware Task Force (2021); Silomon (2020); Cimpanu (2020b).

and cybersecurity actors (Branch et al., 2019). However, the table above shows the variety and the impact these attacks have. Some of the attacks only affect a limited number of systems, such as the attack in the UK. Although these attacks have consequences for the target entity, they do not directly affect the facilities and internal systems, i.e. data extortion and a short-term disruption (UK). Apart from the UK attack, the other attacks in the table demonstrate that attacks cause a substantial and long-lasting impact with consequences for patients' health and safety.

Attacks on CI: The Colonial Pipeline and JBS

In 2003, the US DHS Director, Ridge, argued that for causing significant damage, the terrorist no longer needed bombs or explosives to damage the financial sector or take down a power grid. Instead, they can use computer technologies and interconnected networks to carry out the atrocities (Weimann, 2004, p. 3). The ransomware attacks have a dangerous impact. On national levels, there are a large number of different systems supporting CIs. Systems are interlinked, and there is a high level of cyber dependencies. However, for a conventional terrorist to cause terror, archive strategic goals, or have a notable effect, the attackers need to launch multiple attacks over a long period. Traditional terrorist groups would have to attack multiple targets simultaneously for a long time to create terror, archive the strategic goals, or have a noticeable effect (Lewis, 2002). However, the ransomware attacks are different; one attack can cause a long-term effect for several people and services, cause fear, and get worldwide attention. Two attacks in 2021 were the trigger for the change in the perception of ransomware attacks:

Table 6.7 Two major ransomware attacks in 2021

Company	Attack	Impact
The Colonial Pipeline	Closed down its 5,500 miles of pipeline, which carries 45% of the US East Coast's fuel supplies The pipeline transport daily 2.5 million barrels of refined gasoline, diesel, and jet fuel from the US Gulf Coast to New York	Impacted people and companies are relying on Colonial Pipeline's services. i.e. Hospitals, emergency medical services, law enforcement, fire departments, airports, truck drivers and the public
JBS	Suspended operations at its nine beef processing plants after a ransomware attack JBS controls approximately 20% of the slaughtering capacity for cattle and hogs	Impacted the meat production line, other facilities, sale and distribution, and customers. Concerns about a shortage of meat raised concerns about pricing

Sources: Associated Press (2021); Bing (2021); Otto (2021); Rosenbaum (2021); Polansek & Mason (2021).

Attack on CI: Colonial Pipeline

The first attack was the attack launched towards the Colonial Pipeline operator on the US East Coast. The company shut down the pipeline as a precaution to prevent the attackers from obtaining information that could allow the theme to attack sensitive parts of the line (Sanger et al., 2021; Associated Press, 2021; Otto, 2021). The shutdown lasted several days, led to increased prices, panic buying, and local fuel shortage (Bing, 2021). The US President Biden claimed that his administration would pursue measures to disrupt this foreign ransomware groups' operation ability. It is not ruled out that these measures might include retaliatory cyber attacks (Suderman, 2021b). The FBI attributed the attack to the DarkSide group, and President Biden subsequently claimed this group would be eliminated and prosecuted. However, since the group operates from Russia or one of the former Soviet states, it is unlikely that the US would have a successful prosecution due to the 'one rule' agreement with the Russian authorities (Sanger et al., 2021; Associated Press, 2021).

Attack on Essential Services: JBS

Shortly after the Colonial Pipeline attack, the world's largest meat supplier, JBS, was attacked. This attack impacted several of its pork, poultry, beef, and prepared-food plants in the US, Australia, and Canada (BBC News, 2021a; Sorvino, 2021). Although the production was restored quickly, there have been concerns raised about the production and distribution line and the company's market domination. The food and agriculture sector has not received the same government attention level compared with other CIs and essential services. This area was not considered a CI in the US until 2003 (Rosenbaum, 2021). The attack acts as a wake-up call for the US meat industry, highlighting the vulnerabilities in the food supply chain and the importance of having a more diverse meat processing capacity (Quinn, 2021). The FBI has attributed the JBS attack to the ransomware group REvil (Sodinokibi) (Aggarwal, 2021; Lerman, 2021; BBC News, 2021a).

Responding to the Attacks: DarkSide and REvil

DARKSIDE

The Darkside RaaS group attempted to distance themselves from the Colonial Pipeline attack, arguing that their goal was to make money, not creating societal problems (Palmer, 2021a). The DarkSide stated: "We are apolitical, we do not participate in geopolitics, do not need to tie us with a defined government and look for other our motives [sic]" (KrebsOnSecurity, 2021; Bostrup, 2021). The actors claimed that they now have established a check on their partners to avoid similar disturbances. This step back was caused by the widespread attention and the pressure caused by this attack. The harsh reaction to the attack from the US might have an impact on its future attack routes. Moreover, the reaction should also be considered in line with the JBS attack that triggered the link between ransomware groups, national security threats, and terrorism. It is not the first time this group has tried to make a PR spin regarding their activities. In a modern Robin Hood style, they claim to take from the rich and give something back to the poor. In 2020, the group announced on its public blog that they would donate parts of the ransom income to the non-profit organisations: Child International and The Water Profit (Otto, 2021; Vaas, 2021). After the Colonial Pipeline attack, the pressure on the DarkSide group increased, and they uploaded a message to their affiliates stating that an unnamed law enforcement agency has disrupted a large part of its public infrastructure. Shortly after this public statement, DarkSide's name-and-shame blog, ransom collection site, and breach data delivery network were seized, and their cryptocurrency wallet funds were removed (Afifi-Sabet, 2021; Vaas, 2021).

Yet, this attack has shaken the ransomware community and it has been described as a mistake that transformed a lucrative but overlooked area to become subjected to intensive governmental scrutiny and policy change labelling the activities as national security threats. The administrators for a widely used Russian cybercrime forum, XSS, suddenly banned all ransomware advertising and activities on its platform, including promoting services and discussions (Afifi-Sabet, 2021; DataBreaches.net, 2021). The ransomware Babuk has also ceased its operation, handing over its ransomware source code to a new team (Afifi-Sabet, 2021). This might be an immediate but temporary retreat due to the negative attention. However, most operators are operating in their closed groups. They will resurface under new names and with new, improved ransomware variants and new innovative routes to laundering the money from the attacks (Afifi-Sabet, 2021).

The REvil group claimed on YouTube and the Telegram Channel, Russian OSINT, that the attack on JBS Food was intended for the Brazilian entity – not the US. Therefore, the group did not understand the US reaction and why they began to interfere with this matter. Additionally, to the US' harsh reaction and proposed legislation prohibiting ransomware payments, REvil highlighted that potential ransom prohibition preventing victims from paying the ransom would not affect future ransom demands. Additionally, the group declared that they were not affected by being called terrorists (Spring, 2021; Rubins, 2021; Paganini, 2021). Despite the brazen statement, REvil changed its platform policy, instituting pre-moderation for its partner network. The group also claimed it would ban any attempt to attack governmental or public, educational, or healthcare organisations (Vaas, 2021).

The RaaS group still managed to conduct a new ransomware attack in the aftermath of the JBS attack. Before the 4 July weekend holiday in the US, the group targeted organisations using the Kaseya VSA remote management software and requested a 70-million-dollar ransom. REvil conducted a supply-chain attack by leveraging a vulnerability in the software to target multiple managed service providers and their customers. (Lawler, 2021; Osborne, 2021b). Shortly after this attack, all known websites linked to the group went offline on the Dark Web. This raised speculation that authorities had targeted them, either Russia or the US. It might also be that the group decided to disappear for a while (BBC News, 2021b). The group's public representative, Unknown, went silent too. It is not unusual that ransomware groups go offline for some time to return later or to regroup. It could be that the groups felt the pressure from the media coverage and the US threats to take action if the Russian authorities did not act or internal disagreements (Morris, 2021; Mehrotra, 2021). When the group went offline, they left some victims from the Kaseya attack without access to their system. Some victims had paid the ransom; others negotiated with the group. Kaseya announced later that they had obtained a universal decryptor tool (Mehrotra, 2021).

Strategies and the Game

The Game Payoff

The ransomware groups continue attacking CIs despite the enhanced focus on cyber-security and the means and methods used. As long as these ransomware groups continue to operate from Russia with relative impunity, nothing will change. Yet, the US President Biden administration has increased the rhetoric stating that Russia appears to harbour groups like DarkSide and REvil. Yet, there is no clear evidence that Russia is directly involved in these activities (Khurshudyan & Morris, 2021). The cost–benefit calculation is essential to consider in relation to the accommodation offered by the host government to the groups. The ransomware groups know that they can operate freely if it does not create collateral damage for the host country. However, this position might change if the international society imposes a cost. For example, with the new link between ransomware and terrorism, the targeted states might impose harsher measures as deterrence. For example, the targeted states have different options to change the status quo. They can decide to do nothing or impose costs by retaliating against the groups and their sponsors (Sandler & Arce M, 2003, p. 7). They can also decide to enhance their defensive measures by making it more difficult to launch successful attacks. That would involve closer cooperation with relevant stakeholders, national and transnational. They can also do both by developing a multilayered strategy.

STRATEGIES AND COSTS

The ransomware operators' essential tactics and operations are usually associated with terrorism. The preferred tactic is intimidation, coercion, extortion, property damage, disruption of services, and public order. All these elements are included in terrorism definitions worldwide. This means that the global community should consider all these threats as terrorism based on the apparent threat to economic prosperity and security. However, little has been done to make this link beyond the US stance. It is time for authorities to start managing the threats, including classifying ransomware activities as a form of terrorism (Hathaway, 2021). NATO has highlighted that Russia constitutes a threat due to its intensified hybrid actions against its member states and partners, including proxies' actions. The cyber threats to the member states' security are complex, destructive, and coercive, were systematically and frequent ransomware attacks and other malicious cyber attacks constantly target CIs and democratic institutes (NATO, 2021).

Governmental counter-terrorism strategies are either proactive or reactive. Proactive strategies allow the state actors to go aggressively after the groups to eliminate their operational capacities, such as destroying their resources, infrastructure, and actors. The reactive strategy includes a proactive measure to limit the consequences, such as diverting the attack (Sandler & Arce, 2003, p. 7; Arce & Sandler, 2005, p. 184). Therefore, states should weigh the cost and the payoff for each deterrence and defensive strategy they choose to impose for both the host state and the groups. Russia and the ransomware groups are currently benefiting from their relationship. As long as the cost is not increasing, Russia has no reason to change its strategic position. The groups fulfil Russia's agenda by causing chaos and uncertainty in Western states. However, if the Western states begin to impose costs, such as sanctions and freezing assets, Russia might change its position (Arce & Sandler, 2005, p. 184). The first step to unlock more powerful measures requires that states classify ransomware attacks as terrorism.

After the DarkSide attack on Colonial Pipeline, the White House administration called the attackers 'hackers'. They did not use the stronger narrative of terrorists or terrorism about the attack. Nevertheless, the DarkSide attack meets vital elements of terrorism legislation. For example, 18 USC 2331 focuses less on the motivation of terroristic acts and more on the intent in (i) to intimidate or coerce a civil population (US.Gov, 1991). According to the UN, cyber attacks might bear the characteristics of terrorism, such as install fear of continuance of political or social objectives (UNODC, 2012, p. 11). After the JBS attack, the US DoJ has formed an internal task force to manage ransomware. Subsequently, the US DoJ linked ransomware and terrorism by prioritising the investigation by using structures traditionally reserved for terrorism (Scroxton, 2021c; Bing, 2021; Security, 2021). These attack methods are now considered national and economic security threats to the nation (Bing, 2021). The US DoJ recommended that senior officials pursue cases more aggressively, including the FBI and the US Secret Services. The DoJ sent internal guidance to US Attorney's offices across the country that the new task forces in Washington should centrally coordinate the ransomware investigations (Ransomware Task Force, 2021, p. 25).

INSURANCE PAYMENT

Various areas related to managing ransomware should be incorporated into cybersecurity strategies. For example, it could be a requirement for businesses to report ransomware attacks, and they should also be encouraged not to pay the ransom. In the current climate, companies are unwilling to report these incidents that might delay a solution to the problem, allowing them to return to normal operations. Currently, the investigations are too slow and time-consuming, leaving the victims unable to resume their operations (Security, 2021). A coordinated governmental response is needed to ensure that cyber resilience is enhanced on multiple levels, including international diplomatic efforts and prosecution for cybercriminals.

Asking for ransom is a tactic used by terrorist groups over the years. Groups have deployed an umbrella of means and methods to gain international publicity from their activities and gain large ransom payments (Wilkinson, 2011, p. 27). Over the years, ransomware groups have developed a multibillion-dollar industry based on these attacks. The total amount of ransom paid by victims reached nearly 350 million dollars worth of cryptocurrencies in 2020. Compared with 2019, the amount paid in ransom increased by 311%. However, most payments are shared with a small number of very organised cybercriminals, such as Evil Corp and Darkside. For example, 199 deposit addresses received approximately 80% of all the payments in 2020, where a limited group of 25 addresses received nearly half of these payments (Lee,

2021). For a long time, ransomware groups have considered the insurance companies' practices as facilitating an 'endless pot of money' (Lerman & Vynck, 2021).

Although authorities strongly discourage making ransom payments that only encourage criminal networks to continue these attacks, Colonial Pipeline decided to pay the ransom. The rationale for this payment was the impact the attack had on people and companies relying on Colonials Pipeline's services (Associated Press, 2021). The company paid DarkSide 75 bitcoins, which equals nearly 5 million dollars. However, the US Authorities later recovered a large portion of the ransom (Sabbagh, 2021b; Associated Press, 2021; Shaban et al., 2021). The REvil ransomware group got an impressive 11 million dollars from the attack after having encrypted JBS' files and disrupted its operations in the US and Australia (Halfacree, 2021; Tung, 2021b; Lerman, 2021).

Some insurance companies have argued that the payment is lower than the actual cost of rebuilding systems and data afterwards. The costs of restoring compromised systems, any resulting downtime, or lost business after the attack are often more expensive than paying the ransomware demand. Yet, there is a mounting pressure on these companies not to pay the cybercriminals to discourage more attacks with higher ransom demands. This has forced insurance brokers to rethink their insurance policies (Lerman & Vynck, 2021; Wolff, 2021). Yet, some of the new policies introduced had consequences. The French insurance company AXA officially announced in 2021 that they would no longer cover the ransom. The company decided to take this step due to the uncertainty regarding the legality of making these payments as the French Senate had raised the possibility of introducing a payment ban. Within days after this decision, the company was targeted, too (Perlroth & Satariano, 2021; Ikeda, 2021; Wolff, 2021).

The current issue surrounding ransom payment needs to be addressed. Paying the ransom is still legal as the hacking groups are seldom members of banned terrorist groups (Sabbagh, 2021b; Sabbagh, 2021a). Legislation has been introduced in several countries as a response to kidnappings by terrorist groups. For example, British extortion laws prohibit ransom payments to terrorists. The UK Terrorism Act 2000 criminalises instances of terrorist financing. The UK Terrorism Act 2000 has been amended by Section 42 of the Counter-terrorism and Security Act 2015, which prohibit insurance companies from making payments in response to terrorist demands (GOV.UK, 2015; GOV.UK, 2000). The G8 member states also committed to rejecting ransom payments to terrorists in line with the UN's approach. The UN Security Council Resolution (UNSCR) 2133 from 2014 covers kidnap for ransom. UNSCR 2133 explicitly calling for the member states to prevent making ransom payments, financial assets, or economic resources available for those involved in terrorism (Home Office, 2014; UN, 2014). The background for expanding the legal provision is that paying terrorist organisations will provide the groups with monetary support to strengthen their attacking capabilities, maintain their groups, and recruit, and retain members. (Home Office, 2014).

As long as these ransomware groups are not legally defined as terrorists, the practice will continue, and there is no bar for these payments. The insurance companies are left with a dilemma; if they refrain from paying the ransom, which can restore some of the damage, the insurance payment would be much higher. However, the ransom payment inadvertently funds organised crimes and indirectly laundering money (Sabbagh, 2021a). The surge in attacks pushes insurance companies to rethink how much coverage they can offer and how much they can charge the clients. The insurance companies are beginning to demand detailed proof about the client's cybersecurity measures to vet their cyber resilience and preparedness. This means that the companies restrict their coverage or limit their terms and conditions (Lerman & Vynck, 2021).

Cyber Defence: Deterrence and Defence

It is no secret that Russia and other states are using proxies in their attacks or providing safe havens to attackers. It can be argued that they provide safe spaces similar to what Afghanistan did with Al-Qaeda terrorists (Cerulus, 2021a; Barnes, 2021). The US has made it clear after the string of high-profile attacks against essential CIs that they would respond harshly in retaliation if actors from Russia again violate American sovereignty (Roth & Harding, 2021). The Russian authorities are rarely prosecuting the attackers, and they refuse to extradite them. In a reaction to the Colonial Pipeline attack, US President Biden argued that Russia allowed the cybercriminals to operate within the Russian border. Therefore, Russia has some responsibilities for the increase in attacks (Perlroth & Satariano, 2021). Biden argued that there is mutual self-interest to manage this area. He indicated that if further attacks emanated from the Russian territory, the US also has substantial cyber capabilities to respond to the attacks (Computer Weekly, 2021). After the 2021 Geneva Summit between Russia's President Putin and US President Biden, it was clear from the US side that they expect that Russia would act on the growing number of attacks (Holland & Shalal, 2021; Roth & Harding, 2021).

STRATEGIC REVIEW

By linking ransomware to terrorism, new powers and investigatory practices and processes are accessible to be used by state actors and law enforcement. These are counter-terrorism measures reserved for national security cases. Enacting these powers shows the seriousness of the attacks (Bing, 2021). This new initiative has been critiqued. Shield (2021) argued that linking ransomware and terrorism in a generic sense is likely incorrect and is not nuanced enough as ransomware and terrorism cannot be compared like to like. For example, if an attack is conducted towards a small entity, it is unlikely to act terrorism. However, if the attack takedown CI such as an oil pipeline or a water system, then it would classify as terrorism. This means that the target and the intentions are the determining factors. Yet, if connecting the attacks to terrorism is the way to enact a government response, then the new measure might be the best option as deterrence and defence against these attacks. This initiative cannot stand alone if the current level of ransomware should be reduced (Security, 2021). The US administration has prioritised a more coordinated approach by engaging public–private partnerships nationally and internationally. So far, there is no evidence that the attack rate is slowing down, and the responses to the risks have mainly been insufficient and fragmented (Scroxton, 2021c). Collaboration seems to be the key to break the deadlock of managing these attacks. One of the most important steps is to get the global public and private community involved to address the global threat. The US Deputy National Security Advisor Neuberger urged private actors to take more responsibility to prevent attacks (Scroxton, 2021c; Barnes, 2021)

National Security Threat

Managing attacks require state engagement in protecting vital assets. Intelligence communities and law enforcement should play a more visible role in sharing information and other resources to collect evidence and identify and pursue the attackers (Chapple, 2021; Ransomware Task Force, 2021). The US Ransomware Task Force (2021) forwarded recommendations for urgent implementation. First, coordinated international diplomatic and law enforcement efforts must be engaged to prioritise ransomware using a comprehensive and reduced strategy proactively. This strategy should include a carrot-stick approach to direct states away from providing safe havens to ransomware criminals. Second, governments should enhance resilience towards sustained, aggressive, and intelligence-led ransomware campaigns. The solution is to bring together a multistakeholder framework with public and private entities. Third, governments are urged to establish Cyber Response and Recovery Funds to support the activities to counter ransomware. Fourth, the international coordinated response and efforts should develop a clear, accessible, and broad framework to support organisations to prepare and respond to ransomware. Regulations might be included to drive the adoption in under resources and critical sectors. Finally, the cryptocurrency sector should take responsibility as the ransomware actors use cryptocurrencies as their ransom demand. The sections should be more closely regulated, and governments should demand that cryptocurrency exchanges, crypto kiosks, and over-the-counter trading desks would comply with existing laws (Ransomware Task Force, 2021, p. 6).

The international society needs to stand together in sending a signal to the cybercriminals that this type of crime is a diplomatic and cybersecurity priority. The response and initiatives should be launched on multiple levels, including the G7, G7 finance minister, G20, Interpol, and Europol. The message should be enforced that ransomware is now considered a national security concern and threat to CIs (Ransomware Task Force, 2021, p. 21). There need to be a joint effort on the international, regional, and national levels to deal with the growing number of attacks involving both public and private actors.

In both the G7 and NATO's 2021 Summits, malicious ransomware attacks have been discussed. One of the concerns of the G7 group is the substantial amount of ransomware attacks launched from Russia against foreign targets. The G7 group restated that they want a stable, predictable relationship with Russia. Therefore, they urged President Putin's government to identify, disrupt, and hold the cybercriminals to account for the online attacks, abuse of cryptocurrencies, and other related cybercrimes (Scroxton, 2021b). The UK echoes the US' concerns about ransomware and the growing number of malicious attacks by state-sponsored and state-supported groups. In relation to the G7 meeting, the UK Foreign Secretary promised to take a stricter stance on cybercriminals and other threat actors, such as the state-supported actors engaged in ransomware attacks. The UK indicated an ambition to take a leadership role in establishing international norms and processes to become more resilient and fill in the current legislative vacuum exposed by states and state-supported actors (Scroxton, 2021a).

After the NATO Summit, the Alliance outlined a communique about responding to national security threats (Tung, 2021a). NATO argued that the Alliance is determined to employ its range of cyber capabilities to deter, defend, and counter online threats under international law. NATO also opened the possibility that an attack on one Member State could trigger Article 5, which means an attack on one of the NATO states is an attack on all. However, such a division would be determined on a case-by-case basis. The Alliance considers that the impact of these cumulative cyber attacks can be compared with an armed attack (Computer Weekly, 2021; NATO, 2021). NATO's statement highlighted that those aggressive actions from Russia constitute a security threat to the Euro-Atlantic Alliance. The statement indirectly supports the US argument that ransomware attacks constitute terrorism by claiming that terrorism in all forms and manifestations is a constant threat to the member states (NATO, 2021; Tung, 2021a). However, the threat of using Article 5 does not align with the ransomware attacks unless a clear attribution to the state hosting the attackers can be made.

The EU has also grasped the seriousness of ransomware attacks, particularly after witnessing the devastating impact of the attack on Irelands Health Services. Nevertheless, the EU is falling short of classifying attacks similar to terrorism. Using the term national security issues shows the seriousness of these attacks, moving them from being considered a cybercrime. However, the attacks have increased within the member states, going up from 432 reported incidents in 2019 to 756 in 2021 (Tidy, 2021a). The European Commission focuses on creating a cyber office where diplomats, defence officials, and law enforcement agencies can coordinate their work across the member states to manage cyber threats (WSJ, 2021).

A proposal has been launched to develop a team of multinational cyber experts to be rapidly deployed to the European member states during severe attacks. Previously, these attacks have been linear and, to a certain extent, simple. This is no longer the case, as demonstrated by the attacks on Ireland's Health Service and French public hospitals, but the current structure cannot deal with these types of attacks. The complexity of these attacks requires collaborative actions from all member states, Yet, it takes time to develop response teams (Tidy, 2021a; Murphy, 2021). The EU recommended that national governments put the European Union Agency for Cybersecurity (ENISA) in charge of a similar unit similar to the US-based Ransomware Task Force. The European initiative would coordinate existing work between cyber agencies and EU member states to mirror the national initiatives to boost cybersecurity (Hellard, 2021). In this context, the unit should help develop the member states cyber-defence capabilities. The Joint Cyber Unit will first be operational until 2022 and fully established until 2023 (Tidy, 2021a; Murphy, 2021; Cimpanu, 2021b).

The EU has also joined the US in criticising states harbouring cybercriminals. The 'fight against ransomware' mirrors the well-known rhetoric 'fight against terrorism' used after the US 9/11 attack (Cerulus & Goujard, 2021). The US and EU summit in 2021 also included discussions about ransomware attacks. The two partners aim to revitalise the relations between them and enhance cooperation. The collaboration between the EU and the US have launched initiatives to share information and exchange best practices to manage the attacks (Cimpanu, 2021b). This means more collaboration between law enforcement, awareness-raising about the threat and risk of paying a ransom and putting pressure on states hosting these groups to arrest and extradite or effectively prosecute cyber criminals on their territory (Cerulus & Goujard, 2021).

Conclusion

The ransomware attacks illustrate apparent issues with managing the area and building up a resilience framework based on deterrence and defence. Without any doubt, ransomware attacks constitute a significant challenge for the victims and the wider society. The attacks are getting more severe, and they happen more frequently. Additionally, they have ramifications beyond the original targets. The attacks bear substantial similarities to terrorism. However, there is no clear definition of cyberterrorism suitable for managing the area. The attacks are caught up in a grey zone between conventional terrorism and cybercrime, where none of them is sufficient to cover the offences. Therefore, it is essential that states addressees the legislative lacuna and the missing cybersecurity framework.

References

Acronis, 2021a. *Analysis of Ragnar locker ransomware.* [Online] Available at: www.acronis.com/en-gb/articles/ragnar-locker/ [Accessed 25 07 2021].

Acronis, 2021b. *Threat analysis: DarkSide ransomware.* [Online] Available at: www.acronis.com/en-gb/articles/darkside-ransomware/ [Accessed 27 05 2021].

Afifi-Sabet, K., 2021. *Ransomware operators in turmoil after Colonial Pipeline backlash.* [Online] Available at: www.itpro.co.uk/security/ransomware/359558/ransomware-operators-in-turmoil-after-colonial-pipeline-backlash [Accessed 28 06 2021].

Aggarwal, M., 2021. *Biden 'mulling cyber war' after spate of high profile attacks on US.* [Online] Available at: www-independent-co-uk.cdn.ampproject.org/c/s/www.independent.co.uk/news/world/americas/us-politics/biden-us-cyber-war-russia-b1859538.html?amp [Accessed 27 06 2021].

Arce M, D. G. & Sandler, T., 2005. Counterterrorism: A game-theoretic analysis. *The Journal of Conflict Resolution,* 49(2), pp. 183–200.

Associated Press, 2021. *Colonial Pipeline confirms it paid $4.4m ransom to hacker gang after attack.* [Online] Available at: www.theguardian.com/technology/2021/may/19/colonial-pipeline-cyber-attack-ransom [Accessed 24 06 2021].

Barnes, J. E., 2021. *F.B.I. Director compares danger of ransomware to 9/11 terror threat.* [Online] Available at: www.nytimes.com/2021/06/04/us/politics/ransomware-cyberattacks-sept-11-fbi.html [Accessed 28 06 2021].

Bassiouni, M. C., 2001. *International Terrorism and Multilateral Conventions.* New York: Transnational Publishers.

BBC News, 1999. *World: Americas US cyber terrorism plea.* [Online] Available at: http://news.bbc.co.uk/1/hi/world/americas/260855.stm [Accessed 02 06 2021].

BBC News, 2021a. *JBS: FBI says Russia-linked group hacked meat supplier.* [Online] Available at: www.bbc.co.uk/news/world-us-canada-57338896 [Accessed 28 06 2021].

BBC News, 2021b. *REvil: Ransomware gang websites disappear from Internet.* [Online] Available at: www.bbc.co.uk/news/technology-57826851 [Accessed 28 07 2021].

Benazet, D., 2021. *The key ingredient in recent malware attacks.* [Online] Available at: www.techradar.com/news/the-key-ingredient-in-recent-malware-attacks [Accessed 26 06 2021].

Bing, C., 2021. *Exclusive: U.S. to give ransomware hacks similar priority as terrorism.* [Online] Available at: www.reuters.com/technology/exclusive-us-give-ransomware-hacks-similar-priority-terrorism-official-says-2021-06-03/ [Accessed 28 06 2021].

Bostrup, J., 2021. Mystisk hackergruppe har skabt en kriminel og farlig milliardindustri. *Politiken,* 23 05 2021.

Bowman-Grieve, L., 2015. Cyberterrorism and moral panics: A reflection on the discourse of cyberterrorism. In: *Terrorism Online. Politics, Law and Technology.* Abingdon: Routledge, pp. 98–118.

Branch, L. E. et al., 2019. Trends in Malware Attacks against United States Healthcare Organizations, 2016–2017. *Global Biosecurity,* pp. 15–27 [Accessed 18 11 2021].

Brewster, T., 2021. *Ransomware hackers claim to leak 250GB of Washington, D.C., police data after cops don't pay $4 million ransom.* [Online] Available at: www.forbes.com/sites/thomasbrewster/2021/05/13/ransomware-hackers-claim-to-leak-250gb-of-washington-dc-police-data-after-cops-dont-pay-4-million-ransom/ [Accessed 13 06 2021].

Carver, A., 2016. Parliamentary attempts to define terrorism. *Journal of Applied Security Research,* 06 04, 11(2), pp. 124–138.

Cerulus, L., 2021a. *Biden needs Putin in the fight against ransomware.* [Online] Available at: www.politico.eu/article/biden-zones-putin-fight-against-ransomware-russia-us/ [Accessed 26 06 2021].

Cerulus, L. & Goujard, C., 2021. *EU, US launch initiative against ransomware.* [Online] Available at: www.politico.eu/article/eu-us-launch-ransomware-cooperation-group/ [Accessed 26 06 2021].

Chapple, M., 2021. *Ransomware is a national security risk. It's time to treat it like one.* [Online] Available at: https://amp-cnn-com.cdn.ampproject.org/c/s/amp.cnn.com/cnn/2021/06/10/perspectives/ransomware-attacks-national-security/index.html [Accessed 12 06 2021].

Check Point, 2021. *The new ransomware threat: Triple extortion.* [Online] Available at: https://blog.checkpoint.com/2021/05/12/the-new-ransomware-threat-triple-extortion/ [Accessed 05 06 2021].

Cimpanu, C., 2020a. *Conti (Ryuk) joins the ranks of ransomware gangs operating data leak sites.* [Online] Available at: www.zdnet.com/article/conti-ryuk-joins-the-ranks-of-ransomware-gangs-operating-data-leak-sites/ [Accessed 20 06 2021].

Cimpanu, C., 2020b. *First death reported following a ransomware attack on a German hospital.* [Online] Available at: www.zdnet.com/article/first-death-reported-following-a-ransomware-attack-on-a-german-hospital/ [Accessed 17 09 2021].

Cimpanu, C., 2020c. *Ransomware deploys virtual machines to hide itself from anti-virus software.* [Online] Available at: www.zdnet.com/article/ransomware-deploys-virtual-machines-to-hide-itself-from-antivirus-software/ [Accessed 19 06 2020].

Cimpanu, C., 2021a. *City of Liege, Belgium hit by ransomware.* [Online] Available at: https://therecord.media/city-of-liege-belgium-hit-by-ransomware/ [Accessed 27 06 2021].

Cimpanu, C., 2021b. *EU announces joint cyber-unit to respond to large-scale security incidents.* [Online] Available at: https://therecord.media/eu-announces-joint-cyber-unit-to-respond-to-large-scale-security-incidents/ [Accessed 27 06 2021].

CIS, 2021. *Ransomware: In the healthcare sector.* [Online] Available at: www.cisecurity.org/blog/ransomware-in-the-healthcare-sector/ [Accessed 18 06 2021].

Cluley, G., 2021. *REvil ransomware – What you need to know.* [Online] Available at: https://securityboulevard.com/2021/04/revil-ransomware-what-you-need-to-know/ [Accessed 26 07 2021].

Cohen, D., 2014. Cyber terrorism: Case studies. In: Syngress, ed. *Cyber Crime and Cyber Terrorism Investigator's Handbook.* Waltham: Elsevier, pp. 165–174.

Computer Weekly, 2021. *Biden tackles Putin on ransomware at Geneva summit.* [Online] Available at: https://bit.ly/3cz7LsD [Accessed 24 06 2021].

Conway, M., 2014. Reality check: Assessing the (un)likelihood of cyberterrorism. In: *Cyberterrorism. Understanding, Assessment, and Response.* New York: Springer, pp. 103–121.

Costa, A. M., 2005. *Drugs, Crime and Terrorist Financing. Breaking the Links,* Vienna: Conference on Combatting Terrorist Financing.

Crenshaw, M., 2011. *Explaining Terrorism. Causes, Processes and Consequences.* 1 ed. Abingdon: Routledge.

Cronin, A. K., 2003. Behind the curve: Globalization and international terrorism. *International Security,* 27(3), pp. 30–58.

Crowdstrike, 2021. *Ransomware as a service (RaaS) explained.* [Online] Available at: www.crowdstrike.com/cybersecurity-101/ransomware/ransomware-as-a-service-raas/ [Accessed 27 05 2021].

DataBreaches.net, 2021. *Russian-language hacking forum bans ransomware-related ads.* [Online] Available at: www.databreaches.net/russian-language-hacking-forum-bans-ransomware-related-ads/ [Accessed 28 06 2021].

Davis, J., 2020. *FBI: Ragnar locker ransomware attacks increase with data theft risk.* [Online] Available at: https://healthitsecurity.com/news/fbi-ragnar-locker-ransomw are-attacks-increase-with-data-theft-risk [Accessed 25 07 2021].

Denning, D. E., 2000. *Cyberterrorism. Testimony before the Committee on Armed Services U.S. House of Representatives.* [Online] Available at: https://faculty.nps. edu/dedennin/publications/Testimony-Cyberterrorism2000.htm [Accessed 02 04 2021].

Denning, D. E., 2011. *Whither cyber terror? 10 years after September the 11th.* [Online] Available at: http://essays.ssrc.org/10yearsafter911/whither-cyber-terror/.[Accessed 02 06 2021].

Dogrul, M., Aslan, A. & Celik, E., 2011. Developing an international cooperation on cyber defense and deterrence against cyber terrorism. In: *3rd International Conference on Cyber Conflict.* Tallin: CDD COE, pp. 1–15.

EU, 2017. *Directive (EU) 2017/541 of the European Parliament and of the Council of 15 March 2017 on Combatting Terrorism and Replacing Council Framework Decision 2002/475/JHA and amending Council Decision 2005/671/JHA.* [Online] Available at: https://eur-lex.europa.eu/legal-content/EN/TXT/PDF/?uri=CELEX:32017L0 541&from=en [Accessed 06 06 2021].

European Parliament, 2015. *Understanding definitions of terrorism.* [Online] Available at: www.europarl.europa.eu/RegData/etudes/ATAG/2015/571320/EPRS_ATA (2015)571320_EN.pdf [Accessed 06 06 2021].

Europol, 2012. *TE-SAT 2012. EU Terrorism Situation and Trend Report'.* [Online] Available at: www.europol.europa.eu/activities-services/main-reports/te-sat-2012-eu-terrorism-situation-and-trend-report [Accessed 07 04 2021].

Europol, 2020. *Internet Organised Crime Threat Assessment (IOCTA) 2020.* [Online] Available at: www.europol.europa.eu/activities-services/main-reports/internet-organised-crime-threat-assessment-iocta-2020 [Accessed 07 03 2021].

Europol, 2021. *European Union serious and organised crime threat assessment, A corrupting influence: the infiltration and undermining of Europe's economy and society by organised crime,* Luxenbourg: Publications Office of the European Union.

FBI Flash, 2021. *Conti ransomware attacks impact healthcare.* [Online] Available at: www.aha.org/system/files/media/file/2021/05/fbi-tlp-white-report-conti-ransomware-attacks-impact-healthcare-and-first-responder-networks-5-20-21.pdf [Accessed 20 06 2021].

France24, 2021. *Cyber attacks hit two French hospitals in one week.* [Online] Available at: www.france24.com/en/europe/20210216-cyber-attacks-hit-two-french-hospitals-in-one-week [Accessed 18 06 2021].

Ganor, B., 2002. Defining terrorism: Is one man's terrorist another man's freedom. *'Police Practices and Research,* 3(4), pp. 387–304.

Gatlan, S., 2020. *RagnarLocker ransomware hits EDP energy giant, asks for €10M.* [Online] Available at: www.bleepingcomputer.com/news/security/ragnarlocker-ransomware-hits-edp-energy-giant-asks-for-10m/ [Accessed 20 06 2021].

Gatlan, S., 2021. *PYSA ransomware backdoors education orgs using ChaChi malware.* [Online] Available at: www.bleepingcomputer.com/news/security/pysa-ransomware-backdoors-education-orgs-using-chachi-malware/ [Accessed 27 06 2021].

Goodin, D., 2020. *LockBit is the new ransomware for hire.* [Online] Available at: www.wired.com/story/lockbit-is-the-new-ransomware-for-hire/ [Accessed 20 06 2021].

Goodwin, B., 2020. *Cyber gangsters hit UK medical firm poised for work on coronavirus with Maze ransomware attack.* [Online] Available at: www.computerweekly.com/news/252480425/Cyber-gangsters-hit-UK-medical-research-lorganisation-poised-for-work-on-Coronavirus [Accessed 20 06 2021].

GOV.UK, 2000. *Terrorism Act 2000.* [Online] Available at: www.legislation.gov.uk/ukpga/2000/11/section/1 [Accessed 06 06 2021].

GOV.UK, 2015. *Counter-terrorism and Security Act 2015.* [Online] Available at: www.legislation.gov.uk/ukpga/2015/6/section/42 [Accessed 24 06 2021].

Gross, T., 2021. *Inner workings of darkside cybergang reveal it's run like any other business.* [Online] Available at: www.npr.org/2021/06/10/1005093802/inner-workings-of-darkside-cybergang-reveal-its-run-like-any-other-business?t=1623602735352 [Accessed 13 06 2021].

Gura, D., 2021. *U.S. suffers over 7 ransomware attacks an hour. It's now a national security risk.* [Online] Available at: www.npr.org/2021/06/09/1004684788/u-s-suffers-over-7-ransomware-attacks-an-hour-its-now-a-national-security-risk?t=1627331521989 [Accessed 27 07 2021].

Halfacree, G., 2021. *The Latest REvil ransomware vicitim? Sol Oriwba. Oh, a US Nuclear Weapons Contractor.* [Online] Available at: www.theregister.com/2021/06/15/us_nuclear_weapons_contractor_sol_oriens/ [Accessed 27 06 2021].

Halopeau, B., 2014. Terrorist use of the Internet. In: Syngress, ed. *Cyber Crime and Cyber Terrorism Investigator's Handbook.* Waltham: Elsevier, pp. 123–132.

Hanel, A., 2019. *Big game hunting with Ryuk: Another lucrative targeted ransomware.* [Online] Available at: www.crowdstrike.com/blog/big-game-hunting-with-ryuk-another-lucrative-targeted-ransomware/ [Accessed 25 07 2021].

Hathaway, M., 2021. *Hijacked and paying the price – Why ransomware gangs should be designated as terrorists.* [Online] Available at: www.ineteconomics.org/perspectives/blog/hijacked-and-paying-the-price-why-ransomware-gangs-should-be-designated-as-terrorists [Accessed 28 06 2021].

Hellard, B., 2021. *EU plans to launch bloc-wide cyber task force.* [Online] Available at: www.itpro.co.uk/security/cyber-attacks/359960/eu-draft-plans-for-bloc-wide-cyber-task-force [Accessed 26 06 2021].

HelpNetSecurity, 2021. *Double-extortion ransomware attacks on the rise.* [Online] Available at: www.helpnetsecurity.com/2021/05/18/double-extortion-ransomware-attacks/ [Accessed 25 07 2021].

Hernández, J. S. L., 2021. *What are state-sponsored cyberattacks?.* [Online] Available at: https://blog.f-secure.com/what-are-state-sponsored-cyberattacks/ [Accessed 02 06 2021].

Holbrook, D. & Horgan, J., 2019. Terrorism and Ideology: Cracking the nut. *Perspective on Terrorism*, 13(6), pp. 2–15.

Holland, S. & Shalal, A., 2021. *Biden presses Putin to act on ransomware attacks, hints at retaliation.* [Online] Available at: www.reuters.com/technology/biden-pressed-putin-call-act-ransomware-attacks-white-house-2021-07-09/ [Accessed 28 07 2021].

Home Office, 2014. *Counter-terrorism and security bill.* [Online] Available at: https://assets.publishing.service.gov.uk/government/uploads/system/uploads/attachment_data/file/540539/CTS_Bill_-_Factsheet_9_-_Kidnap_and_Ransom.pdf [Accessed 21 06 2021].

Ikeda, S., 2021. *Ransomware attack reported at Insurance Giant AXA one week after it changes cyber insurance policies in France.* [Online] Available at: www.cpomagazine.com/cyber-security/ransomware-attack-reported-at-insurance-giant-axa-one-week-after-it-changes-cyber-insurance-policies-in-france/ [Accessed 19 06 2021].

Ilascu, I., 2021. *China's APT hackers move to ransomware attacks.* [Online] Available at: www.bleepingcomputer.com/news/security/chinas-apt-hackers-move-to-ransomware-attacks/ [Accessed 20 06 2021].

Kennedy, R., 1999. Is one person's terrorist another's freedom fighter? Western and Islamic approaches to 'just war' compared. *Terrorism and political violence,* 11(1), pp. 1–21.

Kennelly, J., Goody, K. & Shilko, J., 2020. *Navigating the MAZE: Tactics, techniques and procedures associated with MAZE ransomware incidents.* [Online] Available at: www.fireeye.com/blog/threat-research/2020/05/tactics-techniques-procedures-associated-with-maze-ransomware-incidents.html [Accessed 25 07 2021].

Khurshudyan, I. & Morris, L., 2021. *Ransomware's suspected Russian roots point to a long detente between the Kremlin and hackers.* [Online] Available at: www.msn.com/en-us/news/world/ransomware-e2-80-99s-suspected-russian-roots-point-to-a-long-detente-between-the-kremlin-and-hackers/ar-AAKY1M8[Accessed 27 06 2021].

KrebsOnSecurity, 2019. *Who's behind the GandCrab ransomware?.* [Online] Available at: https://krebsonsecurity.com/2019/07/whos-behind-the-gandcrab-ransomware/ [Accessed 20 06 2021].

KrebsOnSecurity, 2020. *REvil ransomware gang starts auctioning victim data.* [Online] Available at: https://krebsonsecurity.com/2020/06/revil-ransomware-gang-starts-auctioning-victim-data/ [Accessed 27 07 2021].

KrebsOnSecurity, 2021. *A closer look at the DarkSide ransomware gang.* [Online] Available at: https://krebsonsecurity.com/2021/05/a-closer-look-at-the-darkside-ransomware-gang/ [Accessed 28 06 2021].

Lawler, R., 2021. *19 Days after REvil's ransomware attack on Kaseya VSA systems, there's a fix.* [Online] Available at: www.theverge.com/2021/7/22/22589643/ransomware-kaseya-vsa-decryptor-revil[Accessed 28 07 2021].

Lee, N., 2021. *As the U.S. faces a flurry of ransomware attacks, experts warn the peak is likely still to come.* [Online] Available at: www-cnbc-com.cdn.ampproject.org/c/s/www.cnbc.com/amp/2021/06/10/heres-how-much-ransomware-attacks-are-costing-the-american-economy.html[Accessed 28 06 2021].

Lerman, R., 2021. *JBS paid $11 million in ransom after hackers shut down meat plants.* [Online] Available at: www.washingtonpost.com/technology/2021/06/09/jbs-11-million-ransom/ [Accessed 28 06 2021].

Lerman, R. & Vynck, G. D., 2021. *Ransomware claims are roiling an entire segment of the insurance industry.* [Online] Available at: www.washingtonpost.com/technology/2021/06/17/ransomware-axa-insurance-attacks/ [Accessed 27 06 2021].

Lewis, J. A., 2002. *Assessing the risks of cyber terrorism, cyber war and other cyber threats.* [Online] Available at: https://csis-website-prod.s3.amazonaws.com/s3fs-public/legacy_files/files/media/csis/pubs/021101_risks_of_cyberterror.pdf [Accessed 27 07 2021].

Livingstone, H., 2021. *New Zealand hospital faces second week of disruption after major cyber attack.* [Online] Available at: www.theguardian.com/world/2021/may/24/new-zealand-hospital-cyber-attack-waikato-disruption [Accessed 18 06 2021].

Luiijf, E., 2014. Definitions of cyber terrorism. In: Syngress, ed. *Cyber Crime and Cyber Terrorism Investigator's Handbook.* Waltham: Elsevier, pp. 11–17.

Lutkevich, B., 2020. *Ransomware.* [Online] Available at: https://searchsecurity.techtarget.com/definition/ransomware?_ga=2.177677222.2020948496.1624124109-2103148593.1623869695 [Accessed 19 06 2021].

Malware Bytes, 2021a. *Ransomware.* [Online] Available at: www.malwarebytes.com/ransomware [Accessed 26 07 2021].

Malware Bytes, 2021b. *Ryuk ransomware.* [Online] Available at: www.malwarebytes.com/ryuk-ransomware [Accessed 25 07 2021].

Malwarebytes Labs, 2021a. *Ransom.Sodinokibi.* [Online] Available at: https://blog.malwarebytes.com/detections/ransom-sodinokibi/ [Accessed 20 06 2021].

Malwarebytes Labs, 2021b. *Trojan.TrickBot.* [Online] Available at: https://blog.malwarebytes.com/detections/trojan-trickbot/ [Accessed 25 07 2021].

Marks, T. A., 2004. Ideology of insurgency: New ethnic focus or old Cold War distortions?. *Small Wars and Insurgencie,* 15(1), pp. 107–128.

Marsili, M., 2019. The war on cyberterrorism. *Democracy and Security,* 15(2), pp. 172–199.

Mathews, L., 2020. *North Korea-Linked Hackers Are Now Spreading Their Own Ransomware.* [Online] Available at: www.forbes.com/sites/leemathews/2020/07/29/north-korea-hackers-lazarus-vhd-ransomware/?sh=536731b05b11 [Accessed 29 07 2021].

Matusitz, J., 2021. *Communication in global Jihad.* Abingdon: Routledge.

McAfee, 2021. *What is ransomware?.* [Online] Available at: www.mcafee.com/enterprise/en-gb/security-awareness/ransomware.html [Accessed 26 07 2021].

Mehrotra, K., 2021. *When Ransomware group REvil vanished, its victims were stranded.* [Online] Available at: www.bloomberg.com/news/newsletters/2021-07-27/when-ransomware-group-revil-vanished-its-victims-were-stranded [Accessed 28 07 2021].

Morris, C., 2021. *REvil ransomware websites go offline, and no one is sure exactly why.* [Online] Available at: https://fortune.com/2021/07/13/revil-ransomware-offline-dark-web/ [Accessed 28 07 2021].

Muncaster, P., 2020. *Energy giant EDP hit with €10 Million ransomware threat.* [Online] Available at: www.infosecurity-magazine.com/news/energy-giant-edp-hit-10-million/ [Accessed 20 06 2021].

Muncaster, P., 2021. *Chinese APT group linked to ransomware attacks.* [Online] Available at: www.infosecurity-magazine.com/news/chinese-apt-group-linked-to/ [Accessed 21 06 2021].

Munk, T. H., 2015. *Cyber-security in the European region: Anticipatory governance and practices.* [Online] Available at: www.escholar.manchester.ac.uk/api/datastream?publicationPid=uk-ac-man-scw:266937&datastreamId=FULL-TEXT.PDF [Accessed 12 08 2020].

Murphy, N., 2021. *EU sets up cyber-security task force to defend bloc from ransomware attacks.* [Online] Available at: www.thenationalnews.com/world/europe/eu-sets-up-cyber-security-task-force-to-defend-bloc-from-ransomware-attacks-1.1247556 [Accessed 26 06 2021].

NATO, 2019. *NATO Glossary of terms and definitions.* [Online] Available at: www. coemed.org/files/stanags/05_AAP/AAP-06_2019_EF.pdf [Accessed 06 06 2021].

NATO, 2021. *Brussels summit communiqué.* [Online] Available at: www.nato.int/cps/ en/natohq/news_185000.htm [Accessed 24 06 2021].

Ogun, M. N., 2012. Terrorist use of internet: Possible suggestions to prevent the usage for terrorist purposes. *Journal of Applied Security Research*, 28 03, 7(2), pp. 203–217.

Osborne, C., 2021a. *FBI identifies 16 Conti ransomware attacks striking US healthcare, first responders.* [Online] Available at: www.zdnet.com/article/fbi-identifies-16-conti-ransomware-attacks-striking-us-healthcare-first-responders/[Accessed 20 06 2021].

Osborne, C., 2021b. *Updated Kaseya ransomware attack FAQ: What we know now.* [Online] Available at: www.zdnet.com/article/updated-kaseya-ransomware-attack-faq-what-we-know-now/ [Accessed 28 07 2021].

OSCE, 2013. *Good practices guide on non-nuclear critical energy infrastructure protection (NNCEIP) from terrorist attacks focusing on threats emanating from cyberspace,* Vienna: OSCE.

Otto, G., 2021. *Here's what we know about DarkSide ransomware.* [Online] Available at: https://intel471.com/blog/darkside-ransomware-colonial-pipeline-attack [Accessed 28 06 2021].

Paganini, P., 2021. *REvil Ransomware spokesman releases an interview on recent attacks.* [Online] Available at: https://securityaffairs.co/wordpress/118639/cyber-crime/revil-ransomware-interview.html [Accessed 28 06 2021].

Palmer, D., 2020. *This ransomware has learned a new trick: Scanning for point of sales devices.* [Online] Available at: https://zd.net/3DIv1jx [Accessed 28 06 2021].

Palmer, D., 2021a. *Have we reached peak ransomware? How the internet's biggest security problem has grown and what happens next.* [Online] Available at: www. zdnet.com/article/have-we-reached-peak-ransomware-how-the-internets-biggest-security-problem-has-grown-and-what-happens-next/ [Accessed 28 06 2021].

Palmer, D., 2021b. *What is ransomware? Everything you need to know about one of the biggest menaces on the web.* [Online] Available at: www.zdnet.com/article/ ransomware-an-executive-guide-to-one-of-the-biggest-menaces-on-the-web/ [Accessed 20 06 2021].

Patel, N., 2021. Cyber and tria: Expanding the definition of an "Act of Terrorism" to include cyber attacks. *Duke Law & Technology Review*, 19(23).

Paulose, R., 2013. *CYBER Terrorism: Fact Or Fiction?.* [Online] Available at: https:// acontrarioicl.com/2013/11/28/cyber-terrorism/ [Accessed 02 04 2021].

Perlroth, N. & Satariano, A., 2021. *Irish hospitals are latest to be hit by ransomware attacks.* [Online] Available at: www.nytimes.com/2021/05/20/technology/ ransomware-attack-ireland-hospitals.html [Accessed 17 06 2021].

Polansek, T. & Mason, J., 2021. *U.S. says ransomware attack on meatpacker JBS likely from Russia.* [Online] Available at: www.reuters.com/world/us/some-us-meat-plants-stop-operating-after-jbs-cyber-attack-2021-06-01/ [Accessed 27 07 2021].

Quinn, C., 2021. *U.S. meat industry becomes latest cyber victim.* [Online] Available at: foreignpolicy.com/2021/06/02/jbs-hack-meat-beef-ransomware/ [Accessed 28 06 2021].

Ransomware Task Force, 2021. *Combatting ransomware. A comprehensive framework for action: Key recommendations from the ransomware task force,* s.l.: Institute for Security and Technology.

RNZ, 2021. *Waikato DHB cyber attack: Documents appear to have been released online.* [Online] Available at: www.nzherald.co.nz/nz/waikato-dhb-cyber-attack-documents-appear-to-have-been-released-online/DY4M5YQ3CBOWQNJ6Y7FAOOWOLM/ [Accessed 26 07 2021].

Rosenbaum, E., 2021. *JBS cyberattack: From gas to meat, hackers are hitting the nation, and consumers, where it hurts.* [Online] Available at: www.cnbc.com/2021/06/02/from-gas-to-burgers-hackers-hit-consumers-where-it-hurts.html [Accessed 27 07 2021].

Roth, A. & Harding, L., 2021. *Biden warns US will hit back if Russia continues with cyber strikes.* [Online] Available at: www.theguardian.com/us-news/2021/jun/16/biden-to-meet-putin-at-highly-anticipated-summit-in-geneva?CMP=Share_AndroidApp_Other [Accessed 27 06 2021].

Rubins, A., 2021. *REvil ransomware gang reveal details of US attacks!.* [Online] Available at: www.cybernewsgroup.co.uk/revil-ransomware-gang-reveal-details-of-us-attacks/ [Accessed 28 06 2021].

Sabbagh, D., 2021a. *Insurers 'funding organised crime' by paying ransomware claims.* [Online] Available at: www.theguardian.com/technology/2021/jan/24/insurers-funding-organised-by-paying-ransomware-claims [Accessed 24 06 2021].

Sabbagh, D., 2021b. *Ransomware is biggest online threat to people in UK, spy agency chief to warn.* [Online] Available at: www.theguardian.com/technology/2021/jun/14/ransomware-is-biggest-online-threat-to-people-in-uk-spy-agency-chief-to-warn [Accessed 24 06 2021].

Sandler, T. & Arce M, D. G., 2003. Terrorism and game theory. *Simulation & Gaming,* 09.

Sanger, D. E., Krauss, C. & Perlroth, N., 2021. *Cyberattack forces a shutdown of a top U.S. pipeline.* [Online] Available at: www.nytimes.com/2021/05/08/us/politics/cyberattack-colonial-pipeline.html [Accessed 13 06 2021].

Schmid, A. P. & Jongman, A. J., 1988. *Political Terrorism: A New Guide to Actors, Authors, Concepts, Data Bases, Theories, and Literature.* New York: New Brunswick.

Scroxton, A., 2021a. *UK promises tougher line on cyber crime.* [Online] Available at: www.computerweekly.com/news/252502300/UK-promises-tougher-line-on-cyber-crime [Accessed 25 06 2021].

Scroxton, A., 2021b. *G7 commits to action on ransomware, digital privacy.* [Online] Available at: www.computerweekly.com/news/252502386/G7-commits-to-action-on-ransomware-digital-privacy [Accessed 24 06 2021].

Scroxton, A., 2021c. *Government action on ransomware epidemic gathers pace.* [Online] Available at: www.computerweekly.com/news/252501907/Government-action-on-ransomware-epidemic-gathers-pace [Accessed 25 06 2021].

Security, 2021. *US to treat ransomware like terrorism.* [Online] Available at: www.securitymagazine.com/articles/95366-us-to-treat-ransomware-like-terrorism [Accessed 12 06 2021].

Shaban, H., Nakashima, E. & Lerman, R., 2021. *JBS, world's biggest meat supplier, says its systems are coming back online after cyberattack shut down plants in U.S.* [Online] Available at: www.washingtonpost.com/business/2021/06/01/jbs-cyberattack-meat-supply-chain/ [Accessed 28 06 2021].

Shield, T., 2021, US to treat ransomware like terrorism. *Security.* [Online] Available at: www.securitymagazine.com/articles/95366-us-to-treat-ransomware-like-terrorism [Accessed 23 11 2021].

Silomon, J., 2020. *The Düsseldorf cyber incident.* [Online] Available at: https://ifsh.de/en/news-detail/the-duesseldorf-cyber-incident [Accessed 27 07 2021].

Sophos, 2021. *The state of ransomware 2021.* [Online] Available at: https://news.sophos.com/en-us/2021/04/27/the-state-of-ransomware-2021/9 [Accessed 23 11 2021].

Sorvino, C., 2021. *JBS cyberattack shines a spotlight on the biggest risk to big meat: Consolidation.* [Online] Available at: www.forbes.com/sites/chloesorvino/2021/06/02/jbs-cyberattack-shines-a-spotlight-on-the-biggest-risk-to-big-meat-consolidation/?sh=5b6e873161db [Accessed 28 06 2021].

Spring, T., 2021. *The REvil ransomware gang is interviewed on the Telegram channel called Russian OSINT.* [Online] Available at: https://threatpost.com/revil-spill-details-us-attacks/166669/ [Accessed 28 06 2021].

Suderman, A., 2021a, *Ransomware gangs get more aggressive against law enforcement.* [Online] Avaliable at: https://apnews.com/article/ransomware-gangs-hacking-police-cybercrime-pipeline-3a38c27c4fafe0c39461fb71bf91a42a [Accessed 18 11 2021].

Suderman, A., 2021b. *DC Police victim of massive data leak by ransomware gang.* [Online] Available at: https://apnews.com/article/police-technology-government-and-politics-1aedfcf42a8dc2b004ef610d0b57edb9 [Accessed 13 06 2021].

Tavares, P., 2020. *Ragnar locker malware: What it is, how it works and how to prevent it | Malware spotlight.* [Online] Available at: https://resources.infosecinstitute.com/topic/ragnar-locker-malware-what-it-is-how-it-works-and-how-to-prevent-it-malware-spotlight/ [Accessed 20 06 2021].

The Maritime Executive, 2020. *USCG: Cyberattack penetrated cargo facility's operating controls.* [Online] Available at: www.maritime-executive.com/article/uscg-cyberattack-penetrated-operating-controls-of-isps-facility [Accessed 13 06 2021].

Theohary, C. A. & Rollins, J. W., 2015. *Cyberwarfare and cyberterrorism: In brief,* Washington DC: Congressional Research Service.

Tidy, J., 2021a. *EU wants emergency team for 'nightmare' cyber-attacks.* [Online] Available at: www.bbc.co.uk/news/technology-57583158 [Accessed 21 06 2021].

Tidy, J., 2021b. *Why cyber gangs won't worry about US-Russia talks.* [Online] Available at: /www.bbc.co.uk/news/technology-57504007 [Accessed 21 06 2021].

Tung, L., 2021a. *NATO: Series of cyberattacks could be seen as the same threat as an armed attack.* [Online] Available at: www.zdnet.com/article/nato-series-of-cyberattacks-could-be-seen-as-the-same-threat-as-an-armed-attack/#ftag=RSSbaffb68 [Accessed 27 06 2021].

Tung, L., 2021b. *Ransomware: Meat firm JBS says it paid out $11m after attack.* [Online] Available at: www-zdnet-com.cdn.ampproject.org/c/s/www.zdnet.com/google-amp/article/ransomware-meat-firm-jbs-says-it-paid-out-11m-after-attack/ [Accessed 28 06 2021].

US Gov, 2001. *Uniting and strengthening America by providing appropriate tools required to intercept and obstruct terrorism (USA Patriot Act) Act of 2001.* [Online] Available at: www.congress.gov/107/plaws/publ56/PLAW-107publ56.pdf [Accessed 25 07 2021].

UN, 2004. *Resolution 1566 (2004).* [Online] Available at: www.un.org/ga/search/view_doc.asp?symbol=S/RES/1566%20%282004%29 [Accessed 06 06 2021].

UN, 2005. *Secretary-General Kofi Annan launches global strategy.* [Online] Available at: www.un.org/press/en/2005/sg2095.doc.htm [Accessed 06 06 2021].

UN, 2014. *Security Council adopts Resolution 2133 (2014), calling upon states to keep ransom payments, political concessions from benefiting terrorist.* [Online] Available at: www.un.org/press/en/2014/sc11262.doc.htm [Accessed 21 06 2021].

UN, 2021a. *Cybersecurity.* [Online] Available at: www.un.org/counterterrorism/cybersecurity [Accessed 11 06 2021].

UN, 2021b. *Text and status of the United Nations conventions on terrorism.* [Online] Available at: https://treaties.un.org/Pages/DB.aspx?path=DB/studies/page2_en.xml [Accessed 06 06 2021].

UNODC, 2012. *The Use of the Internet for Terrorist Purposes,* Vienna: United Nations.

US.Gov, 1991. *18 USC Ch. 113B: Terrorism.* [Online] Available at: https://uscode.house.gov/view.xhtml?path=/prelim@title18/part1/chapter113B&edition=prel [Accessed 06 06 2021].

Vaas, L., 2021. *DarkSide ransomware suffers 'Oh, Crap!' server shutdowns.* [Online] Available at: https://threatpost.com/darksides-servers-shutdown/166187/ [Accessed 28 06 2021].

Veerasamy, N., 2020. Cyberterrorism – the spectre that is the convergence of the physical and virtual worlds. In: *Emerging Cyber Threats and Cognitive Vulnerabilities.* London: Academic Press, p. 252.

Walsh, N. P., 2021. *Serious cyberattacks in Europe doubled in the past year, new figures reveal, as criminals exploited the pandemic.* [Online] Available at: https://edition.cnn.com/2021/06/10/tech/europe-cyberattacks-ransomware-cmd-intl/index.html [Accessed 26 06 2021].

Walter, E. V., 1969. *Terror and Resistance.* Oxford: Oxford University Press.

Weimann, G., 2004. *Cyberterrorism? How Real Is the Threat?.* [Online] Available at: www.usip.org/sites/default/files/sr119.pdf [Accessed 04 06 2021].

Wilkinson, P., 2011. *Terrorism Versus Democracy. The Liberal State Response.* 3 ed. Abingdon: Routledge.

Wolff, J., 2021. *As Ransomware Demands Boom, Insurance Companies Keep Paying Out.* [Online] Available at: www.wired.com/story/ransomware-insurance-payments/ [Accessed 28 06 2021].

WSJ, 2021. *Cyber Daily: EU aims to beef up cybersecurity amid ransomware boom | Apple Plays Privacy, Security Cards.* [Online] Available at: www.wsj.com/articles/cyber-daily-eu-aims-to-beef-up-cybersecurity-amid-ransomware-boom-apple-plays-privacy-security-cards-11624539673 [Accessed 26 06 2021].

Zurier, S., 2021. *Chinese espionage group APT27 moves into ransomware.* [Online] Available at: www.scmagazine.com/home/security-news/ransomware/chinese-espionage-group-apt27-moves-into-ransomware/ [Accessed 20 06 2021].

7 Other Politically Motivated Attacks
Political Activists and Hacktivists

Introduction

Cyberwarfare and cyberterrorism are not the only politically motivated area that is rising. Non-state actors are operating independently outside the state apparatus and launching attacks against public and private entities. Hacktivism is the online version of protest or civil disobedience. The attack forms take two directions. One direction is purely online, where an attack is impacting groups, entities, or online users. The second direction can be online and offline, where a large group of online users conduct a joint action against a particular target (online or offline). In both areas, cyberspace and the Internet actors act as facilitators for progressing a political agenda. Additionally, these actors are more likely to be prosecuted than their state-sponsored or state-supported counterparts. The predominately focus in this chapter is on hacktivism and new forms for online political protest emerging in 2020 and 2021.

Conceptualising 'Other' Politically Motivated Attacks

'Other' politically motivated actors are operating outside the realm of the state, state-sponsored, and state-supported groups. These actors are non-state groups and individuals who are using the online environment for political activism and protest. The actions do not generate a high level of fear and uncertainties among the public. However, the attacks can have disruptive and damaging impacts on targets and customers. Some of the politically motivated groups rely on the online environment to facilitate or enhance the scope of the protest. Other politically motivated groups aggressively use online computer technologies, devices, and networks as vectors to exploit, disrupt, or damage the target. These groups' activities are directly criminalised in national cybercrime legislations imposed to manage illegal intrusions online. Attacks carried out by non-state actors often have a lower level of sophistication than state and state-sponsored/supported as the non-state actors have fewer resources at their disposal. However, the attacks are often innovative and effective, using humour and surprise to gain attention. Due to the nature of the attacks and how they are conducted, the groups are often organised in

DOI: 10.4324/9781003126676-7

a decentralised way, where actors are working together ad hoc depending on the cause and the actors' particular political interests (Cruz & Plaisance, 2021, pp. 1330–1331; Holt et al., 2018, p. 392; Insikt Group, 2019).

Cyberactivism is interlinked with two different areas. First, online political activism refers to political mobilisation, which involves using computer technologies, cyberspace, and networks to enhance or create politically motivated movements. The Internet and social media enable actors to identify or manage alternative channels to distribute information and create awareness about particular cases. The online environment creates endless opportunities for engaging and supporting political causes and ideologies online and offline. Some of these activists groups cultivate loyal and persistent following the group, engaging in the activities, and help to promote the cause online (Cruz & Plaisance, 2021, p. 1330; Sorell, 2015, p. 393).

Secondly and the most well-known form of online protest is hacktivism. Hacktivism is based on political activism, where hacking skills are employed against powerful commercial institutions or governments; or any entity the group decide is either bad or wrong (Check Point, 2021; Sorell, 2015). Hacktivists are stateless, elusive, often lawless, and always anonymous in their actions and organisation. The way they are organised and embrace the online environment has proved beneficial as the actors can quickly join the network to complete the attack to disband upon completion (Cruz & Plaisance, 2021, p. 1330; Sorell, 2015, p. 392). Despite general support by the public, they are still considered to fall outside the realm of acceptable political protests. However, compared with the offline tactics of politically motivated groups, using means and methods such as occupations, blockades, defacements, culture jamming, strikes, and sabotage, there is not much difference between some online and offline protest forms (Baraniuk, 2014; Sauter, 2014, p. 26).

The Legislative Foundation

THE RIGHT TO PROTEST

The right to protest is deeply rooted in the Human Rights Conventions and national constitutions. The freedom of protest is one characteristic of a free and democratic society where the society is prepared to follow some wishes of the population to satisfy the majority. Therefore, democratic governments will tolerate and encourage various political activities, where the public can oppose and form a healthy opposition (Fenwick, 2006, p. 419). Freedom of opinion and expression are fundamentally civil and political rights considered necessary for an individual's development in any given society. It is impossible to enjoy other rights linked to protest without free speech, i.e. freedom of assembly and association (Howie, 2018, pp. 12–13; HRC, 2011, p. 1).

The UN's Universal Declaration from 1948 set out necessary rights for political activism. See Table 7.1.

Table 7.1 The UN protection of the right to protest

The UN's Universal Declaration from 1948	Rights
Article 18	The right to freedom of thoughts
Article 19	The right to freedom of opinion and expression
Article 20	The right to freedom of peaceful assembly and association

Source: UN (1948).

The International Covenant on Civil and Political Rights (ICCPR), implementing the personal and political rights set out in the UN Universal Declaration, states that the freedom of thought is protected and "No one shall be subject to coercion which would impair his freedom to have or to adopt a religion or belief of his choice" (The UN, 1966) The freedom of expression (Art 19) covers

> [F]reedom to seek, receive and impart information and ideas of all kinds, regardless of frontiers, either orally, in writing or in print, in the form of art, or through any other media of a person's choice.
>
> (Howie, 2018; The UN, 1966)

At the same time, the freedom of assembly is recognised in Article 21 and the freedom of association in Article 22. It is a fundamental human right for all individuals to join a peaceful assembly to express themselves, celebrate, or express grievances. Together, these rights constitute the foundation of democratic societies, where changes can be made through discussion and persuasion rather than by using force (Steiner et al., 2007, p. 489; Swaine, 2018, p. 406; UN, 2020).

These rights are protected in various domestic legislation, international treaties, and regional human rights instruments. Table 7.2 outlines the key regional provisions, which forms the basis of national human right's legislations.

Although the central rights of freedom of expression, freedom of assembly, and participation in the democratic system are not respected in all jurisdictions, the rights remain relevant to protests merging online and offline spaces, such as street protests together with online communication. In most politically motivated activities, new technologies act as a medium for organising offline protests. Although the online element becomes prevalent, offline protests are still happening with the broader population's understanding and support. The online environment can indeed be an amplifier for the cause and the activities, but it does not necessarily exclude or overtake participation (Article 19, 2016; Sorell, 2015).

Table 7.2 International definitions

Organisation	Convention	Provisions
The CoE	The European Convention on Human Rights 1953	Article 10, freedom of expression; Article 11, freedom of assembly and association
The OAS	The American Convention on Human Rights 1978	Article 13, freedom of thought and expression; Article 15, right of assembly; Article 16, freedom of association
The OAU	The African Charter on Human and People's Rights 1981	Article 9, the right to receive information and free expression; Article 10, the right to freedom of association; Article 11, the freedom of assembly

Sources: CoE (1950); Organisation of African Unity [OAU] (1981); Organisation of American States [OAS] (1969).

The UN Human Rights Council (HRC) adopted in 2018 an essential resolution, HRC REC 38/11, on human rights and protests stating that human rights must be protected online to enable online protest, similar to the protests protected in the UN's Human Rights Article 19 (Article 19, 2018; UN, 2018a). The new element is that online users also have the right to assembly solely through online conduct (Article 19, 2018). Significantly, the addition to the right comes in the light of state powers trying to control online protests. There has been an increase in states shutting down the Internet, limiting access to online media accounts, and blocking websites as anticipatory measures or responses. The anticipatory tactic limits online and offline users' rights to participate, receive, and distribute information about protests (APC, 2019, p. 2; Article 19, 2018). In 2018, the HRC had also adopted REC 38/7 on the promotion, protection, and enjoyment of human rights on the Internet (UN, 2018b).

Despite the UN resolution, the use of the online environment for public protests is contested. The entire Internet is private. Online use is incorporated in everyday lives to assemble public life. However, no public areas are designed for online protests in virtual spaces, similar to the offline environment where states have a negative obligation to protect the right to protest. This means that the rights are not directly transferrable to the Internet. Public rights regulate the relationship between the state and the citizens. Often the states do not have any interest in challenging this private ownership of the Internet, leaving online users to be subjected to the private services' terms and conditions, such as access to the platforms and association (Baraniuk, 2014; Cruz & Plaisance, 2021, p. 1330; Fenwick, 2006, p. 397). However, the state can regulate some areas within the online environment by criminalising certain behaviours and activities.

Cybercrime Legislation

Although the hacktivist groups are engaged in various types of actions, online and offline, criminal and non-criminal, they are primarily involved in clandestine activities to draw attention to a particular issue, gain attention, and promote their own type of ethics. These groups' modus operandi is linked to illegally breaking into corporations and governmental targets to promote a political end – or prevent the operations of these entities by disturbing or damaging the online structures of services. However, the targets also include religious organisations, terrorists, drug dealers, and paedophiles depending on the groups' cause and what they consider is right or wrong (Frankenfield, 2019; Sorell, 2015, p. 392). The hacktivist groups are far from being on the same level as state-sponsored/supported actors, but they have become proficient in their specialist areas. Although they operate on a lower scale, the groups have considerable capabilities and capacities for conducting attacks; the lack of sophistication is replaced with relentless and innovative actions.

CoE's Convention on Cyberbercrime 2001

To define this area of cybercrime, the CoE's Convention on Cybercrime 2001 is instrumental. The Convention defines vital areas and improves the means to prevent and suppress computer-related crimes on the national and international levels. So far, there are 65 signatory states, whereas 3 states still miss ratifying the Convention (CoE 2021). The states having ratified the Convention have also introduced cybercrime legislation. The different legislative framework covers the hacktivist's main techniques, such as hacking and DDoS attacks.

HACKING

Significantly, the Convention criminalises hacking without explicitly defining it (CoE, 2001a, 2001b, p. 7). The hacking typology encompasses 'illegal access' covering hacking, cracking, computer trespass of various types, and the definitions of the criminal offences are outlined in Articles 2–6 of the Convention. These are developed to protect the confidentiality, integrity, and availability of computer systems or data and separate the illegal activities from the legitimate and common use of computer systems and networks, processes, and practices (CoE, 2001b, pp. 8–9). See Table 7.3.

The Convention aims to harmonise domestic criminal law provisions developed by the signatory States, and it creates a practical cooperative system in an international context (CoE, 2001b, p. 3). An example is the UK Computer Misuse Act 1990, amended by the UK Serious Crime Act of 2015 to update the offences. See Table 7.4.

Table 7.3 CoE definition of illegal access

Name	Criminalisation	Included
CoE 2001a, Article 2	Article 2, illegal access	Committed intentionally Accessed the whole or any part of a computer system without right Committed by infringing security measures, the intent of obtaining computer data or other dishonest intent, or in relation to a computer system connected to another computer system.

Sources: CoE (2001a).

Table 7.4 The UK definition of unauthorised access

Legislation	Definitions	Characteristics
The Computer Misuse Act 1990	Section 1: unauthorised access to computer material	The act does not use the hacking typology. Includes a broader definition of 'Unauthorised access'
	Section 2: unauthorised access with intent to commit or facilitate the commission of further offences	It is not necessary to prove that the intended further offence has been committed.
	Section 3: unauthorised acts with intent to impair, or with recklessness as to impairing the operation of a computer	Linked to activities where the offender performs any unauthorised act in relation to a computer and knows that the access is unauthorised, such as DDoS attacks
	Section 3ZA: unauthorised acts causing, or creating risk of, serious damage	Linked to activities that caused or created a significant risk of serious damage to human welfare or national security. i.e. CIs
	Section 3A: making, supplying, or obtaining articles for use in offence under Section 1, 3, or 3ZA	Linked to the growing market of electronic malware or 'hacker tools' that can be used for breaching or compromising, computer systems

Source: Crown Prosecution Service (2021).

Although the UK has not explicitly mentioned hacking, the UK Crown Prosecution Service has outlined hacking in its Cybercrime Guidance and defined the area as a form of intrusion that target computers, including module phones and tablet devices (The Crown Prosecution Service, 2019). Hacking is generally included in the legislation as it creates a foundation for many cyber-dependent crimes. For example, the French Criminal Code (FCC), Article 323–1, criminalising hacking by relating it to unauthorised access to an automated data processing system (Lecomte, 2020). Similarly, the German Criminal Code Sections 202a and 202b also criminalise hacking (Niethammer et al., 2020).

The US has also introduced similar legislation in the Computer Fraud and Abuse Act 1986 (CFAA), where hacking is referred to as 'without authorisation' or 'exceed authorisation'. The phrase without authorisation is typically linked to external attackers. Whereas the exceed authorisation would be insiders, such as employees (Doyle, 2014, p. 4; Marshall Jarrett & Bailie, 2015, pp. 7–12). The CFAA has been amended to cover several new hackings methods that have evolved beyond the original intent (National Association of Criminal Defence Lawyers, 2021; Office of Legal Education Executive Office for United States Attorneys, 2015). See Table 7.5.

The legislation broadly defines these areas in relation to financial institutions or the US government (Office of Legal Education Executive Office for United States Attorneys, 2015). The definition of protected computers was also expanded in 2008. The definition now includes computers used in or affecting interstate or foreign commerce or communication (Office of Legal Education Executive Office for United States Attorneys, 2015, p. 5). Despite various amendments of the CFAA, it has not fundamentally changed since 1986. It is still problematic legislation, vaguely formulated and unclear about the actual areas covered within the law (Rosenblatt, 2020b).

Table 7.5 The US definition of unauthorised access

Legislation	Definitions
The CFAA	18 U.S.C. 1030, outlaws conduct that victimises computer systems
	Subsection 1030(a) includes:
	Knowingly accessed a computer without authorisation or exceeding authorised access, and using such conduct having obtained information requires protection against unauthorised disclosure
	Subsection 1030(b) included attempt or conspire to commit any of these offences outlined in subsection (a).

Sources: Office of Legal Education Executive Office for United States Attorneys (2015); LLI (2021).

Table 7.6 Definitions covering DDoS attacks

State	Provisions	Characteristics
The United Kingdom	The UK Computer Misuse Act 1990. Section 3: unauthorised acts with intent to impair, or with recklessness as to impairing the operation of a computer	Included preventing or hindering access to computer material by a legitimate user. The modification does not need to have occurred. The impairment can also be temporary.
The United States	The US CFAA 18, section 1030 (a)(5): 1 prohibits a variety of acts that result in damage to a computer	Criminalised not only explicit threats to damage computers but also comprising or committing a computer hacking offence or associated offences
France	The French Criminal code, Article 323–2 FCC, included sanctions on impending or slowing down computer systems	If the offence involves an attack against a public or governmental computer, the sanctions are raised
Germany	The German Criminal Code Section 303b links the DoS/DDoS attacks to computer sabotage	Covers everyone who interferes with data processing operations of substantial importance to another by deleting, suppressing, rendering unusable or altering data, or entering or transmitting data to cause damage to another

Sources: Congressional Research Service (2020); Crown Prosecution Service (2021); Lecomte (2020); Niethammer et al. (2020); Office of Legal Education Executive Office for United States Attorneys (2015, p. 2); Sauter (2014, p. 14).

DDOS

DDoS attacks are the most prominent and disruptive means in the online hacktivists toolbox. There is also a distinction between how the activities are perceived. For example, sit-ins are considered a natural tactical tool for activists by blocking access to a location. Whereas DDoS attacks that disrupt and block online access for a short period is perceived as criminal tactics (Sauter, 2014, p. 7). Both DoS and DDoS attacks are launched to render a service inaccessible. Therefore, it can be the ultimate tool for hackers, hacktivists, organised crimes groups, etc., where the method is used to overload a network or an application layer (NCSC, 2016). The Convention had not directly implemented DoS and DDoS attacks, but several articles in the Convention can be used depending on the attack form, i.e. Article 2, illegal access; Article 4, data interference; Article 5, system interference; or Article 11, attempt, aiding, and abetting (CoE, 2013). States have adopted provisions to manage this area. See Table 7.6.

Table 7.7 Progression

Regional institution	Progress
The OAU	Substantive reforms and progress had been made
The Commonwealth countries	Using a model law to create a legal framework for criminalisation
The OAS	Recommend the member states implement the principle included in the Convention on Cybercrime and acceding to the convention
The EU	Developed a substantive framework to manage this area and harmonise cybercrime legislation
The Asian-Pacific Economic Cooperation	Collectively committed states to enact a comprehensive set of laws following international legal instruments, including UN's General Assembly Resolution 55/63 (2000) and CoE's Convention on Cybercrime

Sources: CoE (2001a, 2020a, 2020b, p. 5); EU (2005); Schølberg & Hubbard (2005, pp. 7–8); The Commonwealth (2017, p. 1); UN (2001).

LEGISLATIVE DEVELOPMENTS

A survey conducted by the CoE in 2020 on the current state of cybercrime legislation globally has sowed. In total, 177 states worldwide were progressing or had already reformed existing legislation. However, 153 of these states have used both the Convention on Cybercrime and the UN guidelines for legislative reforms as a foundation. Other organisations have proposed similar frameworks to the CoE Convention to align regional frameworks with the Convention (CoE, 2020a, p. 5, 2020b).

There is a common consensus for criminalising illegal intrusion/unauthorised access into computer systems and networks that align with the Convention on Cybercrime and various UN's initiatives. There is limited scope for typology hacking, which is the most used phrase to explain these areas. See Table 7.7. This outline of initiatives and directions illustrates that contrary to cyberwarfare and cyberterrorism, a considerable quantity of legislation developed covering hacktivist's attacks.

Motivation

Many hacktivist and politically motivated hacking activities are perceived as an online form of civil disobedience. Often the aim is to use the online environments as a technique for resistance and protest to generate social or political change by peacefully breaking unjust laws (Lavorgna, 2020, p. 60). New forms of activism/hacktivism emerged in 2020 and 2021, setting a direction for future protest forms. Some of the means and methods are illegal, such as hacking, exploitation, and DDoS attacks. Other new innovative attacks operate with the legal framework, allowing attacks to develop similar DDoS attacks. This makes the area of online activism/hacktivism very interesting.

Year 2020 will be remembered for its use of online protest to call for social change while the world was in lockdown due to the COVID-19 pandemic. The pandemic was a game changer of how people interacted and how the online environment was used for political actions (Rosenblatt, 2020a).

The online environment enables political groups and individuals to reach out to geographically distant people with common goals to unite and support a shared goal (Frankenfield, 2019). The objective of hacktivist groups can be similar to traditional protest groups. However, the hacktivists' justification and activities challenge traditional protest forms by extending the scope, ideological foundation, and the means and methods used (Sorell, 2015). Hacktivism is being used alone or in conjunction with more traditional activism forms, such as the actions related to the Occupy Wall Street and the Church of Scientology protests (Frankenfield, 2019; Sorell, 2015).

Hacktivist draws an analogy between hacking, civil rights activities, movements, and civil disobedience. Some supporters claim that the hacktivism protest forms should be recognised in the same way as offline protests. For example, in 2013, Anonymous presented a 'We the People' petition to the US government to get DDoS attacks recognised as a legitimate form of protest similar to the peaceful occupation of the land by linking their activities to the Occupy encampment. This petition was rejected, but it opened the debate whether hacktivist groups' activities should purely be considered in the realm of offline protests and not as a criminal enterprise (Gillespie, 2019, p. 92; Kerr, 2013; Li, 2013, p. 304).

Online Protest Movements

From an early stage in the Internet's development, politically motivated hackers have been drawn to the online environment to launch a protest. Groups and individuals have adopted this platform for various types of activities. These activities are linked to civil disobedience using the online sphere to protest. Although not all online protest groups are organised similarly, some are comparable to the offline groups using the same tactic imposed, i.e. traditional political parties and protest movements. Other groups are operationally different from these by not adhering to the same hieratical structure but are founded ad hoc and anarchistic. These online protest groups are more loosely founded. They are activated by postings on social media online or message boards, similar to large-scale rave parties or impromptu charity events (Sorell, 2015). Advocacy groups embrace the online environment to coordinate their activities among the member groups and associated groups concerning a particular activity. It also allows participants to link with groups online and get information about protests and meetings (Denning, 2010; Yar & Steinmetz, 2019, p. 85).

The way online protests have been linked to the offline environment has changed the management of these activities. The 'Carnival against Capitalism' protest in London in 1999 arranged was particularly violent. It was considered that the trigger was the online exposure that had brought in a large crowd of people. The 1999 N30 London protest followed this event using the virtual space actively in the protest. The ability to anonymously participate and post information online has propelled beyond the reach of conventional media by breeding transnational protest allowing Internet-enabled protesters to gather simultaneously in a global context (BBC News, 1999b). Most protest movements are still engaging in traditional battles regarding power, participation, and democracy. However, they are empowering by new downloadable weapons and protest forms to provide a voice to a global audience (Grammatikopoulou, 2013; Karatzogianni, 2012). A key example of using the digital environment in relation to a political protest is the Arab Spring uprising in 2011. The Arab Spring was the first large-scale revolutionary movement in the digital age, where information was used as the principal weapon based on who had it, who controlled it, and who knew how to use it (Cyber Security, 2021). New actors unaffiliated with formal movements collaborated with traditional grassroots movements. Social networks have been instrumental in mobilising people and enabling individuals and groups to collaborate innovatively and effectively (Bernburg, 2016, p. 20).

NEW DIRECTIONS FOR ONLINE PROTESTS: THE GEN Z AND K-POP STANS

Despite the controversy about the TikTok app, a community formed within the platform has emerged from the PG lip-syncs and viral dance videos to becoming increasingly political. The most exciting development within political online activism and grouping are the Generation Z (Gen Z) and K-pop stans, who began to engage with political protests developing a new breed of 'pop activism'. The Gen Z/K-pop stans are rethinking the millennial generation's social justice warriors by including the use of dark memes, hashtags, and K-pop fancams (Koo, 2020). The emergence of these TikTok Gen Z/K-pop stans challenges the current understanding of online political activism. The app provides a platform for collectivism, agency, and action that fits into the goal of the generation by making 'the personal' political. The generation is hopeful, dynamic, and prepared to exploit various forms of technology to their advantage (Bedingfield, 2020; Hoise, 2020). The TikTokers engage in political expression and dialogue/conflict filtered through their identities and experiences and expressed in their actions (Herrman, 2020; Ohlheiser, 2020b). This generation has often been discounted and underestimated. However, Gen Z/K-pop stans have unexpectedly found their voice and engage in discussions and actions about social and political issues, such as climate change, gun violence, BLM, LGBTQ+, and the COVID-19 pandemic (Hoise, 2020).

Hacktivism

Hacktivism is the combination of hack and activism, and this area covered the actor a hacking or illegal intrusion/unauthorised access to computer systems for politically or socially motivated purposes (Check Point, 2021; Goode,

2015, p. 75; Hampson, 2012, p. 515). A number of groups are interlinked with political activists, anarchists, or movements that have observed the benefit of having an online presence or support. However, hacktivist groups with more fluid ideologies engage with a broad number of activities carried out alone or with other like-minded hackers (Frankenfield, 2019). Although hacktivists and hackers operated in similar ways, the motivation is different. Where the hackers are acting in self-interest, the hacktivist is engaged to archive political or social changes. Hacktivist activities often cover website defacements, information theft, website parodies, DoS attacks, virtual sit-ins, and virtual sabotage (Hampson, 2012, p. 515; Jordan & Taylor, 2004, p. 69).

The motivation for being involved in these online actives can include revenge, political and social incentives, ideology, protest, embarrass organisations or individuals within these organisations – or sometimes the activities mirror vandalism. Yet, the hacktivists groups aim to challenge governments, organisations, and companies that go against the hacktivist groups' moral position (Ablon, 2018, p. 3; Check Point, 2021; Holt et al., 2018, p. 387). Hacktivism's core areas are supporting democracy, protecting free speech online, and promoting access to information. For example, a part of the politically motivated activities is assisting computer users in enhancing online privacy and avoiding surveillance, disputing cooperate or government powers to protest globalisation and capitalism (Frankenfield, 2019). Circumventing governance censorship is another core area of hacktivism. The hacktivists are not only engaged in targeting the censoring governments. They also enable online users to circumvent national firewalls and security restrictions, impacting access to material online and communicating (Frankenfield, 2019).

Over the years, hacktivism has developed as a valuable form of political protest from the early movement of ethical hacking by including the political activist dimension in the 1990s and early 2000s movements. The early hacktivists developed from various phone pranks and computer programmers' curious exploration of computer systems and networks – even before developing the Internet. This movement and the groups' activities formed a subculture of online users with the skills and understanding of the online environment, enabling them to explore the limits of the new space and the new expressive and disruptive tools that are replacing physical protests (Hampson, 2012, p. 515; Jordan & Taylor, 2004; Karagiannopoulos, 2020, p. 64). The activities expanded to include the protection of the online technology-based subcultures and object to the restrictions of downloading music, information, movies, etc. by exploiting the gaps in anti-hacking protection imposed by businesses and public institutions (Jordan & Taylor, 2004, Chapters 1–3; Sorell, 2015). Hacktivist groups in every region have their unique motives to justify their online activities. Groups have emerged from regional conflicts, state-directed initiatives, general governmental disillusionment, or events against a group's worldview (Insikt Group, 2019).

The groups often contradict themselves and their values. Activities are launched to prevent access to particular websites or services. Thereby, they cut off online users from certain services or networks. This contradicts the idea of free speech and the free circulation of information. Attacking to promote own rights and limits others does not comply with freedom of thought and expression. The groups are launching DDoS attacks against webpages and applications, defacing opponents and doxxing those they disagreement do not foster an open and accessible environment (Ablon, 2018, p. 3; Frankenfield, 2019). The groups are also launching attacks for less sympathetic purposes that decrease public support. For example, groups have engaged in harassment and extortion – or stealing and disseminating sensitive, proprietary, or classified material, which impacts the people named in the material (Ablon, 2018, p. 3).

THE EMERGENCE OF NEW HACKTIVIST GROUPS

Some of the former members of Anonymous are also returning the activism, for example, in support of the BLM movement in 2020 (Clayton Rice Q.C., 2021; Menn, 2021). However, a new type of activism and groupings are emerging. These groups are mainly protesting against the operation of cybersecurity actors and the tech companies' distribution of propaganda. One prominent group that has caught attention is APT-69420 Arson Cats (Associated Press, 2021; Panda Security, 2021). The group aims to express its displeasure with the way video surveillance is increasing and how online surveillance is playing with the lives of ordinary citizens. Moreover, the groups are also concerned about a large number of end-point video vulnerabilities. The hackers have accessed and published live video feeds from companies, such as Tesla and Cloudflare, and videos and footage from other Verkada clients, including offices, warehouses, factories, prisons, psychiatric wards, banks, and schools (Clayton Rice Q.C., 2021; Laskey, 2021; Menn, 2021). Groups have launched attacks supporting anti-racist and anti-fascist politics by targeting Parler's archive and hacking Gap, the social networks used by white nationalists and right-wing extremists. New groups of hackers have also focused on Qanon and online hate groups. These hacktivists' preferred actions are to upload material on an online transparency site, Distributed Denial of Secrets (DDoSecrets), similar to WikiLeaks (Reuters, 2021).

Actors

The spectrum of 'other' politically motivated cyber attacks and groups covers every action conducted by entirely non-state political actors. The new moments are interesting as they reinvent hacktivism by merging legal and illegal actions in their target selection and execution. The groups' online presence can be linked to the two previous waves of hacktivism, so it is essential to understand it as a concept. The two new directions are very distinct. One group operated in the realm of traditional online activism, i.e. Gen Z/K-pop stans. The other direction is linked to traditional hacktivism with a new twist, i.e. APT-69420 Arson Cats.

First Activism Wave

Globally, Hacktivism is the most well-known form of online protests and activism. Various groups have developed from the 1990s, including Cult of the Dead Cow (CDC), Hacktivismo, Lulz Security (LulzSec), Anonymous, Legions of the Underground, The Electronic Disturbance Theater (EDT), Young Intelligent Hackers Against Terrorism, Syrian Electronic Army, and

Table 7.8 The first activism wave

Name	Activities	Characteristics
The CDC founded in 1983	Developed tools for testing password security. Developed technique for controlling computers from a distance	The CDC is one of the most respected and famous American hacking groups Invented the term 'Hacktivism' (Hacktivismo) and dubbed the actors 'hacktivists' in 1994.
The Critical Art Ensemble (CAE) founded in 1987	Engaging in media interventions by developing micropolitical means to disrupt, intervene, and educate	Tactics lead to more groups to develop online blockages and trespass
The Strano Network founded in 1995	Launched a one-hour strike against websites operated by governmental agencies. Considered as being an early example of a DDoS attack	Conducted the first electronic civil disobedience by arranging a protest against the French government police on nuclear and social issues
The EDT founded in 1997	Developed the Floodgate tool for an online virtual sit-in	Collaborated closely with Mexico's Zapatista revolutionary movement. The tool was instrumental for the group's online success attacking the Mexican President Zedillo, the Frankfurt Stock Exchange, and a site of the US Department of Defense, defenselink.mil
The Electohippies Collective founded in 1999	Combined online and offline protests. Ran an online protest which included a familiar aspect of hacktivism: DoS	Known for their virtual sit-in campaign during the 1999 Seattle meeting by World Trade Organisation (WTO) and blocking computer network at the event

Sources: BBC News (1999a); Cox (2014); Denning (2010); Insikt Group (2019); Karagiannopoulos (2020, pp. 65, 67); Lecher (2017); Menn (2019); Sauter (2014).

AnonGhost (Frankenfield, 2019). One of the first groups to get wide recognition is CDC. Two years after this group was founded, the US Congress adopted the CFAA legislation criminalising intentional access without authorisation (Insikt Group, 2019). The first groups were primarily involved in creating open-source programmes to prevent attempts from public and private entities to control the online experience (Kahn & Kellner, 2004, p. 90). Yet, the groups were also involved in developing tools for virtual sit-ins. The groups were smaller and more engaged in organising public-participation events following the principle of open and no-harmful protests. These events supplemented civil disobedience in the offline world (Karagiannopoulos, 2020, p. 70; Menn, 2019; Murphy, 2019). See Table 7.8.

The most recognised successors to the first, rather primitive, hacktivist groups are Anonymous. This group, together with LulzSec and WikiLeaks, characterised the second wave. Each of these groups has a different incitement for being involved in the hacktivist movement. Group Anonymous is predominately known for its focus on particular areas and its political stance. Whereas LulzSec is more known for its humour and cheeky campaigns where some were political. Finally, WikiLeaks is known for uploading material online originating from whistle-blowers and online hacks. See Table 7.9.

Second Activism Wave

ANONYMOUS

Group Anonymous' activities have developed from engaging in small, clustered activities to become a global activists group facilitating disruptions by subgroups and affiliates, making the activities less structured and recognisable. The uniqueness of these hacktivist groups is that it has no formal membership, controlling body or internal structure. Everyone can participate in actions at will. The group is one of the first hacktivist groups to have a completely decentralised foundation allowing individuals to create regional subgroups as a part of the Anonymous framework (Anonymous International; Anonymous Italia, etc.) (Afifi-Sabet, 2020; Holt et al., 2018, pp. 13–15; Insikt Group, 2019; Karagiannopoulos, 2020, p. 76; Mueller, 2017, p. 143; Wood, 2020). Being a pioneering social movement linked together with a desire for activism and online activities, they created an alternative form of an organisation aiming to be transnational, stable, open, transparent, accountable, and inclusive where anyone can claim membership. The determining factor is "if you believe in Anonymous, and call yourself Anonymous, then you are Anonymous" (Insikt Group, 2019; Mueller, 2017, p. 143).

Group Anonymous is founded upon the spirit of humorous deviance, including anti-celebrity ethics. Before the group moved onto political hacktivism in 2008, it was widely known for its 'trolling campaigns'. Members of the group used online means and methods to abuse, harass, or bring into disrepute individuals or institutions. These campaigns were pursued for a laugh ('the lulz') (Coleman, 2015, pp. 17, 31; Richards & Wood, 2018, p. 189). Compared with the first hacktivist groups, group Anonymous successfully rebranded hacktivism through their rhetoric and the way they have embraced technological development. The years with the Anonymous domination have led to large-scale recruitment based on highly mediated and media-friendly events with noticeable actions; easy to cover as news events (Karagiannopoulos, 2020, p. 77; Wood, 2020).

The group is very recognisable, and most people will have heard about the group's activities. The group has been praised for its engagement in cyber-vigilante campaigns beyond the hacking communities, including its actions against sex offenders, animal abusers, corrupt politicians, and terrorist organisations (Richards & Wood, 2018, p. 192). A cascade of increasingly political operations has been attributed to the group after its first long-term campaigns, Project Chanology, Operation Payback, etc. (Afifi-Sabet, 2020; Lavorgna, 2020, p. 60). For example, the group has been involved in actions in support of the Occupy Wall Street movement, the Arab Spring protests; campaigns against the CIA and Interpol; against Muslim discrimination in Myanmar; support of the democratic activists in Hong Kong; and attacks against purported members of the Ku Klux Klan (Brooking, 2015; Karagiannopoulos, 2020, p. 74). However, in the fight against ISIS, the members of Anonymous found themselves in an internal turmoil linked to sharing information with the establishment they were supposed to fight. Additionally, the group has always fought all restrictions on Internet use. But in the fight against ISIS, they actively limited access for some online users, i.e. ISIS militants. In online and offline debates, it became clear that self-identifying Anonymous members struggled to reconcile their past goals with the present activities (Brooking, 2015). The Internet conflicts, the diversified actions, and the lack of community feeling decreased the group's support. During the same period, businesses, organisations, and governmental institutions increased their cybersecurity, making it more difficult for lower-level actors to beach the networks (Willams, 2019).

LULZSEC

The group LulzSec was also operational when Anonymous' activities developed. The group name combines lulz (for a laugh) and sec (security), which is the group's primary motivation, and the link to humour is evident in its motto: "Laughing at your security since 2011!" providing "high-quality entertainment at your expense" (Arthur, 2013; Branch, 2011; Gallagher, 2011). LulzSec's cheerful public image undoubtedly helped the group gaining popularity within a short time. The group is similar to other hacking groups that spill over the political environment from time to time without having a clear political profile similar to Anonymous (Arthur, 2011, 2013; Batty, 2011;

Martin, 2011). Although most members of LulzSec came from the same core hacker group as Anonymous, the two groups have had their conflicts. In particular, the groups clashed after LulzSec attacked several video games initiated by a 'DDoS Party' that brought down several gaming servers and websites, such as EVE Online, League of Legends and Minecraft (Lynley, 2011a). The conflict between the two groups was further fuelled by LulzSec publicly mocked 4chan users, the image-sharing message board where Anonymous derived from (Lynley, 2011a, 2011b).

Despite this conflict, the two groups collaborated in an operation against government agencies in actions dubbed Operation Anti-Security, which encouraged hackers worldwide to attack governmental websites and deface them. Despite LulzSec's claims that the hacks on websites like the CIA were for fun (Lynley, 2011b). The two groups also collaborated in an attack on Arizona Police Department and other organisations in the Arizona state government as a reaction to what the groups called an unjust war on drug actions (Gallagher, 2011; Insikt Group, 2019). The LulzSec group allegedly disbanded after some of its members were arrested. However, due to the way the group was organised and the transient nature of their membership, it is unlikely that all of the members were arrested. However, nothing has been attributed to the group since (Davis, 2014).

WIKILEAKS

At the border of hacktivism, it is possible to include WikiLeaks. WikiLeaks claims to be an independent and non-profit online media organisation that does not obtain the documents themselves. However, the website has been instrumental for the hacktivist groups to upload information vital to their political campaigns (Bacon, 2018). Some of the leaks published come from insiders, who reveal sensitive information that might have public interests. This information is secrets or bad practices that the organisations want to keep out of the public sphere, such as documents showing malpractices/discrepancies in organisations' official aspirations and actual practice. In that sense, the leaks appear to be a service to the public by showing the wrongdoing and the consequences of these actual practices (Sorell, 2015; WikiLeaks, 2011). Other types of material published on WikiLeaks are stolen online by hacktivist groups. For example, group Anonymous forwarded in 2012 internal emails from an American Security company Stratfor (Sorell, 2015). The leaks disclosed how the military-industrial complex conspired to spy on citizens, activists, and trouble-causers (Chatterjee, 2012). Some frictions appeared in WikiLeaks and Anonymous' relationship in 2012, and some of the hacktivists distanced themselves from the site claiming that the site has become a personal tribulation for Assange (Halliday, 2012).

Table 7.9 The second activism wave

Name	The group's actions	Most well-known attacks
Anonymous	Originated in 2003 from the image board 4chan Involved with numerous DDoS campaigns and other online actions Know by the use of the Guy Fawkes mask	2008: Project Chanology: long-term campaign against the Church of Scientology 2010: Operation Payback against the music and film industry and associations as revenge for increased actions against copyright infringers 2010: #OPPayback expanded to included operation avenge Assange attacking PayPal, Visa, and Mastercard for withdrawing the server service to WikiLeaks After 2012: the group diversified with several decentralised operations
LulzSec	Founded and dissolved in 2011 Comes from Anonymous Known for its humouristic online attacks Dissolved after law enforcement prosecuted several members	2011: Attacked the InfraGard website dubbed 'F**k FBI Friday' 2011: Attacked the US Senate and released some security information 2011: Attacked the Bank of Portugal, the Portuguese Parliament, and the Ministry of Economy, Innovation and Development in response to police brutality and austerity measures
WikiLeaks	A non-profit organisation founded in 2006 Publishes news leaks and classified information Julian Assange is generally described as its funder	The group has realised classified many documents For example: 2010: The Afghan War Diary with documents of equipment expenditures and holdings 2010: The Iraq War Logs, which included information of insurgents in Iraq 2016: Email and documents from the Democratic National Committee during the US presidential election 2017: The Vault-7 documents about CIA's hacking tools

Sources: Bacon (2018); Batty (2011); Branch (2011); Davis (2014); Insikt Group (2019); Karagiannopoulos (2020); Mueller (2017); Sorell (2015); Van Wie Davis (2021, p. 11).

Third Activism Wave

GEN Z AND K-POP STANS

Gen Z members are a more racially and ethically diverse group than previous generations, such as baby boomers, Gen-X, and millennials. They are also digital natives with little memory of a time before the smartphone (Parker & Igielnik, 2020). The K-pop fanbase, the stans, is operating in the same field as the Gen Z TikTokers. Both groups show a growing political awareness across different interest areas. The groups operate within the legal framework; their means and methods innovatively explore technologies and communication platforms to carry out their activities. The K-pop fan culture developed from the mid-1990s export-oriented popular South Korean music. The music scene relied heavily on Internet and social media exposure and a strategy to cultivate fandom. Since the early days of this K-pop culture, fans have been engaged in online discussion groups, forums, and chat rooms related to Asian popular music. Members communicated intensively based on their musical interests and knowledge of K-pop (Bedingfield, 2020; Park, 2020). The early K-pop fanbase was the young Asian diaspora. However, the notion of K-pop spread fast to other communities of young people of colour who did not feel represented in the American mainstream culture (Ohlheiser, 2020a). K-pop fans and Gen Z are used to dominate the online conversation and embrace an online environment contrary to older generations. K-pop fans have been instrumental in propelling their favourite artist into stardom is based on a group tactic to manipulate the metrics on social media in a way that they resemble a bot (Ohlheiser, 2020a).

The K-pop stan has been written off by online activist groups as screaming, tedious young airheads who have created toxic fanbase siloes. However, these kinds of negative assumptions have united the groups, for example, in their actions related to BLM. The various stan groups are passionate about all types of political activism. A part of their motivation and engagement is linked to the ability to express themselves and be themselves (Koo, 2020). The political and social engagement of the communities are unexpected as some of the fans are attracted to the culture being apolitical, fantastical, and removed from home politics and American hegemony. However, not all fans are engaged in these causes, and there is also space to be fans and have fun (Bedingfield, 2020). Those who protested against the US President Trump during the US election might not be involved in future actions; all actions are linked to the teens' personal experience (Ohlheiser, 2020b). The social and politically active fractions with the K-pop fanbase see themselves as people affected by political decisions, and they are humans before being fans. The fanbase has a platform and the numbers to make a difference (Bedingfield, 2020). The groups should not be seen as monolithic. The groupings have a long history of creating online communities as a safe space for themselves – a space where they set up their own rules with a very intimate affinity with people worldwide (Bedingfield, 2020; Koo, 2020).

APT-69420 Arson Cats are a relatively new group that has emerged in the ashes of Anonymous. Not much has been published about the group, but it has already gained notorious status within a short period. Contrary to the K-pop and Gen Z activities, they are also operating illegally, and their actions can be traced back to 2019. According to the group's spokesperson, Kottmann, the group is motivated by the spirit of activism used to expose the poor security work of corporations before malicious actors do more damage. In this context, they frame themselves as grey hat hackers by doing the companies a favour before the real black hat hackers can exploit the vulnerabilities. However, the group does not hide their dislike for the law and corporate powers. They oppose the concept of intellectual property and how it limits online users understanding of the online systems integrated into everyday life (Reuters, 2021).

The group did not hack themselves, but they found source code repositories through GitLab, Bitbucket Git servers, and SonarQube source code management apps. However, instead of handing over the information to authorities or notified the companies, the group connected to the exposed applications and downloaded the intellectual property material, which was later uploaded on Git.rip (Cimpanu, 2021; Clayton Rice Q.C., 2021). Although the group did not always contact the companies before exposing the material, they claim they tried to prevent the exposure from harming companies when the information was released (Vincent, 2021a).

DDOSECRETS

DDoSecrets follows in the pathway of WikiLeaks. DDoSecrets is different in how they obtain the information. Some data were collected on the Dark Web, published by ransomware groups. The argument is that some of the dumped data available deserve to be scrutinised as they inform the public about bad practices by some actors (DarkReading, 2021; Greenberg, 2021). Yet, the practice opens up some ethical questions. Data on the Dark Web have already been released. However, the exposure of company information has a devastating effect that the release and the double exposure will amplify. The data leaks might encourage the ransomware groups as they can use these exposures to threaten the victims. This type of data would only be visible on the Dark Web for a short period. However, this group preserves these data sets allowing them to stay exposed in the public view. Over time, DDoSecrets would become the only publisher of the data (DarkReading, 2021; Greenberg, 2021). However, this is not the only way the group get data. Anonymous provided data for the BlueLeaks dump in 2020, and DDoSecrets has also obtained data about Gab, the extreme far-right and racial social network launched in 2017. The group claimed no responsibility for the hack, claiming they only reported and distributed information to journalists and researchers (Bradbury, 2021; Cimpanu, 2020).

Table 7.10 The third activism wave

Groups	Group's actions	Most well-known attacks
Gen Z/K-pop stans	A new generation of activism Operated within the legal framework Linked together in the K-pop fandom	2020: The Tusla Campaign tickets event 2020: Dallas Police Department app overloading the webpage with fancams
APT-69420 Arson Cats	Based on a small collective The group is acting independently Their motivation is to have fun, being gay, and create a better world One head figure is Kottmann	2021: Attack on Tesla, Cloudflare and several Verkada's clients: AI-based surveillance
DDoSecrets	Similar to WikiLeaks. A non-profit organisation devoted to enabling free communication in the public interest Collective lead by Emma Best It aims to end online surveillance and Tapping into footage and uploading material	2020: BlueLeaks. Internal US law enforcement data obtained by Anonymous 2021: ParlerLeaks. Videos and images were uploaded to Parler from the January 6th attack on the Capitol. All information was publicly available. 2021: GabLeaks. information from/about users on a white supremacist and racist social media

Sources: AFP (2021); Bedingfield (2020); DDoSecrets (2020, 2021a, 2021b); Laskey (2021); Vincent (2021b).

Means and Methods: Deterrence and Defence

The new groups of politically motivated actors differ from the 2010s hacktivist groups. They are less engaged with launching DDoS attacks to disrupt and destroy computer networks and systems. To a large extent, they operate in a grey zone using available public data, find the information in politically available open source, and then exploit the information. Groups like APT-69420 Arson Cats have carved out their route to conduct politically motivated attacks within this regulatory lacuna. The Gen Z/K-pop stans are slightly different. These groups explore legal routes for political activism, where some mirror DDoS attacks but are launched differently. Law enforcement keeps a close eye on these new groups, and there is already one case underway against Koffmann from APT-69420 Arson Cats. The Federal Bureau of Investigation (FBI) also has DDoSecrets under observation after they published BlueLeaks with information from Anonymous. Law enforcement has been targeted by all these groups, and so have other governmental and political entities, private corporations, and individuals.

Attacks against Public and Private Entities: New and Old Methods

In most political activities in the US and other Western states, politically motivated groups have the power to be a force for change and disrupt through their peaceful actions. A coalition of online protesters used the hashtag #Resistance on Twitter to confront US President Trump on his favourite social media site. However, they have had very little success until the stans got involved and promoted the hashtag to the group. The message was circulated widely, triggering the groups' sense of activism (Ohlheiser, 2020a). This was a popular way to make a political stance, and it is for the social media sites to regulate behaviour on their platforms. The social media site has made changes for political actors online by blocking content and close down accounts. Several US Republicans moved to Parler, a right-wing social media platform after US President Trump was permanently banned from Twitter in 2021. Trump was banned for his potential to incite following the US Capitol Hill insurrection on the 6th of January (Dzhanova, 2021; Pardes, 2020). However, the tech companies, Google, Apple, and Amazon, collectively showed their regulatory powers by withdrawing the platforms hosting web services for Parler forcing the site to close its business (Newhouse, 2021).

THE TUSLA EVENT

The online environment and the interconnectivity have been instrumental in several political actions combining the online and offline environments. Gen Z/K-pop stans joined forces to show their unhappiness with US President Trump during the 2020 election campaign. The young online users explored a legal way to hijack the Tusla political election rally and publicly humiliate the President (Bedingfield, 2020; Herrman, 2020). The planned action gained momentum online within the groups, and a substantial amount of people reserved tickets for the Tusla event without intentions of attending (Bedingfield, 2020; Ohlheiser, 2020b). The action was successful for the Gen Z/K-pop groups as they unexpectedly exposed the weaknesses in the campaign ticket system. Before the event, the Trump campaign expected a crowd size of approximate 1 million participants based on the reservations and data collected online about the event. On the day, only 6,200 people attended the event in a half-empty arena, to a huge surprise to the organisers (Lorenz et al., 2020; Porter, 2020).

The TikTok platform was instrumental in the false registration drive, leading to empty seats in the stadium and outside the arena. The way the Gen Z/K-pop stans engineered the moment was widely celebrated (Herrman, 2020; Lorenz et al., 2020; Ohlheiser, 2020b). Although the Gen Z/K-pop stans members did not have an electoral ability to make a difference, they still had a voice, and they demonstrated that they had strength in the numbers (Hoise, 2020; Lorenz et al., 2020). There is nothing in this action by the Gen Z/K-pop stans that are illegal. The groups exploited a clear security gap in how the event was organised. Reserving tickets for free is a service provided by several event organisers. Nevertheless, the Tulsa event was instrumental in creating the myth of these young people becoming politically radicalised. Other young people joined the #Resistance afterwards to form a powerful coalition of political actors (Ohlheiser, 2020b).

PERCEPTION OF ACTIONS

The actions of the Gen Z/K-pop stans are seen as the liberal's choice of actions similar to the 4chan hacktivist groups were to older generations. They are an army of anonymous Internet warriors, which a majority of people like to praise but do not really understand. The groups follow a personal agenda and do not align with conventional politics (Ohlheiser, 2020b). Although Gen Z/K-pop stans' activities archived media attention similar to the established hacktivists got in their prime time, they are still perceived as a joyful group of pranksters having fun rather than a political force with impact. These young online users archived this outcome by exercising their rights to express themselves through association and assembly. They are likely to continue this form of protest (The UN, 1966). The owners of these online platforms can regulate their use if they want to limit the actions. The monopoly of tech companies and social media businesses has regulatory powers to control their platforms. However, the same companies are driven by data extraction and behavioural modifications, which balances conduct against revenue generated by the use (Fernandez, 2021; Zuboff, 2019). Therefore, it is unlikely they will change terms and conditions to regulate the large group of young and active online users when their actions are not illegal.

Attacking CI Services: Anonymous, and Gen Z/K-pop

Both Anonymous and Gen Z/K-pop have been active in supporting the BLM movement. Anonymous uses their usual tactic, whereas Gen Z/K-pop has exposed new innovative ways to bring down webpages, but they operate within an uncontested grey zone within the law. Protecting computing infrastructure is a policy priority for actors worldwide. CIs such as banking, energy, transportation, and manufacturing rely on interconnected computers that have been vulnerable to exploitation online. These entities operate essential services, and companies and citizens trust their data to distant servers in return for more convenient and reliable services (Lindsay & Gartzke, 2016, p. 1). The latest attacks from state and non-state actors have shown substantial gaps in cybersecurity. However, it is concerning that hacktivists using low-sophisticated tools are still able to attack without much effort. In 2010, Anonymous launched one of its most well-known actions, #OpPayback, to revenge PayPal and other companies for suspending payments and server access to WikiLeaks following the publication of classified US documents (Brooking, 2015). The group also has a history of targeting various US federal and state government entities, such as the CIA and the US Senate. Anonymous was behind the Arizona Department of Public Safety in 2011 (Kelly, 2021, p. 1681). A decade later, the group can launch severe attacks against essential services and obtain and exploit data, showing that there are still issues with the level of cybersecurity.

ANONYMOUS

In 2020, group members actively supported the BLM protests after the police killing of George Floyd (Griffin, 2020; Rosenblatt, 2020a). Tweets and Facebook posts by the hacktivist collectively received millions of supports from new followers. The group indicated it aims to expose the many crimes of police forces worldwide (Griffin, 2020; Mehrotra & Tarabay, 2020; Molloy & Tidy, 2020). Hacktivists, leaktivists, and public disclosure organisations have been highlighted in the US counter-intelligence strategy 2020–2022 as constituting significant threats (AFP, 2020; Menn, 2021; The White House, 2020, p. 2). With this enhanced strategic focus, together with the very public statements from Anonymous about future actions, CI and ICTs providers and operators should see it as a warning to ensure that their cybersecurity is updated and system gaps are patched. Police forces should be particularly concerned as the group has previously targeted them.

After the killing of Floyd, Anonymous threatened to expose crimes within the department. The group launched a DDoS attack against the Minneapolis Police Department, which temporarily brought down the website. However, this is not a particularly new and sophisticated attack form. It would have been possible to prevent the attacks if the police forces had enough cybersecurity enacted (Ropek, 2020; Vaas, 2020). For example, Anonymous attacked in 2020 the Atlanta Police Department in retaliation for killing a black man, Brooks. The cyber attack was embarrassing for the City of Atlanta, which had invested hugely in cybersecurity after a ransomware attack in 2018. Still, the police were unable to detect and prevent such an attack (Vaas, 2020). Law enforcement and other government agencies who provide essential services to the public should have a high level of cyber-resilience, especially as several police forces have been subjected to attacks in the past.

Anonymous is still operating illegally and using the same old means and methods compared with the new groups. This makes it challenging for the group to claim that their actions should be seen as legitimate, similar to peaceful offline protests. The hacktivists often considering themselves as virtual vigilantes working for a cause beyond the individual's self-interest. Despite their noble intentions and aims to improve equality, justice, or human rights, they still act illegally (Crowdstrike, 2021). Yet, the only issue with these attacks is not their legality but how to prevent the attack. Very little attention is given to resilience and preparedness. The legal framework deals with attribution and prosecution of the attacks afterwards. However, the impacts on victims and a wider group of citizens that cannot access services should be included in the preventive strategies to enhance resilience. Most of the challenge is that the national cybersecurity framework relies on the actors to invest sufficient cybersecurity measures to decrease the threats. Only a limited number of private CIs are required to implement a particular cybersecurity level (Chung, 2018, p. 449).

GEN Z/K-POP STANS

Political actions by Gen Z/K-pop stans have highlighted that it is not only the illegal methods that can bring down a webpage; a joint action can have the same effect to halt public services (Alexander, 2020). Like Anonymous, the groups were supportive of the mass protests in response to police brutality in the wake of Floyd's death. These protests resulted in mass arrest and violence against protesters and press members (Alexander, 2020). In June, the K-pop stans took down the Dallas Police Department's app by overloading it with fancams, short clips of Korean K-pop groups, or idols performing live (Bedingfield, 2020).

The groups reacted to a tweet by the Dallas Police Department asking people to send videos of 'illegal activity from the protests' to a special app called iWatch Dallas during the protests. The K-fans took up this request and downloaded the app (Alexander, 2020; Lorenz et al., 2020; Ohlheiser, 2020a). Instead of using the illegal tactic similar to group Anonymous and other hacktivist groups, the fanbased stayed within the law, albeit bending it in an innovative way (Ohlheiser, 2020a). The group uploaded a constant and overwhelming flow of short fan-produced videos, bringing the system down similarly to DDoS attacks (Alexander, 2020; Lorenz et al., 2020). Additionally, numerous one-star reviews appeared on the app's pages on Google Play and Apple's App store marketplace with text including #BLM (Black Lives Matter) and #ACAB (All Cops Are Bastards). Later, the Dallas Police Department announced that the app was offline (Alexander, 2020; Ohlheiser, 2020a). When the app was down, the K-pop fanbase responded to the messages by uploading a mix of clips from K-pop groups performances, games like *Animal Crossing*, anime GIFs, and other pop culture references to celebrate their success (Alexander, 2020). However, it was not only the Dallas Police Department who experienced this form of activism. Similar activities were launched against a portal set up by a Michigan Police Department, where witnesses could upload pictures or videos of protests. Similarly, Kirkland, a Washington Police Department, requested footage of a local demonstration, but their apps were flooded and clogged by K-pop fans (Andrews, 2020).

Although the actions are not prohibited, the actions mirror the illegal use of DoS and DDoS attacks. These means and methods will likely be deployed in the future in a larger context to avoid prosecution. However, to have any effect, there needs to be a substantial number of people involved at the same time. The stans have gained a new and appreciative online audience for their online activism. Other online users praised the K-pop stans for their engagement in political and social causes by pushing for justice beyond their relentless promotion of groups like BTS, Blackpink, or EXO (Ohlheiser, 2020a). By looking at actions like this, it is possible to draw similarities between the K-pop stans and more established hacktivist groups like Anonymous. However, the main differences are the illegal vs legal discourse (Ohlheiser, 2020a). From the security perspective, the new groups are more unpredictable than the old types of activist groups. The actions highlight the need for proactive measures so that public and private services are less vulnerable to disruptions. Yet, it leads to the question about when Human Rights protect actions and when they are not.

Strategies and the Game

There are two groups of actors; the public and private actors on one side and the protesters on the other. Both groups need to weigh up costs and benefits and change the other side's strategic position. The key factor influencing the protestors to take action is the probability of success (Buenrostro et al., 2007). For example, the protester might successfully promote their cause and gain support for social and political change. However, they bear the risk of not being successful. Instead, they might get a negative payoff from costs imposed by the opposition. For example, if they hack into systems or launch DDoS attacks, they might be prosecuted. They might also face costs from other actors. ISPs, tech companies, and businesses provide the protesters with resources to facilitate collective actions, i.e. access to the Internet, social media sites, communication platforms, etc. (Stockemer, 2012, pp. 210–211). Finally, there might be costs in cybersecurity where it becomes challenging to breach the systems due to a lack of skills or time. As a reaction, the protestors might substitute costly activities with lower-cost actions to attain the desired goal (Patil et al., 2018; Pierskalla, 2010, p. 121; TrapX, 2020). Some online activists have decided to fulfil their goals using less intrusive means, but when a large group collaborates, it has the same effect, i.e. the Gen Z/K-pop stans. These methods might not have the same effect, but they still gain attention, and they also manage to bring down webpages in a similar way to DDoS attacks.

The cost–benefit balance would change by enhancing cybersecurity, and it would be more difficult for hacktivists to gain a positive payoff. The key is to make it more difficult to attack the different entities. Cybersecurity is not only about updating computer systems and network security. However, it is also about enhancing training, processes, and practices to work online and protect data, access credentials, and passwords. As long as it is relatively easy to conduct these attacks and gain access to systems and information, the activist will continue to do so. Cybersecurity is complicated as computer technology changes and the attackers change tactics. However, most of these attacks are not sophisticated, and most of them could be prevented with updated security measures. Deterrence and successful protest are decided by the cost–benefit calculation of winning an open conflict, the cost of repression, and the cost of escalation (Pierskalla, 2010, p. 125). The costs are linked to a failure of the attack (deterrence by denial) or retaliation (deterrence by punishment). The essential operation of deterrence is the communication by the defender where the opponent's attacks are made more costly than the benefits it produces (Vogele, 1993, p. 30).

Cybersecurity and Deterrence

The majority of online attacks are conducted on the lower end of the spectrum. These attacks are less likely to have a significant effect that can cause physical damage to the population. Therefore, it is not a surprise that comprehensive public and private strategies are missing. It seems like states are more focusing on preventing the state-sponsored/supported attacks and have overlooked this area. With state and state-sponsored/state-supported actors, some governmental actors cooperate and develop adequate responses, including raising the security level, knowledge exchange, minor sanctions, name and shame tactics, which have not prevented the attacks from developing (Lindsay, 2015). When it comes to hacktivism, it is less likely that the states will cooperate and develop common strategies, and it is left to national strategies and actors to manage the area.

The hacktivists' success is not necessarily linked to their skills, but more of their ability to finding vulnerabilities in weak applications, webpages, and servers with inadequate security (Mansfield-Devine, 2011). It is a challenge for organisations to defend themselves from hacktivist attacks. The threats are multifold, spanning from simple non-sophisticated attacks to well-executed large-scale attacks on multiple levels. Managing the threats is complex and requires protection from internal and external sources (Caldwell, 2015). As a part of developing national cybersecurity strategies, the states have included their cybersecurity resources to enhance their cyber capabilities, such as information sharing, cybersecurity standardisation, and risks management plans. There is no requirement for private entities to do the same, and systematic guidance is not provided to the private sector to ensure that they can withhold attacks (Siboni & Sivan-Sevilla, 2018). A multilayered approach is covering different levels of complex infrastructure and at the same time applying multiple different protective layers. However, it is also a continual process involving monitoring, threat detection, training, etc., to detect vulnerabilities and eliminate malicious activities (Impact, 2020; Jett, 2021). This includes the physical boundaries, network firewalls, and intrusion detection systems. It also includes the different bureaucratic procedures to constantly keep software patches and antivirus definitions updated, educate users about operational security, monitor network activity, investigate suspicious activities, coordinate with cybersecurity actors, and law enforcement before and after an attack (Lindsay & Gartzke, 2016).

INCLUDING COST-IMPOSITIONS

To increase cybersecurity, organisations need to factor in the integrity and resilience of the related businesses and social processes into the constant development of complex technologies. It is not enough to see cybersecurity as purely a matter of protecting the systems and networks (WeForum, 2020). As long as it is relatively easy to conduct these attacks and gain access to systems and information, the activist will continue to do so. Better security practices would have prevented APT-69420 Arson Cats and Kottmann from finding log-in credentials to Verkada's super admin account online (Vincent, 2021a, 2021b).

UNDERINVESTMENT IN CYBERSECURITY

For years public and private entities have underinvested in cybersecurity, processes, and practices to protect vital assets. The vulnerabilities to these actors digital technologies create risks to CIs, business continuity, intellectual property, trade, and consumer secrets and privacy (Siboni & Sivan-Sevilla, 2018). Underinvesting does not mean they are not investing at all. They just do not invest enough to manage the actual threats proactively. Most organisations invest based on a cost–benefit analysis by quantifying the benefits associated with their potential investment opportunities (Gordon et al., 2014, p. 80). However, various organisations tend to take a somewhat reactive approach to significant cybersecurity investments deferring investments unless they need to react to an incident (Gordon et al., 2015). Security strategies should incorporate computer technologies, management, budgets risks assessments, etc., encompassing the whole organisational structure from managers to employees within all aspects of the CI structure (Mansfield-Devine, 2011). These plans could enable public and private entities to become more robust and consider cybersecurity in all steps they take. It concerns how hacktivists managed to DDoS and access data from law enforcement and police forces worldwide during the second wave of attacks. A decade later, they are still vulnerable to attacks.

No business or governmental agencies are immune from attacks; over the years, hacktivism has grown from being a nuisance to pose a significant threat. Hacktivism has exposed the fragile digital systems and infrastructure that underpins most public and private entities (Bradford, 2014; Vamosi, 2011). A DDoS attack, for example, interferes with an organisation's online operations during the attack. However, they often have long-term consequences, such as a monetary impact. Some online users or customers might permanently change to a competing service provided that has a more reliable online service. Revenue loss is one side effect, reputational damage is another. The latter might prevent the actors from getting an opportunity to progress later (The Council of Economic Advisers, 2018). A part of the politically motivated actors' actions is conducted to cause embarrassment and reputational damage. The reason behind the attack is usually communicated to the public (Bradford, 2014).

Prosecution

The CoE Convention on Cybercrime requires that national cybercrime legislation's implementation and applications are compatible with international human rights agreements. The Convention refers directly to Article 15 of the CoE's protection of Human Rights and Fundamental Freedoms and the 1966 UN ICCPR (Hampson, 2012, p. 524), which clearly states that the rights should be considered with the legislative framework. UN Resolutions from 2016 and 2018 are also supporting that the rights that people are enjoying offline should be applied to the online environment. See Table 7.11.

Because cybercrime is criminalised, most hacktivists' means and methods fall within the provisions of national cybercrime legislation. The consequence of the current legal framework is that hacktivists are likely to be punished for something that does not warrant a prosecution offline. The motivation of hacktivists is political or social, which traditionally is not severely punished by law (Knapp, 2015, p. 259). Yet, in some legislation, such as the CFAA, hacktivists have faced severe prison sentences if found guilty. With various types of politically motivated attacks escalating, hacktivism should be considered in the context of these rather than cybercrime. However, it is clear that when hacking is used, the actual 'illegal intrusion' legislation is enacted, and hacking, defacing, and DDoS attacks have taken over from the more innocent short-term virtual sit-ins or blockage of certain websites for a limited number of times. The lines become blurred between the two groups, hackers and hacktivists. Hackers are predominately perceived as engaging in

Table 7.11 Protection of online protest

UN resolutions	Definitions
The UN REC 32/13	"... for the Internet to remain global, open and interoperable, it is imperative that States address security concerns in accordance with their international human rights obligations, in particular with regard to freedom of expression, freedom of association and privacy"
The UN REC 38/7	"... the same rights that people have offline must also be protected online, in particular freedom of expression, which is applicable regardless of frontiers and through any media of one's choice, in accordance with article 19 of the Universal Declaration of Human Rights and of the International Covenant on Civil and Political Rights"

Source: UN (2016, 2018b).

criminal activities. In contrast, hacktivists are more likely to be considered individuals who hack for social or political reasons, as no personal or financial gains are associated with the actions. But the legislation does not separate these two groups (Manjikian, 2021, p. 167).

There should also be a more differentiated approach to the elements included in hacktivism. Finding information publicly available from open sources, social media, or on the Dark Web and leaking is different from hacking into systems and stealing the data. Moreover, DDoS as a virtual sit-in blocking data traffic for a limited amount of time is not different from an offline blockade or sit-in preventing access to a specific location. Offline protests cause inconvenience, annoyance, and distractions. They can stop daily routines and cause unwanted attention. The target can be burdened by being singled out, but if the action in the offline world is protected, it should also be tolerated in the online environment (Hampson, 2012, p. 540).

PREVIOUS PROSECUTIONS

The LulzSec group was dismantled because of prosecutions where one of their own was passing on information to the FBI. The FBI cooperation with one of LulzSec leaders, Monsegur (Saba), resulted in several Anonymous and LulzSec members' arrests (Associated Press, 2014; Pilkington, 2014a). Monsegur's actions enabled the FBI to identify eight of his peers, despite

Table 7.12 Hacktivist prosecution

Name	Sentence	State
Jeremy Hammond	A 10-year prison sentence for hacking and releasing documents	The US
Barrett Brown	A 63-month prison sentence for hacking-related activities, including leaking material online	The US
Jake Davis	A 2-year sentence in a young offender institution for writing press releases, conducting media interviews, and running its Twitter account	The UK
Ryan Cleary	A 32-month prison sentence. Not a central member of the group but a botnet of compromised computers	The UK
Mustafa Al-Bassam	A 20-month prison sentence, suspended for two years for hacking and finding vulnerabilities in websites that could be exploited	The UK
Ryan Ackroyd	A 30-month prison sentence for hacking	The UK
Darren Martyn and Donncha O'Cearrbhail	A probation act and a fine for hacking/DDoS	Ireland

Sources: Arthur (2011); Fish & Follis (2015); Naked Security (2013); Pilkington (2014b); Shirbon (2013).

Monsegur's claim that he merely provided logging and intelligence to the FBI in return for a lenient sentence (Pilkington, 2014a, 2014b). See Table 7.12.

The US CFAA is problematic legislation, and it is unclear what constitutes an illegal hacktivist activity. A hacktivist can be subjected to severe criminal and civil penalties for violating the act simply because this is a fraud statute. The concerning aspect of the act is that the penalties increase depending on how many people are affected by the violation. Therefore, hacktivist indicted under this act often pleads guilty to get a lesser prison sentence or fine. There has not been a test case under the CFAA as people are unwilling to risk a potential severe prison sentence (Wood, 2020).

DDOSECRETS

In 2020, Anonymous was involved in its most significant action by accessing a large number of police data dubbed BlueLeaks and action conducted after the police killing of George Floyd. The leaked archive contains over 16 million rows of data (269 gigabytes). DDoSecrets published the data, including a substantial amount of potentially sensitive files from 2007 until mid-June 2020. The data leak came from a security breach at a Texas web design and hosting company that maintained state law enforcement data-sharing portals (Greenberg, 2020; KrebsOnSecurity, 2020; Lee, 2020). These files revealed, for example, how law enforcement described the anti-fascist movement Antifa. DDOSecrets published the files on its website in a searchable format. Supporters of the site created the #blueleaks hashtag to collect their findings on social media. DDoSecrets, who leaked the files, argued that none of the flies is classified. Although the files might not show illegal behaviour, there are revelations about legal but controversial police practices (Greenberg, 2020).

There is more focus on preventing these leaks from being circulated to a broader audience. Public and private actors are involved in creating restrictions and limit the damage. After the BlueLeaks was published, Twitter permanently banned the DDoSecrets online account because of the link to the files – and Reddit followed this practice. The company claimed the group violated the rules about distributing hacked material, and they used terms and conditions for blocking content and accounts is a growing practice that enables the companies behind the privately owned platform to control content and support public authorities' actions (Cimpanu, 2020; Lee, 2020; Stone, 2020; Winston, 2020). These terms and conditions have never led to a ban of WikiLeaks' Twitter account, although WikiLeaks have included links to hacked material (Lee, 2020). At the same time, the German law enforcement seized the DDoSecrets server that hosted the BlueLeaks data by request from the FBI, resulting in the group's online repository of the records going offline (DDoSecrets, 2020; Lee, 2020; Rosenblatt, 2020b; Winston, 2020). DDoSecrets has also been formally designated as a criminal hacker group by the DHS' Office of Intelligence and Analysis (Winston, 2020).

APT-69420 ARSON CATS AND KOTTMANN

Similar practices have been deployed to APT-69420 Arson Cats and their spokesperson, Kottmann. Law enforcement uses a harsh tactic to indict and prosecute the people behind the attacks when it is possible to identify them. The hacking group APT-69420 breached the video and Artificial Intelligence (AI) security company Verkada's systems enabling the group to access more than 150,000 of the company's surveillance video cameras in various locations, such as Tesla factories, police stations, gyms, schools, prisons, and hospitals. Some of the material is highly personal and sensitive, although no footage appears from private homes (Vincent, 2021b; Patterson, 2021). One video shows how staff are tackling and holding down a man to his bed at Halifax Health, a Florida hospital. Another video shows a man in handcuffs questioned by police officers at a police station in Stoughton, Massachusetts (Clayton Rice Q.C., 2021; Laskey, 2021; Menn, 2021). The group argued that they wanted to inform the public about the dangers of such omnipresent surveillance. The group's overall motive for publishing the data was based on their agenda for promoting freedom of information and fighting against intellectual property and capitalism (BBC News, 2021; Patterson, 2021; Vincent, 2021a, 2021b).

THE INDICTMENT

Kottmann has been accused of hacking several companies and government agencies since 2019. The Swiss authorities executed a search warrant related to Kottmann's activities on the US authorities' request, and Kottmann has been indicted for computer intrusion and data and identity theft (Keane, 2021; Panda Security, 2021; The US DoJ, 2021). Additionally, Kottmann is accused of operating a website called git.rip, which was seized by the FBI for further investigation. The git.rip was used to publish internal documents and source codes of more than 100 entities, i.e. the state of Washington, the Washington Department of Transportation, a microchip processor or manufacturer, and a maker of tactical equipment (Keane, 2021; Panda Security, 2021; Vincent, 2021a). The US authorities stated that stealing credentials and data and subsequently publishing the source code, proprietary, and sensitive information online is not a protected speech. Instead, these actions fall under theft and fraud. These actions will increase the vulnerabilities for everyone spanning from large corporations to individual consumers. The US Authorities claims that a noble motive does not remove the criminal element from the intrusion (Cimpanu, 2021).

The indictment notice also stated that Kottmann could profit from additional activities, such as speaking to the mass media and selling hacking inspired merchandise, i.e. profit from selling shirts with text such as 'Venture anticapitalist', 'catgirl hacker', 'no gender, no crime', and 'I would never do cybercrime' (Reuters, 2021; Turton, 2021). Although the charges no necessarily reflect the outcome of the case, they are severe. The indictment includes conspiracy to commit computer fraud and abuse, giving up to a five-year imprisonment sentence. Wire fraud and conspiracy to commit wire fraud can give up to a 20-year imprisonment sentence. Finally, aggravated identity theft can give a mandatory minimum 24-month imprisonment sentence following any other sentences imposed (The US DoJ, 2021).

Hacktivists are increasingly threatened with investigations and prosecutions, which often includes disproportional long prison sentences. This stance has, to some extent, been successful; since the harsh clampdown on Anonymous and LulzSec hacktivists in 2013, the actions have decreased in the number of attacks, but they have not disappeared, as illustrated above (Fish & Follis, 2015; Karagiannopoulos, 2021). States have been successful in prosecuting prominent hacktivists, and this had a deterrence effect. However, with the pandemic restricting offline protests, and new legislation restricting the rights to protest, hacktivism has slowly gained momentum. New ways of protesting and new groups are gradually emerging, indicating that post-COVID-19 hacktivism could be a popular alternative to traditional offline protest (Karagiannopoulos, 2021).

Conclusion

Hacktivism has developed in 2020 and 2021, leading to new means and methods deployed in online protests. Some new groups operate within the legal framework, whereas others continue the traditionally illegal practices developed by previous groups. The new wave of hacktivists' activities is more intrusive than traditional online activism. However, they are far from having the same impact as the state and state-sponsored/supported actors' actions. The large-scale attack conducted by state actors and their affiliates is attributed publicly but not likely to prosecute. In contrast, the low key non-sophisticated actors are facing prosecution and significant prison sentences.

References

Ablon, L., 2018. *Data thieves: The motivations of cyber threat actors and their use and monetization of stolen data.* [Online] Available at: www.rand.org/content/dam/rand/pubs/testimonies/CT400/CT490/RAND_CT490.pdf [Accessed 07 03 2021].

Afifi-Sabet, K., 2020. *What is hacktivism?* [Online] Available at: www.itpro.co.uk/hacking/30203/what-is-hacktivism [Accessed 22 11 2020].

AFP, 2020. *US adds hacktivists, social media manipulators to top intel threats.* [Online] Available at: https://news.yahoo.com/us-adds-hacktivists-social-media-manipulators-top-intel-203119738.html/ [Accessed 03 08 2021].

AFP, 2021. *Watching the watchers: Hacker group breaches security cameras at Tesla, banks, jails and schools.* [Online] Available at: www.news24.com/news24/World/News/watching-the-watchers-hacker-collective-breaches-cameras-at-tesla-banks-jails-and-schools-20210310 [Accessed 01 08 2021].

Alexander, J., 2020. *K-pop stans overwhelm app after Dallas police ask for videos of protesters.* [Online] Available at: www.theverge.com/2020/6/1/21277423/k-pop-dallas-pd-iwatch-app-flood-review-bomb-surveillance-protests-george-floyd [Accessed 01 04 2021].

Andrews, T. M., 2020. *BTS donates $1 million to Black Lives Matter after K-pop fans flood hashtags to support movement.* [Online] Available at: www.washingtonpost.com/technology/2020/06/07/bts-donation-k-pop-fans-black-lives-matter/ [Accessed 01 04 2021].

APC, 2019. *The promotion and protection of human rights in the context of peaceful protests: Submission to the Office of the High Commissioner for Human Rights by the Association for Progressive Communications (APC).* [Online] Available at: www.ohchr.org/Documents/Issues/RuleOfLaw/PeacefulProtest/CSOs/association-for-progressive-communication.pdf [Accessed 15 03 2021].

Arthur, C., 2011. *From LulzSec to 4chan: a hacking who's who.* [Online] Available at: www.theguardian.com/technology/2011/jun/22/lulzsec-4chan-hacking-whos-who [Accessed 26 02 2021].

Arthur, C., 2013. *LulzSec: What they did, who they were and how they were caught.* [Online] Available at: www.theguardian.com/technology/2013/may/16/lulzsec-hacking-fbi-jail [Accessed 26 02 2021].

Article 19, 2016. *The right to protest: Principles on the protection of human rights in protests.* [Online] Available at: www.article19.org/resources/the-right-to-protest-principles-on-the-protection-of-human-rights-in-protests/ [Accessed 30 07 2021].

Article 19, 2018. *UNHRC: States must protect rights in protests, including online.* [Online] Available at: www.article19.org/resources/unhrc-states-must-protect-rights-in-protests-including-online/ [Accessed 15 03 2021].

Associated Press, 2014. *Prosecutors seek leniency for hacker Sabu who helped tackle Anonymous.* [Online] Available at: www.theguardian.com/technology/2014/may/26/hacker-fbi-anonymous-leniency-prosecutors-monsegur-sabu [Accessed 01 08 2021].

Associated Press, 2021. *Feds charge Swiss 'hacktivist' for data theft and leaks.* [Online] Available at: www.marketwatch.com/story/feds-charge-swiss-hacktivist-for-data-theft-and-leaks-01616120020 [Accessed 31 07 2021].

Bacon, M., 2018. *Hacktivism.* [Online] Available at: https://searchsecurity.techtarget.com/definition/hacktivism [Accessed 28 02 2021].

Baraniuk, C., 2014. *Legalise online protests to safeguard democracy.* [Online] Available at: www.newscientist.com/article/mg22429921-500-legalise-online-protests-to-safeguard-democracy/ [Accessed 15 03 2021].

Batty, D., 2011. *LulzSec hackers claim breach of CIA website.* [Online] Available at: www.theguardian.com/technology/2011/jun/16/cia-website-lulzsec-hackers [Accessed 26 02 2021].

BBC News, 1999a. *'Hippies' declare web war on WTO.* [Online] Available at: http://news.bbc.co.uk/1/hi/uk/543752.stm [Accessed 28 02 2021].

BBC News, 1999b. *Online activists plan global protest.* [Online] Available at: http://news.bbc.co.uk/1/hi/uk/537587.stm [Accessed 28 02 2021].BBC News, 2021. *Hack of '150,000 cameras' investigated by camera firm.* [Online] Available at: www.bbc.co.uk/news/technology-56342525 [Accessed 01 08 2021].

Bedingfield, W., 2020. *How K-pop stans became an activist force to be reckoned with.* [Online] Available at: www.wired.com/story/how-k-pop-stans-became-an-activist-force-to-be-reckoned-with/ [Accessed 30 03 2021].

Bernburg, J. G., 2016. *Economic Crisis and Mass Protest: The Pots and Pans Revolution in Iceland.* Oxon: Routledge.

Bradbury, D., 2021. *Hackers steal 70GB of data from far-right social network gab.* [Online] Available at: www.itpro.co.uk/marketing-comms/social-media/358744/hackers-steal-70-gb-of-data-from-far-right-social-network-gab [Accessed 01 08 2021].

Bradford, J., 2014. *A different motive: Hacktivism by the numbers.* [Online] Available at: www.advisenltd.com/2014/03/21/different-motive-hacktivism-numbers/ [Accessed 03 08 2021].

Branch, P., 2011. *LulzSec takes down CIA website in the name of fun, fun, fun.* [Online] Available at: https://theconversation.com/lulzsec-takes-down-cia-website-in-the-name-of-fun-fun-fun-1858 [Accessed 28 02 2021].

Brooking, E. T., 2015. *Anonymous vs the Islamic state.* [Online] Available at: https://foreignpolicy.com/2015/11/13/anonymous-hackers-islamic-state-isis-chan-online-war/ [Accessed 28 02 2021].

Buenrostro, L., Dhillon, A. & Wooders, M., 2007. Protests and Reputation. *International Journal of Game Theory*, 35, pp. 353–377.

Caldwell, T., 2015. Hacktivism goes hardcore. *Network Security*, 2015(5), pp. 12–17.

Chatterjee, P., 2012. *WikiLeaks' Stratfor dump lifts lid on intelligence-industrial complex.* [Online] Available at: www.theguardian.com/commentisfree/cifamerica/2012/feb/28/wikileaks-intelligence-industrial-complex [Accessed 21 03 2021].

Check Point, 2021. *What is hacktivism?* [Online] Available at: www.checkpoint.com/cyber-hub/threat-prevention/what-is-hacktivism/ [Accessed 15 02 2021].

Chung, J. J., 2018. Critical infrastructure, cybersecurity, and market. *Oregon Law Review*, 96(2), pp. 441–476.

Cimpanu, C., 2020. *Twitter bans DDoSecrets account over 'BlueLeaks' police data dump.* [Online] Available at: www.zdnet.com/article/twitter-bans-ddosecrets-account-over-blueleaks-police-data-dump/ [Accessed 01 08 2021].

Cimpanu, C., 2020. *BlueLeaks: Data from 200 US police departments & fusion centers published online.* [Online] Available at: www.zdnet.com/article/blueleaks-data-from-200-us-police-departments-fusion-centers-published-online/ [Accessed 01 08 2021].

Cimpanu, C., 2021. *Verkada hacker charged in the US for hacking more than 100 companies.* [Online] Available at: https://therecord.media/verkada-hacker-charged-in-the-us-for-hacking-more-than-100-companies/ [Accessed 01 08 2021].

Clayton Rice Q.C., 2021. *Cyberespionage and the new hacktivism.* [Online] Available at: www.claytonrice.com/cyberespionage-and-the-new-hacktivism/ [Accessed 31 07 2021].

CoE, 1950. *The European convention on human rights.* [Online] Available at: www.echr.coe.int/Documents/Convention_ENG.pdf [Accessed 15 03 2021].

CoE, 2001a. *Convention on cybercrime.* [Online] Available at: www.europarl.europa.eu/meetdocs/2014_2019/documents/libe/dv/7_conv_budapest_/7_conv_budapest_en.pdf

CoE, 2001b. *Explanatory reports – ETS 185 – Cybercrime (convention).* [Online] Available at: https://rm.coe.int/16800cce5b [Accessed 15 02 2021].

CoE, 2013. *T-CY guidance note #5.* [Online] Available at: https://rm.coe.int/16802e9c49 [Accessed 30 07 2021].

CoE, 2020a. *Global state of cybercrime legislation: Update!* [Online] Available at: www.coe.int/en/web/cybercrime/news/-/asset_publisher/S73WWxscOuZ5/content/global-state-of-cybercrime-legislation-update- [Accessed 18 11 2021].

CoE, 2020b. *The Budapest Convention on Cybercrime: Benefits and Impact in Practice.* Strasbourg: Council of Europe. [Online] Available at: https://rm.coe.int/t-cy-2020-16-bc-benefits-rep-provisional/16809ef6ac [Accessed 18 11 2021].

Coleman, G., 2015. *Hacker, Hoaxer, Whistleblower, Spy: The Many Faces of Anonymous.* London: Verso.

Congressional Research Service, 2020. *Cybercrime and the law: Computer Fraud and Abuse Act (CFAA) and the 116th Congress.* [Online] Available at: https://fas.org/sgp/crs/misc/R46536.pdf [Accessed 30 07 2021].

Council of Europe, 2021. *Chart of signatures and ratifications of Treaty 185.* [Online] Available at: www.coe.int/en/web/conventions/full-list/-/conventions/treaty/185/signatures?p_auth=6ykZObDS [Accessed 15 02 2021].

Cox, J., 2014. *The history of DDoS attacks as a tool of protest.* [Online] Available at: www.vice.com/en/article/d734pm/history-of-the-ddos-attack [Accessed 06 03 2021].

Crowdstrike, 2021, *Hacktivism: What you need to know.* [Online] Available at: www.crowdstrike.com/cybersecurity-101/hacktivism/ [Accessed 18 11 2021]

Crown Prosecution Service, 2021. *Computer Misuse Act 1990.* [Online] Available at: www.cps.gov.uk/legal-guidance/computer-misuse-act [Accessed 15 02 2021].

Cruz, J. & Plaisance, P. L., 2021. Virtue ethics and a technomoral framework for online activism. *International Journal of Communication,* 15, pp. 1330–1348.

Cyber Security, 2021. *The 10 most (potentially) inspiring cases of hacktivism.* [Online] Available at: www.cybersecuritydegrees.com/faq/the-most-inspiring-cases-of-hacktivism/ [Accessed 28 02 2021].

DarkReading, 2021. *Ransomware victims' data published via DDoSecrets.* [Online] Available at: www.darkreading.com/risk/ransomware-victims-data-published-via-ddosecrets/d/d-id/1339848 [Accessed 01 08 2021].

Davis, D., 2014. *Hacktivism: good or evil?* [Online] Available at: www.computerweekly.com/opinion/Hacktivism-Good-or-Evil [Accessed 25 02 2021].

DDoSecrets, 2020. *BlueLeaks.* [Online] Available at: https://ddosecrets.com/wiki/BlueLeaks [Accessed 01 08 2021].

DDoSecrets, 2021a. *GabLeaks.* [Online] Available at: https://ddosecrets.com/wiki/GabLeaks [Accessed 01 08 2021].

DDoSecrets, 2021b. *Parler.* [Online] Available at: https://ddosecrets.com/wiki/Parler [Accessed 01 08 2021].

Denning, D. E., 2010. *Activitsm, hacktivism, and cyberterrorism: The internet as a tool for influencing foreign policy.* [Online] Available at: www.iwar.org.uk/cyberterror/resources/denning.htm [Accessed 05 03 2021].

Doyle, C., 2014. *Cybercrime: An Overview of the Federal Computer Fraud and Abuse Statue and Related Federal Criminal Laws.* Washington D.C.: Congressional Research Service.

Dzhanova, Y., 2021. *Top conservative figures are tweeting to advertise their Parler accounts after Trump was permanently banned from Twitter.* [Online] Available at: www.businessinsider.com/top-conservatives-moving-to-parler-after-trumps-ban-from-twitter-2021-1?r=US&IR=T [Accessed 03 08 2021].

EU, 2005. *Council Framework Decision 2005/222/JHA on Attacks against Information Systems.* Brussels: EUR-Lex.

Fenwick, H., 2006. *Civil Liberties and Human Rights.* 3 ed. Abingdon: Cavendish Publishing.

Fernandez, R., 2021. *How big tech is becoming the government.* [Online] Available at: www.somo.nl/how-big-tech-is-becoming-the-government/ [Accessed 03 08 2021].

Fish, A. & Follis, L., 2015. *Hactivists aren't terrorists – But US prosecutors make little distinction.* [Online] Available at: https://theconversation.com/hactivists-arent-ter rorists-but-us-prosecutors-make-little-distinction-45260 [Accessed 27 03 2021].

Frankenfield, J., 2019. *Hacktivism.* [Online] Available at: www.investopedia.com/terms/ h/hacktivism.asp#:~:text=An%20example%20of%20hacktivism%20is,Syrians%20 during%20the%20Arab%20Spring) [Accessed 25 02 2021].

Gallagher, R., 2011. *Why hacker group LulzSec went on the attack.* [Online] Available at: www.theguardian.com/technology/2011/jul/14/why-lulzsec-decided-to-disband [Accessed 30 03 2021].

Gillespie, A. A., 2019. *Cybercrime. Key Issues and Debate.* 2 ed. Abingdon: Routledge.

Goode, L., 2015. Anonymous and the political ethos of hacktivism. *Popular Communication*, 13(1), pp. 74–86.

Gordon, L. A., Loeb, M. P. & Lucyshyn, W., 2014. Cybersecurity investments in the private sector: the role of governments. *Georgetown Journal of International Affairs*, 15, pp. 79–88.

Gordon, L. A., Loeb, M. P., Lucyshyn, W. & Zhou, L., 2015. The impact of information sharing on cybersecurity underinvestment: A real options perspective. *Journal of Accounting and Public Policy*, 34(5): 509–519.

Grammatikopoulou, C., 2013. From the Deep Web to the city streets: Hacking, politics and visual culture. *Quaderns-e*, 19(1), pp. 202–219.

Greenberg, A., 2020. *Hack brief: Anonymous stole and leaked a megatrove of police documents.* [Online] Available at: www.wired.com/story/blueleaks-anonymous-law-enforcement-hack/ [Accessed 01 08 2021].

Greenberg, A., 2021. *Anti-secrecy activists publish a trove of ransomware victims' data.* [Online] Available at: www.wired.com/story/ddosecrets-ransomware-leaks/ [Accessed 01 08 2021].

Griffin, A., 2020. *'Anonymous' activitsts return with hugely popular messages of support for George Ffloyd.* [Online] Available at: www.independent.co.uk/life-style/gadgets-and-tech/news/anonymous-george-floyd-black-lives-matter-facebook-twitter-video-k-pop-a9542666.html [Accessed 28 03 2021].

Halliday, J., 2012. *Anonymous distances itself from WikiLeaks.* [Online] Available at: www.theguardian.com/technology/2012/oct/12/anonymous-distances-itself-wikileaks [Accessed 21 03 2021].

Hampson, N. C. N., 2012. Hacktivism: A new breed of protest in a networked world. *Boston College International and Comparative Law Review*, 35(2), pp. 511–542.

Herrman, J., 2020. *TikTok is shaping politics. But how?* [Online] Available at: www. nytimes.com/2020/06/28/style/tiktok-teen-politics-gen-z.html [Accessed 31 03 2021].

Hoise, K., 2020. *More than just Tok: Gen Z's activism on TikTok is outperforming the performative.* [Online] Available at: www.reach3insights.com/blog/tiktok-social-activism [Accessed 31 03 2021].

Holt, T., Bossler, A. M. & Siegfried-Spellar, K. C., 2018. *Cybercrime and Digital Forensics. An Introduction.* 2 ed. Abingdon: Routledge.

Howie, E., 2018. Protecting the human right to freedom of expression in international law. *International Journal of Speech-Language Pathology,* 20(1), pp. 12–15.

HRC, 2011. *General comment no. 34: Article 19: Freedoms of opinion and expression.* [Online] Available at: www2.ohchr.org/english/bodies/hrc/docs/gc34.pdf [Accessed 15 03 2021].

Impact, 2020. *Why you need layered security.* [Online] Available at: www.impactmybiz. com/blog/layered-cybersecurity-why-you-need-it/ [Accessed 03 08 2021].

Insikt Group, 2019. *Return to normalcy: False flags and the decline of international hacktivism*. [Online] Available at: www.recordedfuture.com/international-hacktivism-analysis/ [Accessed 29 03 2021].

Jett, J., 2021. *Building multilayered security for modern threats*. [Online] Available at: https://threatpost.com/multilayered-security-modern-threats/166457/ [Accessed 03 08 2021].

Jordan, J. & Taylor, P. A., 2004. *Hacktivism and Cyberwards. Rebels with a Cause?* Abingdon: Routledge.

Kahn, R. & Kellner, D., 2004. New media and internet activism: from the 'Battle of Seattle' to blogging. *new media & society*, 6(1), pp. 87–95.

Karagiannopoulos, V., 2020. A short history of hacktivism: Its past and present and what can we learn from it. In: *Rethining Cybercrime. Critical Debates*. Chams: Palgrave Macmillan, pp. 63–86.

Karagiannopoulos, V., 2021. *A decade since 'the year of the hacktivist', online protests look set to return*. [Online] Available at: https://theconversation.com/a-decade-since-the-year-of-the-hacktivist-online-protests-look-set-to-return-163329 [Accessed 03 08 2021].

Karatzogianni, A., 2012. WikiLeaks affects: Ideology, conflict and the revolutionary virtual. In: *Digital Cultures and the Politics of Emotion: Feelings, Affect and Technological Change*. Basingstoke: Palgrave Macmillan, pp. 52–72.

Keane, J., 2021. *Hacker that claimed to breach cameras at Tesla charged in the US*. [Online] Available at: www.siliconrepublic.com/enterprise/hacker-breach-cameras-tesla-charged-in-the-us [Accessed 28 03 2021].

Kelly, B. B., 2021. Investing in a centralized cybersecurity infrastructure: Why 'hacktivism' can and should influence cybersecurity reform. *Boston University Law Review*, 92(5), pp. 1663–1711.

Kerr, D., 2013. *Anonymous petitions U.S. to see DDoS attacks as legal protest*. [Online] Available at: www.cnet.com/tech/services-and-software/anonymous-petitions-u-s-to-see-ddos-attacks-as-legal-protest/ [Accessed 03 08 2021].

Knapp, T. M., 2015. Hacktivism – Political dissent in the final frontier. *New End Law Review*, 49(2), pp. 259–296.

Koo, C., 2020. *The boomer's guide to online activism in the age of TikTok and K-pop stans*. [Online] Available at: www.popdust.com/gen-z-activists-2646352753.html [Accessed 31 03 2021].

KrebsOnSecurity, 2020. *'BlueLeaks' exposes files from hundreds of police departments*. [Online] Available at: https://krebsonsecurity.com/2020/06/blueleaks-exposes-files-from-hundreds-of-police-departments/ [Accessed 01 08 2021].

Laskey, S., 2021. *Global hackers raid Verkada's clients' video surveillance data*. [Online] Available at: www.securityinfowatch.com/video-surveillance/article/21213804/global-hackers-raid-verkadas-clients-video-surveillance-data [Accessed 01 08 2021].

Lavorgna, A., 2020. *Cybercrimes. Critical Issues in a Global Context*. London: Macmillan.

Lecher, C., 2017. *Massive attack*. [Online] Available at: www.theverge.com/2017/4/14/15293538/electronic-disturbance-theater-zapatista-tactical-floodnet-sit-in [Accessed 06 03 2021].

Lecomte, F., 2020. *France: Cybersecurty laws and regulations 2021*. [Online] Available at: https://iclg.com/practice-areas/cybersecurity-laws-and-regulations/france [Accessed 06 03 2021].

Lee, M., 2020. *Hack of 251 law enforcement websites exposes personal data of 700,000 cops.* [Online] Available at: https://theintercept.com/2020/07/15/blueleaks-anonymous-ddos-law-enforcement-hack/ [Accessed 03 08 2021].

Lindsay, J. & Gartzke, E., 2016. Coercion through cyberspace: The stability-instability paradox revisited. In: *The Power to Hurt: Coercion in Theory.* Oxford: Oxford University Press, pp. 176–204.

Lindsay, J. R., 2015. Tipping the scales: the attribution problem and the feasibility of deterrence against cyberattack. *Journal of Cybersecurity,* 1(1), pp. 53–67.

Li, X., 2013. Hacktivism and the first amendment: Drawing the line between cyber protests and crime. *Harvard Journal of Law and Technology,* 27(1), pp. 302–330.

LLI, 2021. *18 U.S. code § 1030 – Fraud and related activity in connection with computers.* [Online] Available at: www.law.cornell.edu/uscode/text/18/1030 [Accessed 30 07 2021].

Lorenz, T., Browning, K. & Frenkel, S., 2020. *TikTok teens and K-pop stans say they sank Trump rally.* [Online] Available at: www.nytimes.com/2020/06/21/style/tiktok-trump-rally-tulsa.html [Accessed 01 04 2021].

Lynley, M., 2011a. *Hit the deck: LulzSec and Anonymous start trading blows.* [Online] Available at: https://venturebeat.com/2011/06/15/lulzsec-anonymous-civil-war/ [Accessed 30 03 2021].

Lynley, M., 2011b. *Psych! LulzSec and Anonymous are "bros", hacker groups say.* [Online] Available at: https://venturebeat.com/2011/06/20/lulzsec-anonymous-bros [Accessed 30 03 2021].

Manjikian, M., 2021. *Introduction to Cyber Politics and Policy.* London: Sage.

Mansfield-Devine, S., 2011. Hacktivism: assessing the damage. *Network Security,* 8, pp. 5–13.

Marshall Jarrett, H. & Bailie, M. W., 2015. *Prosecuting Computer Crimes.* Washington D.C.: Office of Legal Education Executive Office for United States Attorneys.

Martin, A., 2011. *LulzSec's Sony hack really was as simple as it claimed.* [Online] Available at: www.theatlantic.com/technology/archive/2011/09/lulzsecs-sony-hack-really-was-simple-it-claimed/335527/ [Accessed 26 02 2021].

Mehrotra, K. & Tarabay, J., 2020. *Anonymous vows to 'Expose' Minneapolis police, site attacked.* [Online] Available at: www.bloomberg.com/news/articles/2020-05-31/anonymous-says-it-ll-expose-minneapolis-police-website-hacked [Accessed 01 08 2021].

Menn, J., 2019. *Cult of the Dead Cow: How the Original Hacking Supergroup Might Just Save the World.* London: Hachette UK.

Menn, J., 2021. *New wave of 'hacktivism' adds twist to cybersecurity woes.* [Online] Available at: www.reuters.com/article/us-cyber-hacktivism-focus-idUSKBN2BH3HJ [Accessed 25 03 2021].

Molloy, D. & Tidy, J., 2020. *George Floyd: Anonymous hackers re-emerge amid US unrest.* [Online] Available at: www.bbc.co.uk/news/technology-52879000 [Accessed 28 03 2021].

Mueller, M., 2017. *Will the Internet Fragment?* 1 ed. Cambridge: Polity Press.

Murphy, H., 2019. *Cult of the Dead Cow: How the Original Hacking Supergroup Might Just Save the World, by Joseph Menn.* [Online] Available at: www.ft.com/content/5250f866-cfe3-11e9-99a4-b5ded7a7fe3f [Accessed 21 02 2021].

Naked Security, 2013. *The LulzSec hackers who boasted they were "Gods" await their sentence.* [Online] Available at: https://nakedsecurity.sophos.com/2013/05/16/lulzsec-hackers-wait-sentence/ [Accessed 28 03 2021].

National Association of Criminal Defence Lawyers, 2021. *Computer Fraud and Abuse Act (CFAA)*. [Online] Available at: www.nacdl.org/Landing/Computer FraudandAbuseAct [Accessed 15 02 2021].

NCSC, 2016. *Denial of service (DoS) guidance*. [Online] Available at: www.ncsc.gov. uk/collection/denial-service-dos-guidance-collection [Accessed 30 07 2021].

Newhouse, A., 2021. *Big Tech's rejection of Parler shuts down a site favored by Trump supporters – And used by participants in the US Capitol insurrection.* [Online] Available at: https://theconversation.com/big-techs-rejection-of-parler-shuts-down-a-site-favored-by-trump-supporters-and-used-by-participants-in-the-us-capitol-insurrection-153070 [Accessed 03 08 2021].

Niethammer, A., Herfurth, C., Rieks, D. & Saerbeck, S., 2020. *Germany: Cybersecurity laws and regulations 2021*. [Online] Available at: https://iclg.com/practice-areas/cybersecurity-laws-and-regulations/germany#:~:text=Denial%2Dof%2Dserv ice%20attacks%20constitute,called%20%E2%80%9Ccomputer%20sabot age%E2%80%9D) [Accessed 07 03 2021].

OAS, 1969. *American convention on human rights "PACT OF SAN JOSE, COSTA RICA" (B-32)*. [Online] Available at: www.oas.org/dil/treaties_B-32_American_Convention_on_Human_Rights.htm [Accessed 15 03 2021].

OAU, 1981. *African charter on human and peoples' rights*. [Online] Available at: www.achpr.org/legalinstruments/detail?id=49 [Accessed 15 03 2021].

Office of Legal Education Executive Office for United States Attorneys, 2015. *Prosecuting computer crimes*. [Online] Available at: www.justice.gov/sites/default/files/criminal-ccips/legacy/2015/01/14/ccmanual.pdf [Accessed 05 03 2021].

Ohlheiser, A., 2020a. *How K-pop fans became celebrated online vigilantes*. [Online] Available at: www.technologyreview.com/2020/06/05/1002781/kpop-fans-and-black-lives-matter/ [Accessed 30 03 2021].

Ohlheiser, A., 2020b. *TikTok teens and K-pop stans don't belong to the "resistance"*. [Online] Available at: www.technologyreview.com/2020/06/23/1004336/tiktok-teens-kpop-stans-trump-resistance-its-complicated/ [Accessed 01 04 2021].

Panda Security, 2021. *Hacktivists breach a security company, get access to 150,000 camera feeds*. [Online] Available at: www.pandasecurity.com/en/mediacenter/mobile-news/hacktivists-150000-camera-feeds/ [Accessed 18 03 2021].

Pardes, A., 2020. *Parler games: Inside the right's favorite 'Free Speech' app*. [Online] Available at: www.wired.com/story/parler-app-free-speech-influencers/ [Accessed 03 08 2021].

Park, T. K., 2020. *U.S. politics should've seen K-pop stans coming*. [Online] Available at: www.vulture.com/2020/06/k-pop-activism-politics-explainer.html [Accessed 31 03 2021].

Parker, K. & Igielnik, R., 2020. *On the cusp of adulthood and facing an uncertain future: What we know about Gen Z So Far*. [Online] Available at: www.pewresearch. org/social-trends/2020/05/14/on-the-cusp-of-adulthood-and-facing-an-uncertain-future-what-we-know-about-gen-z-so-far-2/ [Accessed 03 08 2021].

Patil, A. P., Bharath, S. & Annigeri, N. M., 2018. Applications of game theory for cyber security system: A survey. *International Journal of Applied Engineering Research,* 13(17), pp. 12987–12990.

Patterson, D., 2021. *Hack of video security company Verkada exposes footage from 150,000 connected cameras*. [Online] Available at: www.cbsnews.com/news/verkada-hack-tesla-nissan-equinox-cloudflare/ [Accessed 01 08 2021].

Pierskalla, J. H., 2010. Protest, deterrence, and escalation: The strategic calculus of government repression. *Journal of Conflict Resolution*, 54(1), pp. 117–145.

Pilkington, E., 2014a. *Anonymous superhacker turned FBI informant Sabu remains defiant over snitching.* [Online] Available at: www.theguardian.com/us-news/2014/dec/09/hacker-sabu-defends-informing-anonymous-fbi-interview [Accessed 02 08 2021].

Pilkington, E., 2014b. *LulzSec hacker 'Sabu' released after 'extraordinary' FBI cooperation.* [Online] Available at: www.theguardian.com/technology/2014/may/27/hacker-sabu-walks-free-sentenced-time-served [Accessed 28 03 2021].

Porter, T., 2020. *TikTok teens say they tanked Trump's comeback rally in Tulsa by reserving thousands of tickets and not showing up.* [Online] Available at: www.businessinsider.com/tiktok-teens-and-k-pop-fans-tanked-trumps-tulsa-rally-2020-6?r=US&IR=T [Accessed 03 08 2021].

Reuters, 2021. *New generation of angry & youthful hackers join the 'hacktivism' wave, adding to cyber-security woes.* [Online] Available at: https://economictimes.indiatimes.com/magazines/panache/new-generation-of-angry-youthful-hackers-join-the-hacktivism-wave-adding-to-cyber-security-woes/articleshow/81707844.cms?from=mdr [Accessed 31 07 2021].

Richards, I. & Wood, M. A., 2018. Hacktivists against terrorism: A cultural criminological analysis of anonymous' anti IS campaigns. *International Journal of Cyber Criminology*, 12(1), pp. 187–205.

Ropek, L., 2020. *Anonymous claims responsibility for Minneapolis PD cyberattack.* [Online] Available at: www.govtech.com/security/anonymous-claims-responsibility-for-minneapolis-pd-cyberattack.html [Accessed 02 08 2021].

Rosenblatt, K., 2020a. *A summer of digital protest: How 2020 became the summer of activism both online and offline.* [Online] Available at: www.nbcnews.com/news/us-news/summer-digital-protest-how-2020-became-summer-activism-both-online-n1241001 [Accessed 31 07 2021].

Rosenblatt, S., 2020b. *The state of hacktivism in 2020.* [Online] Available at: www.darkreading.com/the-state-of-hacktivism-in-2020-/d/d-id/1338382 [Accessed 28 03 2021].

Sauter, M., 2014. *The Coming Swarm. DDoS Actions, Hacktivism, and Civil Disobedience on the Internet.* London: Bloomsbury Academics.

Schølberg, S. & Hubbard, A. M., 2005. *Harmonizing National Legal Approaches on Cybercrime.* Geneva: International Telecommunication Union.

Shirbon, E., 2013. *British hacker "Kayla" admits attacks on Sony, Murdoch, Nintendo.* [Online] Available at: www.reuters.com/article/britain-hacker/british-hacker-kayla-admits-attacks-on-sony-murdoch-nintendo-idUSL5N0CW3CZ20130409?edition-redirect=in [Accessed 28 03 2021].

Siboni, G. & Sivan-Sevilla, I., 2018. *The role of the state in the private-sector cybersecurity challenge cybersecurity challenge.* [Online] Available at: www.georgetownjournalofinternationalaffairs.org/online-edition/2018/5/27/the-role-of-the-state-in-the-private-sector-cybersecurity-challenge [Accessed 02 08 2021].

Sorell, T., 2015. Human rights and hacktivism: The cases of WikiLeaks and Anonymous. *Journal of Human Rights Practices*, 7(3), pp. 391–410.

Steiner, H. J., Alston, P. & Goodman, R., 2007. *International Human Rights in Context. Law, Politics, Moral.* 3 ed. Oxford: Oxford University Press.

Stockemer, D., 2012. When do People Protest? – Using a Game Theoretic Framework to Shed Light on the Relationship Between Repression and Protest in Hybrid and

Autocratic Regimes. In: *Social Sciences and Cultural Studies - Issues of Language, Public Opinion, Education and Welfare.* Rijeka: InTechOpen, pp. 215–218.

Stone, J., 2020. *DDoSecrets' mission is 'unchanged' in wake of 'BlueLeaks' Twitter ban.* [Online] Available at: www.cyberscoop.com/blue-leaks-ddosecrets-twitter-ban-anonymous/ [Accessed 01 08 2021].

Swaine, L., 2018. Freedom of thought as a basic liberty. *Political Theory*, 46(3), pp. 405–425.

The Commonwealth, 2017. *Model law on computer related crime.* [Online] Available at: https://thecommonwealth.org/sites/default/files/key_reform_pdfs/P15370_11_ROL_Model_Law_Computer_Related_Crime.pdf [Accessed 15 02 2021].

The Council of Economic Advisers, 2018. *The Cost of Malicious Cyber Activity to the U.S. Economy.* Washington D.C: Executive Office of the President of the United States.

The Crown Prosecution Service, 2019. *Cybercrime – Prosecution guidance.* [Online] Available at: www.cps.gov.uk/legal-guidance/cybercrime-prosecution-guidance [Accessed 08 08 2020].

The UN, 1966. *International covenant on civil and political rights.* [Online] Available at: www.ohchr.org/en/professionalinterest/pages/ccpr.aspx [Accessed 29 07 2021].

The US DoJ, 2021. *Swiss hacker indicted for conspiracy, wire fraud, and aggravated identity theft.* [Online] Available at: www.justice.gov/usao-wdwa/pr/swiss-hacker-indicted-conspiracy-wire-fraud-and-aggravated-identity-theft [Accessed 31 07 2021].

The White House, 2020. *National counterintelligence strategy of the United States of America 2020–2022.* [Online] Available at: www.dni.gov/files/NCSC/documents/features/20200205-National_CI_Strategy_2020_2022.pdf [Accessed 03 08 2021].

TrapX, 2020. *Fighting cyber attacks with game theory.* [Online] Available at: https://threatpost.com/trapx-fighting-cyber-attacks-with-game-theory/156545/ [Accessed 03 08 2021].

Turton, W., 2021. *Swiss hacker's indictment spotlights ethics of activist attacks.* [Online] Available at: www.bloomberg.com/news/articles/2021-03-19/swiss-hacker-s-indictment-spotlights-ethics-of-activist-attacks [Accessed 01 08 2021].

UN, 1948. *Universal declaration of human rights.* [Online] Available at: www.un.org/en/universal-declaration-human-rights/ [Accessed 15 03 2021].

UN, 2001. *55/63 Combating the criminal misuse of information technologies.* [Online] Available at: www.itu.int/ITU-D/cyb/cybersecurity/docs/UN_resolution_55_63.pdf [Accessed 15 02 2021].

UN, 2016. *The promotion, protection and enjoyment of human rights on the Internet: resolution / adopted by the human rights council.* [Online] Available at: www.refworld.org/docid/57e916464.html [Accessed 04 08 2021].

UN, 2018a. *The promotion and protection of human rights in the context of peaceful protests.* [Online] Available at: https://documents-dds-ny.un.org/doc/UNDOC/GEN/G18/213/58/PDF/G1821358.pdf?OpenElement [Accessed 15 03 2021].

UN, 2018b. *The promotion, protection and enjoyment of human rights on the internet.* [Online] Available at: https://documents-dds-ny.un.org/doc/UNDOC/GEN/G18/215/67/PDF/G1821567.pdf?OpenElement [Accessed 15 03 2021].

UN, 2020. *UN human rights committee publishes interpretation on the right of peaceful assembly.* [Online] Available at: www.ohchr.org/EN/NewsEvents/Pages/DisplayNews.aspx?NewsID=26133&LangID=E [Accessed 29 07 2021].

Vaas, L., 2020. *'Anonymous' takes down Atlanta Police Dept. site after police shooting.* [Online] Available at: https://nakedsecurity.sophos.com/2020/06/16/anonymous-takes-down-atlanta-police-dept-site-after-police-shooting/ [Accessed 01 08 2021].

Vamosi, R., 2011. *How hacktivism affects us all.* [Online] Available at: www.pcworld.com/article/239594/how_hacktivism_affects_us_all.html [Accessed 03 08 2021].

Van Wie Davis, E., 2021. *Shadow warfare.* London: Rowman & Littlefield.

Vincent, J., 2021a. *'Anti-capitalist' Verkada hacker charged by US government with attacks on dozens of companies.* [Online] Available at: www.theverge.com/2021/3/19/22339625/tillie-kottmann-swiss-hacker-verkada-charged-us-government-verkada [Accessed 18 11 2021].

Vincent, J., 2021b. *Tens of thousands of Verkada cameras were easily accessible to employees as well as hackers.* [Online] Available at: www.theverge.com/2021/3/11/22324876/surveillance-camera-firm-verkada-breached-hacked-super-admin-access-employees [Accessed 18 11 2021].

Vogele, W. B., 1993. Deterrence by civilian defence. *Peace and Change,* 18(1), pp. 26–49.

WeForum, 2020. *Cybersecurity, emerging technology and systemic risk.* [Online] Available at: www3.weforum.org/docs/WEF_Future_Series_Cybersecurity_emerging_technology_and_systemic_risk_2020.pdf [Accessed 03 08 2021].

WikiLeaks, 2011. *What is WikiLeaks.* [Online] Available at: www.wikileaks.org/About.html [Accessed 20 03 2021].

Willams, O., 2019. *Why is the number of active hacktivist groups plummeting?* [Online] Available at: https://tech.newstatesman.com/security/hacktivist-groups [Accessed 07 03 2021].

Winston, A., 2020. *Feds are treating BlueLeaks organization as 'a criminal hacker group', documents show.* [Online] Available at: www.theverge.com/2020/8/13/21365448/blueleaks-dhs-distributed-denial-secrets-dds-ddosecrets-police [Accessed 28 03 2021].

Wood, M., 2020. *Hacktivism on the rise in wake of national protests.* [Online] Available at: www.marketplace.org/shows/marketplace-tech/computer-hacking-activism-anonymous/ [Accessed 01 04 2021].

Yar, M. & Steinmetz, K. F., 2019. *Cybercrime and Society.* 3 ed. London: Sage.

Zuboff, S., 2019. *The Age of Surveillance Capitalism.* 1 ed. London: Profile Books.

8 Conclusion

Introduction

Society's dependencies on computer technologies, systems, and communication platforms have exposed significant vulnerabilities by politically motivated actors. These attacks have increased their scope and reach with severe consequences. The book has demonstrated a rise in cyber attacks against CI, and these attacks are linked to obtaining information, disturbing data traffic, or destroying vital assets. The attacks have significant political, economic, and societal implications, short term as well as long term. The analysis of current attacks has revealed definitional, legal, and strategical issues with the responses to the problems. The book chapters have focused on three main areas, motivation, actors, and means and methods used. Having analysed these areas, it is clear that issues need urgent attention to enhance the cybersecurity level to withstand these attacks and change the strategic payoff.

Concluding Remarks

The book highlighted problems in two overarching areas. First, the politically motivated attacks are escalating, and different types of groups are becoming more involved in attacks. The attacks might differ in sophistication, but the attackers are using similar types of means and methods. One type of group appears to be independent of the state, but the state sponsors their actions. These groups act under the direction of the state, but they decide how to carry out the tasks by acting as direct proxies for the state (Chapter 5). Another important group is non-state actors acting independently, but these actors benefit from following the state's political agenda (Chapter 6). Finally, there is a group of politically motivated actors acting entirely outside the realm of the state (Chapter 7). There are also serious issues with how these groups are managed, and the legislative framework applied. The regulatory framework and the offences are not designed to manage these cyber attacks.

DOI: 10.4324/9781003126676-8

Second, the number of attacks on CIs has demonstrated that the resilience and preparedness of these vital structures and services are not fully developed to withstand the attacks. This calls for closer cooperation between public and private entities to develop a cybersecurity framework and standards that can minimise the payoff for the attackers.

The Actors

The overarching research objective was to investigate whether a clear conceptualisation of the area is useful beyond the traditional fragmented definitions and legislative framework. The research revealed that there are several politically motivated actors and formations. However, these activities and grouping have been considered in the realm of offline offences for a long time. There are areas within the current classifications that make this area challenging. It would be helpful to rethink the whole area and create distinct classifications outside the laws of war, counter-terrorism, and cyber-crime legislation.

There is a problem with categorising the attacks and attackers, when the attackers are considered in isolation using offline conventions, norms, and legislation to identify and prosecute the actors. The different areas outlined in the table should be reconsidered to enhance cybersecurity and impose costs on the actors. Managing cyber attacks is a constant process; the attacks are getting more complex and require more comprehensive responses. Different initiatives should be launched; developing a regulatory framework is just one of many initiatives included in a multilayered approach (Galen, 2021).

Table 8.1 Key problems with the current framework: Legislative framework

Areas	*Areas for improvements*	*Behaviours*
Cyberwar and cyberwarfare	Developing international norms for acceptable cyber capabilities and capacities Develop an international framework for the protection of cyber territory, assets, and populations	States claim to respect international law in their online actions while building up cyber capabilities and capacities that have a damaging effect on targets No protection of non-governmental entities and online users/ populations
	Addressing the use of state-sponsored actors in an international context	By using state-sponsored groups, the state creates a buffer between the actions and the actual attack

Table 8.1 Cont.

Areas	Areas for improvements	Behaviours
Cyberterrorism	Developing an international framework to address the current gaps in cyberterrorism legislation and definitions regarding state-supported attacks	Ransomware is considered a national security threat/ terrorism. The current national counter-terrorism framework is developed to manage offline offences, but ransomware attacks are unclear
	Developing a classification of ransomware attacks needs to be considered, and a consistent framework for managing these attacks: do the actions fall under the scope of counter-terrorism or cybercrime legislation	Some states are enabling the ransomware groups to attack by offering near impunity if they follow the political agenda of the host state
Political activism/ hacktivism	Developing a content response enabling protection of the right to protest online	Some actions conducted have the same effect as those criminalised in current cybercrime legislation. However, hacktivists do not enjoy the protection of the right to protest
	Developing a proportional framework for criminalising hacktivists hacking attacks consistent with offline legislation for violent protests	Some means and methods used by hacktivists give more severe sentences compared with criminalised actions during offline protests

Rethinking the Current Legislative Framework

In managing the rise of politically motivated attacks, it would be useful to rethink the current situation to progress a new foundation developing from the outset of existing law regulating offline war and warfare. However, these should act as a starting point as they are inadequate to comprehend all the different areas that have been highlighted. Yet, key areas should be addressed to adjust the framework to the different categories of attackers. One fundamental area is to include all the actors and not only states. However, this comes with a new set of challenges as these attacks cannot be considered like for like. Therefore, there needs to be a hieratical structure due to the attacks' sophistication and impact. This categorisation would include the actors and the impact to be able to respond proportionally to the attacks: protactive and reactive. The hierarchy would have the states at the top, followed by state-sponsored actors, state-supported actors/terrorists, and finally politically motivated actors that should have particular protection due to the right to protest.

Currently, cyberwar and warfare are considered in the light of international law and custom, national counter-terrorism, and cybercrime legislation which creates a complex, fragmented, and disproportional approach. The jurisdiction and legislative issues regarding cyber terrorists, hackers, and cybercriminals are considered under national criminal laws and associated jurisdictional considerations (Barletta et al., 2011, p. 79).

As evidenced by the numerous examples in the book, there are severe issues with developing international regulations and norms of behaviours and weapons in cyberspace. The gaps in the framework allow actors to manoeuvre around within any significant obstacles or consequences to progress. Mistrust among states and their conflicting political interests have been exposed due to the constant attacks, and the lack of collaboration enhances the risks. States should move beyond their geopolitical positions and negotiate a legal framework for acceptable behaviour in cyberspace and protection of vulnerable targets (Wegener, 2011, p. 95)

However, the rise of attacks, the cross-border nature, and the capabilities and capacities of the actors raise calls for action to reconsider the offences' status and characteristics. A new way of assessing and categorising these offences would help by assessing motivation and attack forms and routes to establish a common approach to politically motivated cyber attacks. The classifications derive from the widespread harm with political incitement, increased difficulties in identifying, capturing, and prosecuting the offenders. The strong presence of political motivation aimed at destabilising societies, creating uncertainties, and disrupting and destroying should be seen in a context with merger criminal law and international law regulating war and armed conflicts (Barletta et al., 2011, p. 79). The attacks are instrumental for disabling or belittle governments and organisations following underlying political or social agendas. The attacks can disable part of the CI, with widespread consequences to the target, suppliers, and/or the wider populations, or they aim to obtain confidential and sensitive information (McAlpine & Oldham, 2018).

Managing the Area

There have been drafts proposed in the UN to develop cybercrime treaties, but geopolitics has stalled the development. The attempts have predominately been a diplomatic front showing willingness. However, it is questionable whether an agreement can be reached due to underlying tensions between the actors and how they currently benefit from having a lawless space. These areas are incorporated as deterrence and defence measures in national cybersecurity strategies, but in reality, they boost political, financial, and military advantages. It is, therefore, unlikely that states are willing to enter into agreements that limit these powers unless the strategic payoff is changing for these actors (Barletta et al., 2011, p. 77; Congressional Research Service, 2009). States should create a global and cross-sectoral legal framework that sets out rules and penalties for cyber conflicts by introducing a set of structured internationally negotiated binding agreements. Compared with current international rules regulating conflict between states, the frameworks should impose obligations on the signatory states to control their own and non-governmental groups and actors operating within these limitations (Barletta et al., 2011, p. 79).

Only by creating an international cybersecurity regime and concerted effort of participants, the proliferation of these cyberpowers can be improved. An international regime covering a legislative framework regarding behaviours, attack types, and targets can reduce the threats of politically motivated attacks, such as cyberwarfare, cyberterrorism, and political online activism/ cybercrime (Barletta et al., 2011, p. 77). Currently, the world is in a perpetual state of cyber conflict that borders cyberwarfare. This fight cannot be ended in the same way as conventional conflicts where one state will surrender, and the conflict will end. Currently, states are continually testing opponents defences by attacking technologies, devices, and networks (Kolbe, 2020). There are currently no consequences for the attackers to propel change in operations based on a negative payoff. If this area is addressed, it will signal the adversaries that specific actions are prohibited and have associated costs beyond the benefits. This is currently missing in the international framework and national cybersecurity strategies (Valeriano, 2020).

All existing instruments can all be amended to include various types of politically motivated attacks similar to laws covering norms for conventional warfare on land, air, and sea, i.e. the UN Charter, NATO Treaty the Genevan, and the Hauge Conventions (ICRC, 1899; ICRC, 1907; ICRC, 1977; ICRC, 1949; United Nations, 1980; UN, 1945; NATO, 1949). A new framework would address areas such as territorial integrity, actors, and protection of the civil population and essential CIs. In this book, it has been highlighted that attacks can impact beyond the actual target, transnational, and cross-border – as well as online users and populations. Similar to exiting international law, there should be a prohibition of the transmission of cyber attacks through the neutral states not included in the conflict. However, this should not only be related to states. To prevent the widespread effect of cyber attacks, initiatives should be launched to protect neutral companies, groups, and individuals (Westby, 2011, p. 92). Collaboration and communication is a core factor for developing protective measures and a legislative framework, and states should make an effort to actively participate in the UN and other organisations initiatives to promote cybersecurity. Even though it takes time to develop a framework, the state should refrain from using cyberspace in conflicts, for revenge or to further their prosperity by using illegal methods (Wegener, 2011, p. 96; McAlpine & Oldham, 2018).

Prohibiting certain weapons should be included in a framework of the production, proliferation, and application of cyberweapons to cover single-purpose weapons created for attacking CI, CII, NCI and ICTs components to mirror the rules in the Geneva and Hague laws, such as the use of weapons based on program codes, such as malicious malware and the means of their delivery (Barletta et al., 2011, p. 77). Yet, it is unlikely that this area would gain support from states that already have developed significant cyber powers and successfully deployed them in the past. Managing non-state actors, such as cyberterrorist and hacktivist, are also problematic as these actors are following their agenda outside the reach of the states.

Although all these areas are desirable and valuable to manage cyber attacks, the problem with geopolitics stays in the way of reaching agreements. Attention should be made to manage the non-state actors included in these attacks, i.e. state-sponsored and state-supported actors that have links to the state or following the state's agenda. The state's position is more apparent as they are regulated by international law and custom; thus, the other groups' classification is more challenging

STATES

The attacks are conducted as a part of a broader political agenda. Contrary to personal and financial cybercrime, there is a link to political ideologies incorporated in the motivations. Some are stronger than others. There are state and non-state actors involved in these actions. Sometimes, the political link is not visible, but it is possible to see how the attacks fit the state and non-state actors' strategies by analysing them. For state actors, their actions are linked to their political, military, and economic plans. Most of them are pursuing particular long-term plans, where one is to become a leading cyber power and ensure that the state thrives politically and financially. For example, the actions of China align with the 'Made in China 2025' plan (UNIDIR, 2020a). Like the US, there is an incitement to be a world power on multiple levels, political, military, and fiscal, which aligns with the developed cybersecurity strategies (Chapter 4) (UNIDIR, 2020c). Similar to China, the US wants to be a leading cyber power. Russia is following the same agenda by cementing its geopolitical status and becoming less reliant on foreign technology (UNIDIR, 2020b). In comparison, North Korea is different as it increased its cyber capabilities and capacities to strengthen its military reputation and the state's survival (Casear, 2021).

In contrast to offline warfare, online warfare does not require massive investments in weapons. Moreover, the attackers do not need expensive investments to conduct attacks; good computing skills, software, and understanding of the target victim are enough to launch a powerful attack (Barletta et al., 2011, p. 80). In the offline environment, economic strength and high military capabilities create an unbalanced relationship in the bargain situation between states. These factors are less influential with cyberconflicts.

The asymmetric means used in cyber attacks enable actors with limited financial and technical resources to compromise high-value targets (Kshetri, 2014, p. 10; Masters, 2011).

Contrary to nuclear weapons or sophisticated conventional arms, various types of cyberweapons are much cheaper to produce, proliferate significantly, and their use is not restricted by borders. States like Russia, China, Iran, and North Korea cannot match US' spending on conventional weapons, but they become equal with cybertools. These states have exposed the US' weaknesses. Compared with these states, the US is more reliant on financial, commercial, and governmental networks, which leaves the system vulnerable to attacks (Kolbe, 2020).

STATE-SPONSORED AND STATE-SUPPORTED GROUPS

One of the issues that the states need to solve is the increasing use of state-sponsored and state-supported actors. Pervasive state-sponsored online actions are becoming systemised and used as a cover-up for the states' engagement in the processes. These activities make it difficult to identify intrusions and disturbances by organised crime groups, sub-national organisations, and hackers. The number of non-state actors involved in the cyber attacks interferes with the criminal prosecution using the existing computer crime legislation. Therefore, it might be time to reconsider how these attacks are managed (Barletta et al., 2011, p. 81).

In hybrid cyberwarfare, these actors have obtained a prominent position distancing the state from the attacks. In the attacks covered in the previous chapters, the state-sponsored actors are often linked to three different objectives. They are likely probing for and exploiting national infrastructure vulnerabilities. Finally, the attacks can also be linked to exploiting money from systems and people. Businesses have become a favourite target of these attackers because their cybersecurity is often lacking or outdated, making it easy to exploit vulnerabilities undetected in systems (Quostar, 2020). The state predominately uses these actors to carry out timely or large-scale attacks to access information or retaliate. The distance between what is publicly perceived as non-state actors and the state is beneficial as the state can deny these attacks, even when they are part of the internal cyber. (Westby, 2011). All the states included in Chapter 5 are using distanced cyber units and state-sponsored actors.

Cyberterrorists or state-supported actions are not different from state-sponsored groups, hacktivists, and politically motivated cybercriminals using the same means and methods to conduct online attacks. These activities align with the state objectives, and there is no negative payoff associated with providing a safe haven to these actors. Compared with state and state-sponsored actors, there is no difference in the ability to disrupt and destroy various ICs, causing political and economic damage to the target and society. However, managing the state-supported groups can only be obtained with collaboration with the host states.

ACTIVISTS AND HACKTIVISTS

This part of politically motivated attacks is not comparable to the state and state-sponsored/supported actions. However, the actors have a profound political and social foundation, and they are using the same means and methods as the other actors. It would be useful to consider these attacks in conjunction with the other groups, but issues regarding the human rights protection of online attacks need to be established. Currently, hacktivism is considered to be less severe compared with the other two areas. However, hacktivists face a disproportionate level of prosecution compared with more severe costs associated with prison sentences. There are different definitions of hackers in national legislation, and there are also different perceptions in societies about the seriousness of hacktivism and online protest. Political activists and hacktivists consider themselves having the right to protest online and offline against what challenges their political or social beliefs (McAlpine & Oldham, 2018). Although the prosecution has a deterrence effect, they are also likely to conflict with the right to protest. So criminalisation and prosecution should be weighed up against political and personal rights.

Protection of CIs

Another important conclusion drawn from the book chapters is the importance of enhancing the cybersecurity level to change the payoff for the attackers. One way to do this is to enhance the capabilities and capacities for managing these attacks on state levels. However, it is equally important to consider a multilayered approach where proactive and reactive measures are developed on multiple levels. One of the most critical areas is developing cybersecurity for public and private entities owning or operating the CIs. This would change the costs as it would become more challenging to attack the sites, and if attacked, the CIs would quickly be able to restore its operations.

This book has also highlighted the issues with the protection of CI. There has been a steady increase in attacks against CIs, and over the years, there have been significant attacks that should have prompted more awareness about resilience and preparedness. The Estonia 2007 attack raised concerns about public and private actors, but not enough to create an international framework for protecting these vital assets (BBC News, 2007). Other high-profile attacks, such as the Stuxnet worm (2010), the Wannacry and NotPetya (2017), should also have acted as a facilitator for change (Hern, 2017; Zetter, 2014). It is not until 2020–2021, where the high profiled attacks against SolarWinds, COVID-19 research, healthcare facilities, the Microsoft Exchange hack, that the pressure for developing more comprehensive cybersecurity frameworks have emerged (Constantin, 2021; Osborne, 2021; Burt, 2020; Stilgherrian, 2020). Ransomware attacks on businesses, military units and contractors, governmental departments, education, health care, and other vulnerable areas have shown the powers of these attacks and the impact they have on

Table 8.2 Key problems with the current framework: Public and private actors

Actors	Areas for improvements	Behaviour
State actors	Developing international and national regulation for cybersecurity Developing proactive and reactive security measures to protect CIs Support private actors in developing cybersecurity plans and standards Developing support and funding opportunities to enhance cybersecurity	States have predominately been involved in developing national deterrence and defence, yet they need to be equally involved in building a multilayered approach to support public and private entities to create cybersecurity plans and protective structures
Private actors	Developing own security plans Investing in security solutions Engage in public and private partnerships	Private entities have a responsibility to enhance cybersecurity to decrease the chances of becoming a target. Security should be included on multiple levels, both technical and non-technical measures

society. Colonial Pipeline and JBS ransomware attacks have impacted the public, increasing the pressure for more cybersecurity (Associated Press, 2021; Rosenbaum, 2021). Recent attacks, such as the BlueLeaks and the attacks on Dallas Police Department in the US, have opened a discussion about preparedness and security of public entities that have been subjected to a substantial amount of attacks for decades (KrebsOnSecurity, 2020; Alexander, 2020).

The risks to these vital services and structures increase at a concerning level. Due to the interdependencies and connectivity of these entities, the impact of an attack goes beyond the original target. The attacks have exposed gaps in cybersecurity, strategies, and legislation. CIs underpin all actions online, and they are interlinked with the physical world. The situation where CIs are an attractive target for cyberactors is not likely to change. It is nearly impossible for private entities to match the security defence capabilities to prevent the state-funded attackers from innovative and sophisticated attacks. The different entities do not have the funding to invest in automated defence or security personal to match these attacks (O'Mally, 2019). However, this should not be an excuse for doing nothing. It is still a concern how easy it is for less skilled actors to compromise systems. Building a security culture means that it is not just the responsibility of underresourced entities to manage the area. Instead, it requires security to be built into the structure on multiple levels and incorporated into everyday routines (Galen, 2021).

Protecting CIs is becoming a significant challenge, and the number of attacks has revealed numerous vulnerabilities in the current structure. The escalating cyber attacks and the complexity of systems are some of the main issues (Gilligan, 2021). Public and private entities are operating in a complex, global, and digital ecosystem. The reliance on CIs is growing. People are beginning to understand the damage these politically motivated attacks can inflict on society, where computer systems run services at hospitals, emergency services, power and water plants, etc. (Janicke, 2018). The systems are primarily interlinked entities with customers, suppliers, and managed system providers. All these entities form a complex system that creates obstacles for the actors to assess their vulnerabilities: Due to the interconnectivity, they are equally exposed to those of their participants. Additionally, the actors are trying to implement cybersecurity and standards and adhere to fragmented regulations in this area (Bravo, 2020).

The number of attacks highlighted in Chapters 5, 6, and 7 demonstrate that the current security level is patchy. There is a constant flow of attacks targeting CIs which are depending on the online environment to function. Attackers are testing the resilience level of different systems. So far, they have been successful in finding substantial weaknesses (Gilligan, 2021). With the current structure, it is not likely that this is going to change. Therefore, a more comprehensive approach is needed, which includes cooperation between key public and private stakeholders to enhance the resilience level across sectors. Although most states have developed cybersecurity strategies, there needs to be a more interactive approach for cooperation in the boderless online space. It is in both the public and private interest that the security level increases. Like the national strategies, the private sectors should develop similar policies that link into a multilayered approach covering both the technical and human sides.

In the aftermath of the breach on the Colonial Pipeline, US President Biden signed an exclusive order to enable specific security mitigation to enhance the security and responses to the attack (Huey et al., 2021). Similarly, CISA and the FBI issued a list of recommendations for owners and operators to reduce the risk of ransomware attacks. These recommendations included multifactor authentication for remote access to the information technology and the operational technology, etc. (Magill, 2021; CISA, 2021). It is good that initiatives are launched to secure these areas, but these reactive responses came too late when several attacks had caused substantial damage. Attacks on CIs are not new, and they should already be a high level of cybersecurity awareness and measures to create resilience towards attacks. Additionally, there should be a requirement of introducing proactive measures to ensure the facilities, the networks, and the computer systems. Proactive measures would preemptively identify security weaknesses and threats before the attack. Yet, this should be combined with reactive measures to immediately mitigate the incidents and prevent repeating attacks (ThinkTech Advisors, 2021).

Private Sector Engagement

Private entities also need to enhance their cybersecurity level. Competitive interests have for a long time influenced the area. On the one hand, the protection of computer systems, networks, CIs, and services had been overshadowed by geopolitical tensions and state interests that has increased the risks and decreased cooperation on the political level (Bravo, 2020). This focus has created a vacuum. Many businesses and organisations have been left alone to create a cybersecurity framework by establishing a reactive legal structure without support and guidance from the state (McAlpine & Oldham, 2018).

On the other hand, the cybersecurity issues are filtered down through the systems. The private sector has significant power to impact resilience and preparedness, and actions could have been taken earlier. However, global tech companies have advocated for open digital borders to incorporate a global supply chain and enable online connectivity worldwide. These actors have also challenged core competencies of the states, i.e. standard-setting and monetary policies. Technological supremacy and national competitiveness are interlinked. Therefore, the lack of global tech governance has enabled the companies to influence standard settings, foreign participation in CIs, foreign purchase of national technology, offshoring data, and transfer technologies to gain access to the international market (Bravo, 2020). Cybersecurity needs to be factored into the private sector's competitiveness, business structures, and policies.

The book has exposed the public and private sectors' vulnerabilities and lack of preparedness if attacked. Governments and international organisations and institutions have been preoccupied with establishing their role and operations in cyberspace for a long time. Actors on multiple levels ought to participate actively in enhancing anticipatory responses. Governments, organisations, the private sector, and individuals should implement and maintain cybersecurity processes and practices based on internationally accepted norms and standards, including privacy protection and security technologies. Software and hardware developers significantly enhance cybersecurity by including resilience and preparedness to gap vulnerabilities in an anticipatory framework (Wegener, 2011, p. 96; Munk, 2015; McAlpine & Oldham, 2018).

Cybersecurity and Strategies

What can be done about these issues? The current diplomatic climate for developing a framework mirrors the Cold War. The tit-for-tat games between the states are becoming more prominent, with harsh rhetoric in public exchanges public, which does nothing to manage the current situation. Competitions between the states to become the most cyber power are based on mistrust and revenge, escalating the ongoing conflict holding several entities and online users hostages.

The US and allied have developed a practice of attribute states and actors in public; sanctions have been imposed, and individuals have been indicted (EC, CoEU, 2020; The White House, 2021; Carrega, 2020; Paganini, 2018). The victims cannot identify the attackers at the beginning of an attack where they are indistinguishable from other attackers. The attacker can be an insider, a hacker, a rough actor, an organised criminal, a lone wolf, a terrorist, or a national state. It is a difficult task to track and trace the attackers and criminal activities. Often, it is impossible to attribute the attack to a particular individual, group, or state. Often the attribution is based on a group's known means, method, and motivation rather than a precise identification (Westby, 2011, p. 90).

These actions have been taken to impose costs on the attacking states and actors. So far, there has not been any notable effect. The prosecution will only be possible if the actors are located in states with extradition agreements. Russia has refused to investigate and prosecute the ransomware actors, claiming that there is no legislation in place. However, there is a lack of willingness as long as the actions of the state-supported actors align with the state's cyber strategies, and there is not imposed a negative payoff. The only actors that are likely to be prosecuted are hacktivists.

DETERRENCE AND DEFENCE

States have changed their defence strategies; for example, the US has taken a more proactive approach in the 'defend forward' strategy. Other Western states are more cautious as these actions can escalate the attacks. According to the UN Charter, states are obliged according to Article 2(4) to refrain "from the threat or use of force against any state's territorial integrity or political independence" (UN, 1945; Gopalan, 2018; Waxman, 2011, p. 426). However, Article 51 highlights that the states still possess a right of individual or collective self-defence. The challenging point is when this right to use forces equalarmed attacks. It also needs to be considered if the attacks violate the territorial integrity of the state. If an attack has a physical consequence, it might fulfil the requirements under international law. However, it is not clear when it is permissible to launch a cyber attack in self-defence (Gopalan, 2018; Waxman, 2011).

The Way Forward – Some Initiatives

Private Collaboration

Initiatives have been launched to increase resilience against attacks. In 2018, 34 companies, including multinational companies such as Facebook, LinkedIn, Dell, and Cisco, signed a Cybersecurity Tech Accord pleading to uphold four vital principles to enhance cybersecurity. These principles are as follows: Protect all online users and customers everywhere; Oppose cyber attacks on innocent citizens and enterprises from anywhere; Empower users, customers, and developers to strengthen cybersecurity protection; and partner with each other and with like-minded groups to enhance cybersecurity. This initiative is a step in the right direction, but more private sector engagement is needed (Meyer, 2020; Smith, 2018). One lesson to be learned from the SolarWinds attack is that everyone can become a target, and interconnectivity and interdependencies make companies more vulnerable (Schneier, 2020).

Growing Concern about Attacks on Healthcare Services

During the COVID-19 pandemic, many attacks have been launched towards healthcare organisations and research facilities. In the 2020 Paris Forum, more than 65 healthcare-related organisations joined the Paris Call for Trust and Security in Cyberspace. This initiative includes organisations and businesses working on vaccines, hospitals, and governmental institutions. The Paris Call is a robust multistakeholder coalition addressing online attacks against the health sector. The first principle developed is to prevent malicious cyberactivities threatening indiscriminatory or systematic harm to people and critical infrastructure (Burt, 2020; Paris Call, 2018).

In May 2020, the Oxford Process, which includes 136 of the world's most prominent international law experts, stated that all medical facilities are protected by international law at all times. Later, a second statement was published a second statement stating that organisations involved in researching, manufacturing, and distributing COVID-19 vaccines are also protected (Burt, 2020; Oxford Institute for Ethics, Law and Armed Conflicts, 2020a; Oxford Institute for Ethics, Law and Armed Conflicts, 2020b). The Oxford statement emphasised that cyberoperations do not occur in a normative vacuum or a law-free zone. The UN General Assembly, international law, and the Charter of the UN are applicable. The rules outlined by these key international institutions and conventions are essential to maintaining peace and stability and promoting an open, secure, stable, accessible, and peaceful information and communications technology environment (Oxford Institute for Ethics, Law and Armed Conflicts, 2020a).

Similarly to these statements, the CyberPeace Institute, the International Committee of the Red Cross, and 40 international leaders also launched a call for governments to stop attacking the healthcare sector (Burt, 2020). The same institute joined forces with the WHO to highlight that the practices used in cyberspace endanger human life (CyberPeace Institute, 2020). Grassroot movements, experts businesses are becoming concerned about the current situations, and they are not raising their voices to pressure the politicians to find a solution to these issues.

The US–Russia Summit in 2021

Diplomacy still exists, at least on the surface, and talks have emerged between the US and Russia at a summit in Geneva in 2021. US President Biden and Russia's President Putin agreed to develop a cybersecurity arrangement between the two countries. This agreement aims to protect healthcare, utilities, and other CI to ensure that the public is safe from these attacks (Tidy, 2021; Paul, 2021; Nichols, 2021; Computer Weekly, 2021). However, these talks are likely to drag out as the two sides disagree about the high-profile cyber attacks launched against the US. During the Summit, President Biden gave President Putin a list of 16 targets of 'off-limits' targets that the US would seek to agree with Russia about (Tidy, 2021; Roth & Harding, 2021). Although the US and Russia, in principle, agreed that something should be done about the surge in cyber attacks, and particularly about ransomware, it remains uncertain if the Russian authorities will take action on these matters (Computer Weekly, 2021; Cerulus, 2021).

Nevertheless, the idea of an online CI truce is unlikely if it is only binding state actors. The use of state-sponsored and state-supported is the core problem in the escalation of attacks. The state-supported actors can easily hide within this formation and continue to attack and terrorise governments, businesses, and populations on foreign soil if state-sponsored groups are tied up to a bilateral agreement (Nichols, 2021). Therefore, it is required that both countries in 2021 work together to identify what is included in the 'off-limits' statement and follow up on cases originating in order countries (Computer Weekly, 2021). The positive element is that CI protection was discussed, and the two states agreed, in principle, to take these matters forward. The international society will closely watch what is happening in the future. In this sense, the payoff might change slightly.

Russia might appear willing to engage with the US. But de facto, the status quo will continue as the Russian authorities deny the problem. President Biden also voiced scepticism about the possible outcome of these talks when he stated: "It's about self-interest and the verification of self-interests. Or, as the old expression goes, the proof of the pudding is in the eating" (Roth & Harding, 2021).

References

Alexander, J., 2020. *K-pop stans overwhelm app after Dallas police ask for videos of protesters.* [Online] Available at: www.theverge.com/2020/6/1/21277423/k-pop-dallas-pd-iwatch-app-flood-review-bomb-surveillance-protests-george-floyd [Accessed 01 04 2021].

Associated Press, 2021. *Colonial Pipeline confirms it paid $4.4m ransom to hacker gang after attack.* [Online] Available at: www.theguardian.com/technology/2021/may/19/colonial-pipeline-cyber-attack-ransom [Accessed 24 06 2021].

Barletta, G. A., Barletta, W. A. & Tsygichko, V. N., 2011. Cyber conflict. In: *The Quest for Cyber Peace.* Geneva: ITU, pp. 53–65.

BBC News, 2007. *Estonia hit by 'Moscow cyber war'.* [Online] Available at: http://news.bbc.co.uk/1/hi/world/europe/6665145.stm [Accessed 11 03 2018].

Bravo, T., 2020. *Wild wide web.* [Online] Available at: https://reports.weforum.org/global-risks-report-2020/wild-wide-web/ [Accessed 07 08 2021].

Burt, T., 2020. *Cyberattacks targeting health care must stop.* [Online] Available at: https://blogs.microsoft.com/on-the-issues/2020/11/13/health-care-cyberattacks-covid-19-paris-peace-forum/ [Accessed 03 01 2021].

Carrega, C., 2020. *6 Russian military officers charged with a worldwide cyberattack.* [Online] Available at: https://edition.cnn.com/2020/10/19/politics/russian-nationals-charged-justice-department/index.html [Accessed 07 01 2021].

Casear, E., 2021. *The incredible rise of North Korea's hacking army.* [Online] Available at: www.newyorker.com/magazine/2021/04/26/the-incredible-rise-of-north-koreas-hacking-army [Accessed 15 07 2021].

Cerulus, L., 2021. *Biden needs Putin in the fight against ransomware.* [Online] Available at: www.politico.eu/article/biden-zones-putin-fight-against-ransomware-russia-us/ [Accessed 26 06 2021].

CISA, 2021. *DarkSide ransomware: Best practices for preventing business disruption from ransomware attacks.* [Online] Available at: https://us-cert.cisa.gov/ncas/alerts/aa21-131a [Accessed 08 08 2021].

Computer Weekly, 2021. *Biden tackles Putin on ransomware at Geneva summit.* [Online] Available at: www.computerweekly.com/news/252502593/Biden-tackles-Putin-on-ransomware-at-Geneva-summit?_ga=2.4748019.1599825627.1624525693-2103148593.1623869695 [Accessed 24 06 2021].

Congressional Research Service, 2009. *Information Operations, Cyberwarfare, and Cybersecurity: Capabilities and Related Policy Issues,* Washington DC: Congressional Research Service.

Constantin, L., 2021. *SolarWinds attack explained: And why it was so hard to detect.* [Online] Available at: www.csoonline.com/article/3601508/solarwinds-supply-chain-attack-explained-why-organizations-were-not-prepared.html [Accessed 05 07 2021].

CyberPeace Institute, 2020. *Securing healthcare to achieve cyberpeace: A joint WHO-cyberpeace institute moderated workshop.* [Online] Available at: https://cyberpeaceinstitute.org/event/a-joint-moderated-workshop-securing-healthcare-to-achieve-cyberpeace/ [Accessed 03 01 2021].

EC, CoEU, 2020. *EU imposes the first ever sanctions against cyber-attacks.* [Online] Available at: www.consilium.europa.eu/en/press/press-releases/2020/07/30/eu-imposes-the-first-ever-sanctions-against-cyber-attacks/ [Accessed 17 12 2020].

Galen, R. v., 2021. *Stop playing catchup: Move from reactive to proactive to defeat cyber threats.* [Online] Available at: www.darkreading.com/attacks-breaches/stop-playing-catchup-move-from-reactive-to-proactive-to-defeat-cyber-threats/a/d-id/1341372 [Accessed 08 08 2021].

Gilligan, J. M., 2021. *It is time to get serious about securing our nation's critical infrastructure.* [Online] Available at: www.cisecurity.org/blog/it-is-time-to-get-serious-about-securing-our-nations-critical-infrastructure/ [Accessed 06 08 2021].

Gopalan, S., 2018. *Is counter-attack justified against a state-sponsored cyber attack? It's a legal grey area.* [Online] Available at: https://theconversation.com/is-counter-attack-justified-against-a-state-sponsored-cyber-attack-its-a-legal-grey-area-94023 [Accessed 08 08 2021].

Hern, A., 2017. *WannaCry, Petya, NotPetya: how ransomware hit the big time in 2017.* [Online] Available at: www.theguardian.com/technology/2017/dec/30/wannacry-petya-notpetya-ransomware [Accessed 29 08 2020].

Huey, C., Marshall, J. & Pope., T., 2021. *What's past is prologue – A new world of critical infrastructure security.* [Online] Available at: https://blog.talosintelligence.com/2021/06/new-world-after-pipeline-ransomware-ONG.html [Accessed 08 08 2021].

ICRC, 1899. *Convention (II) with respect to the laws and customs of war on land and its annex: Regulations concerning the Laws and Customs of War on Land. The Hague,*

29 July 1899. [Online] Available at: https://ihl-databases.icrc.org/ihl/INTRO/150 [Accessed 28 12 2020].

ICRC, 1907. *Convention (IV) respecting the Laws and Customs of War on land and its annex: Regulations concerning the Laws and Customs of War on land. The Hague, 18 October 1907.* [Online] Available at: https://ihl-databases.icrc.org/ihl/INTRO/ 195 [Accessed 28 12 2020].

ICRC, 1949. *The Geneva Conventions of 12 August 1949.* [Online] Available at: www. icrc.org/en/doc/assets/files/publications/icrc-002-0173.pdf [Accessed 29 12 2020].

ICRC, 1977. *Protocol additional to the Geneva Conventions of 12 August 1949, and relating to the protection of victims of international armed conflicts (Protocol I), 8 June 1977.* [Online] Available at: https://ihl-databases.icrc.org/ihl/INTRO/470 [Accessed 29 12 2020].

Janicke, H., 2018. *Cyber peacekeeping is integral in an era of cyberwar – Here's why.* [Online] Available at: https://theconversation.com/cyber-peacekeeping-is-integral-in-an-era-of-cyberwar-heres-why-90646 [Accessed 08 08 2021].

Kolbe, P. R., 2020. *With hacking, the United States needs to stop playing the victim.* [Online] Available at: www.nytimes.com/2020/12/23/opinion/russia-united-states-hack.html?smid=em-share [Accessed 01 01 2021].

KrebsOnSecurity, 2020. *'BlueLeaks' exposes files from hundreds of police departments.* [Online] Available at: https://krebsonsecurity.com/2020/06/blueleaks-exposes-files-from-hundreds-of-police-departments/ [Accessed 01 08 2021].

Kshetri, N., 2014. *Cybersecurity and International Relations: The U.S. Engagement with China and Russia.* Greensboro: FLACSO-ISA Joint International Conference, Buenos Aire.

Magill, J., 2021. *Critical infrastructure companies rise to meet cyber threat.* [Online] Available at: www.forbes.com/sites/jimmagill/2021/07/26/critical-infrastructure-companies-rise-to-meet-cyber-threat/?sh=709323057c87 [Accessed 07 08 2021].

Masters, J., 2011. *Confronting the cyber threat.* [Online] Available at: www.cfr.org/ backgrounder/confronting-cyber-threat [Accessed 16 11 2020].

McAlpine, A. & Oldham, M., 2018. Threats. In: *Cyber security: Law and guidance.* Haywards Heath: Blooomsbury Professional, pp. 1–30.

Meyer, P., 2020. Norms of responsible state behaviour in cyberspace. In: Springer, ed. *The Ethics of Cybersecurity.* Cham: Springer, pp. 347–360.

Munk, T. H., 2015. *Cyber-security in the European Region: Anticipatory governance and practices.* [Online] Available at: www.escholar.manchester.ac.uk/api/ datastream?publicationPid=uk-ac-man-scw:266937&datastreamId=FULL-TEXT.PDF [Accessed 12 08 2020].

NATO, 1949. *The North Atlantic Treaty.* [Online] Available at: www.nato.int/cps/en/ natolive/official_texts_17120.htm [Accessed 16 12 2020].

Nichols, S., 2021. *Biden proposes critical infrastructure safe zones for hacking.* [Online] Available at: https://bit.ly/32kUYI9 [Accessed 24 06 2021].

O'Mally, M., 2019. *Protecting enterprises from state-sponsored hackers.* [Online] Available at: www.lightreading.com/protecting-enterprises-from-state-sponsored-hackers/a/d-id/752468 [Accessed 08 08 2021].

Osborne, C., 2021. *Everything you need to know about the Microsoft Exchange server hack.* [Online] Available at: www.zdnet.com/article/everything-you-need-to-know-about-microsoft-exchange-server-hack/ [Accessed 19 07 2021].

Oxford Institute for Ethics, Law and Armed Conflicts, 2020a. *The Oxford Statement on the International law protections against cyber operations targeting the health care sector.* [Online] Available at: www.elac.ox.ac.uk/the-oxford-statement-on-the-international-law-protections-against-cyber-operations-targeting-the-hea [Accessed 03 01 2021].

Oxford Institute for Ethics, Law and Armed Conflicts, 2020b. *The Second Oxford Statement on International Law Protections of the healthcare sector during Covid-19: Safeguarding vaccine research.* [Online] Available at: www.elac.ox.ac.uk/article/the-second-oxford-statement [Accessed 03 01 2020].

Paganini, P., 2018. *US charges North Korea agent over Sony Pictures hack and WannaCry.* [Online] Available at: https://securityaffairs.co/wordpress/75994/intel ligence/north-korea-agent-indictment.html [Accessed 18 07 2021].

Paris Call, 2018. *Paris call for trust and security in cyberspace.* [Online] Available at: https://pariscall.international/en/ [Accessed 03 01 2021].

Paul, K. 2021, How remote work opened the floodgates to ransomware [Online]. *The Guardian* 17.06.2021. www.theguardian.com/technology/2021/jun/17/ransomware-working-from-home-russia [Accessed 18 11 2021].

Quostar, 2020. *Are state-sponsored cyber-attacks a serious threat to your businesses?.* [Online] Available at: www.quostar.com/blog/are-state-sponsored-attacks-a-risk-to-businesses/ [Accessed 23 07 2021].

Rosenbaum, E., 2021. *JBS cyberattack: From gas to meat, hackers are hitting the nation, and consumers, where it hurts.* [Online] Available at: www.cnbc.com/2021/06/02/from-gas-to-burgers-hackers-hit-consumers-where-it-hurts.html [Accessed 27 07 2021].

Roth, A. & Harding, L., 2021. *Biden warns US will hit back if Russia continues with cyber strikes.* [Online] Available at: www.theguardian.com/us-news/2021/jun/16/biden-to-meet-putin-at-highly-anticipated-summit-in-geneva?CMP=Share_AndroidApp_Other [Accessed 27 06 2021].

Schneier, B., 2020. *The US has suffered a massive cyberbreach. It's hard to overstate how bad it is.* [Online] Available at: www.theguardian.com/commentisfree/2020/dec/23/cyber-attack-us-security-protocols?CMP=Share_AndroidApp_Other [Accessed 26 12 2020].

Smith, B., 2018. *34 companies stand up for cybersecurity with a tech accord.* [Online] Available at: https://blogs.microsoft.com/on-the-issues/2018/04/17/34-companies-stand-up-for-cybersecurity-with-a-tech-accord/ [Accessed 03 01 2021].

Stilgherrian, 2020. *Cyber attacks on COVID-19 vaccine production are not quite a war crime.* [Online] Available at: www.zdnet.com/google-amp/article/cyber-attacks-on-covid-19-vaccine-production-are-not-quite-a-war-crime/ [Accessed 03 01 2021].

The White House, 2021. *The United States, joined by allies and partners, attributes malicious cyber activity and irresponsible state behavior to the People's Republic of China.* [Online] Available at: www.whitehouse.gov/briefing-room/statements-releases/2021/07/19/the-united-states-joined-by-allies-and-partners-attributes-malicious-cyber-activity-and-irresponsible-state-behavior-to-the-peoples-republic-of-china/ [Accessed 19 07 2021].

ThinkTech Advisors, 2021, proactive vs. reactive Cybersecurity [Online]. Available at: https://thinktechadvisors.com/2020/01/proactive-vs-reactive-cybersecurity/ [Accessed 18 11 2021].

Tidy, J., 2021. *Why cyber gangs won't worry about US-Russia talks.* [Online] Available at: www.bbc.co.uk/news/technology-57504007 [Accessed 21 06 2021].

UN, 1945. *Charter of the United Nations.* [Online] Available at: www.un.org/en/sections/un-charter/un-charter-full-text/ [Accessed 07 12 2020].

UNIDIR, 2020a. *China. Cybersecurity policy*. [Online] Available at: www.google. com/url?sa=t&rct=j&q=&esrc=s&source=web&cd=&ved=2ahUKEwjhw_ 3iha3rAhVFY8AKHW2MAwUQFjAJegQIChAB&url=https%3A%2F%2Funi dir.org%2Fcpp%2Fen%2Fstate-pdf-export%2FeyJjb3VudHJ5X2dyb3VwX2lkIjo iNTkifQ&usg=AOvVaw1xFziGmoNVDz3GanCZKcwg [Accessed 21 08 2020].

UNIDIR, 2020b. *Russian Federation*. [Online] Available at: https://unidir.org/cpp/en/ states/russianfederation [Accessed 21 12 2020].

UNIDIR, 2020c. *United States of America. Cybersecurity policy*. [Online] Available at: https://unidir.org/cpp/en/states/unitedstatesofamerica [Accessed 21 04 2020].

UN, 1980. *The convention on prohibitions or restrictions on the use of certain conventional weapons which may be deemed to be excessively injurious or to have indiscriminate effects*. [Online] Available at: https://treaties.un.org/Pages/ViewDetails. aspx?src=TREATY&mtdsg_no=XXVI-2&chapter=26&lang=en [Accessed 28 12 2020].

Valeriano, B., 2020. *Cost imposition is the point: Understanding U.S. cyber operations and the strategy behind achieving effects*. [Online] Available at: www.lawfareblog. com/cost-imposition-point-understanding-us-cyber-operations-and-strategy- behind-achieving-effects [Accessed 27 12 2020].

Waxman, M. C., 2011. Cyber-attacks and the use of force: Back to the. *The Yale Journal of International Law*, Volume 36, pp. 421–459.

Wegener, H., 2011. Cyber peace. In: ITU, ed. *The Quest for Cyber Peace*. Geneva: ITU, pp. 77–85.

Westby, J. R., 2011. A call for geo-cyber stability. In: ITU, ed. *The Quest for Cyber Peace*. Geneva: ITU, pp. 66–76.

Zetter, K., 2014. *An unprecedented look at Stuxnet, the world's first digital weapon*. [Online] Available at: www.wired.com/2014/11/countdown-to-zero-day-stuxnet/ [Accessed 13 07 2021].

Index

Note: Page numbers in **bold** indicate tables on the corresponding pages.

Printed in the United States
by Baker & Taylor Publisher Services